ORGANIZATIONAL BEHAVIOR: EXPERIENCES AND CASES

SECOND EDITION

by Dorothy Marcic

University of Wisconsin–LaCrosse

West Publishing Company

St. Paul • New York • Los Angeles • San Francisco

Table of Contents

CONTENTS (cont)

CONTENTS (cont)

CONTENTS (cont)

Preface

Written for the introductory organizational behavior course, this second edition has been significantly revised. Half of the existing exercises and cases are new.

Organizatonal Behavior (OB) is a discipline which has both theoretical and practical elements. Most OB textbooks do a decent job of developing the theoretical foundation, but many have less emphasis on the practical aspects. This book was designed to fill that gap. It has been developed with the following assumptions:

1. Learning can be interesting and fun. It does not have to be painful or boring.

2. Most theories of learning place application at a higher level than intellectual understanding. (Imagine a statistics course where you learned theories but never worked any problems.)

3. Organizational Behavior is particularly suited to learning through application by the use of experiential exercises.

4. Most OB instructors can incorporate some types of experiential exercises into their courses, depending on their own interests and inclinations.

5. A person who has a better understanding of herself and how groups function will make a better manager because she will be more aware of her own resources and how to utilize them effectively.

In order to provide a diversity of experiences, the following types were used:

1. Group or individual activities.
2. Diagnostic instruments.
3. Role-Plays.
4. Case Studies.

Because some teachers prefer group activities, while others use more role-plays, the attempt was made to cover all four areas. In addition, the exercises go from very simple to more complex, so that seasoned as well as newer experiential exercise users can find ones they are comfortable with.

Times given for each exercise are variable and can be done with the lesser time for shorter classes and more time can be used with longer classes.

Another difference is that some of the exercises use "real-world" examples, while others use the university or the classroom as a focus for studying organizations and groups. This second type was chosen also, because students can usually relate quite easily to managerial and organization issues on campus or in the classroom.

Many OB textbooks and exercises deal with mainly cognitive issues and ignore or gloss over the affective or emotional. Craig Lundberg of the University of Southern California gave a presentation on this at a recent Organizational Behavior Teaching Conference. A general feeling of the more than 50 participants was that there indeed was a lack of affective material in texts and this ought to be corrected.

At that same OBTC meeting, several of us spent two hours with Robert Tannenbaum, discussing the importance of helping students to understand themselves better. Tannenbaum feels OB professors have generally been negligent in giving students direction in terms of knowing who they are, where they would "fit" best and therefore, how to live and work more productively. Some of the exercises in this book are designed to overcome this deficiency.

A final note is given on how students should "use" experiential exercises. To gain maximum benefit, keep the following points in mind:

1. Try to take the exercises seriously. If you take them as jokes, you will not learn much.

2. If you have a disagreement with one instructor or part of an instrument, try not to let that overtake the potential learning. Do not lose sight of the bigger goal.

3. Even if you do not understand why you have to do something, still try to get into the exercise, otherwise you probably will not learn from it.

4. Take responsibility for your own learning. The teacher is a facilitator and you need to be an important part of the learning model.

And finally, remember--learning can be fun--and at times, unsettling. One of my professors used to say, "It's good when you are confused, because it shows you are learning."

CONTRIBUTORS TO THIS EDITION

So many people have given tremendous support and assistance for the second edition. My editor, Esther Craig was always willing to give a helping hand and her positive attitude smoothed over many a bumpy road. Don Hellriegel, John Slocum and Dick Woodman gave invaluable time and effort in the first and second editions.

In addition, numerous colleagues provided useful and productive feedback. Wilf Zerbe of the University of Calgary offered advice and suggestions as well as critical feedback. Others who helped include Bob Marx of the University of Massachusetts, Ella Bell of Yale, Larry Michaelson and Alice Watkins of the University of Oklahoma, Andre Delbecq of Santa Clara University, and Ken Murrell of the University of Western Florida. Two departmental colleagues who helped, often at crucial times, were Susan Willey and William Ross. What cannot be forgotten is the support and encouragement from friends. Those cheerleaders include Rose Horne, Monte Hanson, Roy Auerbach, Margaret Clayton, Georgann Bolig Nirva (who also offered invaluable advice on layout and design), Bob Cerwin, and my dear sister, Janet Mittelsteadt.

Adminstrators here at the University of Wisconsin-La Crosse could not have been of more assistance. Dean Ron Bottin and department chair Fikru Boghossian created an environment and provided needed resources to make this project possible.

Several OB faculty members reviewed the first edition and offered worthwhile suggestions during the revision process. Special appreciation go to Teresa Joyce Covin of Kennesaw College, Hamid Akbari of Northeastern Illinois University, Eser Uzun Belding of the University of Michigan at Flint, Pamela L. Cox of Syracuse University, Douglas M. Fox of Western Connecticut State University, Morris A. Graham of Brigham Young University, and Lynda L. Moore of Simmons College.

Huge thanks go to those who offered hours and hours of their time working on the at times overwhelming clerical tasks. Mary Clements performed super-human feats while typing and printing the manuscript, Jan Gallagher and Stephanie Swedal did numerous jobs and Brenda Kuhle was there for months filling in the cracks and keeping track of details, the most crucial and challenging being permissions. Our departmental secretary, Lois Olson, helped to make my teaching responsibilities less stressful by cheerfully completing last minute work for me when deadlines were approaching.

And lastly, my family. My three daughters, Roxanne, Solange and Elizabeth became used to waving goodbye to Mom to work on "the book." Their love and support carried me through many a rough day.

To my three daughters --

Roxanne, Solange

and Elizabeth

Chapter 1   **Icebreakers**

1. A SOCIALIZATION EXERCISE: LEARNING THE ROPES IN AN EXPERIENTIAL COURSE[*]

PURPOSE:

1. To present a socialization instrument and its conceptual base.
2. To explore student expectations about experiential learning.

GROUP SIZE:

Any number of groups of four to five members.

TIME REQUIRED:

45-65 minutes; in order to use the exercise in 45 minutes, steps 1 and 2 of Part A must be completed before class.

RELATED TOPICS:

Learning

---

[*]Adapted from Patricia Sanders and John N. Yanouzas from <u>Exchange</u>, Vol. 8(4), 1983, pp. 29-34. Used with permission.

INTRODUCTION:

Experiential Learning is one part of the whole learning process which can go from actual experiences to analyzing them and applying what you have learned. This exercise is designed to help you understand the importance of experiential learning.

EXERCISE SCHEDULE:

PART A - INVENTORY

1. (5 min.) Experiential Socialization Index

Below you are asked to indicate how much you agree with several statements describing students' behavior, attitudes, and beliefs related to learning in classroom activities. Please respond to all items individually. Do not make ties between statements. Use the following scale for reference:

Strongly Disagree (SD) 1	Disagree (D) 2	Mildly Disagree (MD) 3	Neutral (N) 4	Mildly Agree (MA) 5	Agree (A) 6	Strongly Agree (SA) 7

As a student in this class, my role is to...

1. Accept personal responsibility for becoming involved in learning experiences 　　1 2 3 4 5 6 7

2. Be willing to participate actively in classroom analysis of learning activities 　　1 2 3 4 5 6 7

3. Accept affective (feeling) learning as an important source of learning 　　1 2 3 4 5 6 7

4. Recognize the importance of integrating cognitive (thinking) learning 　　1 2 3 4 5 6 7

5. Be willing to engage in self assessment 　　1 2 3 4 5 6 7

6. Be willing to learn from one's classmates 　　1 2 3 4 5 6 7

7. Be willing to make connections between classroom experiences and cognitive content 　　1 2 3 4 5 6 7

8. Be willing to learn from observing one's own behaviors and the behaviors of others 　　1 2 3 4 5 6 7

9. Believe that information learned will be useful in the future 　　1 2 3 4 5 6 7

10. Accept the instructor's authority to conduct the class 　　1 2 3 4 5 6 7

11. Complete assignments and readings prior to class 　　1 2 3 4 5 6 7

12. Maintain a formal student/teacher relationship 　　1 2 3 4 5 6 7

13. Be willing to come to class on time 　　1 2 3 4 5 6 7

14. Be willing to do extra work when needed 　　1 2 3 4 5 6 7

15. Accept the instructor's authority to
    make decisions about the relevance of
    course content and assignments   1 2 3 4 5 6 7

16. Contribute to maintaining a structured
    classroom atmosphere   1 2 3 4 5 6 7

17. Believe neatness on assignments is
    important   1 2 3 4 5 6 7

18. Be willing to share with others personal
    strengths and weaknesses   1 2 3 4 5 6 7

2. (10-15 min.) The instructor passes out data collection forms to fill
   in the responses to the index. Based on this, the instructor prepares
   class medians for the 18 items.

> Items 1-9:   pivotal norms
> Items 10-18: peripheral norms

3. (10 min.) Socialization Matrix

   Task: Plot your score on the matrix below and answer the two
   questions on the next page.

SOCIALIZATION MATRIX

PERIPHERAL
NORM ACCEPTANCE

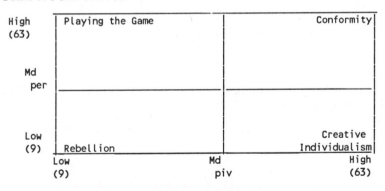

PIVOTAL NORM ACCEPTANCE

Conceptual Model. The ESI is based on Schein's (1968) model of socialization. According to Schein, not all organizational values and norms are equally important for the organization. Some are pivotal in importance while others are only peripheral for membership in the organization. Pivotal norms represent those behaviors which are central and necessary for productive membership in the organization. As applied to experiential learning, pivotal norms of learning would include: (1) the locus of responsibility for learning must be shared between student and instructor; (2) affective as well as cognitive processes are involved in learnings; (3) learning goals include transference of knowledge as well as development of skills and attitudes; and (4) the student must be an active participant in the learning process (Bowen, 1980). If the pivotal norms are to be accepted, the instructor must actively seek to enhance their value through appropriate socialization.

Peripheral norms are those behaviors which are not absolutely necessary to embrace for group membership, but are peripherally related to group goals and productivity. The peripheral norms of experiential learning include values such as: being punctual; completing assignments neatly; willing to do optional work; and accepting the authority of the instructor. These are not absolutely necessary for the attainment of learning in the experiential method but can contribute towards learning.

Questions: 1. How does your score differ from others in class and from class norms? Were you surprised with the results?

2. Do you agree or disagree with your socialization type?

PART B - Group Discussion

1.(20 min.) Form groups of 4 to 5 members and discuss their scores and answers to the above two questions.

Each group is to generate a list of issues and questions related to their expectations of the course and prepare a summary to report. Some guidelines are:

a. What are the instructor and student's roles in this course?
b. Do you agree or disagree with the pivotal and peripheral norms indicated on the ESI? Why or why not? What could you add to this list?
c. What should the students expect from this course?
d. What resources do the students have to offer?
e. What does the instructor expect from the students?
f. What is the hoped-for outcome of the course?
g. What application does the concept of organizational socialization have for membership in a work organization?

2. (15 min.) Each group presents summaries to whole class.

Reference

Schein, E.H. "Organizational Socialization and the Profession of Management," Industrial Management Review, Vol. 9, 1968, pp. 1-26.

2. MY ABSOLUTE WORST JOB: AN ICEBREAKER*

PURPOSE:

To become acquainted with one another.

GROUP SIZE:

Any number of dyads.

TIME REQUIRED:

35-60 minutes.

EXERCISE SCHEDULE:

1. (5 min.) Write answers to the questions below.

    a.   What was the worst job you ever had? Describe:
           (1)   The type of work you did
           (2)   Your boss
           (3)   Your co-workers
           (4)   The organization and its policies
           (5)   What made the job so bad?

    b.   What is your dream job?

2. (5-10 min.) Find someone you don't know and share your responses.

3. (5-10 min.) Get together with another dyad (preferably new people). Partner "A" of one dyad introduces "B" to the other dyad, then "B" introduces "A". The same process is followed by the other dyad.

The introduction should follow this format:

> "This is Mary Cullen. Her very worst job was putting appliques on bibs at a clothing factory and the reason she disliked it was because of the following. What she would rather do is be a financial analyst for a big corporation.

4. (5-10 min.-- optional) Each group of four meets another quartet and gets introduced, as before.

---

5.   (5 min.) The instructor asks for a show of hands on the number of people whose worst jobs fit into the following categories:
      a.   Factory
      b.   Restaurant
      c.   Manual labor
      d.   Driving or delivery
      e.   Professional
      f.   Health care
      g.   Phone sales or communications
      h.   Other

6.   (5-10 min.) Instructor gathers data from each group on worst jobs and asks groups to answer:
      a.   What are any common characteristics of the worst jobs in your group?
      b.   How did your co-workers feel about their jobs?
      c.   What happens to morale and productivity when a worker hates the job?
      d.   What was the difference in your own morale/productivity in your worst job versus a job you really enjoyed?
      e.   Why do organizations continue to allow unpleasant working conditions to exist?

7.   (5-10 min.) The instructor leads a group discussion on a-e above.

3. THE TINKERTOYS EXERCISE*

PURPOSE:

1. To help class members feel more comfortable with one
     another.
2. To examine issues of group dynamics, conversation,
     leadership.

GROUP SIZE:

Any number of groups of three to eight members.

TIME REQUIRED:

35-40 minutes.

MATERIALS: One box of tinkertoys for each group.

RELATED TOPICS:

Dynamics within groups, interpersonal communication, leadership.

OBJECT:

To build the tallest self-support structure with the contents of one box of tinkertoys.

EXERCISE SCHEDULE:

1. (20 minutes) Each group is given a box of tinkertoys. The first step is planning and groups have
     20 minutes to plan. No assembly is allowed during this time. Pieces may be looked at,
     but not even trial assembly of two parts is allowed. At the end of 20 minutes, pieces
     go back in the box.

2. (< 1 minutes) Construction Phase. **ONLY 40 SECONDS.**

3. (4 minutes) Group views each others towers.

4. (10-15 minutes) The instructor leads a discussion:

    a. How did groups plan?
    b. Did a leader emerge?
    c. How were conflicts resolved?
    d. What behaviors emerged during construction?

---

* Adapted from <u>Organizations and People</u> by J. B. Ritchie and Paul Thompson (St. Paul: West Publishing, 1984,) p. 56. Used with permission. Tinkertoys is a registered trademark of the Questor Corp.

Chapter 2   **Personality**

4. PERSONALITY ASSESSMENTMENT: JUNG'S TYPOLOGY[*]

PURPOSE:

To determine your personality type according to Carl Jung's Personality Topology.

TIME REQUIRED:

15-20 minutes to complete and score inventory.

Your personality is what you are. You have similarities and differences from other people. The differences measured here are not better or worse, merely different. Complete and score the inventory below to find out your personality type. Then look in Appendix D to learn what it means.

PERSONALITY INVENTORY

For each item, circle either "a" or "b." If you feel both "a" and "b" are true, decide which one is more like you, even if it is only slightly more true.

1. I would rather:
    a. Solve a new and complicated problem
    b. Work on something I have done before

2. I like to
   a.   Work alone in a quiet place
   b.   Be where "the action" is

3. I want a boss who
   a.   Establishes and applies criteria in decisions
   b.   Considers individual needs and makes exceptions

4. When I work on a project, I
   a.   Like to finish it and get some closure
   b.   Often leave it open for possible changes

5. When making a decision, the most important considerations are
   a.   Rational thoughts, ideas and data
   b.   People's feelings and values

6.   On a project, I tend to
   a.   Think it over and over before deciding how to proceed
   b.   Start working on it right away, thinking about it as I go along

7. When working on a project, I prefer to
   a.   Maintain as much control as possible
   b.   Explore various options

8. In my work, I prefer to
   a.   Work on several projects at a time, and learn as much as possible
        about each one
   b.   Have one project which is challenging and keeps me busy

9. I often
   a.   Make lists and plans whenever I start something and may hate to
        seriously alter my plans
   b.   Avoid plans and just let things progress as I work on them

10. When discussing a problem with colleagues, it is easy for me to
    a.   To see "the big picture"
    b.   To grasp the specifics of the situation

11. When the phone rings in my office or at home, I usually
    a.   Consider it an interruption
    b.   Don't mind answering it

12. Which word describes you better?
    a.   Analytical
    b.   Empathetic

13. When I am working on an assignment, I tend to
    a.   work steadily and consistently
    b.   work in burst of energy with "down time" in between

14. When I listen to someone talk on a subject, I usually try to
    a.   Relate it to my own experience and see if it fits
    b.   Assess and analyze the message

15. When I come up with new ideas, I generally
    a. "Go for it"
    b. Like to contemplate the ideas some more

16. When working on a project, I prefer to
    a. Narrow the scope so it is clearly defined
    b. Broaden the scope to include related aspects

17. When I read something, I usually
    a. Confine my thoughts to what is written there
    b. Read between the lines and relate the words to other ideas

18. When I have to make a decision in a hurry, I often
    a. Feel uncomfortable and wish I had more information
    b. Am able to do so with available data

19. In a meeting, I tend to
    a. Continue formulating my ideas as I talk about them
    b. Only speak out after I have carefully thought the issue through

20. In work, I prefer spending a great deal of time on issues of
    a. Ideas
    b. People

21. In meetings, I am most often annoyed with people who
    a. Come up with many sketchy ideas
    b. Lengthen meetings with many practical details

22. Are you a
    a. Morning person?
    b. Night owl?

23. What is your style in preparing for a meeting?
    a. I am willing to go in and be responsive
    b. I like to be fully prepared and usually sketch an outline of the meeting

24. In a meeting, would you prefer for people to
    a. Display a fuller range of emotions
    b. Be more task oriented

25. I would rather work for an organization where
    a. My job was intellectually stimulating
    b. I was committed to its goals and mission

26. On weekends, I tend to
    a. Plan what I will do
    b. Just see what happens and decide as I go along

27. I am more
    a. Outgoing
    b. Contemplative

28. I would rather work for a boss who is
    a. Full of new ideas
    b. Practical

In the following, choose the word in each pair which appeals to you more:

29. a. Social
    b. Theoretical

30. a. Ingenuity
    b. Practicality

31. a. Organized
    b. Adaptable

32. a. Active
     b. Concentration

SCORING KEY

Count one point for each item listed below which you have circled in the inventory.

SCORE FOR I	SCORE FOR E	SCOREFOR S	SCORE FOR N
2a	2b	1b	1a
6b	6b	10b	10a
11a	11a	13a	13b
15b	15a	16a	16b
19b	19a	17a	17b
22a	22b	21a	21b
27b	27a	28b	28a
32b	32a	30b	30a

Total

Circle the one with more
points--I   or   E   Circle the one with more
points--S   or   N

SCORE FOR T	SCORE FOR F	SCORE FOR J	SCORE FOR P
3a	3b	4a	4b
5a	5b	7a	7b
12a	12b	8b	8a
14b	14a	9a	9b
20a	20b	18b	18a
24b	24a	23b	23a
25a	25b	26a	31b
29b	29a	31a	32b

Total

Circle the one with more
points--T   or   F   Circle the one with more
points--J   or   P

YOUR SCORE IS

I or E _____

S or N _____

T or F _____

J or P _____

5. PERSONALITY AND ORGANIZATION*

PURPOSE:

To analyze how different personalities function in organizations.

GROUP SIZE:

Any number of groups of 4 to 6 members (of mixed personality types).

TIME REQUIRED:

Each option has a different time, from 30 to 50 minutes.

PREPARATION REQUIRED:

1. For Option 1, 2, and 3 complete the Personality Assessment in the previous exercise.
2. For Option 2, complete the Like and Do Well grid.
3. For Option 3, read the Helen Kelly Case Study.

ROOM ARRANGEMENT REQUIREMENT:

Enough room for subgroups to meet.

EXERCISE SCHEDULE:

OPTION 1

MOST IMPORTANT FEATURE OF AN IDEAL JOB (30 minutes)

Purpose:

To relate research findings about the most important features in an ideal job to the participants' responses and personality types.

1. (15 min.) In personality-similar groups, discuss the following:
   What's the Most Important Feature of an Ideal Job?
2. (15 min.) Compare the responses with other groups.
3. See "What's The Most Important Feature of an Ideal Job?" in the Appendix.

---

*Adapted from Sandra Krebs Hirsch and reproduced by special permission of the Publisher, Consulting Psychologists Press, Inc., Palo Alto, CA 94306, from <u>Using the Myers Briggs Type Indicator in Organizations</u>, 1985.

OPTION 2

LIKE AND DO WELL (30 minutes or more depending on number of small groups.)

Purpose:

To analyze aspects of a job that an individual does and does not like and does and does not do well.

1. (Before class) Complete The Like and Do Well Grid.
2. (15 min.) In personality-similar groups, discuss your answers.
3. (15 min.) Compare with other groups.

LIKE AND DO WELL GRID

Things I like and I do well:	Things I like but do not do well:
Things I do not like but I do well:	**Things I do not like and I do not do well:**

OPTION 3

HELEN KELLY CASE STUDY (50 minutes)

PURPOSE:

To apply knowledge of personality type to a problem between two people at work.

FORMAT
1. (5 min.) Divide into small groups of four to six members of mixed personality types.
2. (20 min.) Have each group answer the questions at the end of the case study.
3. (25 min.) Have each small group present its analysis to the entire class.

HELEN KELLY

Helen Kelly has worked for the same company for seven years. Until last year she was the administrative secretary for the marketing department. Her job duties included typing, filing, and answering the telephone. She generally did what was assigned to her. Last year the Marketing Coordinator left the company. Rather than fill this position, the responsibilities of the position were divided between the Marketing Director, Henry Long, and Helen. Since that time, the problems listed below have arisen in the Marketing Department between Henry and Helen.

1. Henry believes that Helen is not assertive enough. She is responsible for preparing monthly reports and submitting bids on projects. Both of these tasks require that she get information from others. Helen has not gotten the information at the proper time; she does not "get after people" to give it to her.

2. Henry wants Helen to "run" the marketing department on a daily basis and keep track of what needs to be done, what he needs to do, what is coming up, etc. She does not want to do this.

3. Helen waits to be told what to do rather than initiate activity herself.

4. Helen seems unconcerned about her work and uninterested in "taking hold" of these new responsibilities.

5. From Helen's point of view she is being criticized unjustly.

6. Helen says that she will do what is wanted, but that Henry does not tell her what he wants her to do.

7. Helen has told the consultant working with her that she feels hurt and unappreciated, but says she would never tell Henry that.

8. When Helen is asked what she thinks about the new job and whether she likes it, she is quiet. She says that sometimes she thinks she might want to develop her career, but she doesn't know.

9. When talking with Henry, Helen gets confused because she does not know what he wants, yet he pressures her to be more assertive. She says that she wants to do her job well, but she does not think she wants to "pound the table" like Henry.

Helen has taken the MBTI; she is an ISTP. Her scores are I=43, S=41, T=7, and P=55. Henry has not taken the MBTI, but the consultant working with the two of them guesses he is probably an ENTJ.

Using type, explain the problems between Helen and Henry from the point of view of each person focusing on the following questions:

1. How does each see the problems?

2. What problems do Helen and Henry have with each other trying to resolve their conflicts?

3. What do you think each needs to consider when working with the other; that is, Helen with Henry and Henry with Helen?

4. Using type, develop strategies for resolving the problems between Helen and Henry. What could each do?

6. LOCUS OF CONTROL[*]

PURPOSE:

To measure Locus of Control.

GROUP SIZE:

Any number.

TIME REQUIRED:

15-20 minutes to complete and score inventory.

RELATED TOPICS:

Motivation

DIRECTIONS:

Answer the following questions the way you feel. There are no right or wrong answers. Don't take too much time answering any one question, but do try to answer them all.

One of your concerns during the test may be, "What should I do if I can answer both yes and no to a question?" It's not unusual for that to happen. If it does, think about whether your answer is just a little more one way than the other. For example, if you'd assign a weighting of 51 percent to "yes" and assign 49 percent to "no," mark the answer "yes." Try to pick one or the other response for all questions and not leave any blanks.

In the column, mark a Y for Yes and a N for No next to each question. When you are finished, turn the page to score your test.

Put "Y" to indicate Yes and "N" to indicate No.

_____ 1. Do you believe that most problems will solve themselves if you just don't fool with them?

_____ 2. Do you believe that you can stop yourself from catching a cold?

_____ 3. Are some people just born lucky?
_____ 4. Most of the time do you feel that getting good grades meant a great deal to you?

_____ 5. Are you often blamed for things that just aren't your fault?

[*]By Stephen Nowicki, Jr. and B. Strickland in The Mind Test by Rita Aero and Elliot Weiner. New York: William Morrow, 1981, pp. 20-23. Used with permission.

____ 6. Do you believe that if somebody studies hard he or she can pass any subject?

____ 7. Do you feel that most of the time it doesn't pay to try hard because things never turn out right anyway?

____ 8. Do you feel that if things start out well in the morning it's going to be a good day no matter what you do?

____ 9. Do you feel that most of the time parents listen to what their children have to say?

____ 10. Do you believe that wishing can make good things happen?

____ 11. When you get punished does it usually seem it's for not good reason at all?

____ 12. Most of the time do you find it hard to change a friend's opinion?

____ 13. Do you think that cheering more than luck helps a team to win?

____ 14. Did you feel that it was nearly impossible to change your parents' minds about anything?

____ 15. Do you believe that parents should allow children to make most of their own decisions?

____ 16. Do you feel that when you do something wrong there's very little you can do to make it right?

____ 17. Do you believe that most people are just born good at sports?

____ 18. Are most of the other people your age stronger than you are?

____ 19. Do you feel that one of the best ways to handle most problems is just not to think about them?

____ 20. Do you feel that you have a lot of choice in deciding who your friends are?

____ 21. If you find a four-leaf clover, do you believe that it might bring you good luck?

____ 22. Did you often feel that whether or not you did your homework had much to do with what kind of grades you got?

____ 23. Do you feel that when a person your age is angry at you, there's little you can to do stop him or her?

____ 24. Have you ever had a good-luck charm?

____ 25. Do you believe that whether or not people like you depends on how you act?

____26. Did your parents usually help you if you asked them to?

____27. Have you felt that when people were angry with you it was usually for no reason at all?

____28. Most of the time, do you feel that you can change what might happen tomorrow by what you do today?

____29. Do you believe that when bad things are going to happen they just are going to happen no matter what you try to do to stop them?

____30. Do you think that people can get their own way if they just keep trying?

____31. Most of the time do you find it useless to try to get your own way at home?

____32. Do you feel that when good things happen they happen because of hard work?

____33. Do you feel that when somebody your age wants to be your enemy there's little you can do to change matters?

____34. Do you feel that it's easy to get friends to do what you want them to do?

____35. Do you usually feel that you have little to say about what you get to eat at home?

____36. Do you feel that when someone doesn't like you there's little you can do about it?

____37. Do you usually feel that it was almost useless to try in school because most other children were just plain smarter than you were?

____38. Are you the kind of person who believes that planning ahead makes things turn out better?

____39. Most of the time, do you feel that you have little to say about what your family decides to do?

____40. Do you think its better to be smart than to be lucky?

SCORING THE SCALE

Using the Scoring Key below, compare your answers on the previous page to the ones on the key. Give yourself one point each time your answer agrees with the keyed answer. Your score is the total number of agreements between your answers and the ones on the key.

SCORING KEY

1. Yes _____
2. No _____
3. Yes _____
4. No _____
5. Yes _____
6. No _____
7. Yes _____
8. Yes _____
9. No _____
10. Yes _____
11. Yes _____
12. Yes _____
13. No _____
14. Yes _____
15. No _____
16. Yes _____
17. Yes _____
18. Yes _____
19. Yes _____
20. No _____
21. Yes _____
22. No _____
23. Yes _____
24. Yes _____
25. No _____
26. No _____
27. Yes _____
28. No _____
29. Yes _____
30. No _____
31. Yes _____
32. No _____
33. Yes _____
34. No _____
35. Yes _____
36. Yes _____
37. Yes _____
38. No _____
39. Yes _____
40. No _____

TOTAL
SCORE

INTERPRETING YOUR SCORE

Low Scorers (0-8) - Scores from zero to eight represent the range for about one third of the people taking the test. As a low scorer, you probably see life as a game of skill rather chance. You most likely believe that you have a lot of control over what happens to you, both good and bad. With that view, internal locus of control people tend to take the initiative in everything from job-related activities to relationships and sex. You are probably described by others as vigilant in getting things done, aware of what's going on around you, and willing to spend energy in working for specific goals. You would probably find it quite frustrating to sit back and let others take care of you, since you stressed on the test that you like to have your life in your own hands.

Although taking control of your life is seen as the "best way to be," psychologists caution that it has its own set of difficulties. Someone who is responsible for his or her own successes is also responsible for failures. So if you scored high in this direction, be prepared for the downs as well as the ups.

Average Scorers (9-16) - Since you've answered some of the questions in each direction, internal and external control beliefs for you may be situation specific. You may look at one situation, work, for example, and believe that your rewards are externally determined, that no matter what you do you can't get ahead. In another situation, love perhaps, you may see your fate as resting entirely in your own hands. You will find it helpful to review the questions and group them into those you answered in the internal direction and those you answered in the external direction. Any similarities in the kinds of situations within one of those groups? If so, some time spent thinking about what it is in those situations that makes you feel as though the control is or is not in your hands can help you better understand yourself.

High Scorers (17-40) - Scores in this range represent the external control end of the scale. Only about 15 percent of the people taking the test score 17 or higher. As a high scorer, you're saying that you see life generally more as a game of chance than as one where your skills make a difference.

There are, however, many different reasons for any individual to score in the external control direction. For example, psychologists have found that people in many minority and disadvantaged groups tend to score in the external direction.   One recent suggestion for such scores is that people in these groups perceive their life situations realistically. In general, blacks, women, and lower-socioeconomic-class individuals really do have more restrictions on their own successes --fewer job options, lower pay, less opportunity for advancement--in many cases no matter what they do or don't do. An internal locus of control belief in such situations would be quite unrealistic and inappropriate. Thus your own high external control score could be a realistic perception of your current life circumstances.

On the other hand, your score may represent a strong belief in luck or superstition and a concurrent feeling of helplessness in controlling your life. Research studies have shown a relationship between unrealistic external control beliefs and problems like anxiety, depression, low self-concept, and poor physical health. Only you can decide exactly how much of your external belief system is accurate and how much of it is inappropriate given your life situation. If any of the emotional and/or physical problems listed do fit your view of your own life, professional help is definitely called for and very likely to produce positive results. But you'll have to take the initiative and make the first major move to regain control--or the belief of control--over your own life.

ABOUT THE SCALE

Do you believe in luck? Is it something like luck or chance or the actions of others that determines what happens to you? Or do you see the direction of your life determined by your own actions? These two views represent the extremes of a personality concept labeled "locus of control." This concept is concerned with whether an individual believes in an internal or an external control of his life.

In 1954, psychologist Julian Rotter was supervising Dr. E. Jerry Phares as he conducted therapy with a single, twenty-three-year-old man in a Veterans Administrative Hygiene Clinic. As therapy moved along, Drs. Rotter and Phares noted that Karl's (not his real name) problems were not of the common variety--at least not common to the Freudian understanding used in therapy before and during the 1950's. In recalling the therapy, Dr. Phares writes, "It gradually dawned on the clinician that Karl did not perceive any causal relationship between his behavior and the occurrence of rewards. He attributed such occurrences to luck or other factors over which he had no control.   Once the clinician realized this, Karl's behavior made sense."

Over the next twelve years, Drs. Phares and Rotter jointly and separately pursued the concept labeled "locus of control." Dr. Rotter culminated this work in 1966 by publishing the first Locus of Control Scale. That test attempted to measure how we perceive the relationship between our own actions and the consequences of those actions. Dr. Rotter felt that we learn from past life experiences whether to believe that our rewards and punishments depend on our own actions or on those of people around us.

After hundreds of research studies investigating Rotter's test and the locus of control concept, psychologists Stephen Nowicki, Jr., and B. Strickland developed a related but significantly different test. With the publishing of their scale, Drs. Nowicki and Strickland attempted to deal with certain criticisms that had been leveled at Rotter's test and, in addition, make it possible to measure locus of control in children. In 1974, Dr. Nowicki and a colleague, Dr. Marshall Duke, revised the earlier Nowicki-Strickland scale into the adult test we have included here.

Chapter 3   **Values and Ethics**

7. SOCIAL VALUES EXERCISE[*]

PURPOSE:

> To examine differences in social values.

GROUP SIZE:

> Any number of groups of 5 to 8 members.

TIME REQUIRED:

> 40-60 minutes.

PREPARATION REQUIRED:

> Complete the Social Values Inventory.

ROOM ARRANGEMENT:

> Enough space for students to sit in groups of 5 to 8.

EXERCISE SCHEDULE:

1. Rank order the following social values individually.

2. (10-15 min.) In groups of 5 to 8 members, rank order the following social values.

SOCIAL VALUES INVENTORY

Rank order with "1" being most desirable and "18" being least desirable:

	Individual	Group
Personal freedom	1	1
A comfortable life	2	4
A world at peace	7	2
Freedom from infectious diseases	3	
Jobs for everyone	14	
Low taxes	15	17
Good transportation system	8	
Good defense system	18	18
A world of beauty	9	
Spiritual/Religious fulfillment	17	4
Freedom from cancer	4	3
Good educational system	12	
Efficient business	13	
Good welfare system	16	
Equal opportunity for everyone	11	
Stable world economy	10	
Elimination of poverty	5	
Freedom from corruption and crime	6	

3. Based on the group ranking of the social values, now decide as a group what type of society would result from this type of values priority.

Questions to be answered:

A. What would be the relative amount of resources put into each item below (under B)?

B. What would be the aspects of each system below.

   1. Major industries
   2. Educational system
   3. Religious orientation
   4. Leisure activities
   5. Physical environment

6. Level of taxes: state whether high, medium or low (relative)
   amount would be spent on:

   a. social security
   b. defense
   c. welfare
   d. education
   e. health care

C. Would this now be your "ideal" society?

Explain.

8. A DIFFERENT SITUATION[*]

PURPOSE:

To examine ethical foundations of bribery in an international setting.

GROUP SIZE:

Any number of groups of 6-8 members.

TIME REQUIRED:

50-70 minutes.

PREPARATION REQUIRED:

1. Read the Case Study and answer the questions before class.
2. Preferably have some background on the Foreign Corrupt Practices Act.

RELATED TOPICS:

Decision-Making

EXERCISE SCHEDULE:

1. Read the case study below.

CASE STUDY: A DIFFERENT SITUATION

While Jane Welch was growing up in Texas, she was an excellent student. Her parents and teachers thought of her as "college capable"; in fact, she never seriously considered any option other than college.   She chose to major in marketing because one of her goals was, in her own words, "not to get stuck in Civil Service like my dad did. Private industry is the place for me where I have more of an opportunity to be promoted on my own merits and not necessarily on seniority." Jane entered college and, as usual, did well scholastically.

As college graduation neared, Jane began to interview with a number of companies. The college placement counselor advised Jane to make a list of aspects that she would find desirable or undesirable in a job. One of the items on her list was that the company and its product or goal had to be socially justifiable. This item had come to mind because many of her classmates were going to work for oil companies. Jane believed that in spite of the oil companies' slightly higher pay scale, she would not want to work for a company that made its money selling a non-renewable resource.

Another of the items on her list was that she wanted to travel in her job. Her family had traveled in the U.S. on vacations when she was a child and she had been to Mexico and Canada, but she wanted to see something of other parts of the world. Although Jane did not care to live in

---

[*]By Paul N. Keaton and Patricia A. Watson-Kuentz. Used with permission.

another country, she did think that a job which took her periodically to other countries for short trips would be desirable.

One day during the spring semester of her senior year, Jane talked with one of her marketing professors, Dr. Mayfield, about her career goals, and Dr. Mayfield suggested that perhaps Jane should look into the exporting business. Dr. Mayfield said he had a friend in Memphis who was a vice president in a cotton exporting firm, Cotton Belt Exporting. Things fell into place and Jane received and accepted an offer of a job in the firm.

For the first couple of years, Jane's responsibilities included traveling throughout the Southern U.S. and California buying cotton from farmers and gins, but the company promised that once she had proven herself in a couple of positions she would be promoted into a position where she would be dealing directly with people in foreign countries. After about six years and two positions in the firm, she was promoted to Manager of Export Sales to Japan.

It took Jane some time to become accustomed to dealing with Japanese businesspeople, but in doing so she became fascinated by the differences in customs. She learned to understand that just because Mr. Tanaka said "yes" while Jane was talking to him, he did not mean that he agreed to what was being said--instead, he meant merely that he understood what was being said. Each trip to Japan was a learning experience.

Jane also became acquainted with the mechanics of selling cotton to Japan. She learned that disagreements between cotton sellers in the U.S. and cotton buyers in Japan were arbitrated to a large degree by two associations, one in the U.S. (the American Cotton Shipping Association) and one in Japan (the Cotton Trade Association). The two associations agreed on many rules for trade but when their rules conflicted, the cotton contracts themselves specified which rules would apply.

On one trip to Japan, Jane heard rumors from importers that the Cotton Trade Association was contemplating some rule changes in the near future that could affect her company's ability to trade with Japan. She paid a visit to the Association but her usual contact was on vacation in Hawaii, so she had to see another gentleman, Mr. Kodama. Mr. Kodama said that he knew little about the pending changes but he intimated that, although he was a busy man, for a small fee he could probably find out "many" details. Jane left the office promising to get back to Mr. Kodama.

Jane considered her options. She decided that although she had never approved of paying to obtain such information, the urgency of the situation and the probable need for immediate action dictated that she should make the payment. The next day she returned to Mr. Kodama's office with an envelope containing 22,170 yen (equivalent to about $100 U.S.) which was, from her experience, the going rate for such payments.

Mr. Kodama told Jane that a middle level government official, Mr. Nakamura, was pressuring the cotton importing people to diversify their source of cotton in order to reduce Japan's dependency on one country. The Association reacted by considering rule changes that would encourage importers to buy from sources other than their largest ones.   Since the U.S. was the largest supplier of cotton to Japan, this action was certain to reduce the total amount of cotton it could sell to Japan.

Jane checked with her company, and her boss approved Jane's suggestion that she do some lobbying while she was in Japan. After obtaining the appropriate introductions, Jane arranged to have lunch with Mr. Nakamura. At the restaurant, Jane explained her company's situation, giving Mr. Nakamura facts about the promise of larger crops in the U.S., reduced prices because of technological advances in production, improved strains of cotton, etc. After much discussion, Mr. Nakamura indicated that, having given some thought to the specifics of the problem, he believed he might be able to see Jane's side of the argument.

Later in the conversation, Mr. Nakamura began to discuss the increasing cost of living, especially since his son had been admitted to Harvard in the U.S. He wondered if Jane's company might see fit to give the boy some type of scholarship--according to the Harvard catalog, his son would need about $20,000 per year to attend school. Mr. Nakamura subtly (but unmistakably) intimated that financial aid to his son might help him see the cotton situation more clearly.

Jane found herself in a dilemma. She had rationalized the payments for information, but somehow this situation seemed different.

2. (20-30 min.) In groups of 6-8 members, discuss the following questions:

    a. Is there a difference between the legal and the ethical in business practice?

    b. Does American law (e.g., Corrupt Practices Act) say anything relevant to the situation Jane finds herself in?

    c. How responsive should Americans be to cultural differences that may approve of or even encourage business practices that would be frowned upon or outlawed in the U.S.?

    d. How does a person resolve conflicts between personal values held by the individual and "commonly accepted practices"?

    e. Would the situation be any different if something other than money were requested?

3. (20-25 min.) Groups will report on the major points of their discussion to the whole class.

4. (10-15 min.) The instructor will lead a discussion on the Case Study examining values, ethics and conflicts present in this case.

9. THE INSTITUTIONAL REVIEW BOARD CASE[*]

PURPOSE:

To experience ethical dilemmas in decision-making.

GROUP SIZE:

Any number of groups of 5-8 members.

TIME REQUIRED:

40-60 minutes.

PREPARATION:

1. Lecture on reading on ethics.
2. Read case below and answer the questions.

RELATED TOPICS:

Behavioral research

EXERCISE SCHEDULE:

1. (Pre-Class) Students read case and answer the questions.

2. (20-30 minutes) Groups discuss the case and answer the two questions. You should act as a mock IRB and decide whether the company should be allowed to implement such a program.

3. (20-30 minutes) The instructor leads a group discussion on the case.

BACKGROUND:

In recent years changes in legislation have required closer scrutiny of research projects at universities using human subjects. Generally, a group of professionals, called an Institutional Review Board (IRB) reviews research proposals to ascertain whether the projects would violate any ethical guidelines.

CASE STUDY

The K. Insurance Company has proposed a program which it believes can improve sales. The names of each of its salesperson are placed in the office's cafeteria on a large poster, followed by the days of the week. Listed under each day of the week is the total dollar amount (in thousands) of insurance policies sold by that salesperson. At the end of the week, the salesperson with the highest sales total receives a $25 gift certificate to a local department store.
A. example of such a chart is listed below

---

[*]Adapted from Robert A. Giacalone, Assistant Professor of Management, University of Richmond. Used with permission.

Name	Mon.	Tues.	Wed.	Thurs.	Fri.
Joel Davis	.	.	.	.	.
Pete Smith	.	.	.	.	.
Jenny Jones	.	.	.	.	.
Alice Barnes	.	.	.	.	.

Management proponents of this program have noted that it has been used in a variety of companies, works very well, and could even help to double sales. They note that it is based on psychological concepts that have been tested by various experts in the fields of psychology and management. Employees in those companies where the program has been implemented never complain about the program and some even say that they like the rewards.

A number of employees at the K. Company, however, have quietly expressed reservations about the program. First, they note that the program violates the employee's privacy. It is part of the job for management to know how you are doing, they argue, but advertising your performance to others violates your rights of privacy. Second, they note that most employees really do not like the program, but keep quiet or express liking in order to avoid retribution from management. Third, the employees note that they do not doubt that the program will work. Essentially, they believe that the employees fear humiliation (from mediocre performance) and will stress themselves in order to increase sales. This, they say, is both physically and psychologically unhealthy. k Finally, the employees noted that management should not cloak the program under the guise of a benevolent psychological intervention. The psychologists tested the efficacy of the program, not its effects on the participants of the program.

Questions

1. What are the major ethical issues that are raised by this case?

2. If you were a member of an IRB, how would you vote on this matter?

10. THE ETHICS OF EMPLOYEE APPRAISAL

PURPOSE:

To examine ethics in hiring and appraising employees.

GROUP SIZE:

Any number of groups of 5-8 members.

TIME REQUIRED:

40-55 minutes.

RELATED TOPICS:

Leadership.

BACKGROUND:

Much attention has been given in recent years to ethics in business, yet one area often overlooked is ethical issues when hiring or appraising employees. Marion Kellogg developed a list of principles to keep in mind when recruiting or appraising.

How to Keep Your Appraisals Ethical
A Manager's Checklist[*]

1. Don't appraise without knowing why the appraisal is required.

2. Appraise on the basis of **representative** information.

3. Appraise on the basis of **sufficient** information.

4. Appraise on the basis of **relevant** information.

5. Be honest in your assessment of all the facts you obtain.

6. Don't write one thing and say another.

7. In offering an appraisal, make it plain that this is only your personal opinion of the facts as you see them.

8. Pass appraisal information along only to those who have good reason to know it.

9. Don't imply the existence of an appraisal that hasn't been made.

10. Don't accept another's appraisal without knowing the basis on which it was made.

EXERCISE SCHEDULE

1. (5-10 min.) The instructor discusses each of the 10 rules in Kellogg's checklist.

2. (5 min.) Students read each incident and decide which of the ten rules is violated, marking the appropriate number on the right. In some cases, more than one rule is violated.

3. (15-20 min.) Groups go over each "case" and come to a consensus on which rules are violated.

4. (15-20 min.) The instructor leads a discussion on each incident and "rule violations."

INCIDENT #1   Violates Rule #

1. Steve Wilson has applied for a transfer to Department Q, headed by Marianne Kilbourn. As part of her fact-finding, Marianne reads through the written evaluation which are glowing, then asks Steve's boss, Bill Hammond, for information on Steve's performance. Bill starts complaining about Steve, since his last project was not up to par, but does not mention Steve's wife has been seriously ill for two months. Marianne then decides not to accept Steve's transfer.

   _____

2. Maury Nanner is a sales manager and is having lunch with several executives. One of them, Harvey Gant, asks him what he thinks of his subordinate George Williams and he gives a lengthy evaluation.

   _____

3. Phillip Randall is working on six-month evaluations of his subordinates. He decides to rate Elisa Donner less-than-average on initiative because he thinks she spends too much time and energy and money making herself look attractive. He thinks it distracts the other male employees.

   _____

4. Paul Trendant has received an application from an out-standing candidate, Jim Fischer. However, Paul decides not to hire Jim because he heard from someone that Jim moved to town last month because his wife got a good job here and he thinks Jim will quit whenever his wife gets transferred.

   _____

5. Susan Forman is on the first-track and tries to make herself look good to her boss, Peter Everly. This morning she has a meeting with Pete to discuss which person to promote. Just before the meeting, Pete's golf buddy, Harold, a co-worker of Susan, tells Susan that Alice, Jerry and Joe are favored by Pete. Susan had felt Darlene was the strongest candidate, but goes into the meeting with Pete and suggests Alice, Jerry and Joe as top candidates.

   _____

6. Sandy is a new supervisor for seven people. After several months, Sandy is certain that Linda is marginally competent and frequently cannot produce any useful work. Looking over past appraisals, Sandy sees all of Linda's evaluations were positive and she is told that Linda "has problems" and not to be "too hard on her." Realizing this is not healthy, Sandy begins documenting Linda's inadequate performance and several supervisors hint that she should "lighten up, because we don't want Linda to feel hurt."

—————

11. SPIRITUALITY IN ORGANIZATIONS[*]

PURPOSE:

To examine how concepts of spirituality are used in organizations.

GROUP SIZE:

Any number of groups of 5-7 members.

TIME REQUIRED:

30-45 minutes.

PREPARATION REQUIRED:

Students complete "Spirituality Form".

EXERCISE SCHEDULE:

1.   (20-30 min.) Either in groups of 5-7 or as a whole class, discuss definitions and answers to questions 2-6.

2.   (10-15 min.) Discuss the relevance of spirituality in organizations.

SPIRITUALITY FORM

1. Define:

> Higher consciousness
> Vision
> Charisma
> Spirit
> Spiritually dead
> Inspiration
> Love of work
> Integrity

2.   List as many common phrases as possible using the word "spirit," such as school spirit, etc.
3.   What is the meaning of spirit in the above phrases?
4.   a. How do you know spirit?
     b. How can managers foster it?
5.   What is the difference between a group that has spirit and one that doesn't? (i.e., group seems up--or down, group has energy, etc.)
6.   List activities religious leaders have done through the ages to foster development of spirit.

---

[*]By Peter Vaill and Dorothy Marcic. Copyright 1988. All rights reserved.

Chapter 4 Perception and Attribution

12. JOHARI WINDOW[*]

PURPOSE:

1. To introduce the concept of the Johari Window.
2. To permit participants to process data about themselves in terms of self-disclosure and feedback.

GROUP SIZE:

Any number of groups of four to six members.

TIME REQUIRED:

50-70 minutes.

RELATED TOPICS:

Interpersonal Communication
Interpersonal Relationships

---

[*]Adapted by Joseph Luft and Harry Ingham from <u>Group Processes: An Introduction to Group Dynamics,</u> by Joseph Luft by permission of Mayfield Publishing Company. Copyright (c) 1984, 1970 and 1963 by Joseph Luft. Used with permission.

BACKGROUND: by Dorothy Marcic

```
                         SELF
                  Known        Unknown
            ┌─────────────────┬─────────────┐
            │                 │             │
     Known  │      Open       │   Blind     │
            │      Arena       │   Spot      │
OTHERS      │                 │             │
            ├─────────────────┼─────────────┤
            │                 │             │
   Unknown  │     Facade      │   Unknown   │
            │   Hidden Area    │             │
            │                 │             │
            └─────────────────┴─────────────┘
```

The drawing above represents the Johari Window, which is named after its originators, Joseph Luft and Harry Ingham.

The Johari Window is a model of perception because it looks at how we see ourself compared to how others see us, and it has four windows examining both known and unknown areas.

The open window, or ARENA, relates to things known to myself or others. For example, a person's height, eye color, and occupation may all fall under the Open Area. The more you know about yourself and the more you reveal to others, means that you have a large arena.

The BLIND SPOT is the window showing things other people know about me, but which I don't know about myself; and it is therefore sometimes called the "Spinach in the tooth" or "halitosis" window. Also included here may be such things as physical mannerisms and certain personality characteristics (for example a man who gets angry quite easily, but sees himself as a calm individual).

The FACADE, or Hidden Area, relates to things I know about myself, but other people don't know, which means I wish to keep them hidden. This, of course, depends on how close we are to the other person as we usually reveal more about ourselves to people we trust. Included in the Facade window may be such things as previous bad school or work experiences, unwanted personality characteristics, and negative reactions toward the other person.

The final window is called "UNKNOWN" because it relates to things neither I nor the other person know about myself--things which are usually hidden in the unconscious. We know the unconscious exists because occasionally we act out certain behaviors and have trouble tracing back the reasons for them.

An addition I have made to the Johari Window is the False Facade Area (not included in the table above), which relates to things I think are hidden from the other person, but which really are not.

For example, you may dislike another person yet try to be nice, however, she sees through your false facade and detects the underlying hostility.

The Johari Window is a good model for understanding the perceptual process in interpersonal relationships.

EXERCISE SCHEDULE:

(Steps 1, 2 - 10 min.)

1. Divide into groups of four to six members.

2. Johari Window Feedback Sheet

Write your impressions of the major assets and liabilities of each group participant, including yourself, in the space below. These will be read later as Feedback.

Participant	Assets	Liabilities
_____	_____	_____
_____	_____	_____
_____	_____	_____
_____	_____	_____
_____	_____	_____
_____	_____	_____

(Steps 3,4 - 35-50 min.)

3. Johari Window Self-Knowledge and Recording Sheet

   a. Share your perceptions with the other group members. Each member, in turn, reads aloud his/her assets and liabilities to the other members of his/her group and other members share what they wrote about that person. Group members use the right column of the sheet below to record perceptions of themselves held by other group members.

   b. List in the left column below the major assets and liabilities of your personality. Then place a check mark in front of those aspects which you have revealed so far to participants.

PERCEPTIONS OF ME

ASSETS	ASSETS
Self-Perceptions	Other's Perceptions

LIABILITIES	LIABILITIES
Self-Perceptions	Others' Perceptions

4. In your groups, discuss the perceptions that were shared in the step above.

5. (5-10 min.) The instructor will lead a group discussion on interpersonal perception. Any group member who wishes to may share experiences in that group.

13. INTERPERSONAL PERCEPTION EXERCISE

PURPOSE:

To compare your perception of yourself with others' perception
of you.

GROUP SIZE:

Any number of groups of 4 to 5 members.

TIME REQUIRED:

30-40 minutes.

INTRODUCTION:

We often do not get a chance to know how other people see us. This exercise is designed to
have you look at yourself in a different light and find out how others see you, using the same
categories.

EXERCISE SCHEDULE:

1. (10 min.) Form groups of four to five members. Each member fill out Interpersonal
    Perception Sheet 1.

2. (20-30 min.) Share your perceptions with the other group members. Person 1 tells how
    she/he sees herself/himself and in turn, all other group members tell how they see that
    person. Person 2 repeats the same procedure, followed by all other group members (until
    everyone has had their turn). While perceptions are being shared within the group,
    members should fill out Interpersonal Perception Sheet 2.

INTERPERSONAL PERCEPTION SHEET 1

MY PERCEPTIONS

Type Person Description	Self Perception	How You Perceive Person #1	How you Perceive Person #2	How You Perceive Person #3	How You Perceive Person #4
One sentence description.					
Animal					
Type of Music (e.g., jazz, rock, classical)					
Song					
Movie or TV Star					

INTERPERSONAL PERCEPTION SHEET 2

OTHERS' PERCEPTIONS OF ME*

Type Person Description	Person #1	Person #2	Person #3	Person #4
One sentence description.				
Animal				
Type of Music (e.g., jazz, rock, classical)				
Song				
Movie or TV Star				

*You may wish to use this space to record others' perceptions of you as members begin to share their matrices in the second part of this exercise.

14. ATTRIBUTION THEORY AND PERFORMANCE COMPARISONS[*]

PURPOSE:

1. To explore the applicability of attribution theories
    to performance diagnoses in work settings.
2. To understand the difference between "internal" and
    "external" attributions.
3. To understand the way in which Kelley's cues (consistency,
    consensus, and distinctiveness) may influence supervisor's
    diagnosis of performance problems.

GROUP SIZE:

Any number.

TIME REQUIRED:

50-70 minutes.

EXERCISE SCHEDULE:

1. (5 min.) Read the "A-Plus Aeronautics" case below and
    then read either Performance Charts for Group A or
    Performance Charts for Group B (at end of exercise).
    Your instructor will tell you which one to read.
    DO NOT read both of them.

2. (5 min.) Answer the questionnaire below the case.

3. (10-15 min.) In groups of 6-12 members of Groups A
    and Groups B, tabulate and average each questionnaire
    response. Then come to a consensus on the three
    questions.

4. (5 min.)   Write the group average for each question on the
    blackboard or a grid prepared by the instructor.

5. (10-15 min.)   The instructor will give some background in
    attribution theory (also read the section "Background on
    Attribution Theory" towards the end of this exercise).

6. (15-25 min.)   In a class discussion answer the following
    questions:

---

[*] Adapted from Karen A. Brown and Terence R. Mitchell, from <u>Exchange</u>, Vol. 8(4), 1983, pp.
23-38. Used with permission.

a. Which of the three information cues (consistency, consensus, distinctiveness) is likely to have the greatest influence on supervisors' diagnostic judgments?

b. Which of the three information cues is likely to be the most readily available to supervisors?

c. How will diagnostic judgments infuence a supervisor's actions to correct a performance problem?

d. Of what value would graphical displays of performance comparisons be in work settings?

e. What kinds of internal attributions might a supervisor make? What kinds of external attributions?

f. In addition to the three performance cues included in the exercise, what other sources of information might the supervisor use in making a diagnosis?

A-PLUS AERONAUTICS

A-Plus Aeronautics is an electronics firm that manufactures components for instrument control panels used in commercial jets. The company operates as a large job shop, routing custom-ordered products through the work centers in three major shop areas:

Fabrication, Assembly, and Testing. There are several work centers in each shop. The custom-ordered products are manufactured in lots of approximately 100 to 1000, with each item flowing through at least 30 work centers on its way to completion.

Sub-components such as circuit boards are assembled in the Assembly Shop, where there are 15 different work centers dedicated to particular kinds of technologies and tasks. The 100 employees in this shop are highly skilled and most of them have been with the company for five or more years.

Hanna Yates is a first line supervisor for the employees in Work Center 7 of the Assembly Shop. She was transferred to this position from Testing and has not previously held a strictly supervisory position. There are 15 people reporting to her, 10 of whom are on the day shift, and five of whom are on the night shift. The performance of day-shift employees is the easiest to monitor because it is possible for Hanna to observe them. Performance of night-shift employees is more difficult to monitor, however, and she relies heavily on daily performance charts generated by the company computer as a source of information about this group. Hanna has learned through informal channels that there may be a performance problem, having to do with declining output, during the night shift. She refers to her performance charts to see what the problem might be. These charts are shown at the end of the exercise.

QUESTIONNAIRE

Answer the following questions as if you were Hanna, using only the information available to you. Respond to each one by circling the number that best represents your assessment of the situation.

1.   How would you rate the seriousness of employee "C's" output decline?

```
1     2     3     4     5     6     7
Not               Moderately      Extremely
Serious           Serious         Serious
```

2.   What is the likelihood that the problem has something to do with employee "C" him/herself (e.g., effort, ability, attitude)?

```
1     2     3     4     5     6     7
Not               Moderately      Extremely
Serious           Serious         Serious
```

3.   What is the likelihood that the problem has something to do with the work environment (e.g., task difficulty, materials, equipment, available information)?

```
1     2     3     4     5     6     7
Not               Moderately      Extremely
Serious           Serious         Serious
```

BACKGROUND ON ATTRIBUTION THEORY

Attribution theory originally was conceptualized by Heider (1958) and has become increasingly popular in the behavioral literature. Attributions are defined as interpretations of the causes of behavior. People may make attributions about the causes of their own behavior, and they also may make attributions about the causes of other people's behaviors. These causal interpretations have been shown to affect people's behaviors in relation to themselves and toward others.

Three basic information cues originally described by Kelley (1967) may influence supervisors' attributions about the causes of a subordinate's poor performance. These information cues are known as: consistency, consensus, and distinctiveness. In work settings, consistency cues provide information about an employee's performance over time, consensus cues provide opportunity for comparisons among employees, and distinctiveness cues allow for comparisons across tasks.

The three cues have been shown to influence observers' attributions about the causes of other people's behaviors (e.g., MacArthur, 1972), and there are indications that they affect supervisors' diagnoses in a similar manner (e.g., Brown, Mitchell, Newell, and Schmitt, 1983). That is, if a subordinate is performing poorly and the supervisor knows that this employee usually performs well (low consistency), he or she is likely to make a different attribution than if the subordinate has continually failed at the job (high consistency). Similarly, if the poor performance is associated with a specific task but not with other tasks performed by the employee (high distinctiveness), the perceived cause of the problem is likely to be different than when the employee has performed poorly on most other tasks (low distinctiveness). Finally, if all of the subordinate's co-workers also are doing poorly (high consensus) the attribution will be different than in situations where just one subordinate is performing poorly (low consensus).

Regardless of the information cues available to observers, there appears to be a tendency toward internal attributions (Jones, 1979; Kelley and Michela, 1980). This tendency is known as the actor-observer error or as the fundamental attribution error (Reeder, 1982). Based on theory and empirical research, it is recognized that observers tend to view the undesirable behaviors or behavior outcomes of actors as being caused by the actors themselves. Actors, on the other hand focus on factors in their environment that may have caused the behavior or outcome. In work settings, these differences may translate into disagreements between supervisors and employees over the causes of poor performance.

References and Supplemental Reading

Brown, K. A. "Explaining Group Poor Performance: An Attributional Analysis." Academy of Management Review, 9(1), 1984, pp. 54-63.

Brown, K. A., T. R. Mitchell, W.T. Newell, T.G. Schmitt. "Diagnosing Poor Performance in Manufacturing Settings." AIDS Proceedings, 1984.

Heider, F. The Psychology of Interpersonal Relations. New York: Wiley, 1958.

Jones, E. E. "The Rocky Road from Acts to Dispositions." The American Psychologist, 34, 1979, pp. 107-117.

Kelley, H. H., J. L. Michela. "Attribution Theory and Research." Annual Review of Psychology. Eds. M. Rosenzweig and L. Porter. Palo Alto: Annual Reviews, 1980. 31: pp. 457-501.

Latham, G., L. L. Cummings, and T. R. Mitchell.   "Behavioral Strategies for Enhancing Productivity." Organizational Dynamics, 1981, pp. 4-23.

MacArthur, L. A. "The How and What of Why: Some Determinants and Consequences of Causal Attributions." Journal of Personality and Social Psychology, 22, 1972, pp. 171-193.

Mitchell, T. R., and L. S. Kalb. "The Effects of the Job Experience on Supervisor Attributions for a Subordinate's Poor Performance." Journal of Applied Psychology, 67, 1982, pp. 181-188.

Mitchell, T.R., and R. E. Wood. "Supervisors' Responses to Subordinate Poor Performance: A Test of an Attributional Model." Organizational Behavior and Human Performance, 25, 1980, pp. 123-138.

Reeder, G. D. "Let's Give the Fundamental Attribution Error Another Chance." Journal of Personality and Social Psychology, 43, 1982, pp. 341-344.

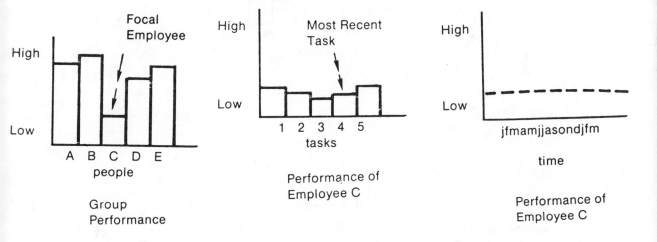

Figure 1   Performance Charts for Group A

Figure 2   Performance Charts for Group B

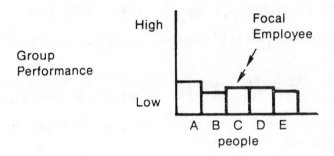

Group
Performance

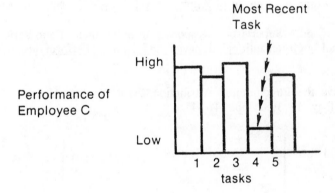

Performance of
Employee C

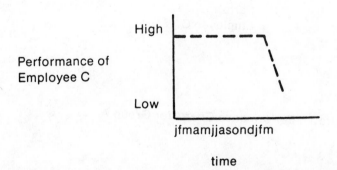

Performance of
Employee C

time

Chapter 5   Learning, Reinforcement and Problem-Solving

15. THE LEARNING-MODEL INSTRUMENT

PURPOSE:

To determine what type of learner students are.

GROUP SIZE:

Any number.

TIME REQUIRED:

30-40 minutes.

PREPARATION REQUIRED:

Complete and score the instrument.

EXERCISE SCHEDULE:

1. (Pre-Class) Complete and score the instrument.

2. (15-20 minutes) Instructor divides class into four groups: Thinker-Planners, Feeling-Planners, Task Implementors and Participative Implementors. Each group discusses:
   a.   What is the ideal learning environment?
   b.   Describe the best learning situation for your opposite type.
   c.   What was your worst learning experience?

3. (15-20 minutes)   The instructor gets reports from each group and leads a discussion on learning styles.

THE LEARNING-MODEL INSTRUMENT[*]

Instructions: For each statement choose the response that is more nearly true for you. Place an X on the blank that corresponds to that response.

1. When meeting people, I prefer
   _____ (a) to think and speculate on what they are like.
   _____ (b) to interact directly and to ask them questions.

2. When presented with a problem, I prefer
   _____ (a) to jump right in and work on a solution.
   _____ (b) to think through and evaluate possible ways to solve the problem.

3. I enjoy sports more when
   _____ (a) I am watching a good game.
   _____ (b) I am actively participating.

4. Before taking a vacation, I prefer
   _____ (a) to rush at the last minute and give little thought beforehand
             to what I will do while on vacation.
   _____ (b) to play early and daydream about how I will spend my vacation.

5. When enrolled in courses, I prefer
   _____ (a) to plan how to do my homework before actually attacking the
             assignment.
   _____ (b) to immediately become involved in doing the assignment.

6. When I receive information that requires action, I prefer
   _____ (a) to take action immediately.
   _____ (b) to organize the information and determine what type of action
             would be most appropriate.

7. When presented with a number of alternatives for action, I prefer
   _____ (a) to determine how the alternatives relate to one another and
             analyze the consequences of each.
   _____ (b) to select the one that looks best and implement it.

8. When I awake every morning, I prefer
   _____ (a) to expect to accomplish some worth while work without
             considering what the individual tasks may entail
   _____ (b) to plan a schedule for the tasks I expect to do that day.

9. After a full day's work, I prefer
   _____ (a) to reflect back on what I accomplished and think of how to
             make time the next day for unfinished tasks.
   _____ (b) to relax with some type of recreation and not think about
             my job.

---

[*]Copyright 1987 by Dr. Kenneth L. Murrell, University of West Florida. Used with permission.

10. After choosing the above responses, I
_____ (a) prefer to continue and complete this instrument.
_____ (b) am curious about how my responses will be interpreted and prefer some feedback before continuing with the instrument.

11. When I learn something, I am usually
_____ (a) thinking about it.
_____ (b) right in the middle of doing it.

12. I learn best when
_____ (a) I am dealing with real-world issues.
_____ (b) concepts are clear and well organized.

13. In order to retain something I have learned, I must
_____ (a) periodically review it in my mind.
_____ (b) practice it or try to use the information.

14. In teaching others how to do something, I first
_____ (a) demonstrate the task.
_____ (b) explain the task.

15. My favorite way to learn to do something is
_____ (a) reading a book or instructions or enrolling in a class.
_____ (b) trying to do it and learning from my mistakes.

16. When I become emotionally involved with something, I usually
_____ (a) let my feelings take the lead and then decide what to do.
_____ (b) control my feelings and try to analyze the situation.

17. If I were meeting jointly with several experts on a subject, I would prefer
_____ (a) to ask each of them for his or her opinion.
_____ (b) to interact with them and share our ideas and feelings.

18. When I am asked to related information to a g roup of people, I prefer
_____ (a) not to have an outline, but to interact with them and become involved in an extemporaneous conversation.
_____ (b) to prepare notes and know exactly what I am going to say.

19. Experience is
_____ (a) a guide for building theories.
_____ (b) the best teacher.

20. People learn easier when they are
_____ (a) doing work on the job.
_____ (b) in a class taught by an expert.

THE LEARNING-MODEL INSTRUMENT SCORING SHEET

Instructions: Transfer your responses by writing either "a" or "b" in the blank that corresponds to each item in the Learning Model Instrument.

Abstract/Concrete		Cognitive/Affective	
Column 1	Column 2	Column 3	Column 4
1. _____	2. _____	11. _____	12. _____
3. _____	4. _____	13. _____	14. _____
5. _____	6. _____	15. _____	16. _____
7. _____	8. _____	17. _____	18. _____
9. _____	10. _____	19. _____	20. _____

Total
Circles _____   _____   _____   _____

Grand Totals _____   _____

Now circle every "a" in Column 1 and Column 4. Then circle every "b" in Column 2 and in Column 3. Next, total the circles in each of the four columns. Then add the totals of Columns 1 and 2; plot this grand total on the vertical axis of the Learning Model for Managers and draw a horizontal line through the point. Now add the totals of Columns 3 and 4; plot that grand total on the horizontal axis of the model and draw a vertical line through the point. The intersection of these two lines indicates the domain of your preferred learning style.

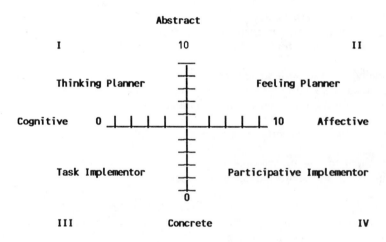

The Learning Model for Managers

THE LEARNING-MODEL INSTRUMENT INTERPRETATION SHEET

The cognitive-affective axis or continuum represents the range of ways in which people learn. Cognitive learning includes learning that is structured around either rote storing of knowledge or intellectual abilities and skills, or both. Affective learning includes learning from experience, from feelings about the experience, and from ones' own emotions.

The concrete-abstract axis or continuum represents the range of ways in which people experience life. When people experience life abstractly, they detach themselves from the immediacy of the situation and theorize about it. If they experience life concretely, they respond to the situation directly with little subsequent contemplation.

The two axes divide the model into four parts or domains. Most people experience life and learn from it in all four domains but have a preference for a particular domain. Liberal arts

on-the-job training usually takes place in the lower quadrants, particularly domain III.

Occupations representative of the four styles include the following: domain I, philosopher or chief executive officer; domain II, poet or journalist; domain III, architect or engineer; domain IV, psychologist or personnel counselor.

Managerial jobs require an ability to learn in all four domains, and a manager's development depends on his or her ability to learn both cognitively and affectively. Thus, management education and development demand the opportunity for the participants to learn how to learn in each domain.

Scoring the Instrument

The scoring sheet indicates which answers receive a score of one point. The rest of the answers receive a score of zero. The total of the scores in the first half of the instrument is plotted on the vertical axis and horizontal line is drawn from the point. The total of the scores in the last half is plotted on the horizontal axis and vertical line is drawn through that point. The point of intersection of the two lines indicates the domain of the respondent.

Interpreting the Scores

The next four paragraphs give an interpretation of the four end points of the axes in the Learning Model for Managers. Following these are explanations of the four domains in the model.

Cognitive Learning

A person who scores low on the cognitive-affective axis shows a marked preference for learning through thought or other mental activity. People who grasp intellectually very quickly what they are trying to learn or who simply prefer to use controlled thought and logic will be found on the cognitive end of this axis. Rationality appeals to these individuals, as do logic and other thinking skills that are necessary for this type of learning. Although this statement is not based on hard research, it appears that a high cognitive orientation correlates with a high task orientation rather than with a people orientation. The research about possible left-versus-right brain functioning correlates a cognitive orientation to individuals who are left-brian dominant. Therefore, the left side of the axis was deliberately assigned to the cognitive orientation to serve as an easy reminder.

Affective Learning

A person who scores high on the cognitive-affective axis shows a marked preference for learning in the affective realm. Such an individual is more comfortable with and seeks out learning from his or her emotions and feelings. These individuals desire personal interaction and seek to learn about people by experiencing them in emotional ways. This type of learner would potentially be highly people oriented. A manger with this orientation would probably seek out social interaction rather than to focus exclusively on the task components of the job. In right-brain research, affective learners are said to be more intuitive, more spontaneous, and less linear. They seek out feelings and emotions rather than logic.

Concrete Life Experiencing

People with a preference for the concrete enjoy jumping in an getting their hands dirty. Hands-on experiences are important to them. As managers, these people want to keep busy, become directly involved, and physically approach or touch whatever they are working with. If they work with machines, they will get greasy; if they work with people, they will become involved.

Abstract Life Experiencing

Individuals preferring this style have no special desire to touch, but they want to keep active by thinking about the situation and relating it to similar situations. Their preferred interaction style is internal-inside their own heads.

The Four Learning Domains

A person is unlikely to be on the extreme end of either axis, and no one type of learning is "best." Any mixture of preferences simply represents a person's uniqueness. The model is useful in helping people differentiate themselves, and it offers a method for looking at the way different styles fit together. This section describes the four domains that are represented in the model.

The descriptions of these domains could be of special interest to managers, because they will help the manager understand the relationship between managerial action and learning style. A manager should be capable of learning and functioning well in all four domains, especially if he or she expects to face a variety of situations and challenges. The successful manager is likely to be the one who can operate in both a task and a people environment with the ability to see and become involved with the concrete and also use thought processes to understand what is needed. The normative assumption of the model is that a manager should learn how to learn in each of the four domains. IN doing this, the manager may well build on his or her primary strengths, but the versatility and flexibility demanded in a managerial career make clear the importance of all four domains.

Domain I, the Thinking Planner. A combination of cognitive and abstract preferences constitutes domain I, where the "thinking planner" is located. This domain might well be termed the place for the planner whose job is task oriented and whose environment contains primarily things, numbers, or printouts. The bias in formal education is often toward this learning domain, and Mintzberg (1976) was critical of this bias. In this domain things are treated abstractly and often their socio-emotional elements are denied.

The domain-I learner should do well in school, should have a talent for planning, and is likely to be successful as a staff person, or manager in a department that deals with large quantities of untouchable things. This domain represents an important area for management learning. Of the four domains, it seems to receive the heaviest emphasis in traditional university programs and in management-development seminars, particularly those in financial management.

Domain II, the Feeling Planner. A combination of affective and abstract preferences constitutes domain II, where the "feeling planner" is located. The managerial style associated with this domain is that of the thinker who can learn and who enjoys working with people but has limited opportunity to get close to them. This domain is important for the personnel executive or a manager with too much responsibility to interact closely with other employees. Social-analysis skills are represented in this area. Managers in this domain should be able to think through and understand the social and emotional factors affecting a large organization.

Difficulties in this area sometimes arise when good first-line supervisors who have a natural style with people are promoted into positions that prevent hem from having direct contact with others and are expected to determine without concrete experience the nature of and solutions to personnel problems.

Domain III, the Task Implementor. A combination of cognitive and concrete preferences constitutes domain III, where the "task implementor" is located. This domain contains decision makers who primarily want to understand the task and who can focus ont he details and specifics of the concrete in a thoughtful manner. If these people are allowed to think about a situation, they can emotional climate is not a problem, this person is likely to do well.

Domain IV, the Participative Implementor. A combination of affective and concrete preferences constitutes domain IV, where the "participative implementor" is located. The manager with people skills who has the opportunity to work closely with people is found in this category. This is the place where implementors and highly skilled organization development consultants reside. This domain is for those who like to become involved and who have the ability and interest in working with the emotional needs and demands of the people in an organization. This is the domain that is emphasized by most of the practical management programs, and it can be used to complement the traditional educational programs of domain I.

References

Blake, R.R., and J. S. Mouton. Managerial Grid. 3rd ed. Houston, Texas: Gulf, 1984.

Jung, C.G. Second impression Trans, H. Godwin. New York: Harcourt Brace, 1924.

Kolb, D.A., I.M. Rubin and J. M. McIntyre. Organizational Psychology. An Experiential Approach. 2nd ed. Englewood Cliffs, NJ: Prentice-Hall, 1974.

Mintzberg, H. "Planning on the Left Side and Managing on the Right." Harvard Business Review, July-August, 1976, pp. 49-58.

Peters, D. Directory of Human Resource Development Instrumentation. San Diego, CA: University Associates, 1985.

Pfeiffer, J. W., R. Heslin, and J.E. Jones. Instrumentation in Human Relations Training. San Diego, CA: University Associates, 1976.

Rogers, C.R. Freedom to Learn. Columbus, OH: Charles E. Merrill, 1982.

16. THE SELF SHAPING PROJECT[*]

PURPOSE:

1. To understand the complexities involved in changing our own behavior and the behavior of others.

2. To more fully understand the principles and theory underlying Behavior Modification.

GROUP SIZE:

The project may be done with or without support groups. If groups are used, optimum size is 4-6 members.

TIME REQUIRED:

This project generally lasts for 4-6 weeks, although variations have been successfully utilized. Your instructor will provide guidelines for the project length.

PREPARATION REQUIRED:

Each student should become familiar with the theoretical principles underlying Behavior Modification. A list of Suggested Readings appears at the end of this project description. Consult with your instructor in choosing the most appropriate reading(s).

RELATED TOPICS:

Learning
Motivation
Change
Control systems
Feedback

INTRODUCTION:

This project challenges you to change your own behavior. The managerial rationale behind this approach can be summarized by the following statement: "If you can't change your own behavior, how can you expect to change someone else's behavior?" The project has been designed to introduce you to the complexities of behavior change.

You will use behavior modification techniques to change any personal behavior of your choice: the target behavior. Over the years we have witnessed student projects designed to modify a wide range of target behaviors including getting to school or work on time, increasing studying, reducing eyelash or nail picking, learning new words, and meeting new people. Choose any target behavior that has importance to you. This will make the project a lot more fun, and you will learn more in the process. Also, choose a behavior that is specific, observable, measurable and controllable.

EXHIBIT I outlines the steps of the project. Take the time to review this exhibit. The two crucial phases of the project are the baseline period and the intervention period. A detailed discussion of these follows.

---

[*]By Rae Andre and Brendan Bannister. Used with permission.

EXHIBIT I

Managerial Uses of Behavior Modification:
Steps in Self Shaping

1. **DEFINE THE PROBLEM:** State the problem in terms of your behavior in particular situations... behavior that doesn't occur, but should, or behavior that does occur, but shouldn't. Write down whatever you know about the problem. Be specific.

2. **TAKE BASE-LINE DATA.** Gather base-line data on your target behavior--frequency, length of occurrence, situation, etc. Take note of when, where, why, and with whom the target behavior occurs, plus your own thoughts and feelings at the time. Your data recording apparatus should be portable and present whenever the target behavior occurs. Reinforce yourself for taking base-line data. Take base-line data for one week.

3. **ANALYZE YOUR DATA.** Go over your baseline and list probably antecedents and consequences for your target behavior. Make a list of the resources available that might aid your project-- friends, time, money, etc. List your potential reinforcers.

4. **DESIGN YOUR PROGRAM.** Specify all of the following:

    --- the behavior to be shaped
    --- the goal or terminal behavior
    --- your reinforcers
    --- the schedule of reinforcement
    --- feedback/record-keeping procedures
    --- steps for fading out reinforcement (if desirable)

5. **INTERVENTION.** Do it... carry out your plan. Monitor it to see if it is working. Why or why not? Change your plan if necessary... most problems occur because the steps taken toward the goal are too big, or because the reinforcers chosen are either too small or are used nonbontin- gently (otherwise known as 'cheating' on oneself or using 'bootleg' reinforcement).

6. **MAINTENANCE.** How to make the changes stick...

    --- stop and reinstate the program as needed
    --- keep recording data on your target behavior
    --- fade out the reinforcement
    --- use difference reinforcers to avoid satiation
    --- switch to non-tangible reinforcers, or to naturally occurring reinforcers

7. **WRITE-UPS OF SELF-SHAPING PROJECTS.** May be organized according to the plan of this sheet, from determining the target behavior and taking a baseline through results by the end of the term and plans for maintenance. Grades do not depend on how well the project went, that is, they do not depend on whether or not you obtained your goal, but rather they depend on your design and on your efforts to improve that design. At least one full page of the paper should be devoted to your assessment of the applicability of this experience to managing.

Papers must be typed, at least four pages (1,000 words) in length, and must include (beyond the four-page minimum) graphs or charts showing your progress.

THE BASELINE PERIOD

During the baseline period, which usually lasts one week, you will observe <u>antecedent</u> conditions which will serve to either enhance or inhibit changes in your target behavior. For example, you may identify getting to school on time as your target behavior. During the baseline period you may notice that you are usually late if you stay up too late the night before or if you haven't prepared the next day's clothes the prior night. Gathering this kind of information can be quite instructive. For example, it my lead to the realization that you are targeting the wrong behavior; perhaps it is late nights out that should be changed. One thing to remember about the baseline period - DO NOT USE REINFORCEMENT OR PUNISHMENT TO SHAPE THE TARGET BEHAVIOR DURING THE BASELINE - JUST OBSERVE AND LEARN.

During the baseline period, you should also measure your target behavior as you will during the intervention period. Measuring your behavior during the baseline can help you to set realistic goals. It also gives comparison data against which change can be evaluated.

During the baseline period you should also be working on the <u>design</u> of your intervention program. The design should incorporate both the <u>strategies</u> and <u>schedules</u> of reinforcement. Strategies of reinforcement include positive reinforcement, negative reinforcement, punishment, and extinction or omission. Schedules of reinforcement include fixed and variable interval, and fixed and variable ratio schedules. The importance of strategies and schedules of reinforcement should not be underestimated. The reading(s) and discussion with your instructor will help clarify important distinctions.

THE INTERVENTION PERIOD

Although your instructor may decide on some variation, the usual time frame for intervention is four weeks. Be prepared that all may not go as you planned. You may find that the chosen strategies, schedules, or rewards do not work as you expected. Don't dismay! These "mini-failures" are exactly the experiences that provide wonderful insights into the "workings" of the theory. The key attitude to maintain during the intervention period is flexibility. Make adjustments! Change your strategies, schedules or rewards to get yourself back on track. During this period your group (if you have been assigned to one) can be very helpful in discussing issues that come up in your project and may act as a reinforcer for your efforts.

At the end of the intervention period you will probably be asked to provide a project write-up and analysis. Our experience has been that the students who do "best" in the write-up are those who invest most in the project. This does not necessarily mean that these were the students who enjoyed the most "success" in changing their behavior. Instead, students who put a good deal of time into understanding <u>why</u> their program was going well or poorly and who made <u>insightful</u> changes and adaptations seem to understand the project best. This is typically reflected in their writing. **EXHIBIT II** illustrates the major topical areas that should be considered in your project write-up.

EXHIBIT II

Suggested Paper Outline

I.   Target Behavior - Why Selected

II.   Measurement of Target Behavior

III.   Strategies of Reinforcement - Are you using positive reinforcement (PR), negative reinforcement (NR), Extinction, Punishment, some combination? What was the rationale for your choice?

IV.   Schedules of Reinforcement - Continuous Reinforcement (CR), Fixed Interval (FI), Fixed Ratio (FR), Variable Interval (VI), Variable Ratio (VR), combinations?
        Again explicitly identify the rationale for your choice(s)?

V.   Description of Baseline Period - Activities/Insights

VI.   Results of Intervention Period (with references to graphs, tables, visual displays). Don't analyze here, just present the data.

VII.   Analysis of what went "Right" and "Wrong" - Very Important

VIII.   Analysis of Managerial Implications, Generalizations and Extensions -Very Important.

SUGGESTED READINGS:

Hamner, W.C. "Reinforcement Theory and Contingency Management in Organizational Settings." In <u>Organizational Behavior and Management: A Contingency Approach</u>. Eds. H. L. Tosi and W. C. Hamner. Chicago: St. Clair Press. [Also reprinted in R.M. Steers and L.W. Porter, <u>Motivation and Work Behavior</u> (all four editions). New York: McGraw-Hill, 1975, 1979, 1983, 1987].

Hamner, W. C., and R. Hamner. "Behavior Modification on the Bottom Line." <u>Organizational Dynamics</u>, 4, 1976, pp. 8-21. [Also reprinted in R.M. Steers and L.W. Porter referenced above.] Kerr, S. "On the Folly of Rewarding A While Hoping for B." <u>Academy of Management Journal</u>, 18, 1975, pp. 769-783. [Also reprinted in R. M. Steers and L. W. Porter referenced above.]

Luthans, F. and T. Davis. "Behavioral Self-Management -- The Missing Link in Managerial Effectiveness." <u>Organizational Dynamics</u>, 8, pp. 42-60.

Manz, C. and H. Sims. "Self-Management as a Substitute for Leadership: A Social Learning Theory Perspective." <u>Academy of Management Review</u>, 5, pp. 361-367.

17. POSITIVE AND NEGATIVE REINFORCEMENT

PURPOSE:

To examine the effects of positive and negative reinforcement on behavior change.

GROUP SIZE:

Any number, although it is especially effective in large classes.

TIME REQUIRED:

25-35 minutes for Part A.
10-15 minutes for Part B.

RELATED TOPICS:

Motivation
Interpersonal Communication

INTRODUCTION:

Behavior Modification (Behavior Management) and Reinforcement are based on the work of B. F. Skinner and have proven to be effective in behavior change in organizations. The following exercise will help you to see what happens when positive and negative reinforcement are used.

EXERCISE SCHEDULE:

PART A - POSITIVE AND NEGATIVE REINFORCEMENT EXERCISE[*]

(Steps 1-4, 5 minutes)

1. Two (or three) volunteers are selected to receive reinforcement from the class while performing a particular task. The volunteers leave the room.

2. The instructor identifies an object for the student volunteers to locate when they return to the room. (The object should be unobtrusive but clearly visible to the class. Examples that have worked well include a small triangular piece of paper that was left behind when a notice was torn off a classroom bulletin board, a smudge on the chalkboard, and a chip in the plaster of a classroom wall.)

3. The instructor specifies the reinforcement contingencies that will be in effect when the volunteers return to the room--for negative reinforcement students should hiss, boo and throw things (although you should not throw anything harmful) when the first volunteer

---

[*]By Larry Michaelson. Used with permission.

is moving away from the object; cheer and applaud when the second volunteer is getting closer to the object; and, if a third volunteer is used, students should use both negative and positive reinforcement.

4. The instructor should assign a student to keep a record of the time it takes each of the volunteers to locate the object.

(Steps 5 & 6, 5-10 minutes)

5. Volunteer number one is brought back into the room and is instructed that "Your task is to locate and touch a particular object in the room and the class has agreed to help you--you may begin."

6. Volunteer number one continues to look for the object until it is found while the class assists by giving negative reinforcement.

(Steps 7 & 8, 3-5 minutes)

7. Volunteer number two is brought back into the room and is instructed that "Your task is to locate and touch a particular object in the room and the class has agreed to help you--you may begin."

8. Volunteer number two continues to look for the object until it is found while the class assists by giving positive reinforcement.

(Steps 9 & 10, 3-5 minutes--Optional)

9. Volunteer number three is brought back into the room and is instructed that "Your task is to locate and touch a particular object in the room and the class has agreed to help you--you may begin."

10. Volunteer number three continues to look for the object until it is found while the class assists by giving both positive and negative reinforcement.

11. (1-15 min.) In a class discussion answer the following questions:
    a. What was the difference in behavior change of the volunteer when different kinds of reinforcement (positive, negative or both) were used?

    b. What were the emotional reactions of the volunteers to the different kinds of reinforcement?

    c. Which type of reinforcement is most common in organizations, positive or negative? What effect do you think this has on motivation and productivity?

PART B   REINFORCEMENT: ITS APPLICATION AND RESULTS[**]

In order to better understand the impact reinforcement can have on the behavior, attitudes, and reactions of others, this exercise requires you to experiment and analyze its application.

_____

[**]By Mary Gander. Used with permission.

1. During the next week, look for a situation where you can practice reinforcement.

   Be alert for situations in which someone does something which you consider to be worthy of a compliment. When such a situation occurs, make a deliberate effort to give them a compliment in a sincere and specific way (e.g., perhaps a roommate washes a sink full of everyone's dirty dishes, or your boss provides you with some helpful information, or a fellow student gets an interview request from a good company, etc.)***

2. After you have completed the experiment, answer the following questions:

   Analyze:
   1) What kind of reinforcement did you use? Why?
   2) What was the other person's reaction?
   3) What short term and/or longer term outcomes, if any, were
       achieved or do you expect to occur?
   4) How did you feel after the incident?

   Briefly describe an incident in which another person used reinforcement on you. How did you feel/respond?

3. (10-15 min.) In class, the instructor will ask for volunteers to explain their experiences and may ask you to turn in this page or another sheet with answers to the above four questions.

***As a variation on this experiment, select a person to compliment whom you normally would never think of reinforcing such as your boss, your father, a professor, or someone with whom you do not feel you have a very good relationship--the results will probably be very interesting! Try using reinforcement more than once on the same person if it is appropriate in situations which occur.

18. FIRING*

PURPOSE:

1. To learn how to make lay-off/firing decisions.
2. to examine values in decision-making.

GROUP SIZE:

Any number of groups of 5-8 members.

TIME REQUIRED:

35 to 50 minutes.

PREPARATION REQUIRED:

Rank order employees in terms of lay-off decisions.

BACKGROUND:

Most organizations go through periods where budgets are cut and numbers of personnel reduced. The following exercise will help you look at various characteristics in the lay-off decision.

EXERCISE SCHEDULE:

1. (Pre-class) Rank order employees.
2. (20-30 min.) Groups of 5-8 members (one observer may be assigned in larger groups) meet and prepare a group ranking.
3. (5 min.) Groups report rankings or write them on the board.
4. (10-15 min.) Instructor leads a discussion on firing decisions and values.

DIRECTIONS:

You are a top-level executive in QLT corporation. Choose one of the following areas as your responsibility in the company.

> Production
> Marketing
> Accounting
> Finance
> Public Relations
> Personnel

62

QLT is in a period of market downturn and needs to slash budgets to avoid major financial setbacks. In a few hours you will be meeting with several other top executives to decide which personnel to lay off. Out of the twelve employees you may need to cut somewhere between two and seven. Rank order them according to their level of "expendability." "1" is first to fire, "12" is last. The more money you save in salaries, the better for the company, and your group will be further rewarded.

Name	Position	Accomplishments	Age	Personal	Salary	Other Data	Ranking*
1. John Ringold	Asst. Dir. of Customer Relalation	Started new customer Satisfaction Program	49	Divorced, 4 children, pays alimony and child support.	$43,000	Had been hard worker but recently work slacking off. Tends to give a lot of negative feedback & puts others off.	
2. Maureen Brown	Senior Accountant	Major force in developing new Control System	38	Married, 2 children, Husband is successful attorney.	$39,500	Works more than almost anyone else. Frequently comes in on weekends. Tends to be isolated from group.	
3. William Brighton	Production Analyst	Researched new system for reducing production costs	31	Single	$34,600	Comes in early and stays late. Always does quality work. Gets along with co-workers, but sometimes seems aloof.	
4. Stephanie Sweetal	Marketing Manager	Responsible for bringing in several major customers	33	Divorced, 1 child, gets no alimony, minial child support.	$33,700	Work is adequate, though not exemplary. Everyone likes her and wants to work with her.	
5. George Devense	Asst. Director of Employee Assistance Programs	Started successful alcohol/drug abuse program	40	Married, 3 children, Wife works part-time as sales clerk.	$41,000	Used to be star employee. Last two years quality has suffered. Work is now mediocre, ever since his mother went in for intensive care treatment. Pleasant personality.	

Name	Position	Accomplishments	Age	Personal	Salary	Other Data	Ranking*
6. Susan Clark	Senior Financial Analyst	Revamped stock and investment programs	43	Single	$44,000	Sometimes outstanding employee, but she goes through "low" periods as well. She is often helpful to other workers.	
7. Barry Morris	Production Research Assoc.	Introduced computerization to production process	34	Married, 3 children, wife is full-time homemaker	$37,800	He tries hard, but sometimes does not make the mark.	
8. Edwina Stolwarth	New Product Analyst	Researched new markets which brought significant profits	35	Married, 1 child, husband is Physician.	$36.500	Always does excellent work, more than expected.	
9. Ray Oswald	Accounting Manager	Developed new system for improving accounts receivable	53	Divorced, 3 children, pays no alimony, all children are in college - pays full expenses.	$46,000	Does adequate work, occasionally misses assignments. Known as a "ladies" man.	
10. Elizabeth Warren	Finance Manager	Developed long range program to help company recover from current difficulties	44	Divorced, no children	$44,000	Hard worker, but her reputation around town is not high--too much partying.	
11. Randy Arbach	Director of Recruitment Testing	Instituted successful system of using a battery of physical tests to screen applicants.	42	Married, 2 children	$42,500	Going through a divorce and previously outstanding work has slipped dramatically. Usually part of the "team."	

Name	Position	Accomplishments	Age	Personal	Salary	Other Data	Ranking*
2. Cindy Miller	Community Liaison	Started program to link company with community organizations	48	Married, 2 teenagers, husband is seasonal construction worker	$33,000	Gets along well with others. Adequate worker.	

*Ranking on lay-off "1" is first to go.

Chapter 6 **Work Motivation**

19. THE MERIT BONUS ACTIVITY[*]

PURPOSE:

1. To familiarize the individual with various criteria
   that can be used to make decisions regarding organizational
   rewards.
2. To introduce issues of money as motivator, the use of
   bonus systems and the concept that people tend to
   behave in ways for which they are rewarded.

GROUP SIZE:

Any number of groups of 4-6 members.

TIME REQUIRED:

25-65 minutes depending on options.

PREPARATION REQUIRED:

Read the "Merit Bonus Case" and assign a merit bonus
to each person on the list.

---

[*]Adapted from E. Gil Boyer (St. Joseph's University), Steven I. Meisel
(La Salle University), Joseph Seltzer (La Salle University), and Joan Weiner (Drexel University).
Used with permission.

EXERCISE SCHEDULE:

1. (Before Class) Read the Merit Bonus Case and assign a merit bonus to each person on the list.

2. (20-30 min.) In groups of 4-6 members, reach a consensus on merit bonus assignments. (This step is optional. The exercise may be done as individuals, in which case Step 5 would have individuals discussing differences in scores.)

3. Identify and write below criteria which can be used when giving rewards.

4. Write down the criteria you would use as a manager.

5. (10-15 min.) Groups report their decision and record them on the blackboard. Where discrepancies exist between groups, they must then defend their decisions.

6. The instructor will generate a list of the responses for #4 on the blackboard.

7. (5 min.) The instructor will give the scoring key to you so that you can obtain total scores for each criteria. Individuals should total scores and each group's decision should be totaled as well.

8. (10 min.) The instructor will lead a discussion on how rewards affect behavior.

THE MERIT BONUS CASE

You are a manager of a department that was formed just under a year ago. At that time, ten recent technical graduates were hired to perform a variety of maintenance tasks. You have finished the annual performance reviews except for one new form that the Personnel Department introduced this year. Under an innovative agreement with the Union, it requires you to make a recommendation for a percentage increase that will be given as a <u>merit bonus</u>. Then the division General Manager will review your recommendations and make the final decision. You are not happy about having to do the task because it's hard to tell how well each person is doing and also the G.M. said at a meeting that "all employees aren't the same." I want to see the managers give their employees different bonuses. I wouldn't want more than a third of your department to get the same amount. I also don't think anyone deserves more than 15%." The company has a cost of living pay raise, so you just have to make recommendations about the merit bonus. All ten should add up to 100%.

_____ ALICE ADAMS - Alice puts a lot of effort into her work and, because of her superior ability and the respect she has earned from others, seems to have a good performance record.

_____ BOB BURNS - Bob is a real nice fellow. He is very friendly and tries hard to do a good job. You think he has the skills, but he makes a lot of mistakes.

_____ CHARLENE CARLSON - Charlene is a hard worker, but tends to be a loner. She is quite skilled and has good performance.

_____   DAN DUNN - Dan is lazy and doesn't get much done. The only
reason he got the job in the first place is that his uncle is
the Assistant General Manager.

_____   ED ENDERS - Ed is very skilled at his job and therefore doesn't
have to work too hard to have good performance. He is quite
friendly with the others.

_____   FRAN FOX - Fran has been an important member of the work group.
She understands the technical details and often tries to help
others. She might be called the informal group leader, but she
seems bored with her present job and doesn't work very hard.
As a result, her performance seems to have been below average.

_____   GUS GROOM - Gus has excellent technical skill and seems to have
good performance even though he often gets into arguments with
the other employees and rarely puts much effort into his job.

_____   HARRY HALL - Harry is not very good at his job but puts in more
time than anyone else, and often works through breaks and
lunch. He gets along well with others both on and off the job.

_____   IRENE ILLMAN - Irene didn't do well in technical school, but
she puts a lot of effort into her job.   She has good
performance except when she has to work with others and her
temper gets in the way.

_____   JOHN JANIS - John has a lot of influence with the other members
of the group and is well liked. You think his performance is
good because he works hard at whatever tasks he is assigned
to do and makes the most of his limited skills.

_100%_ TOTAL

20. EXPECTANCY THEORY ACTIVITY*

PURPOSE:

To see how expectancy theory works in practice.

GROUP SIZE:

An even number of up to ten (10) groups of 5 to 8 members.

TIME REQUIRED:

50-75 minutes.

PREPARATION REQUIRED:

Read the "Background" below and each of the case studies.

RELATED TOPICS:

>Motivation
>Need Theory
>Organizational Research
>Job Design

BACKGROUND:

The essence of expectancy theory is that people choose actions that benefit themselves the most: they maximize the value of their actions. Seen another way, from the point of view of the organization, individuals are motivated to perform behaviors that are in their best interest. In other words, employees will work hard when they are rewarded for working hard. If they are not rewarded they will not work hard, it is in their better interest to expend less effort. If we are talking about motivating choice of tasks rather than effort, then we can say that people will choose tasks that benefit them.

Expectancy theory is of course more complicated in its completeness than the simple description above. It specifies the components of the connection between behavior and reward, saying that for rewards to motivate behavior (1) rewards must be valued, (2) performance must lead to rewards, and (3) behavior must lead to performance. Each of these components is necessary, if one is missing or weak the entire connection is weak and behavior is poorly motivated. These three components are called (1) valence, (2) instrumentality, and (3) expectancy, and are described more fully below. The theory also specifies how these components are combined to calculate motivational force. This is also described below.

Valence - This refers to the value of the rewards of performance for the individual. Some people value money, for example, more than other things or more than other people do. Some

---

people may value the personal satisfaction they get from doing their job well most of all. Some people may value their relationships with co-workers. Different people will value different job or task rewards differently. These rewards have differing valence, therefore, and have differing potential to motivate behavior.

Expectancy theory does not specify all the rewards that must be considered. We do know, though, that pay, co-worker relationships, personal satisfaction, promotions, and the characteristics of the job are common job rewards. To measure valence we must determine how valuable or important to a person the rewards offered by the job are. Valence is best measured on a scale from 0 to 1. The valence of a particular reward is high, or close to 1, when that reward is highly valued. When a reward is not valued it has 0 valence. To make calculations simpler in the exercise that follows, rather than estimating expectancy between 0 and 1 you will use a scale from 0 to 100.

Because jobs have multiple rewards and individuals value more than just one reward, all relevant job outcomes should be taken into account to best predict or enhance motivation. In the exercise that follows, though, you will be considering only the two most important rewards.

Instrumentality - This refers to the perceived relationship between performance and rewards, or how well performance on a job leads to job rewards. Often this component is called Performance-Reward Expectancy, sometimes it is referred to as E_2. Here we will call it instrumentality. This comes from the idea that performance is instrumental for rewards, it is the means to achieve rewards.

Because jobs have multiple rewards they also have more than one instrumentality. For each reward, instrumentality is the degree to which performance on the job is perceived to cause the reward to be received. If high performance and only high performance leads to high amounts of the reward and low performance and only low performance leads to low reward, then instrumentality is high - performance causes the reward to follow. If a reward is achieved whether performance is high or not then performance is not instrumental for the reward and instrumentality is low. In some jobs people get paid the same whether their performance is high or low.

Instrumentality for each reward is best measured on a scale from -1 to +1. When high performance and only high performance leads to high pay, for example, and low performance and only low performance leads to low rewards, then performance is highly instrumental for pay and instrumentality for that reward is high and positive, or close to +1. If there is no relationship between performance and promotions, for exmaple, the instrumentality is absent or close to 0. It is even possible that performance on some jobs leads to lower rewards, such as when doing well in a job lessens the chance of a transfer. In this case instrumentality is negative, or between 0 and -1. In the exercise, though, you will estimate instrumentality on a scale from -100 to +100.

Instrumentality is measured between performance and each reward. For example, if two rewards, pay and promotions, are present, there is an instrumentality of performance of pay (we'll call this first instrumentality I_1 in the exercise) and an instrumentality of performance for promotions (which we will call I_2 in the exercise). These multiple instrumentalities are combined with the multiple valences in the way described below, "Combining Valence, Instrumentality, and Expectancy." In the exercise you will estimate instrumentality for the two most important rewards.

Expectancy - This refers to the perceived relationship between effort and performance. Often this component is called effort-performance expectancy, sometimes it is referred to as E_1. Here we'll call if expectancy.

Expectancy is the degree to which effort is perceived to cause performance. If effort leads to performance and lack of effort leads to lack of performance then expectancy is high. If no matter how much effort a person expends performance does not change, that is, it remains low or high, then is not what is required to cause performance.

Another way of thinking about expectancy is as the amount of control a person perceives they have over their performance. If they can believe that they control performance with their behavior then expectancy is high.

Expectancy is best measured on a scale from -1 to +1. When high effort and only high effort leads to high performance and low effort and only low effort leads to low performance, then expectancy is high and positive, or close to 1. When there is no relationship then expectancy is absent or close to 0. Because it is possible for more effort to lead to lower performance (such as when working harder interferes with productivity) expectancy can be negative. The stronger this negative relationship the closer expectancy is to -1. You will estimate expectancy on a scale from -100 to +100 in the exercise.

Combining Valence, Instrumentality and Expectancy - In order for rewards to motivate effortful behavior, the rewards must be valued, performance must lead to rewards and effort must lead to performance. From the employee's perspective, the "line of sight" from effort to rewards must be clear. Each link in the chain is necessary: effort causing performance, performance causing rewards, and rewards being valued.

In expectancy theory motivational force, which is a person's tendency to choose to expend effort, is equal to the product of expectancy, instrumentality, and valence. It is each of these multiplied by each other. In this way, if any one is absent, or equal to 0, then the whole equation is equal to 0, no force is present.

Specifically the formula is written as follows:

$$MF = E \; x \quad (I \; x \; V)$$

The formula can be read as "motivational force is equal to the product of expectancy times the sum of the product of each instrumentality times each valence." To illustrate, once all components are measured, (1) each reward valence (V_1, V_2, ...) is multiplied by each instrumentality for the corresponding reward (I_1, I_2, ...), (2) these products (VI_1, VI_2, ...) are summed or added together, and (3) this total (VI) is multiplied by expectancy. the resulting figure is what we would predict the force to expend effort to be. For exmaple, if V_1 and V_2 are equal to .8 and .6, I_1 and I_2 are equal to .8 and .9, and E is equal to .7, then

$$MF = .7 \; x \; [(.8 \; x \; .8) + (.6 \; x \; .9)] = .83$$

In the following exercise you will be estimating or measuring the valence, instrumentality, and expectancy that is present for the individuals described in the following case studies. You will also calculate motivational force. To test the validity of expectancy theory you will also be predicting how hard the individuals described are likely to work. Your motivation calculations will be compared to the effort predictions made by other groups, and vice versa. If expectancy theory works then we would expect predictions of level of effort to match calculated motivational force.

CASE STUDIES

CASE A. Arthur has been working for the same insurance firm for twenty years. He was recently transferred to a position where he supervises a group of young managers-in-training. As a senior employee he is well paid. Money, though, doesn't mean much to Arthur. His investments have done well and he has no family to support. Arthur's principal interest has always been the work itself. If he is diligent Arthur is able to do a good job. But the transfer has taken him away from his previous work and he finds supervision uninteresting. In recognition of this, Arthur has been given

If he is diligent Arthur is able to do a good job. But the transfer has taken him away from his previous work and he finds supervision uninteresting. In recognition of this, Arthur has been given a raise and promised more of the same work.

CASE B. Barbara is an entry level accountant for a small bookkeeping firm. One of the things that attracted her to this firm is their way of paying people - Barbara receives a share of the firm's monthly profit based on her monthly performance. As a young person Barbara wants to be successful and for her that means earning money and moving upward in the firm. When Barbara works hard she feels that she accomplishes a lot; more, she thinks, than her co-workers. But when her bosses appraise her performance she feels unfairly treated. On months that she has done well she doesn't get any more profit than other months. What really angered her was when she was overlooked for a promotion after her best month yet.

CASE C: The assembly line at the Mayfair Appliance Plant runs at a steady one foot per second. Charles' job is attaching refrigerator door hinges for which he's not paid very much. Whether he works harder or takes it easy it make no difference - the line moves on. Mayfair's slogan is "Quality Comes First." But though Charles pays special attention to quality no one notices. Although he'd like to socialize, his co-workers ignore him - Charles is the only Native Indian in his plant.

CASE D: Diane works as a software designer for an innovative microcomputer manufacturer. She enjoys her work because it provides her with challenging and interesting work and it pays well. In her firm, bonuses are awarded every quarter on the basis of individual employee accomplishments. People who perform well are also given first choice of new projects. As a well trained and competent worker Diane is able to do her job very well so long as she works hard.

CASE E: Earl only wants two things out of his job - the friendship of his buddies in the machine shop and his paycheck. Earl is paid on a piece rate basis - the harder he works and the more parts he finishes, the more money he makes. Earl is a good machinist and can be very productive if he tries. Unfortunately when Earl outperforms the rest of his work group, they scorn him as a "rate-buster." the more he produces the worse the scorn. It seems that in the past the shop's owners have used high performance ot lower the amount workers receive for each piece produced.

CASE F: Fay recently returned to the workforce after a long absence. During that time much of the way her job is done has changed. It used to be that hard work and creativity was necessary to do a good job, which earned her praise and a good salary. She is still recognized for high performance but she doesn't feel personally responsible. Now a computer program does most of her work for her - her effort or creativity isn't required. Fay's work is always good.

EXERCISE SCHEDULE:

1. (5-10 min.) The instructor will discuss the expectancy model of motivation and will divide the class into an even number of groups, each with about 5 members.

2. (30-45 min.) Each group will first use the expectancy model to calculate the motivational force present in half of the case studies by judging their valence, instrumentality and expectancy. For the remaining cases each group will predict how hard the individual described is likely to work. Groups with odd numbers will calculate motivation for cases in Set I (A, B and c). Even-numbered groups will calculate motivation for cases in Set II (D, E, F) and predict motivation for cases in Set I (A, B, C).

   a. First, read one case study at a time int he appropriate set and come to a group consensus on the two most salient rewards present for the individual. For each of these rewards assign a number between 0 and 100 representing the importance or value or

performance and each reward, or instrumentality, that is present. Use the description of instrumentality in the background and assign numbers between -100 and +100. Record the instrumentality of performance for the first reward in Column 2 and that of the second reward in Column 5.

c.   Third, achieve consensus on the degree of expectancy, or the strength of relationship between effort and performance, that is present. Again, refer to the background and assign a number between -100 and +100. Record this in Column 8.

d.   Fourth, perform the appropriate calculations:
       - multiply Column 1 and Column 2 and divide by 100, place the result
       (which should be between 0 and ±100) in Column 3;

       - do the same for Columns 4 and 5, placing the result in Column 6;

       - add Columns 3 and 6 and place the result in Column 7;

       - multiply Column 7 and 9 and divide by 100, place this result in
       Column 9. This represents the degree to which effort is rewarded in the case. The maximum is 200. Transfer Column 9 to the CLASS TALLY SHEET in the appropriate column of the CALCULATED section.

3.   (5 min.) For each of the case studies in the other set (Set I for even number groups, Set II for odd numbered groups), as a group, predict how motivated to expend high effort the individual described in the case is likely to be. Don't do the calculations in the way you just did, rather think about how hard you would work if you were the individual described. Assign a number between 0 and 100 to how hard you would work, place this number in the appropriate column of the PREDICTED section of the CLASS TALLY SHEET.

4.   (10-15 min.) Each group reports to the class on their calculated and predicted motivational force for cases A through F to complete the CLASS TALLY SHEET. Together the class will compute the average calculated and predicted scores for each force and discuss the match between them. Instructor leads a discussion of the questions below.

Discussion Questions:

1.   Did the average calculated motivational force for the cases match the predicted effort? How would you explain instances where the match is poor?

2.   In your small group discussion, did you notice differences in how people rated valence, instrumentality, or expectancy? What are the implications of these differences for motivating people?

3.   In those cases where predicted motivation or calculated force was low, what would you do to redesign the job so that it was motivating?

GROUP TALLY SHEET

Calculated Force

Group #: ___	(1) V_1	(2) I_1	(3) VI_1	(4) V_2	(5) I_2	(6) VI_2	(7) VI	(8) E	(9) E VI
CASE A \ / D									
CASE B \ OR (E									
CASE C / (F									

$$\frac{(1) \times (2)}{100} = (3) \qquad \frac{(4) \times (5)}{100} = (6) \qquad (3) + (6) = (7) \qquad \frac{(7) \times (8)}{100} = (9)$$

Predicted Effort

(10)

CASE D \   / A

CASE E) OR (B

CASE F /   \ C

CLASS TALLY SHEET

GROUP	Calculated Force (9)					*	Predicted Effort (10)					**
	1	3	5	7	9	$\bar{x}$	2	4	6	8	10	$\bar{x}$
CASE A												
B												
C												

GROUP						$\bar{x}$						$\bar{x}$
	2	4	6	8	10	$\bar{x}$	1	3	5	7	9	$\bar{x}$
CASE D												
E												
F												

21. WORK VS. PLAY*

PURPOSE:

To introduce the concept of motivation.

GROUP SIZE:

Any member of groups of four to five members.

TIME REQUIRED:

40-55 minutes.

EXERCISE SCHEDULE:

1. (20-30 minutes)   Groups discuss:

What drives you to expend energy on play activities?
That is, assuming you have some amount of leisure, non-work oriented time, why do you choose those play activities?
Keep the focus on <u>why</u> not <u>which</u> particular activities.   Choose a reader to present ideas to class.

2. (10-15 minutes)   Each group presents its main discussion points to
class.   The instructor lists these on a blackboard or newsprint.

3. Class discussion on:

a. How can you build some of these motive for play into a work environment?

b. What prevents you from making work more intrinsically motivating,
like play is?

c. If you have already covered motivation theorists, which are relevant here?

---

*Adapted from Phil Anderson, College of St. Thomas. Used with permission.

22. BILL ALLEN IS ALIVE AND WELL IN HIS OFFICE*

PURPOSE:

To explore options for motivating employees.

GROUPS SIZE:

Any number of groups of 4-8 members.

TIME REQUIRED:

35-65 minutes.

PREPARATION REQUIRED:

Read the Bill Allen Case and answer the questions at the
end of the case.

RELATED TOPICS:

Leadership

EXERCISE SCHEDULE:

1. (20-30 min.) In groups of 4-8 members, try to achieve
    a consensus on the answers to the questions at the end
    of the case.

2. (10-20 min.) Groups will report their answers to the
    whole class.

3. (5-15 min.) The instructor will lead a discussion
   explaining the issues of reward vs. motivation.

BILL ALLEN CASE

It had been a while since my last visit to the department store (a large chain in Canada), and as usual some feelings of nostalgia began to surface. I had spent many years with the organization before taking up a career in teaching an consulting. During a sabbatical from my teaching responsibilities, I had returned to the organization for a summer several years ago. Now I was returning at the express request of the organization, and as I approached the main building, my thoughts turned to that request.........

Fred Vaughn, Director of Personnel and Staff Training had asked me to meet with him the next

*By Patrick Doyle and C. Richard Tindal. Of Management for Tomorrow Co., Ontario, Canada.
Used with permission.

time I was in Toronto. In our brief phone conversation, however, we had touched on little more than the date and time of our meeting, and the fact that he wanted to discuss an organizational problem with me. After some brief pleasantries with Fred, I soon learned what that problem was.

FRED VAUGHN: Pat, the problem we are wrestling with is the same one we discussed when you were here on your sabbatical a few years ago. Do you remember those discussions?

PAT DOYLE: Do you mean the concern about the focus of the activities of the sales personnel? Has nothing changed in that area?

FRED VAUGHN: Not really, except that we now have some senior managers who are determined to deal with this problem.

[....As we talked, my thoughts returned to that summer of my sabbatical. I had asked to be assigned to the sales floor in at least four different departments for up to one week periods. While on these assignments, I observed that two of the departments were doing very well in meeting their sales quota while the other two were having difficulties, with one of them falling well short of its planned sales. There were no obvious explanations for the differing performances. However, one factor which Fred and I had discussed at the time was that the departments not performing as well had sales managers with much less visibility on the sales floor than the successful departments. I also recalled that the departments with larger sales volumes were also causing concerns in some instances because of the pattern of those sales.]

PAT DOYLE: Are you hoping to tackle your problem by concentrating on one particular area?

FRED VAUGHN: Initially, yes, but we are hopeful that any solution we arrive at can be applied more broadly, since we know that the same problem is happening in several areas.

PAT DOYLE: So where are you going to start? Somehow I don't think that it is with one of the departments not meeting its sales objectives.

FRED VAUGHN: That's right. In fact, the department I would like you to look at is meeting its sales objectives very well. It is how it is meeting its objectives which concerns the Group Sales Manager, George Mandy and also Sharon McKendry, the Company Controller. I'd like you to talk to them and give some thought to the problem which we are experiencing.

GEORGE MANDY was the Group Sales Manager for the fourth and fifth floors of the store. If any single Group Sales Manager was the key to the success of the store, it was George. While he had come up through the ranks like most other sales managers, there was one vital difference with George. He had spent part of his career with the financial side of the organization, and was therefore aware of the relationship between sales and profitability. His combined experiences gave him credibility with both the accounting and merchandising sides of the organization - a position not usually enjoyed by sales managers.

SHARON MCKENDRY, the Comptroller, appreciated that the sales arm of the organization is its life blood. She made it clear that if someone was interested in improving not only sales but also profitability, then she would try to help them in any way she could.

Both George and Sharon conveyed a sense of urgency and enthusiasm about their work. The key exchanges in our conversations are outlined below.

GEORGE MANDY: Fred was correct, Pat. The department we want to examine is more than meeting its sales objectives. It is the Sporting Goods Department and it is enjoying a high volume of sales because of the concern for fitness which most people now have.

SHARON MCKENDRY: If the department weren't so successful, we couldn't use it as a pilot project.

PAT DOYLE: So, what's wrong with this department if it is selling so well? Is it over stock allotment; is the sales/wage percentage over budget?

GEORGE MANDY: No, the figures are all in line. However, we are concerned about the profitability of the department.

SHARON MCKENDRY: That is the one area in which we do not set objectives for the sales floor the way we do for sales targets, wage percentages, and stock situations.

PAT DOYLE: What makes you think that this department is a problem?

SHARON MCKENDRY: The gross gain figures - we have set figures for these, but we don't believe they are as appropriate as they might be.

GEORGE MANDY: They are also built on historical data.

PAT DOYLE: Why do you feel they may be low?

SHARON MCKENDRY: We have analyzed the sales pattern of the department. The sales targets are being met primarily through the sale of promotional merchandise.

GEORGE MANDY: As you know, one of the main reasons to have promotions is to generate traffic and to create sales in other areas and products besides the specific ones advertised. We are finding that this spillover effect is not happening, however. The sales personnel are meeting the departmental quotas by concentrating their efforts on whatever is being promoted at the time.

PAT DOYLE: I assume that the first thing you considered was a change in the method of compensating sales personnel, so that commissions could be paid on profitability or even gross gain rather than sales volume? What problems did you encounter in considering such a change?

SHARON MCKENDRY: There were several problems. First of all, it would be expensive to develop a system which could calculate a profit by item. With price variances, the calculations would have to be done almost daily - a major undertaking even with the use of computers.

GEORGE MANDY: Another problem we faced was the appropriateness of such a change in compensation. There are just too many factors influencing gross gain to use it as a fair basis for determining a salesperson's compensation. To take matters a step further, and pay salespeople on the basis of profit, would be judging them on even more factors over which they have no control. For example, a salesperson should not be held responsible for warehousing costs! Yet, that is the implication of assigning commissions on the basis of profit.

SHARON MCKENDRY: Besides, that approach could lead us into the problem of salespeople only concentrating on the most profitable items - thereby potentially changing the store's target market. We certainly wouldn't want that to happen.

GEORGE MANDY: What we want to do is use the Sales Managers, more effectively by having them work with their sales people in developing a better balance in the products which they sell. We believe that this approach is possible, and it is certainly more desirable than changing the whole compensation system.   However, our Sales Managers have the same problem we have seen in most other sales managers.

PAT DOYLE: What is that?

GEORGE MANDY: The sales managers are moved to various department as part of their training program. As a result, they are often in charge of areas for which they do not have the technical knowledge which the sales staff have. They also perceive that they do not have the sales skills that their staff have, and appear to be somewhat intimidated by these considerations. Understandably, a sales manager hesitates to train someone if he feels that person has superior knowledge and skills. At least, that is the perceptual hang-up which appears to be affecting many of our sales managers.

SHARON MCKENDRY: What we'd like you to do is meet with one of our sales managers and sales staff, and then offer any suggestions as to how we can get our managers to undertake more initiative with their sales staff in resolving this problem of imbalance in sales.

The two people I was to meet with were Bill Allen, Sales Manager from the Sporting Goods Department, and Paul Barry, one of the sales staff. I was told to expect some frank discussions about the whole situation - and that certainly proved to be true.

Bill Allen looked physically fit, but he was not what one would consider the athletic type. His interests and hobbies were in gardening and microcomputers. On the other hand, Paul Barry - while older than Bill - was obviously a "fitness nut." He had been on the track team at college and had been a first-string offense end on the football team until an automobile accident cut short any thought of a pro career. An aggressive and outspoken individual, Paul had given credible performances in the Toronto and New York marathons over the past two years.

The key discussions with Bill and then Paul are outlined below.

BILL ALLEN: I've had some discussions with George about this situation, but the real problem is the compensation system we use. If you are going to pay people a sales commission based on sales volume, then they will get that volume any way they can! I can't go out there on the floor and tell them to distribute their sales more evenly between promotion and non-promotion items unless there is a change in the structure of the commissions.   I have gone out and said this in the past, but it doesn't have any effect. As far as the salespeople are concerned, they are meeting their quotas - and getting their commissions. I can't fight the system.

PAT DOYLE: So you feel that in the face of the present commission system you are powerless to influence the sales pattern?

BILL ALLEN: I wouldn't have worded it quite that way. I guess my point is that no matter what I may say to them, they know that the fastest, easiest way to get the job down is the way they have chosen. If "the powers that be" want change, they should go back to the old system where promotional merchandise was given a lower commission rate than regularly priced merchandise.

PAT DOYLE: I don't want to get into a long discussion of commission systems, but when that particular approach was tried, it didn't produce the desired results did it?

BILL ALLEN: It is true that there were complaints about it. But, my problem is that without some change in the commission system, I can't go out there and start telling my salespeople how to sell. For one thing, most of them have a lot more experience in this business than I do. Moreover, I can't be on the floor all the time to see what is happening. I have to handle the complaints and produce the endless reports for the buyer and everyone else in the world! Truthfully, I can get a lot more done in the office than I can on the floor where I am constantly being interrupted. If you have any suggestions, I'll be glad to consider them.

[At this point, I was not about to offer any suggestions until I had a clearer picture of what all of the participants in the issue felt. Bill Allen's perception of the problem, however, was very much on my mind when I met with Paul Barry.]

PAUL BARRY: Bill and I have discussed what he calls a problem. I don't see it as a problem. If the organization wants to have sales spread over promotion and non-promotion items, it should give a higher commission to the non-promotion items. As it is, however, I make my quota, and so does the overall department. I don't see why there should be any change. We have promotions so that the company can make money, and we need them to remain competitive.

PAT DOYLE: Do you see the company's point at all - that the present sales pattern does not generate the best profit that it could?

PAUL BARRY: Look, they advertise a product, put it on promotion - so naturally people come into the store looking for that product. Are you recommending that I don't sell it to them, or that I try to switch them to a higher priced product?

PAT DOYLE: I'm not recommending anything at this point. I'm just trying to understand the views of the various people involved so that a solution can be found.

PAUL BARRY: Well, I don't know of any alternatives.

PAT DOYLE: What about Bill helping you and the other sales staff to find methods of spreading out the distribution of the current sales pattern?

PAUL BARRY: There is something which you should understand about this business. We are selling a product which requires a great deal of knowledge. I'm an experienced runner; I know what products are good for running under what conditions. What is Bill Allen going to teach me about that? Besides, I have been in sales much longer than Bill, and I think that I know my job better than he does. We work well together in this department because Bill sticks to his area and handles the customer complaints and lets the rest of us handle the sales floor. It works well that way.

[As I reviewed my notes of the various conversations, I was struck by the varying perceptions of the problem facing the organization.]

QUESTIONS FOR DISCUSSION

1. How do the central characters of George Mandy, Bill Allen and Paul Barry perceive themselves and each other?

2. How would you respond to the opinions of both Paul Barry and Bill Allen about the latter's credibility with the sales staff?

3. How would you describe the problem(s) they are facing?

4. Besides money, what other kinds of motivational rewards can influence the behaviors in this case - especially with respect to Paul Barry and Bill Allen?

5. How should Bill Allen go about influencing the sales pattern of his staff, including Paul Barry?

23. JOB DESIGN

PURPOSE:

To redesign a job using job characteristics theory (Hackman and Oldham, 1976).

GROUP SIZE:

Any number of groups of four to six members.

TIME REQUIRED:

50-70 minutes.

PREPARATION REQUIRED:

Read overview of job characteristics theory.

APPLYING JOB CHARACTERISTICS THEORY: A JOB REDESIGN EXERCISE[*]

Job Characteristics Theory: An Overview

Generally speaking job design is concerned with the specific tasks which are performed on a job, how those tasks are performed, and the types of reactions employees experience as a result of performing the job. The most comprehensive model of job design which exists today is called job characteristics theory (Hackman and Oldham, 1976). Specifically, this theory is concerned with how various job characteristics influence worker reactions (see Figure 1).

Core Job Characteristics

According to Hackman and Oldham (1976), there are five critical characteristics of a job:

1. **Skill variety.** The extent to which a job involves a variety of different activities which require different skills and abilities.

2. **Task identity.** The extent to which a job involves the completion of a whole, identifiable task from beginning to end.

3. **Task significance.** The extent to which the worker perceives that the job is important and has a significant impact on other people.

4. **Autonomy.** The extent to which the job allows the worker to determine how his or her work will be completed.

5. **Feedback.** The extent to which performing the job results in the worker receiving clear information regarding his or her level of performance.

---

[*]Based on a case by Loren W. Kuzuhara and Randall B. Dunham, to appear in the Instructor's Resource Manual for Management by Randy Dunham and J. L. Pierce, Glenview, IL: Scott Foresman, 1989. Used with permission.

Critical Psychological States

The five core job characteristics combine to determine the degree to which a worker experiences three critical psychological states. As shown in Figure 1, skill variety, task identity, and task significance are said to determine the extent to which the worker will perceive the job as being a meaningful work experience. Autonomy determines the level of responsibility for work outcomes which a worker experiences. Finally, feedback provides the worker with knowledge about the results of his or her work activities.

Personal and Work Outcomes

The three critical psychological states combine to determine the following personal and work outcomes: work motivation, work performance, work satisfaction, and absenteeism and turnover behavior.

Growth Need Strength (GNS)

Growth-need strength (GNS) may be defined as the degree to which an individual values complex, challenging work. Its role in the job characteristics model may be described as follows: 1) High GNS individuals will experience high levels of the critical psychological states, if the core job dimensions are high, and lower levels of the critical psychological states if the core job dimensions are low; 2) High GNS individuals will react favorably to high levels of critical psychological states by exhibiting high internal motivation, high work performance, high work satisfaction, and low absenteeism and turnover; 3) Low GNS individuals will still respond favorably to core job characteristics but not as strongly as will high GNS people.

(Pre-class) Schedule

1. Read the overview of job characteristics.

2. (10-20 min.) In groups of 5-7 members, analyze the levels of the core job characteristics in the case relative to the national norm scores.

3. (15-20 min.) Based on the analysis conducted in step two, formulate a new job design which will increase the levels of the core job characteristics.

4. (15-20 min.) Have each group present a brief description of its job redesign plan.

5. (10 min.) The instructor leads a discussion on job design.

Questions for Discussion

1. Explain why you chose to redesign the clerical worker jobs at Wyatt-Boyer Insurance in the way you did.

2. Describe the expected effects of the job redesign on core job characteristics.

3. Describe the expected worker reactions to the changes in core job characteristics.

4. How do you think the workers would respond to the changes in core job characteristics if they had low growth-need strength?

5. Compare and contrast your job redesign plan with the actual job redesign plan which was used at Wyatt-Boyer Insurance. Which job redesign plan do you prefer? Why?

6. Discuss the changes in core job characteristics and personal and work outcomes which resulted form the actual job redesign plan used at Wyatt-Boyer Insurance. Why do you think they changed in the direction expected or not expected? (**Note:** Refer to Figure 5 to answer this question.)

Optional : Self-Generated Personal Experiences
a) Think of a job you have held which you did or did not like.
b) Describe the specific tasks which the job involved.
c) Assess the levels of core job characteristics with respect to your job.
d) If you could, how would you redesign your job? What impact would you expect the job redesign to have on levels of core job characteristics?

Summary

The basic aim of job characteristics theory (Hackman and Oldham, 1976) is to explain how various aspects of a job can influence worker reactions. The fundamental argument of this theory is that for individuals with high growth-need strength, high levels of core job characteristics will lead to high levels of critical psychological states which will result in favorable personal and work outcomes (see Figure 1 for a summary of how job characteristics theory works).

BACKGROUND:
The Wyatt-Boyer Insurance Company

Wyatt-Boyer Insurance is a multiline insurance firm located in a major city of a midwestern state. The company's primary functions are to accept policy applications from agents, rate (price) the policies and prepare and issue the policies.

Figure 2 illustrates the initial work flow layout (i.e., job design) at Wyatt-Boyer Insurance. Policy applications received (new work) were first routed to a general sorting room, where policies were separated by type (A, B, or C). The sorted policies were then sent to the appropriate policy type sort rooms (sort room A, B, or C) where they were prepared for distribution to policy type supervisors. These supervisors assigned the work to entry clerks, who entered policy information in to a computer and sent the work on to underwriters. The underwriters authorized the policies and sent them to rating clerks, who were responsible for pricing (rating) the policies. The rated policies were then printed out and set to a policy type sorting room, where the work was processed and assigned to distribution clerks. Three copies of each policy were made by distribution clerks and then sent on to the mailroom. The mailroom sent one copy of the policy to Wyatt-Boyer files, one copy to the policy holder, and one copy to the appropriate insurance agent.

Recently, management at Wyatt-boyer administered a survey to clerical workers in order to assess core job characteristics and worker responses. Results of this survey are displayed in Figure 3. The dotted line running across each of the bar graphs represents the national norm (i.e., average value) for a large, representative sample of clerical workers in the United States. The top graph shows clerical worker perceptions of core job characteristics. The bottom graph represents workers' satisfaction with various aspects of their jobs, along with attendance levels and an index of productivity. Finally, it should be noted that the clerical workers at Wyatt-Boyer Insurance were generally very competent individuals who had a strong desire to engage in challenging work (i.e., they had high growth-need strength).

Figure 1: Job Characteristics Theory

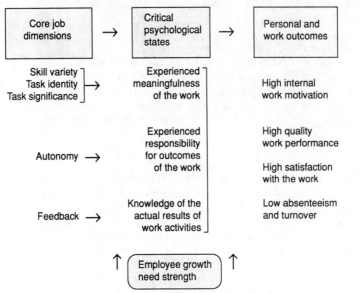

Source: J. R. Hackman and G. R. Oldham (1976). Motivation through the design of work: Test of a theory, *Organizational Behavior and Human Performance*, 16, 250-279.

Figure 2: Initial Work Flow (Job Design) at Wyatt-Boyer Insurance

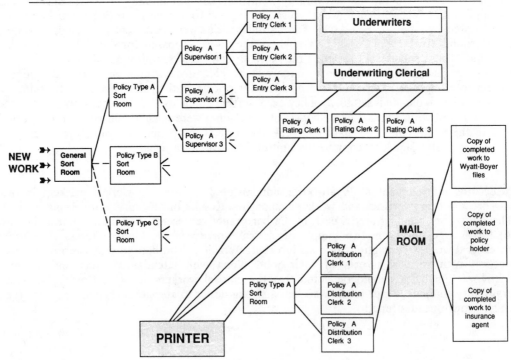

Figure 3: Core Job Characteristics and Worker Reactions for the Initial Work Flow (Job Design) at Wyatt-Boyer Insurance

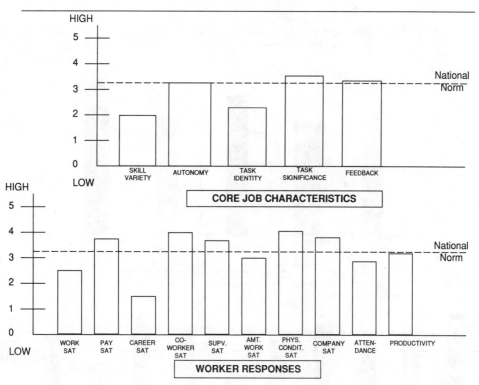

Figure 4: Work Flow at Wyatt-Boyer Insurance after the Job Redesign

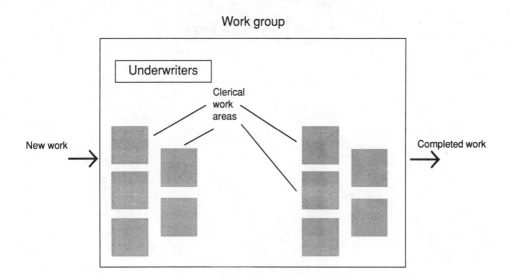

Figure 5: Core Job Characteristics and Worker Reactions to the Job Redesign at Wyatt-Boyer Insurance

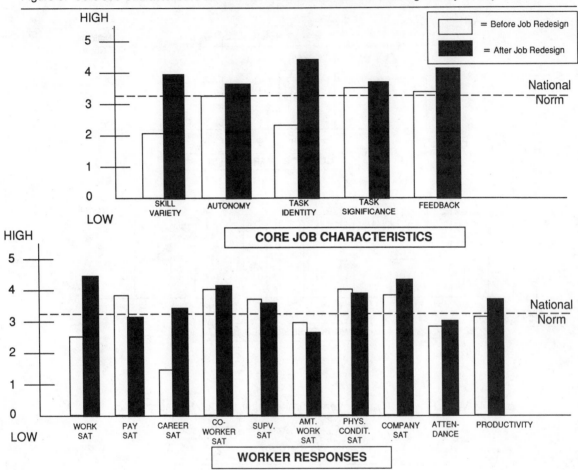

Chapter 7   Interpersonal Communication

24. FIRST IMPRESSION, BEST IMPRESSION*

PURPOSE:

1. To gain information as to the sort of first impressions one makes.
2. To get feedback as to how effective (or ineffective) is one's body language.
3. To learn the impact of one's voice upon others.
4. To illustrate the power of nonverbal and vocal communication in establishing one's power and credibility.

GROUP SIZE:

Any number of triads.

TIME REQUIRED:

40-50 minutes

PREPARATION REQUIRED:

Read the "Introduction" and "Background" below.

ROOM ARRANGEMENT REQUIREMENTS:

Large room or break-out areas where triads can work in relative quiet.

---

*By Janet G. Elsea, Ph.D. from <u>The Four Minute Sell: How to Make a Dynamic First Impression</u>, Simon and Schuster, 1984. Used with permission.

INTRODUCTION:

This exercise can help you manage the impression you want to make and will show you how to "read" other people. It will help you find answers to the four key questions that define a successful communicator:

- What do I LOOK like?
- What do I SOUND like?
- What do I SAY?
- How well do I LISTEN?

By answering these questions you will give a great deal of valuable information about how well or how ineffectively you communicate.

Knowing what kind of communicator you are is critical to success, for communication is what we people--especially business people--do most:

- As much as eighty-five percent of your day may be spent in some form of communication--most of it speaking with and listening to others, according to a survey of businesspeople conducted at Arizona State University's College of Business Administration.

- The typical working American gives about a dozen "speeches" a year--oral presentations to staff, clients, community groups, labor unions and professional associations.

- You spend two to four times as much time talking on the telephone as you do using any other technology, including computers and word-processors. Executives spend about fourteen percent of their days on the phone.

- Communication skills rate high as important factors in a business person's success.

Although nearly every waking moment is spent listening or speaking to someone or something, the truth is most of us haven't the faintest notion of what we look like, how we sound, what we say or whether we are good listeners. And yet scientific research verifies that when meeting someone for the first time, how you say something and what you look like when you say it are much more important than the words you actually speak.

If people aren't quickly attracted to you or don't like what they see and hear in those first two to four minutes, chances are they won't pay attention to all those words you believe are demonstrating your knowledge and authority. They will find your client guilty, seek another doctor, buy another product, vote for your opponent or hire someone else.

During your first few minutes of interaction with others, their attention span is at its greatest and their powers of retention highest: their eyes and ears focus on you and tell their brains what they see and hear. That process of creating first impressions is intriguing but somewhat predictable. Depending on the other person's background and expectations, as well as the context of the interaction, here is what experts tell us typically happens when you meet someone for the first time.

First, people tend to focus on what they can see such as:

-gender	-appearance	-movement
-skin color	-facial expressions	-personal space
-age	-eye contact	-touch

So much meaning is conveyed by these eight components of nonverbal communication that a number of communication experts believe "what you look like" constitutes more than half the total message. An astonishing fifty-five percent of the meaning is conveyed by facial expressions and body language alone. And you haven't yet opened your mouth.

Next, people focus on what they can hear. When you speak, out comes a voice with additional characteristics, among them rate of speech, loudness, pitch, tone and articulation. These give the other person more information about you. Your voice--not including your actual words--may transmit as much as thirty-eight percent of the meaning in face-to-face conversations; it conveys a great deal more information on the telephone, because the other person is deprived of your body language--facial expressions, gestures, eye contact and all the rest.

Last, and certainly least in terms of those first few moments, the other person gets around to your words, which contribute a mere seven percent to the meaning.

It's not that your words are unimportant. But if others do not like what they see, or if they get past your body language only to be stopped by something in your voice, they may not care at all about what you say. Their minds already may be made up, their first impressions indelibly formed.

BACKGROUND:

When you meet someone for the first time you have but 2-4 minutes to make a positive or negative first impression. If that impression is positive, studies say you will be granted higher credibility and trust than if the first impression is negative. Additionally, it is difficult--perhaps impossible--to change a negative first impression unless you have time and opportunity to do so. Finally, when you can be seen (as opposed to say, telephone communication), people take in information about you visually first. Thus, your nonverbal communication accounts for 55% of the meaning's message. Next, people process what their ears hear in your voice; hence, vocal variables of rate, loudness, pitch, quality and articulation are approximately 38% of meaning (and over 70% when telephoning). Thus, the words you use are worth only 7% of the meaning within the first few moments of a new interaction.

EXERCISE SCHEDULE:

1. Read the background on nonverbal communication.

(Steps 2 & 3, 5 min.)

2. Divide into triads.

3. Move to your assigned locale (be it around the room or into another room).

(Steps 4, 5 & 6, 15 min.)

4. Person 1 stands and begins to speak for a minute about her/himself; meanwhile, the others look, listen closely, and take notes using the check sheets on the following page.

5. Person sits down and the other triad members give feedback based on what they wrote on their check sheets.

6. Repeat steps 4 and 5, allowing Person 2 and then Person 3 to speak and receive feedback.

7. (10 min.)   Answer the discussion questions below in your triads.

    a. What did you notice first about each other?
    b. When there was a contradiction between what people looked like, sounded like and/or said, which did you trust or believe?
    c. Was there any one thing that stood out about each person as they talked (appearance, facial expressions, tone of voice, rate of speech, and the like)?
    d. Did your first impressions change as you got to know the people in your trio?
    e. Note situations where first impressions are crucial.
    f. In which sorts of professions is appearance more important than body language, or where the voice is more critical than what one looks like?
    g. When do words begin to play their part in the communication process?

8. (10-20 min.) With the whole class, the instructor wraps up with an overview on how crucial body language and vocal skills are to first impressions; after which generalizations and and conclusions are discussed.

APPEARANCE CHECKLIST*

CHARACTERISTIC	PERSON #1	PERSON #2
gender		
age		
appearance		
facial expressions		
eye contact		
movement		
personal space		
touch		

VOICE CHECKLIST

CHARACTERISTIC	PERSON #1	PERSON #2
rate		
pitch		
loudness		
quality		
articulation		

*Fill in boxes with comments on qualities you noticed for each characteristic--including strengths and weaknesses.

25. LISTENING EXERCISE[*]

PURPOSE:

To examine common means of disrupting communication through poor listening.

GROUP SIZE:

Any number of groups of 4-5 members.

TIME REQUIRED:

30-45 minutes.

ROOM ARRANGEMENT REQUIREMENTS:

So it is possible for 4-5 members to sit facing one another.

RELATED TOPICS:

Interpersonal Relationships

EXERCISE SCHEDULE;

1.   (2 min.) Divide into groups of four to five members each. Any class members left over and not in a group can act as group observers.

2.   (2-3 min.) One volunteer in each group will talk for two to three minutes on any topic. The task for the other three members in each group is to make irrelevant comments every time there is a break in the "speech." For example, if the speaker is describing a trip he or she took recently, the other group members intervene with statements like "I had a hamburger for supper last night," or "Gee, you're nice." Members can also key their nonverbal behavior to this mode of response. One person can act as observer.

3.   (3 min.) Each group should discuss the experience within the group. In particular the speaker should indicate how this kind of response made him or her feel. How many times have you had this kind of response happen to you, have observed it, or done it to others? What impact does it have on the speaker?

4.   (3 min.--optional) The instructor will lead a general class discussion to see whether different groups had different experiences. The observers can relate their observations at this time.

---

[*]By Frederic E. Finch, Halsey R. Jones and Joseph A. Litterer, Managing for Organizational Effectiveness: An Experiential Approach. New York: McGraw-Hill, 1976, pp. 163-164. Used with permission.

5. (15-27 min.) Steps 2, 3, and 4 will be repeated three more times. Another volunteer will speak each time, and the other group members will respond in the ways noted below.

    a. Tangential responses: The second time the task of the group members, whenever they can, is to make tangential responses--i.e., to move the focus of attention from the speaker to the person making the response. For example, if the speaker is talking about a recent trip, the responder might break in and start describing a trip of his own, picking up something in the talk which enables him to "butt in" and take over the conversation. This is a widely used technique which you all recognize. You will find that you can be very creative in moving the conversation back and forth between people. In your discussion you should note its impact on how people feel and on the organization of the interaction.

    b. Interrogative responses: As with tangential responses you will proceed through steps 2, 3, and 4 above. Another volunteer will be given a topic, and the task of the other three members is to make interrogative responses. With interrogative responses you question the speaker. It may seem that you are interested in the speaker, but questioning limits the speaker and takes the conversation in directions dictated by the questioners. Interrogative responses are very useful in keeping the focus of the conversation on the speaker--sometimes in ways he or she does not intend. The responder in this mode is really in control of the conversation. This response can be useful in clarifying misunderstandings, but it can also be used to manipulate the conversation.

    c. Reflective responses: Again a volunteer (some may volunteer twice--it is not necessary for all to be a speaker) will speak on any topic. The task for the other three members is to make reflective responses. These should reflect both content and the feelings behind the content. (Reflective responses are described more fully in the section on "Non-Directive Interviewing.") Try to match your nonverbal behavior to this mode of responding. You will probably feel uncomfortable using this mode (afterward check to see which responses you were most comfortable in using). Proceed through steps 3 and 4.

GENERAL DISCUSSION

6. (5-10 min.) The instructor will lead a general discussion of the exercise.

26. NONVERBAL COMMUNICATION EXERCISES

PURPOSE:

To understand and practice the dynamics of non-verbal communication.

GROUP SIZE:

Any number.

TIME REQUIRED:

OPTION 1 - Class explanation - 5-10 minutes.
　　　　　　 Observation - 3 class sessions.
　　　　　　 Report - 30-40 minutes.
OPTION 2 - 40-50 minutes.

ROOM ARRANGEMENT REQUIREMENTS:

OPTION 2 - One group of six chairs in a circle, remaining
　　　　　　 chairs around this circle.

RELATED TOPICS:

Dynamics Within Groups
Work Motivation

OPTION 1 - Nonverbal Communication Observation
　　　　　　 by Communication Research Associates[*]

INTRODUCTION:

　　Most of us are not completely aware of the nonverbal messages that we send to others. In this exercise someone will observe you and give you feedback on the nonverbal cues you send.

EXERCISE SCHEDULE:

PART A - (5-10 min.) Explanation

　　The teacher will hand out slips of paper, each with a student's name on it. This will be the name of the person you will observe. You will not know who is observing you. If the class is larger than 50, partners may be assigned by the teacher.

---

[*]From <u>Communicate!</u> 3rd ed. Communication Research Associates. Dubuque, IA: Kendall-Hunt. Used with permission.

Procedure:

1. You are to observe_____during the
    (class member)
    next three class sessions. Do not disclose the name of the
    individual you are observing either to that person or to any
    other class member.

2. Take notes concerning the nonverbal communication you observe.
    Be sure to comment on at least the following:
    a. What the person wears that may communicate something about
        that person's personality or mood.

    b. What feelings the person communicates nonverbally.

    c. What other nonverbal cues communicate something (values,
        personality, moods, intelligence, ability as a
        communicator, etc.) about this person.

3. Following your instructor's directions, meet with the person
    you were observing and discuss your observations and
    conclusions.

PART B - (3 class periods) Observation of assigned partner during
       class.

PART C - Report

1. (20-30 min.) Observers will give feedback to their assigned
    partner.

2. (10 min.) Class discussion on the exercise.

    a. What types of messages were communicated during the last
        few class periods?

    b. How accurate did you find the observations?

    c. What is necessary to make certain that your observations
        are correct?

    d. What conclusions can you draw about nonverbal communication
        as a result of your study?

OPTION 2 - The Blind Decision-Makers (The Role of the Nonverbal Communication) by David Bradford[**]

EXERCISE SCHEDULE:

PART A - (20-30 min.)

1. Six class members sit in a circle in front of the class.

2. They must face outward so they can't see each other.

3. The group's task is to rank in order the importance of the eight characteristics of a good leader listed below. The group should discuss the items and their merits to come up with a decision of high quality. The only constraint is that they are not to look at each other.

> Technical knowledge Ethical
> Listening skills Oral communication skills
> Good planner Empathetic
> Writing skills Emotionally secure

4. The task of the observers is to notice the effect of the absence of nonverbal communication in group decision making. The group members are not to give any verbal or nonverbal cues to the members.

PART B - (20 min.) Class Discussion

1. What problems were there in coming to a consensus without seeing the nonverbal signals of others?

2. In what ways do we use nonverbal signals in continuing conversations or group discussions?

[**]From <u>Exchange</u>, Vol. 1(1), 1975, p. 32. Used with permission.

27. FEEDBACK: INTERPERSONAL RELATIONSHIPS IN GROUPS*

PURPOSE:

1. To learn effective methods of interpersonal feedback.
2. To develop a cohesive group.

GROUP SIZE:

Small ongoing (intact) groups of four to eight members.

TIME REQUIRED:

50-75 minutes.

PREPARATION REQUIRED:

Read "Giving and Receiving Feedback" in the Appendix of this book.

ROOM ARRANGEMENT REQUIREMENTS:

Preferably a room large enough so that group members could give feedback in relative privacy.

EXERCISE SCHEDULE:

1. (5 min.) The exercise and purpose are discussed as a whole class.

2. (35-60 min) The class is divided into groups of four to eight members. These should be groups which have worked together before. Each group member is to think about how to fill out the Feedback Statements/Questions below. You are to be as specific as possible and use other group members' names when responding. Next, you are to discuss your responses with all group members. Suggestion: One person at a time gives his/her answers to the statements and other group members give additional feedback.

3. (10 min.) The instructor will lead a group discussion processing this exercise, discussing the importance of giving positive feedback and of resolving issues and conflicts in order for a group to function more efficiently.

Feedback Statements/Questions:

1. What I like most about this group is:

---

*Original idea adapted from Brian Holleran, Professor of Speech Communications, State University of New York, Oneonta. Used with permission.

2. In this group, I have most difficulty in discussing the following topics:

    a.
    b.

3. Things that group members do and bother me the most are:

    a.
    b.
    c.

4. In this group, I would like to change:

5. I wish (_____) would:
          name(s)

6. If I could, I'd like to tell (_____) :
               name(s)

7. A. In this group, the person with whom I have the strongest relationship is:

    B. The strong relationship exists because:

8. I would like to ask (_____) how he/she sees me.
         name(s) or address to whole group

9. I would like to ask if (_____) is angry or upset with me?

10. I would like to ask (_____) what my best contribution to the group is:

11. I would like to ask (_____) if I have seemed to change since entering the group.

12. I would like to ask (_____) what he/she is confused about me.

28. LISTENING THROUGH NON-DIRECTIVE INTERVIEWING[*]

PURPOSE:

To practice skills in listening and non-directive interviewing.

TIME REQUIRED:

20-35 minutes.
40-65 minutes with optional role-play.

PREPARATION REQUIRED:

1. Read "Non-Directive Interviewing" in the Appendix
   of this book.

2. Complete exercises 1-5 on the following pages.

RELATED TOPICS:

Interpersonal Relationships
Conflict Management and Assertiveness

EXERCISE SCHEDULE:

1. (Before class) Complete exercises 1-5 below

Exercise 1[**]

Example

Subordinate: I know I'm supposed to work with Stan, but he's
such a pain. Sure he's bright but he never lets
me forget it. Can't you put us on separate
projects?

(Boss) Evaluating and advice giving: Come on, George, don't
be so critical. You know you can work with him if you have to.
Now write two more evaluating and advice giving responses:

[**]I would like to thank Gerald Egan, whose You & Me (Brooks/Cole, 1977) gave me the idea
to develop exercises 1-5. Idea used with permission.

a._____

_____

b._____

_____

An appropriate reflective response might be:

You feel angry because you're having a bad time working with Stan.

For some practice on reflecting back feelings, respond to the following situations:

<u>Example</u>

<u>Co-worker</u>: That project is turning out to be a mess. Why can't those other three quit fighting with each other?

<u>You</u>: You feel frustrated.
    or
You feel angry.

<u>Exercise 2</u>

1. <u>Subordinate</u>: I deserve more than just a "satisfactory" rating. My gosh! I work my tail off for this organization and is this all the recognition I get?

   a. You feel_____

   b. You feel_____

2. <u>Co-worker</u>: Listen, I'm getting tired of having you interrupt me whenever I talk. Honestly, I can't get a word in edgewise with you!

   a. You feel_____

   b. You feel_____

3. <u>Co-worker</u>: Listen, that **** boss just called me on the carpet for something that wasn't my fault. But how can I squeal on someone else?

   a. You feel_____

   b. You feel_____

4. Co-worker: I want to go for that Senior management position.
   But I really don't have a chance. After all, no woman has
   ever held such a position here before. But I'll try anyway.

   a. You feel_____

   b. You feel_____

In order to really effectively communicate, it is often important
to also let the speaker know you understood why there is such an
emotion being felt.

Example:

Co-worker: That project is turning into a mess!   Why can't those
           other three quit fighting with each other?

    You: You feel frustrated because the squabbles are getting
         in the way of the group's productivity.

Exercise 3:

Now complete the statements from Exercise 1.

1. You feel unappreciated because_____

    _____

2. You feel annoyed because_____

    _____

3. You feel angry because_____

    _____

4. You feel anxious because_____

    _____

Sometimes when people first start using nondirective interviewing
it sounds phony and stilted, often because the listener is essentially
"filling in the blanks" as we did in Exercises 1 and 2.   The way to
avoid this is to think through the "correct" way, but then change the
idea into your own words, so that it sounds more natural.

Subordinate: I'm supposed to be working with four other people from
that other department on this new project. But they never listen to
my ideas and hardly seem to know I'm there.

   a. (Using "Correct" response)   You feel uneasy in the group
       because you don't know anyone and you're not sure if your
       input will be heard.

b. (Using own style)   It's very difficult for you to interact in that group of people who work with one another every day. You don't feel part of "the group."

Now respond to the following situations:
Exercise 4

1. <u>Subordinate</u>: I get really ticked off because our group gets more work to do--and it's more difficult to boot--but then at raise time top management evaluates us on the same standards as the other groups. It's grossly unfair!

    a._____

    _____

    b._____

    _____

2. <u>Co-worker</u>: My boss gets so bogged down in details--and he wants to drag me down there too. My productivity has gone down because I have to watch so many details lately. What a waste of time!

    a._____

    _____

    b._____

    _____

3. <u>Co-worker</u>:   Hey, this idea is really good. Who do you think you are questioning it?   After all, I've worked with this project for four years now. Nobody knows it better.

    a._____

    _____

    b._____

    _____

4. <u>Spouse or boy/girlfriend</u>: You never have any time for me these days. It's always work, work, work. I'm sick and tired of it!

    a._____

    _____

    b._____

    _____

Now you've had a chance to practice nondirective interviewing in make-believe situations. The next step is to recreate some experiences you have had where there was poor communication because Person A did not listen reflectively. Briefly write down the situation, then an emotionally charged statement Person B made. After this, describe what was actually said by Person A as well as what would have been an appropriate nondirective response.

Exercise 5

Situation 1:_____

_____
_____
_____

    Emotional Statement by Person B:_____

    _____
    _____
    _____

    Actual Response by Person A:_____

    _____
    _____
    _____

    More effective response:_____

    _____
    _____
    _____

Situation 2:_____

_____
_____
_____

    Emotional Statement by Person B:_____

    _____
    _____
    _____

    Actual Response by Person A:_____

    _____
    _____
    _____

    More effective response:_____

    _____
    _____

2. (10-20 min.) In groups of 3-4, share your responses for exercises 1-4.

3. (10-15 min.) As a class, several groups report responses to exercises 1-4. The instructor will give appropriate answers too.

ROLE PLAY (OPTIONAL)

4. (10-15 min.) In same groups of 3-4, choose one problem situation from Exercise 5 and practice role playing an appropriate non-directive response to the emotionally charged statement. Those members not in the role play will act as observers, giving feedback in the non-directive communication.

5. (10-15 min.) Several groups will role play, in front of the whole class, receiving feedback from other class members and the instructor.

Chapter 8   Interpersonal Relationships

29. INTERPERSONAL COMMUNICATION/CONFLICT ROLE PLAYS*

PURPOSE:

To practice different means of resolving interpersonal difficulties.

TIME REQUIRED:

20-40 minutes for each of the first three role plays;
35-55 minutes for the fourth one.

RELATED TOPICS:

Conflict Mangement and Assertiveness
Leadership
Interpersonal Communication

INTRODUCTION:

Below are four short role plays relating to interpersonal conflict and communication on the job. Your instructor may choose to do one or more of them.

INSTRUCTIONS: For Role Plays #1, 2 and 3 (20-40 min. for each one.)

1. (Steps 1 and 2, 5 min.) Volunteers are selected as shown:

   a. One person to play subordinate role.
   b. Two or three for the supervisors role.

---

*By Joseph Seltzer. Used with permission.

2. All volunteers go into the hall and read only their own part. Meanwhile, the instructor briefs the class on the role play. Class members do not read role at this time.

3. (5-15 min.) The subordinate and one supervisor come in to play the situation. Other supervisors then play their roles one at a time with the same subordinate.

4. (5-10 min.) As a class compare the different styles of interaction and leadership. Which ones were most effective?

5. (Optional, 5-10 min.) Divide the class into pairs and each person read one of the roles. Each pair does the role play and then the class as a whole discusses it. How did your interaction compare with those done in front of the class? What seemed to work well in resolving the problem?

INSTRUCTIONS: (For Role Play #4--Chris Wilson)

1. (5 min.) Divide into groups of eight. Four read the Chris Wilson role, the other four each read one of the subordinate's roles--Paula Jaynes, Jim Lamp, Alice Pako and Jack Kramer. (Change the names to match sexes if necessary.)

2. (5 min.) Team up Wilson (A) with Paula Jaynes, Wilson (B) with Jim Lamp, etc. Play the roles.

3. (5-15 min.) Switch partners so that Wilson(A) is with Jim Lamp, Wilson(B) with Alice Pako, etc. Role play. Do this up to three times, when every subordinate will have played the role four times with each Wilson.

4. (10-15 min.) In the groups of eight, discuss the different problem-solving styles. What would be best? Which leadership styles were most effective?

5. (10-15 min.) Groups report their interactions to the whole class.

ROLES--ONLY READ THE ROLE YOU ARE ASSIGNED

Role Play #1 -- Mary Smith

a. Role for Mary Smith (subordinate)

You have worked in the Human Resources Department for 32 years and in your time have seen good managers and bad managers. Your current boss, John Johnson has been there for six years. He has generally been friendly and reasonable, but never seems to tell you about your performance unless you make a mistake. But if you do, he'll let you have it. No praise, no encouragement, but he's quick to blame; and he's like that with everyone. The job you do is pretty routine and a bit boring, but everyone has to work. You don't really mind it, except that recently Johnson has been getting on your nerves. He asked you to come to his office after lunch, so you must have done something wrong again. It's getting so you don't want to get out of bed in the morning anymore.

b. Role for John Johnson (supervisor)

You are a manager in the Human Resources Department. Usually you
help other managers with their problem employees, but for the
first time in your six years in this position, you have one of
your own. Mary Smith is a long-term employee and was working in
this department before you started with this organization. In the
past, she worked at a reasonable pace with few errors. Her
clerical job is routine and she knows how to do it well.
Recently, you have had to correct a number of mistakes in the
paperwork that she processes. In addition, she seems to be less
motivated. She has always been conscientious and has had a very
good attendance record, but she has missed a lot of days recently.
When she or anyone else is absent, there is a lot of grumbling
from other employees in the department because they each have to
work a little faster. While none of the problems with Mary Smith
is major, you think it is about time to try to get her back on the
right track and you asked her to come to your office after lunch.

Role Play #2 -- Hal Brown

a. Role for Hal Brown (subordinate)

You have been working in the Finance Department for almost a year.
It's a much better job than any of those you held previously.
While you went to school you had to work part-time to support your
wife and two children. Last year you were putting 20 hours on one
job and 25 on another and taking two courses. But you finally
finished college after eight years. You were pleased to be hired
by this organization because you can finally use all of your
expensive education while making enough money to live comfortably.
You still have to pay off a large amount of money in student
loans, however. You get along well with the other people in your
department, but find your job to be somewhat boring, especially
when you have to work with Purchasing. Some of those people don't
know what they are talking about. Your boss, Jane Jones never
seems to pay much attention to what you do and rarely asks you if
you have finished a project before giving you a new one. For most
of the past year you haven't been overworked, but three weeks ago,
you had some trouble getting started on one particular job and
then Jane gave you the ABCD project. You didn't think the project
was too important and tried to catch up on your work. Last week
Jane asked about ABCD and you said you would get right on it.
Unfortunately, your kids have been sick and you have not been
getting much sleep at nights, so you just didn't get ABCD done by
this morning as you promised. It will probably be finished
sometime tomorrow or the day after. Since Jane rarely gives you
any feedback on your work and doesn't seem all that concerned, you
don't think it will make any difference. She has asked you to
come to her office.

b. Role for Jane Jones (supervisor)

You have been a manager in the Finance Department for 5 years and previously worked in the department for 12 years. There are some real advantages being the manager in a place where employees behave as individuals who see themselves as professionals. Not many departments in this organization are like that. The people you supervise are friendly and get along well with each other. You are able to keep on schedule because each person pulls his share of the load; or at least they used to. About a year ago, you hired Hal Brown right after he finished college. He had been an evening student for eight years. He previously worked at two part-time jobs to support his wife and two young children and was delighted to finally get a job where he could use his education and still make a reasonable living. Initially he took awhile to get adjusted, but eventually seemed to fit in with the rest of the department. About three months ago you became concerned about the quality of the work he was doing. Some of his ideas and approaches seemed "off-the-wall" and not well thought out. Additionally, he seemed to have some difficulty dealing with Purchasing, but you wanted him to learn on his own and did not want to be a "pushy boss." After all, he is a professional. However, last week you finally had to say something since his reports on the ABCD project weren't finished on time. You gave him until this morning, but they still weren't done. You asked him to come to your office.

Role Play #3 -- Pat Jones

a. Role for Pat Jones (subordinate)

You have worked for several years as a case worker for Childhood Abuse Referral (CARE) which provides family counseling in homes where there are abused children. You have an M.S.W. and are very effective, often finding creative solutions to client problems. You really enjoy your job, except for the extensive and routine paperwork which is tedious and boring. To make things worse, the State is now requiring that an additional form be completed. It is a bit complicated and Terry Locke, your supervisor has mentioned several times that your forms often contain errors. Terry is a good supervisor and you respect him(her), but they are wasting your skills with paperwork. Usually you just try to get it done as quickly as possible. This morning Terry asked you to come to his(her) office and you are about to enter it now.

b. Role for Terry Locke (supervisor)

You have recently been appointed Director of Childhood Abuse Referral (CARE) which provides family counseling in homes where there are abused children. Today you called Pat Jones into your office for a discussion about a problem that you have noted. Pat is an excellent case worker and often finds creative solutions to client problems. However, he(she) seems to always be behind on the paperwork. An additional form is now being required by the State and Pat can't or won't do it correctly. You have mentioned the fact that he(she) has made errors several times, but there are still mistakes on the forms. They are long and somewhat complicated, but Jim Smith figured out a method for keeping his records that seems to make it easier to complete the State form. You believe that you have a good relationship with Pat and are respected by him(her).

What you observed this morning may have given you a clue what the problem with Pat's forms might be. You saw him(her) filling out a form while having a conversation with two other members of the staff. Pat just isn't concentrating. He(she) has just arrived at your office.

Role Play #4 -- Chris Wilson - Background (all read this):

Chris Wilson works for the Regional Port Authority, a public transit organization. It is usually referred to by employees as "the Authority." He(she) was recently promoted to General Foreman (a second level supervisor) and supervises a maintenance department with nine foremen and a total of 134 workers. Today, he(she) asked to meet with four foremen individually for about five minutes each.

a. Role for Chris Wilson (supervisor)

Chris Wilson was recently promoted and now has as his(her) subordinates several of his(her) former peers. However, there is no resentment of Wilson's promotion on the part of the subordinates, because they like him(her) and recognize that he(she) is the best person available for the job. Gordon knows from past associations and experiences that three of his(her) subordinates may prove to be major problems unless he(she) takes effective action. Also, there is a new person who has just started as foreman.

Jack Kramer is rather hostile toward the Authority although he is an effective leader with his own men. He is a person with a chip on his shoulder and has been that way for the five years that Chris has known him. Kramer is very knowledgeable about electric wiring, is a perfectionist about having the work done right and is known to run a tightly-knit, closed work group. The problem is that he almost always sides with his men against the Authority and constantly complains about the defects in the Authority, in general and in higher managers, by name. Kramer does not get along well with other foremen and seems to do his job only grudgingly.

Jim Lamp supervises a crew of 18 unionized employees who average 16 years of service with the Authority. Lamp is very friendly, but he has trouble keeping up with the details of his job. His department is almost constantly behind schedule, often because needed parts have not been ordered or because work orders have been misplaced. He just doesn't seem to work very hard.

Alice Pako has only been a foreman for about a year, but instead of running her department, they seem to be running her. Pako worked for 19 years with most of the people she now supervises and appears to have trouble giving orders. If anyone argues with her, she just backs down. Also, she often lends a hand to get the job done, but gets so involved that she ends up doing much of the work herself. When she gets busy like this, other workers often just stand around and watch.

Paula Jaynes has been foreman for only 8 weeks but is bright and hard working and should do well. So far, Chris hasn't noticed any problems. Yesterday was the first time Paula had to handle a discipline situation.

IN YOUR ROLE AS CHRIS WILSON, YOU WILL MEET WITH YOUR SUBORDINATES

INDIVIDUALLY, FOR FIVE MINUTES EACH. PLAN HOW YOU WILL ACT WITH EACH ONE.

b. Role for Paula Jaynes (subordinate)

Paula has been with the Authority for four years and was promoted to a foreman's job less than two months ago. You are proud that you were promoted so rapidly and want to show that you can do a good job. Chris Wilson is your General Foreman and seems to be a good boss. So far everything is going well.

Yesterday, you gave a green sheet to Bob Smith for poor work performance. Ever since you were promoted, his performance has gone down-hill. A month ago you talked to him about it and gave him two weeks to straighten up.   Two weeks ago you talked to him again and wrote up a warning. Yesterday, you talked to him again and told him that he will get one day off. You still aren't sure what the problem is, but his carelessness has almost gotten other people hurt.   Smith is hardly getting anything done and you knew that you had to take action. You feel that you have done the right thing.

c. Role for Jim Lamp (subordinate)

Jim Lamp has worked for the Authority for twenty-seven years and has been foreman of a department for the last nine years. You have eighteen subordinates who are long term employees (average sixteen years of service) and active members of the union. You get along well with the others and are quite happy in your job. When Chris Wilson was recently promoted, you didn't mind, because Wilson was OK as a foreman and besides, you didn't want all that extra work.   You figure being a foreman is just the right job, until you retire.

Generally, your department gets the work done, but occasionally you run behind schedule. The last few months haven't been quite as good, because it's hard keeping track of all the parts needed on the new vehicles.

d. Role for Alice Pako (subordinate)

Alice Pako has been with the Authority and worked in the same

department for eleven years. About a year ago, the foreman
retired and someone had to take his place. Some of your friends
convinced you to apply and you were promoted. Most of the time
things go alright, but occasionally, you have to lend a hand.
Somehow that just slows it down more. You are confused because
you used to be one of the best workers. You have realized how
tough it is being the foreman.   The part you like least of all is
having to tell someone to do a job that they don't want to do.
Sometimes, you just let it slide, especially if Billie or Pat
(your two best friends) is involved.

When Chris Wilson was recently promoted, you were pleased.
He's(she's) a nice person and has been helpful in the past.

e. Role for Jack Kramer (subordinate)

Jack Kramer has nineteen years of experience with the Authority
and has for the past eight years been foreman of an electrical
wiring group. You started with most of the men in this group and
feel strongly loyal to "your people." You have learned more about
wiring than almost anyone else in the Authority and are proud that
in your group, the work is done right.   You never have any
problems with your own people, just the "damn" foremen and
supervisors from other departments. They are always trying to
tell you what to do and they don't even know their "a--- from a
hole in the ground." If they would just leave you alone, you
could get your work done. You aren't too happy about the Payroll
Department either. It seems that they mess up your withholding
every few months and you still haven't gotten your Social Security
records straight. They are just a bunch of incompetents.

Your boss is Chris Wilson.   He(she) used to be a foreman and was
one of the few that didn't get on your nerves. Since you didn't
want the promotion, Wilson seems a good choice. You haven't had
much interaction with him(her) yet.

30. INTIMACY PROGRAM: DEVELOPING PERSONAL RELATIONSHIPS[*]

PURPOSE:

1. To accelerate the getting-acquainted process in groups.
2. To study the experience of self-disclosure.
3. To develop authenticity in groups.

GROUP SIZE:

An unlimited number of dyads.

TIME REQUIRED:

50-75 minutes.

ROOM ARRANGEMENT REQUIREMENTS:

A room large enough for dyads to talk privately without disturbing each other.

EXERCISE SCHEDULE:

1. (5-10 min.) Discussion on building trust.

(Steps 2 & 3, 5 min.)

2. Divide into dyads, preferably with someone you know least well.

3. Read and discuss the guidelines and instructions for the Intimacy Program.

4. (35-50 min.) Meet with your partner and answer the questions in the program.

5. (5-10 min.) The instructor will lead a class discussion on the exercise examining how trust was built in this short time period.

---

[*]Reprinted from: J. William Pfeiffer and John F. Jones, eds. A Handbook of Structured Experiences for Human Relations Training, Vol. III, San Diego, CA: University Associates, 1974. Used with permission.

INTIMACY PROGRAM QUESTIONS[**]

Ask your partner a question and after the answer, the partner asks you a question. Continue taking turns. Do not go through the questions in order, but rather choose the ones which interest you the most, following the rules below:

1. Anything said must be held in confidence.
2. You do not have to answer every question your partner asks.
3. Do not ask your partner a question unless you are willing to answer the same one.
4. Do not write down the answers to the questions. Do them orally.

1. Who is the most important person in your life?

2. As a child, what did you want to be when you grew up?

3. What qualities do you look for in a prospective date or mate?

4. Are you proud of your grades?

5. What was the most "successful" experience you've ever had.

6. How do you have fun?

7. Do you want children?

8. Describe your parents.

9. Who is your best friend?

10. Has anyone ever betrayed your trust?

11. If you could be anything you wanted, what would it be?

12. What do you value most?

13. What is your favorite course? Your worst?

14. Where would you really like to live?

15. What do you want to be doing 10 years from now?

16. What makes you angry or annoyed?

17. What is difficult for you?

18. What kind of people do you like best?

19. What are your political views?

---

20. Are you a religious person?

21. Are you always truthful?

22. Do you have a serious romantic relationship?

23. Do you think women can combine career and motherhood?

24. Are there situations where men are stronger or better than women?

25. Are there situations where women are stronger or better than men?

26. How do you feel about people of other races and cultures?

27. What do you want people to say about you after you've died?

28. Do you usually show your feelings or hide them?

29. Describe yourself in three words.

30. What's your best personal quality?

31. Is money an important goal for you?

32. Describe a unique communication problem you have had.

33. How do you feel about professor-student dating?

34. What is your favorite music?

35. Are you a leader or a follower?

36. Do you want to be like your parents?

37. What are you fascinated by?

38. What bores you?

39. What would be an "ideal life" for you?

40. Where would you like to travel?

41. What's your ethnic background?

42. Do you think a college degree is worthwhile?

43. Why did you come to college?

44. How do you pay for your living/school expenses?

45. What do you think of me?

46. Do you like yourself?

47. What are your favorite and worst foods?

48. Who do you want to like you? Is there a good chance?

49. What is your favorite TV program or movie?

50. Is there anyone else you'd rather be?

51. Who do you admire most?

52. Who was your favorite president and why?

53. What is your favorite color?

54. Do you play a musical instrument or wish you could?

31. TEACHING INTERPERSONAL SKILLS TO SUBORDINATES[*]

PURPOSE:

To provide students with basic skills for helping their future subordinates develop competencies in interpersonal skills.

GROUP SIZE:

Any number from five to six member groups.

TIME REQUIRED:

Semester Assignment. At least six 40-60 minute time periods scheduled in the second half of the course.

PREPARATION REQUIRED:

Lecturette for early in the course on the basic parts or steps of effective skills or competency based training, e.g., (1) learner pre-assessment, (2) concept presentation, (3) concept examples for learner analysis, (4) learner practice (see also behavior modeling techniques).

ROOM ARRANGEMENT REQUIREMENTS:

The five- to six-member student groups will need to meet in separate rooms, each of the groups meeting alone for 40-60 minutes once a week for six weeks. Student groups should arrange for their own meeting time and place, providing information to the instructor on how to locate them. It is helpful for the instructor to provide an open class period on six consecutive weeks to ensure that students have at least one commonly open time period per week during which to schedule a training session.

INTRODUCTION:

You will likely have at some time in your professional career a management or supervisory position. Key to your success will be not only your understanding of and ability to use the interpersonal skills we examine in this course, but also your ability to impart these same valuable skills to your subordinates. Their effective performance is also greatly dependent upon these skills, and their performance will reflect upon you as their supervisor. This assignment is designed to help you learn how to develop effective interpersonal skills training for your future subordinates.

Please refer to the following notes for specific information and a checklist for preparing for and fulfilling this assignment:

---

[*]Adapted with permission from Charles M. Vance, Loyola Marymount University, "Extending Academic Impact: Teaching Students How to Teach Interpersonal Skills to Their Future Subordinates. Organizational Behaivor Teaching Review, 11(3), 1986-87 pp. 86-94.

SUMMARY STUDENT NOTES FOR ASSIGNMENT ON INTERPERSONAL SKILLS DEVELOPMENT FOR SUBORDINATES:

On an appointed day and time of your choosing during the weeks indicated in your syllabus, you will meet with your group for 40-60 minutes and train them in some specific skill of your choice. You must clearly identify who the members of your group represent, (i.e., subordinates, line managers), and what specific skill objective or objectives you have for the group. The skill objective should be of a practical "how to" nature, and related in some way to this course.

Each member of your group will also conduct a training session of your group. Thus, you will act as a trainer once, and as a trainee several times. You will be graded in this project on both your training performance (30 points), and your awareness and understanding of effective subordinate training, as reflected in the quality of your evaluation of others' training (20 points).

Please use the following as a checklist:

1. Set objectives -- clearly identify the specific skill or small set of skills. (Keep it simple!)

2. Meet with your assigned group as often as needed early int he course to identify a different training topic for each group member. be sure that the topics are different enough to be sure that no two training sessions cover the same information or skills. ONce you have identified your different training topics, decide upon the time and place in which each group member will conduct his or her training session. Then hand in to your instructor as early as possible a sheet of paper indicating <u>which</u> group member is conducting a training session on <u>what</u> (date and time) and <u>where</u>.

3. Go to the library and get as much resource material as you can on your topic. Now is your time to become a subject matter expert on your specific topic. After you become very familiar with the subject matter, then begin to focus on how to design and actually conduct the training. Don't try to teach your group everything you've learned on the topic. Again, keep it simple!

4. See your class instructor early for help or suggestions ont he design of your training session, or for assistance in obtaining the audiovisual resources you'll need.

5. Conduct your session. Don't just lecture to the group! Reserve 10 minutes at the end for individual group member written evaluation of your performance.

   Collect the evaluations. A handwritten evaluation on a a blank sheet of paper is acceptable. The quality of each of these evaluations will also be assessed. <u>The individual evaluations should be based on the steps for effective skill training as presented in class by your instructor.</u> Be sure that you are very familiar with those steps, for your instructor will look for your awareness of them when you evaluate your fellow students' training performance.

   To facilitate the instructor's grading of your perceptiveness in evaluating the skill training conducted by each of your group members, be sure to write the last four digits of your I.D. on the back of each of the individual, otherwise anonymous, evaluations you hand in to the group trainer.

6. Hand in at class the following Monday (late papers docked points) a four-to five-page two-part report containing (1) <u>Design</u>: your intended training design, including learner objectives, planned delivery outline with justification for methods used, and references; (2) <u>Evaluation</u>: your personal evaluation of your actual training performance and your analysis of your group members' handwritten evaluations of your training with thoughtful recommendations for

improvement if you were to do the assignment over again. Also attach the handwritten evlautions of your group members.

Consider the following interpersonal skill topics for your training session, but don't be limited by them:

Handling angry customers	Correctional interview
Giving feedback	Discipline interview
Soliciting feedback	Termination interview
Asserting oneself	Managing interpersonal conflict
Active listening	Managing group conflict
Employee selection interview	Disagreeing effectively
Nonverbal communication	

32. EXECUTIVE ETIQUETTE[*]

PURPOSE:

To discuss issues of social relations in business.

GROUP SIZE:

Any number of groups of 5-8 members.

TIME REQUIRED:

(15-60 minutes)

PREPARATION REQUIRED:

Read the seven letters and answer the questions. DO NOT read Miss Trueheart's responses.

RELATED TOPICS:

Women in Management (#1, #2, #3, #7)
Leadership (#2)
Interpersonal Perception (#1)
Organization Culture and Norms (#2, #7)
Conflict Management (#6)
Dynamics Within Groups (#4)
Interpersonal Communication (#5, #6)

BACKGROUND:

Our mythical business person, Mr. Fast-Tracker, has a Plethora of etiquette problems. In order to get intelligent advice, Mr. Fast-Tracker has written to Prudence Trueheart, the quintessence of knowledge in social interactions.

EXERCISE SCHEDULE:

1. (Pre-class) Read the seven questions and answer questions after each letter. The instructor may assign one letter at a time in different class sessions.

2. (5-30 minutes, depending on number of letters discussed) For one or more letters, groups discuss answers to questions and etiquette/social interaction issues.

3. (10-30 minutes) Instructor reads aloud Miss Trueheart's responses for appropriate letters and conducts a class discussion.

LETTERS

---

[*]Adapted by Jack Brittain and Sim B. Sitkin from Judith Martin, excepted from Miss Manners' Guide to Excruciatingly Correct Behavior. Copyright (c) 1982, United Feature Syndicate, Inc. Reprinted with the permission of Atheneum Publishers, an imprint of MacMillan Publishing Company. Copyright on original material by Jack Brittain and Sim B. Sitkin.

#1 Dear Miss Trueheart:

I am a young, single, female executive. I work for the regional office of a major bank, and must occasionally travel to our corporate office in New York to work on a deal. My problem is this: a friend from work recently bumped into a woman from the New York office while on vacation. The woman asked my friend if she knew me, and then inquired about a "rumor" she heard in New York. Apparently the "gossip" in New York is that I had a torrid affair with a married man with whom I worked on a deal. This rumor is supposedly widely circulated, much to my embarrassment. There was no affair.

My friend rose to my defense and quickly denied the rumor, but I doubt it had any impact. What should I do, ignore it and assume that if my managers hear the rumor, they know me well enough to ignore it? I am also concerned that my hard-earned professional image will be damaged in the eyes of Senior Management in New York. Do you have any advice?

Sincerely,
Fast-Tracker

Questions

1. Given what we know about how people make social judgement, what advice would you offer in this situation? Should Fast-Tracker go around denying the affair to anyone who will listen?

2. What steps can Fast-Tracker take to influence the boss's perceptions of what occurred? How can the discussion be managed so that the boss will be guided toward a positive attribution?

3. How important is behavior in this situation? Why?

4. How does the behavior we exhibit "enact" our reality in this situation?

#2 Dear Miss Trueheart:

I am an unmarried businesswoman. I am occasionally invited out to dinner with out-of-town executives and their local managers. I am leery of these situations and have turned down all such invitations, but know my male counterparts have sometimes come away from the table with valuable information that can be used to the company's and their benefit.

How should I act as the only female member of a dinner party? Should I invite a date to accompany me to such a dinner in order to retain respectability and keep weird ideas out of the head of some gentleman who is half smacked by the time the salad is served? What should I wear to such an event--a business suit or dinner dress? Should I meet the gentleman at the restaurant, or allow him to pick me up at home? When I travel out of town on business, am I expected to invite my hosts out to dinner? This problem is easier, because then I could invite their wives as well.

Your advice on this matter is going to be appreciated--not only by me, but by our managers, who are chary of allowing their female subordinants enough rein to become involved in such situations.

Sincerely,
Fast- Tracker

Questions

1. What does this person's dilemma tell us about how people understand social situations?

2. What is the difference between a business and social situation? How do we know if we are in one or the other?

3. What factors can this executive control in influencing the behavior of her dinner guests?

4. Can a manager learn anything abut influencing employees' behavior from this situation?

#3 Dear Miss Trueheart:

The event that has created a permanent state of embarrassment for me happened several months ago at a semiformal Christmas party. Please confirm whether my behavior was so atrocious that my career is ruined and I must look forward to spending the rest of my days without stock options.

My date and I were introduced to Mr. and Mrs. CEO in this way: "Mr. and Mrs. Fast-Tracker..." --at which time I extended my hand.." and Miss Holstein." Mr. CEO ignored my hand and turned to the lady with me. My open hand was left hanging in midair for what seemed like an eternity before it fell, shaky but unshaken, to my side. I have been confounded every since, and so unraveled that I have taken refuge in the company of accountants, where good manners are irrelevant as long as one is suitably dressed.

Does a man not offer a handshake until after his female companion has been introduced and/or shaken the hands of the party to whom whey are being introduced? Am I a bumbler, or did I just have the misfortune of running into an arrogant stick-in-the-mud? My habit has always been to extend my hand immediately upon being introduced.

Questions

1. What is this social ritual all about? What is the relationship between rules of etiquette and the concept of norms?

2. How important is "normatively correct" behavior for business success? Why?

#4 Dear Miss Trueheart:

I recently took over as local manager for a national service firm. The local newspaper was doing a feature on women in business, and asked if I would submit to an interview on the "life-style" my husband and I share. A pleasant and seemingly professional young woman came to my house for tea one afternoon, and we chatted for some time about many things, including her social life. We got quite friendly and I even considered including her in our social circle. You can imagine my horror when I saw that she had violated the spirit of the visit by printing everything I said, even those things which look insulting to friends and associates in print.

It is true, as she said when I complained to her boss, that I had not specified that anything was "off the record." I did not think I needed to, because I assumed she had the good sense to know what was proper for her article and what not. I was not, after all, holding a press conference: I was acting as a hostess in my own home. I wish you would say something about this particular form of rudeness. I personally plan to avoid the press in the future, rather than expose myself to such public inspection.

Question

1. What are the boundary differences in friendships and working relationships?

2. What expectations of loyalty are there with friends and in professional relationships?

3. Give examples of problems you have encountered when professional and personal boundaries were blurred.

#5 Dear Miss Trueheart:

I trust that Miss Trueheart will not find this inquiry too indelicate to comment on. I am a successful young MBA who is fortunate to have an exceptionally well-qualified administrative assistant. She has performed her job brilliantly, and contributed a great deal to my own rapid climb up the corporate ladder. As a result of working closely together over the past year, my feelings of appreciation and respect for her are now, I detect, taking on romantic characteristics. As I have not expressed these feelings I have no idea if she shares them, and am not experienced enough in such matters to "read" any subtle indications on her part.

What, if anything, should I do, and how should it be done? The options I see are business-as-usual, frank revelation and discussion, or graduate encouragement of her to indicate her feelings. I am not a seducer, and do not wish to lose my assistant as a result of some foolish action on my part. Also, I am married. Would Miss Trueheart please suggest what and how she thinks I ought to do?

Questions

1. What are the advantages/disadvantages for both Fast-Tracker and the administrative assistant of "getting involved"?

2. Does it make a difference in such an involvement if one or both are married?

3. How can romantic feelings at work be managed?

4. What should a manager do when two workers are "involved"?

#6 Dear Miss Trueheart

I fear I have inadvertently insulted a co-worker. I offer no excuses, I behaved badly. How might I go about making amends?

Questions

1. In normal office conflicts and snafu, how are problems often resolved when one person goofs up?

2. Is it better to smooth over problems or directly apologize?

#7 Dear Miss Trueheart

I want to be fair and responsible, but there are some things I cannot get used to about the "new manners." Specifically, I am embarrassed when a woman I am lunching with grabs the check. Some of them do this quite aggressively. My company is perfectly willing to pay for any business lunches I consider necessary, and my lunch partner does me no favor by making a show of paying for me herself. What is the woman's real objective here, to prove she is my equal?

Miss Trueheart Replies:

#1 Dear Fast-Tracker:

You have every right to be outraged, for you have been subjected to a social sneak attack. The question of what you should do is difficult, but what you should not do is quite obvious: do not run about wildly denying all present and future rumors. This only leads others to believe you have something to cover up, which you do not. The better course is to let your professional behavior speak for itself and act completely naive about any gossip that is boiling around you. You need to remember that most people recognize gossip for what it is: idle speculation. You will be judged by your actions, and if they are professional and honest, your reputation will reflect those actions. The other supposedly involved party may not have these traits, and as a result the story is widespread in his office.

If you have a good relationship with your boss, you may want to talk the situation over with her. Be forthright and explain that you upset over the rumor that has been circulating about you and want to get professional advice on how to deal with it. Regardless of how useful the advice you receive, your boss will think well of you for seeking her professional wisdom. Furthermore, once the boss has considered the situation from your standpoint, she will interpret all subsequent information from the perspective you have created.

Finally, it is probably best to remember that what to you seems like a central life crisis is of little more than passing interest to your co-workers. If you react calmly and do not make a big fuss, everyone will soon forget and be gossiping about someone else. These things have a way of achieving the importance we assign to them, so if you treat it as the idle gossip that it is, then that is what it will remain.

#2 Dear Fast-Tracker:

Miss Trueheart would dearly love to see "semi-business semi-social" entertainment abolished, for the very reason that it presents so many unpleasant possibilities. However, if businessmen have them, businesswomen must, and unfortunately they must protect themselves against men who try to give them the business.

The surest way to make people behave is to make them aware that many people will know about it if they do not. Yes, invite their wives, if you can. Yes, bring an escort if you can. If neither is possible, you might bring along a junior colleague and explain she is responsible for reporting on the meeting. If you can establish contact with the wives of these gentlemen, then you can mention--in the event of an improper suggestion--that you hope to speak to their wife soon. Threatening blackmail while smiling and being sociable is an indispensable business technique. In your dress and arrangements, you should treat the occasion as a pleasant, informal extension of the work day, not a date. Your dinner companion does not pick you up at home, and you do not dress up.

It is unfortunate that business women must protect themselves, but it is wrong for managers to concern themselves with the problem. They will only use it as an excuse for not promoting women. If one attempts to discuss the problems, however sympathetically, ask him what he does to protect the chastity of his male subordinates.

#3 Dear Fast-Tracker

If Miss Trueheart were to banish you to the company of accountants, she would also have to include Mr. CEO and the person who did the introducing, and the last thing any company needs is more accountants. The proper introduction, with accompanying gestures, would have been: "Mrs. CEO, may I present Miss H ...and Mr. Fast-Tracker. Mrs. CEO then extends her hand, first to Miss H. then to you--or does not, in which case there is no handshaking. The choice is hers. Then "Miss H this is Mr. Bigshot CEO. Mr. CEO, this is Mr. Fast-Tracker." Miss H decides whether to shake hands with Mr. CEO, and Mr. CEO decides whether to offer a hand to you, unless of course you are heir to the company, in which case his job is in jeopardy.

The point is that the socially higher-ranking persons--which means women before men, except in the case of presidents, kings, or popes, and the greater age and more exalted positions before the younger and less significant--either sticks out a hand, or does not. The worst error is to pass by a hand that has been extended, however erroneously. Therefore, the CEO is demoted and your career is launched. Congratulations on your first corporate coup.

#4   Dear Fast-Tracker

Miss Trueheart feels you would be advised to learn the difference between friends and working people. It is true that the same people can be both at different times, and also that a great deal of money and effort is put into blurring the distinction to gain professional advantage. Your privacy will be protected to the degree that you learn to see clearly through the blur.

Your interview was not a social occasion. You tried to make it seem so in the hope that you would inhibit your visitor with the restriction people have when they visit their friends socially to speak well of them afterwards. The interviewer added to the social air in the hope that you would feel the conversational freedom of a hostess among friends. The evidence shows that you were taken in by her ruse, but she was not taken in by yours. MIss Trueheart cannot condemn her for not having the good sense to censor the remarks you did not have the good sense to refrain from making.

The ability to distinguish between business being conducted in social settings and a true social life among real friends will be of enormous value to you now and later in life. Have a good time with your professional friends, but learn to distinguish real friends from those people you see because of mutual professional advantage.

#5   Dear Fast-Tracker:

Thank you for your consideration in assuring Miss Trueheart that you are not a seducer, but actually that was not her worry. Who seduces whom seems a moot point these days. Who hires, fires, and promotes whom is somewhat clearer. The reassurance Miss Trueheart would like for herself and your assistant is that you are not a harasser. You must realize that no matter what happens, you will only hurt the one you love. If she returns your sentiments and the romance progresses happily, she will be subject to the criticism of colleagues who refuse to believe that you admired her performance before noticing anything else about her. If she rejects you, or you want to end the romance, she will have difficulty separating her personal problems from her personnel problems. Miss Trueheart believes the best course of action is to do nothing. However, she does not believe for a minute that this is the sort of advice anyone ever takes.

Presumably your assistant is aware of the hazards of such an involvement. So what Miss Trueheart is most anxious about is that you should present your play in such a way that it is clear that she is free to reject it without fearing that it will affect your professional relationship. Paradoxically, a "frank discussion" will not achieve this. The franker your protestations, the more threatening they will sound. What you must do--as you would know if you were a trained diplomat, a noble and respected profession practiced by rapscallions of every stripe--is provide her with an excuse for not accepting, then wait to see if she takes it. Your marriage is an excellent excuse, as may have noticed on other occasions. If you declare your interest, then add, "But I understand perfectly if you feel you can't get involved because I'm married," you give her the chance to look at you regretfully and say, "No, I wish I could, but I don't feel it's right."

If, however, she says, "So what? So am I," you are in business and your etiquette problems are just beginning.

#6 Dear Fast-Tracker

Now that the duel is illegal, most insults are resolved with apologies. A humble speech, a graceful letter, a box of flowers--what fault will these not erase? Well, Miss Trueheart will tell you.

Miss Trueheart was once asked by an acquaintance what he should do after failing to attend a small, seated dinner party that a kind friend had given in his honor. The engagement had simply been forgotten by both he and his wife, and the thought of these good people standing around as the food congealed was beginning to cause he and his wife to lose sleep. Miss Trueheart was quick to realize that there was only one thing this couple could do: change their name, move out of town, and take up a life of anonymous service to others. There are, indeed, unforgivable social sins for which there is no need to apologize, because no apology is adequate.

Ordinary crimes of forgetfulness should be redeemed by an excess of thoughtfulness. One bombards the offended person with abject words, both spoken and written, and with flowers and other gifts until the person is exhausted enough to soften. The only excuse one should offer, as in so many acts better left uncommitted, is temporary insanity. To say "I was terribly busy" is another insult, meaning, "I had more important things to do than make the effort to be considerate to you." To say "That was such a dreadful, hectic time that I went out of my mind and neglected the very things that mattered most" is more like it.

In general, exclamations of "Oh, no, don't give it another thought" by the offended party should be steadfastly ignored. After all, how often do you believe a hostess who says "Oh, don't leave yet, it's early" as she escorts you to the door. One should never confuse social grace on the part of the offended party with the full discharge of social obligations.

#7 Dear Fast-Tracker:

Yes.

Chapter 9   Dynamics within Groups

33. TOWER BUILDING EXERCISE: A GROUP DYNAMICS ACTIVITY*

PURPOSE:

1. To study dynamics of a group in a task-oriented situation.
2. To examine the dynamics of leadership and power in a group.

GROUP SIZE:

Any number of groups of 6-8 members.

TIME REQUIRED:

50-80 minutes.

MATERIALS:

Each group brings materials for building a tower; these must fit in a box no greater than 8 cubic feet.

ROOM ARRANGEMENT REQUIREMENTS:

Space for each group to build a tower in.

---

*Idea from Philip Hunsaker, in Exchange, 4(4), 1979, p. 49. Additional parts adapted from Mary Gander. Used with permission.

RELATED TOPICS:

    Power & Influence
    Leadership
    Interpersonal Relationships
    Interpersonal Communication
    Creativity

EXERCISE SCHEDULE:

1. (5 min.) Each group is assigned a meeting place and a work place. One or two observers should be assigned in each group. Instructor may assign a manager to each group.

2. (10-20 min.) Each group plans for the building of the paper tower (no physical construction is allowed during this planning period). Towers will be judged on the basis of height, stability, beauty, and meaning. (Another option is to have the groups do the planning outside of class and come prepared to build the tower.)

3. (15-25 min.) Tower construction.

4. (5 min.) Groups inspect other towers, and all individuals rate towers other than their own. See evaluation sheet below. Each group turns in its point totals (i.e., someone in the group adds up each person's total for all groups rated) to the instructor, and the instructor announces the winner.

TOWER EVALUATION SHEET

GROUPS

CRITERIA	1	2	3	4	5	6	7	8
HEIGHT								
STABILITY/ STRENGTH								
BEAUTY								
MEANING/SIG-NIFICANCE								
TOTALS								

Rate each criteria on a scale of 1-10, with 1 being lowest or poorest, and 10 being highest or best.

5. (10-15 min.) Group Dynamics Analysis.
Obsrvers report observations to their own groups and each group analyzes the group dynamics which occurred during the planning and building of the tower.

6. (5-10 min.) Groups will report on major issues in group dynamics which arose during the tower planning and building. (Homework) Complete the following Tower Building Aftermath to be turned in to your instructor.

TOWER BUILDING PROJECT AFTERMATH ANALYSIS
by Mary Gander

YOUR NAME_____ GROUP_____

1. Were you a manager? yes____ no____ Who was informal leader?

    _____. Did you have a deviant or isolate?

    yes____ no____.

2. Did you feel like you "fit" the group or its norm? yes____ no____.
    Explain briefly:

3. Was there any conflict? Briefly explain. Was it resolved?

4. Did any problems arise? How were they handled?

5. How cohesive were you as a group by the end of the project?

    very____ moderately____ not very____ not at all____

6. How do you feel about your personal performance/contribution
    to the work group?

    excellent____ good____ fair____ poor____
    Explain:

7. How do you feel about the functioning of your group as a whole?

8. Do you feel your group produced a good product?

    very much____   it's okay____   no____

9. Please express your opinion of the usefulness of this project involving workgroup dynamics and supervising peers:

   a. great, we learned a lot____

   b. not bad, learned some things____

   c. a waste of time, don't do it next semester____

   d. It was fun, I didn't learn much but it was good to apply things from class____.

   Any additional comments:

10. How much planning did your group do?

   a lot____   some____   we were pretty spontaneous____

11. How many times did you meet (if applicable)?

   once____   twice____   three times____   more than three times____

12. A. Group members: Evaluate your manager's performance (if applicable).

     effective____   somewhat effective____   ineffective____

     Explain:

   B. Managers: Evaluate each of your subordinates (if applicable).

     1.

     2.

     3.

     4.

     5.

     6.

34. WHAT MOTIVATES EMPLOYEES? GROUP RANKING TASK*

PURPOSE:

1. To examine decision-making behavior in groups
2. To study group dynamics
3. To look at perceptions of motivating factors

GROUP SIZE:

Any number of groups of 5-9 members.

TIME REQUIRED:

55-85 minutes.

PREPARATION REQUIRED:

Rank order the 10 priorities in Table I below (use Column B).

ROOM ARRANGEMENT REQUIREMENTS:

Enough space for subgroups to meet.

RELATED TOPICS:

Motivation
Leadership
Interpersonal Communication

BACKGROUND:

Sometimes group decision-making is more effective than doing it alone. Research shows that if the decision is simple it is better to have one person responsible; however, if the problem is more complex, group decision-making is more effective. In this exercise you'll get a chance to compare the results of individual and group decision-making.

Several years ago employees in U.S. organizations; i.e., offices and factories, were given questionnaires by psychologists. All workers were given a list of ten items and asked to list them in their order of importance to themselves. Supervisors were given the same list and invited to predict how their subordinates would answer. The test instrument is shown in Table 1.** Although there are no "correct" answers, your reply will be a good measure of your grasp of what makes people tick.

**From Jurgensen, Clifford, "Job Preferences," Journal of Applied Psychology: 63(3), June 1978, pp. 267-76. Copyright by The American Psychological Association. Reprinted by permission of the author.

EXERCISE SCHEDULE:

PART A - EXERCISE

1. (Pre-class) Rank order (in Table 1, Column B) the ten motivating factor items, with "1" being highest and "10" lowest.

2. (20-30 min.) In groups of 5-9 members, come to a consensus on the ranking of the 10 items (Use Table 1, Column B). Do not vote or "horse-trade." Really try to get agreement in each ranking. If someone disagrees, listen to that view; and when you feel strongly, use persuasive techniques.

3. (Optional) Choose 1-2 observers for each group. They will use What To Observe in a Group," which is in Appendix of this book. Unlike regular group members, observers may not participate in the discussion. They will take notes and later give feedback.

4. (5 min.) The instructor will share the study findings with the class. Put the actual answers in Column C of Table 1.

5. (10 min.) Computation of Table 1.

a. Compare your answer, listed under Column B, with the correct answer, listed under Column D. Subtract D from B for each row, taking the absolute value, and that will be the individual error which should be listed under Column A.

   Example:

If you answered	If correct answer was	Difference is
2	11	9
10	5	5
12	1	11

b. Total up the numbers in Column A (none of which should be negative numbers). This give you your Individual Score.

c. Subtract Column D from Column C on each row, again using the absolute value, to get the group error which should be listed under Column E.

d. Total up the numbers in Column E (none of which should be negative members). This gives you your Group Score.

e. Subtract the numbers in Column C from Column B taking the absolute value, and put the results under Column F. This is your Persuasion Score. The persuasion score measures how much you are able to influence other group members to your thinking. Spend a few minutes in your group discussing the Persuasion Scores. Who had the lowest (this person was the most persuasive) and who had the highest (this person has the least persuasive) score? Table 1 should now be complete.

TABLE 1

Items	A (B-D) Individual Error	B Your Rankings	C Group Rankings	D Employee Ranking	E (C-D) Group Aim	F (B-C) Persuasion
Sympathetic help on personal problems						
Feeling "in" on things						
Good wages						
Good working conditions						
Job security						
Full appreciation of work done						
Tactful disciplining						
Personal loyalty to workers						
Interesting Work						
Promotion and growth in company						

Individual Score (Total of A)   _____

Group Score (Total of E)   _____

Persuasion Score (Total of F)   _____

6. (10 min.) Computation of Table 2.

 a. Average Member Score
    Add up the Individual Score (Step b; Column A) of all group members and divide by the number of members in the group. Put this number in the indicated column.

 b. Group Score (Step d, Column E)
    Put this number in the indicated column.

c. Synergy.
If your Group Score is lower than your average member score, then put "yes" in the column for Synergy. If your Group Score is higher than your Average Member Score, then put "no" in the column for Synergy.

d. Best Member Score
This is the number of the member who has the lowest Individual Score. Put this score in the indicated column.

TABLE 2

Groups

	1	2	3	4	5	6
Average Member Score						
Group Score						
Synergy						
Best Member Score						

7. (10-15 min.--Optional) Observers give specific feedback to their respective groups.

PART B - (10-15 min.) Group Discussion

As a class discuss the following questions:

1. To what extent did group discussion change accuracy of the answers?

2. Which behaviors helped/hindered the decision-making process?

3. What happened if a person had a very accurate Individual Score, but was not very persuasive in the group; and conversely, what if a person had a poor Individual Score and was very persuasive in the group?

35. HOLLOW SQUARE: A GROUP COMMUNICATIONS EXPERIMENT*

PURPOSE:

1. To study dynamics involved in planning a task to be carried out by others.
2. To study dynamics involved in accomplishing a task planned by others.
3. To explore both helpful and hindering communication behaviors in assigning and carrying out a task.

GROUP SIZE:

Any number of groups of at least twelve participants each.

TIME REQUIRED:

50-75 minutes.

MATERIALS:

Hollow Square puzzle pieces in four envelopes for each group.

ROOM ARRANGEMENT REQUIREMENTS:

A room large enough to accommodate the experimental groups comfortably. One other, preferably two, room where the planning and operating teams can be isolated.

RELATED TOPICS:

Interpersonal Communication
Planning and Goal Setting
Leadership
Organization Change and Development

INTRODUCTION:

Often in organizations people who plan a project or task are not the ones who carry it out. Because of this, group and communications problems can occur. This exercise is designed to examine the dynamics of such a situation.

EXERCISE SCHEDULE:

1. (5-10 min.) Class is divided into groups of 12 (or more). In each group, four are assigned to be the Planning Team, four are the Operating Team and four (or more) the Observing Team. Each team goes to its assigned area and read ONLY the briefing sheet relevant for its role. In addition, the observes may use "What To Observe in a Group: in the Appendix of this book.

---

*Reprinted from William Pfeiffer, and John Jones. A Handbook of Structured Experiences for Human Relations Training. Vol. II, 1974, pp. 32-40.

for its role. In addition, the observes may use "What To Observe in a Group: in the Appendix of this book.

2. (20 min.) the Planning Team is given four envelopes with the Hollow Square puzzle pieces. One envelope is for each member. The Planning Team then plans how to instruct the Operating Team, using the guidelines on the Planning Team Briefing Sheet. If there is more than one group, a contest to see who completes the puzzle first will be part of the exercise.

3. (5-15 min.) The Planning Team instructs the Operating Team, which then assembles the Hollow Square. If there is more than one group, a "winner" is declared.

4. (10-15 min.) Observers meet with Planners and Operators to give feedback.

5. (10-15 min.) The instructor leads a discussion around the points illustrated by the exercise. Observers and others may comment also, using the following questions:
    a. What behaviors were most effective in the planning phase?
    b. Did communications break down between planners and operators?
    c. Were the planners secretive or open?
    d. In an organization, how can communication between planners and operators be improved?

FOR PLANNING TEAM ONLY

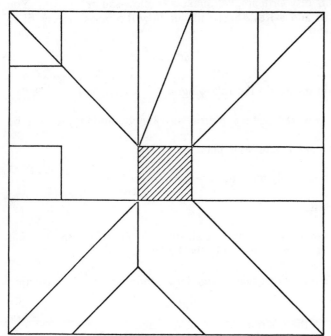

HOLLOW-SQUARE KEY

HOLLOW-SQUARE PATTERN

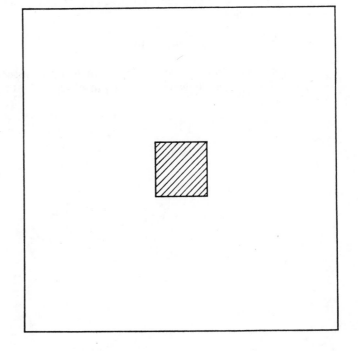

HOLLOW SQUARE PLANNING SHEET

Each of you has an envelope containing four cardboard pieces which, when properly assembled with the other twelve pieces held by members of your team, will make a "hollow-square" design. You also have a sheet showing the design pattern and a Key Sheet showing how the puzzle pieces fit to form the hollow square.

Your Task

During a period of twenty minutes you are to do the following:

1. Plan to tell the operating team how the sixteen pieces distributed among you can be assembled to make the design.
2. Instruct the operating team how to implement your plan.

(The operating team will begin actual assembly after the twenty minutes is up.)

Ground Rules for Planning and Instructing:

1. You must keep all your puzzle pieces in front of you at all times (while you both plan and instruct), until the operating team is ready to assemble the hollow square.

2. You may not touch other member's pieces or trade pieces during the planning or instructing phases.

3. You may not show the Key Sheet to the operating team at any time.

4. You may not assemble the entire square at any time. (This is to be done only by the operating team.)

5. You may not mark on any of the pieces.

6. When it is time for your operating team to begin assembling the pieces, you may give no further instructions; however, you are to observe the team's behavior.

HOLLOW SQUARE OPERATING TEAM SHEET

1. You have the responsibility of carrying out a task according to instructions given by your planning team. Your task is scheduled to begin no later than twenty minutes from now. The planning team may call you in for instructions at any time. If you are not summoned, you are to report anyway at the end of this period. No further instructions will be permitted after the twenty minutes has elapsed.

2. You are to finish the assigned task as rapidly as possible.

3. While you are waiting for a call from your planning team, it is suggested that you discuss and make notes on the following questions.

   a. What feelings and concerns are you experiencing while waiting for instructions for the unknown task?
   b. How can the four of you organize as a team?

4. Your notes recorded on the above questions will be helpful during the discussion following the completion of the task.

HOLLOW SQUARE OBSERVER BRIEFING SHEET

You will be observing a situation in which a planning team decides how to solve a problem and gives instructions on how to implement its solution to an operating team. The problem is to assemble sixteen pieces of cardboard into the form of a hollow square. The planning team is supplied with the key to the solution. This team will not assemble the parts itself but will instruct the operating team how to do so as quickly as possible. You will be <u>silent</u> throughout this whole process.

1. You should watch the general pattern of communication, but you are to give special attention to one member of the planning team (during the planning phase) and one member of the operating team (during the assembling period).

2. During the planning period, watch for the following behaviors:
   a. Is there balanced participation among planning-team members?
   b. What kinds of behavior impede or facilitate the process?
   c. How does the planning team divide its time between planning and instructing? (How soon does it invite the operating team to come in?)
   d. What additional rules does the planning team impose upon itself?

3. During the instructing period, watch for the following behaviors?
   a. Which member of the planning team gives the instructions? How was this decided?
   b. What strategy is used to instruct the operating team about the task?
   c. What assumptions made by the planning team are not communicated to the operating team?
   d. How effective are the instructions?

4. During the assembly period, watch for the following behaviors:
   a. What evidence is there that the operating team members understand or misunderstand the instructions?
   b. What nonverbal reactions do planning team members exhibit as they watch their plans being implemented?

36. GROUP SOCIALIZATION: THE UNITED CHEMICAL COMPANY

PURPOSE:

To explore issues of socialization in groups.

GROUP SIZE:

Any number of groups of 6-9 members.

TIME REQUIRED:

45-65 minutes.

PREPARATION REQUIRED:

Read the Case below and answer the questions at the end.

RELATED TOPICS:

Organization Culture and Socialization
Interpersonal Communication

PART A:

THE UNITED CHEMICAL COMPANY CASE.[*]

The United Chemical Company is a large producer and distributor of commodity chemicals with five chemical production plants in the United States. The operations at the main plant in Baytown, Texas, include not only production equipment but also is the site of the company's research and engineering center.

The process design group consists of eight male engineers and the supervisor, Max Kane. The group has worked together steadily for a number of years, and good relationships had developed among all members. When the workload began to increase, Max hired a new design engineer, Sue Davis, a recent masters degree graduate from one of the foremost engineering schools in the country. Sue was assigned to a project whose goal was expansion of one of the existing plant facility's capacity. Three other design engineers were assigned to the project along with Sue: Jack Keller (age thirty-eight, fifteen years with the company); Sam Sims (age forty, ten years with the company); and Lance Madison (age thirty-two, eight years with the company).

As a new employee, Sue was very enthusiastic about the opportunity to work at United. She liked her work very much because it was challenging and it offered her a chance to apply much of the knowledge she had gained in her university studies. On the job, Sue kept fairly much to herself and her design work. Her relations with her fellow project members were friendly, but she did not go out of her way to have informal conversations during or after working hours.

---

[*]From <u>ORGANIZATIONAL BEHAVIOR AND PERFORMANCE</u>, 3/e by Andrew D. Szilagi and Marc J. Wallace. Copyright (c) 1983 by Scott, Foresman and Company. Reprinted by permission.

Sue was a diligent employee who took her work quite seriously. On occasions when a difficult problem arose, she would stay after hours in order to come up with a solution. Because of her persistence, coupled with her more current education, Sue completed her portion of the various project stages usually a number of days before her colleagues. This was somewhat irritating to her because on these occasions she went to Max to ask for additional work to keep her busy until her fellow workers caught up to her. Initially, she had offered to help Jack, Sam, and Lance with their portion of the project, but each time she was turned down very tersely.

About five months after Sue had joined the design group, Jack asked to see Max about a problem the group was having. The conversation between Max and Jack was as follows:

MAX: Jack, I understand you wanted to discuss a problem with me.

JACK: Yes, Max, I didn't want to waste your time, but some of the other design engineers wanted me to discuss Sue with you. She is irritating everyone with her know-it-all, pompous attitude. She just is not the kind of person that we want to work with.

MAX: I can't understand that, Jack. She's an excellent worker whose design work is always well done and usually flawless. She's doing everything the company wants her to do.

JACK: The company never asked her to disturb the morale of the group or to tell us how to do our work. The animosity of the group can eventually result in lower quality work for the whole unit.

MAX: I'll tell you what I'll do. Sue has a meeting with me next week to discuss her six-month performance. I'll keep your thoughts in mind, but I can't promise an improvement in what you and the others believe is a pompous attitude.

JACK: Immediate improvement in her behavior is not the problem, it's her coaching others when she has no right to engage in publicly showing others what to do. You'd think she was lecturing an advance class in design with all her high-power, useless equations and formulas. She'd better back off soon, or some of us will quit or transfer.

During the next week, Max thought carefully about his meeting with Jack. He knew that Jack was the informal leader of the design engineers and generally spoke for the other group members. On Thursday of the following week, Max called Sue into his office for her midyear review. Certain excerpts of the conversation were as follows:

MAX: There is one other aspect I'd like to discuss with you about your performance. As I just related to you, your technical performance has been excellent; however, there are some questions about your relationships with the other workers.

SUE: I don't understand--what questions are you talking about?

MAX: Well, to be specific, certain members of the design group have complained about your apparent "know-it-all attitude" and the manner in which you try to tell them how to do their job. You're going to have to be patient with them and not publicly call them out about their performance. This is a good group of engineers, and their work over the years has been more than acceptable. I don't want any problems that will cause the group to produce less effectively.

SUE: Let me make a few comments. First of all, I have never publicly criticized their performance to them or to you. Initially, when I was finished ahead of them, I offered to help them with their work, but was bluntly told to mind my own business. I took the hint and concentrated only on my part of the work.

MAX: Okay, I understand that.

SUE: What you don't understand is that after five months of working in this group I have come to the conclusion that what is going on is a "rip-off" of the company. The other engineers are "goldbricking" and setting a work pace much less than they're capable of. They're more interested in the music from Sam's radio, the local football team, and the bar they're going to go for TGIF. I'm sorry, but this is just not the way I was raised or trained. And finally, they've never looked on me as a qualified engineer, but as a woman who has broken their professional barrier.

MAX: The assessment and motivation of the engineers is a managerial job. Your job is to do your work as well as you can without interfering with the work of others. As for the male-female comment, this company hired you because of your qualifications, not your sex. Your future at United is quite promising if you do the engineering and leave the management to me.

Sue left the meeting very depressed. She knew that she was performing well and that the other design engineers were not working up to their capacity. This knowledge frustrated her more and more as the weeks passed.

Case Questions

1. Does Sue value her membership in the group? Explain.

2. What is Sue seeking from membership in the design group?
   Are the other members seeking from membership in the group?

3. How do you rate the way Max handled his meeting with Sue?

4. Discuss this situation in terms of the stages of group development.

5. Discuss this situation in terms of structural dimensions of the group.

6. What should Sue do next? What should Max do next?

EXERCISE SCHEDULE

1. (10-15 min.) In groups of 6-9 members, discuss the answers to the six questions at the end of the case.

2. (5 min.) Discussion is stopped and the instructor asks for two volunteers for each group, one to be an observer and one a "risk-taker." These members go out in the hall with the instructor.

3. (10-15 min.) Members return to class and groups continue discussion.

4. (10-15 min.) Class discusses group process.

5. (10-15 min.) Continue class discussion on the United Chemical Company relating it to the experienced group process.

37. SUNSET COMMUNITY HOSPITAL: USING NOMINAL GROUP TECHNIQUE*

PURPOSE:

To practice using the Nominal Group Technique

GROUP SIZE:

Any number of groups of seven members, where one person is designated as "leader."

TIME REQUIRED:

50-95 minutes.

PREPARATION REQUIRED:

Read the case study on Sunset Community Hospital.

MATERIALS REQUIRED:

1. Flip chart/markers or chalkboard for each group.
2. 3 x 5 index cards (about 7 per class member)

RELATED TOPICS:

Interpersonal Communication

INTRODUCTION:

To resolve the problem in the case below, your group will use the Nominal Group Technique (NGT), which has proven to be an effective means of idea generation for a group examining new issues.

CASE STUDY

A Student Service HMO: Sunset Community Hospital

Fred Feister was meeting with Joseph Collins, Academic Vice President of a neighboring Ivy League University. Sunset Community Hospital itself is located in a New England community and has traditionally found a substantial portion of its patient population drawn from area colleges and universities.

---

*By Andre Delbecq. Used with permission.

However, universities as well as local industries were expressing increased concern about the cost of medical care. At a recent meeting of faculty and students at Mr. Collins' University, both the faculty and student senate voted on a motion requesting their school explore the possibility of an HMO in collaboration with an area hospital. The University has also asked that the HMO include a relationship with a physician group practice so that outpatient services as well as hospital care be included.

Mr. Feister would like his hospital and a physician group practice which utilizes his hospital to be selected as joint providers for the university HMO plan. In order to respond in a way that is both sensitive as well as competitively astute, he is proposing to Mr. Collins that his staff be allowed to meet with a "focus group" composed of faculty members, and a focus group composed of students to examine their special preferences with respect to medical care. He has suggested that a focus group of 24 students (divided into four subgroups representing each class) be arranged. A similar faculty group of the same size across faculty ranks has also been suggested. The central questions for the focus groups would be as follows:

Student Question:

What are the Attributes of Medical Care that are important to you as a student while living in residence away from your family?

Faculty Question:

What are the Attributes of Medical Care that are important to you and your family at this stage of your professional career?

Mr. Collins: "Fred, if you did meet with groups of students and faculty I wonder if this question can be answered in one meeting? We know that everyone is concerned with quality and reasonable cost. But beyond this, what exactly do you expect the students and faculty will say that you don't already know? I'm going to have some problems selling this idea. We're close to the end of the quarter and both faculty and students are busy trying to wind up their spring! They have limited time."

Fred Feister: "The purpose for using this broad question, Mr. Collins, is exactly for me not to prescribe what the students or faculty may say. Students living in dormitory residences away from their families are going to think about medical care in a different manner than they have in the past. It's no longer seeing their family doctor but perhaps a stranger. What are the circumstances that will make this experience comfortable for them?   What hours of the day are going to be critical in the provision of services, etc."

The same is going to be true for faculty. They are particularly insightful health care consumers and will have special concerns that we might be able to respond to. INdeed, your faculty and students may help us develop an HMO that is not simply effective and efficient in terms of medical quality and cost, but also particularly responsive to the special problems of your academic community. Believe me, I know that students participating in such a group will present ideas to us that we as providers will be able to respond to in order to serve them better."

Mr. Collins: "Well Fred, I'm willing to try this once and see whether or not it's worth going through the trouble of recruiting a larger group of students and faculty. Suppose I arrange for you to meet the officers of the Student Senate and have them participate in this focus group you are talking about. Let's see what happens and determine whether or not the ideas produced are worth the energy I would have to invest to get a broader campus sample."

Assignment

Imagine that you are Fred Feister negotiating with your university in competition with several different medical clinics and hospitals to provide prepaid care. You must conduct the focus group for purposes of idea generation, and you have decided to utilize the Nominal Group Technique (NGT) for structuring the meeting.

The NGT question for the meeting with students is:

> "What are the <u>Attributes of Medical Care</u> that are important to you as a student while living in dormitory residences away from home?"

EXERCISE SCHEDULE:

1. (pre-class) Read the Case Study.

2. (5-10 min.) Silent generation of ideas in writing. In groups of seven, the question is read aloud by the leader after which each member individually writes ideas in brief phrases or statements. It is important for each member to work silently and independently.

3. (10-20 min.) Round-robin recording of ideas on a flip pad or blackboard. Each person presents ideas in brief words or phrases, going one-at-a-time. Any member may "pass" if his/her ideas are duplicates and may "re-enter" later. It is important not to start any discussions on ideas until the listing is complete.

4. (10-20 min.) Serial discussion for clarification. Each member takes a turn discussing the various ideas in order to clarify the meaning of the items and explain reasons for agreement or disagreement.

5. (5-10 min.) Preliminary vote on item importance. Group chooses between 5-9 items as "priority items." Each priority item is written down on a 3 x 5 index card. Members then individually and silently rank orders the items. A member writes a "1" in the upper right hand corner for the most important item, "2" for the next most important, and so on. Cards are collected by the leader and shuffled so that anonymity is retained. Votes are then tallied and posted on the flip chart or board in front of the group.

6. (5-10 min.) Discussion of the preliminary vote. Each person has a chance to <u>briefly</u> clarify issues.

7. (5-10 min.) Final Vote. Repeat "Preliminary Vote" step. (number 5)

8. (10-15 min) The instructor will lead a discussion on the benefits of the Nominal Group Technique.

<u>Reference</u>

Delbecq, Andre L., Andrew H. VandeVen and David H. Gustafson. <u>Group Techniques for Program Planning</u>. Middleton, Wis: Greenbriar Press, 1986, pp. 15-82.

Chapter 10   **Dynamics Between Groups**

38. PRISONERS' DILEMMA: AN INTERGROUP COMPETITION

PURPOSE:

1. To explore trust and its betrayal between group members.
2. To demonstrate effects of interpersonal competition.

GROUP SIZE:

Groups of no more than eight members each.

TIME REQUIRED:

50-65 minutes.

ROOM ARRANGEMENT REQUIREMENTS:

Enough space for the opposing teams to meet separately without overhearing each other.

EXERCISE SCHEDULE:

(Steps 1 and 2, 5 min.)

1. The instructor explains what will take place in this exercise and assigns people to groups.

    Two types of teams are formed and named Red and Blue (with no more than eight per group) and are not to communicate with the other team in any way, verbally or nonverbally, except when told to do so by the instructor.

2. Groups are given time to study the Prisoner's Dilemma Tally Sheets.

3. (3 min.) Round 1. Each team has three minutes to make a team decision. Write your decisions when the instructor says time is up.

4. (2 min.) The choices of the teams are announced for Round 1. The scores are entered on the Tally Sheet.

5. (4-5 min.) Round 2 is conducted in the same manner as Round 1.

6. (6 min.) Round 3 is announced as a special round, for which the payoff points are doubled. Each team is instructed to send one representative to chairs in the center of the room. After representatives have conferred for three minutes, they return to their teams. Teams then have three minutes, as before, in which to make their decisions. When recording their scores, they should be reminded that points indicated by the payoff schedule are doubled for this round only.

7. (8-10 min.) Rounds 4 and 5 are conducted in the same manner as the first two rounds.

8. (6 min.) Round 6 is announced as a special round, in which the payoff points are "squared" (multiplied by themselves: e.g., a score of 4 would be $4^2 = 16$.) A minus sign should be retained: e.g., $(-3)^2 = -9$. Team representatives meet for three minutes; then the teams meet for three minutes. At the instructor's signal, the teams write their choices; then the two choices are announced.

9. (6 min.) Round 7 is handled exactly as Round 6 was. Payoff points are squared.

10. (10-20 min.) The point total for each team is announced, and the sum of the two team totals is calculated and compared to the maximum positive or negative outcomes (+108 or -108 points). A discussion on win-lose situations, competition, etc., will be conducted.

PRISONERS' DILEMMA TALLY SHEET

Instructions: For seven successive rounds, the Red team will choose either an A or a B and the Blue Team will choose either an X or a Y. The score each team receives in a round is determined by the pattern made by the choices of both teams, according to the schedule below.

PAYOFF SCHEDULE

AX - Both teams win 3 points.
AY - Red Team loses 6 points; Blue Team wins 6 points.
BX - Red Team wins 6 points; Blue Team loses 6 points.
BY - Both teams lose 3 points.

SCORECARD

ROUND	MINUTES	CHOICE		CUMULATIVE POINTS	
		RED TEAM	BLUE TEAM	RED TEAM	BLUE TEAM
1	3				
2	3				
3*	3(reps.) 3(teams)				
4	3				
5	3				
6**	3(reps.) 5(teams)				
7**	3(reps.) 5(teams)				

*Payoff points are doubled for this round.
**Payoff points are squared for this round. (Retain the minus sign.)

39. WINDSOCK, INC.*

PURPOSE:

To explore intergroup relationships.

TIME REQUIRED:

50-110 minutes.

MATERIALS:

Plastic milk straws (500) and a box (750) of straight pins.

RELATED TOPICS:

Leadership and Interpersonal Communications

EXERCISE SCHEDULE:

1. (5 min.) Class is divided into four groups: Central Office, Product Design, Marketing/Sales and Production. Central Office is a slightly smaller group. If groups are large enough, assign observers to each one.

   Central Office is given 500 straws and 750 pins. Each person reads ONLY the role description relevant to that group.

2. (30-60 min., depending on length of class) Groups perform functions and prepare for a two-minute report for "stockholders."

3. (8-10 min.) Each group gives a two minute presentation to "stockholders."

4. (Optional, 10-15 min.) Observers share insights with subgroups.

5. (5-20 min.) Instructor leads class discussion in areas of intergroup cooperation and coordination, open vs. closed communication, leadership.

---

*Adapted from Christopher Taylor and Saundra Taylor in "Teaching Organizational Team-Building Through Simulation ," Organizational Behavior Teaching Review, Vol. XI(3), 86-87. Used with permission.

ROLES

Central Office

Your team is the central management and administration of WINDSOCK, INC. You are the heart and pulse of the organization, because without your coordination and resource allocation, the organization would go under. Your task is to manage the operations of the organization, not an easy responsibility because you have to coordinate the activities of three distinct groups of personnel: the Marketing/Sales group, the Production group, and the Product Design group. In addition, you have to manage resources including materials (pins and straws), time deadlines, communications, and product requirements.

For the purpose of this exercise, you are to do whatever is necessary in order to accomplish the mission and to keep the organization operating in a harmonious and efficient manner.

WINDSOCK, INC. has a total of 30 minutes (more if instructor assign) to design an advertising campaign and ad copy, design the windmill, and to produce the first windmill prototypes for delivery. Good luck to you all.

Product Design

Your team is the research and product design group of WINDSOCK, INC. You are the brain and creative aspect of the operation, because without an innovative and successfully designed product the organization would go under. Your duties are to design products which will compete favorably in the marketplace, keeping in mind function, aesthetics, cost, case of production, and available materials.

For the purpose of this exercise, you are to come up with a workable plan for a product which will be built by your production team. The windmill you are to design must be light, portable, easy to assemble, and aesthetically pleasing. Central Office controls the budget and allocates material for your division.

WINDSOCK, INC. as an organization has a total of 30 minutes (more if instructor assigns) to design an advertising campaign, design the windmill (your group's task), and to produce the first windmill prototypes for delivery. Good luck to you all.

Marketing/Sales

Your team is the market/sales group of WINDSOCK, INC. You are the backbone of the operation, because without customers and sales the organization would go under. Your task is to determine the market, develop an advertising campaign to promote your company's unique product, produce ad copy, and develop a sales force and sales procedures for both potential customers and the public at large.

For the purpose of this exercise, you may assume that a market analysis has been completed. Your team is now in a position to produce an advertising campaign and ad copy for the product. To be effective, you have to become very familiar with the characteristics of the product and how it is different from those products already on the market. The Central Office controls your budget and allocates materials for use by your division.

WINDSOCK, INC. has a total of 30 minutes (more if instructor assigns) to design an advertising campaign and ad(your group's task), design the windmill, and to produce the first windmill prototypes for delivery. Good luck to you all.

Production

Your team is the production group of WINDSOCK, INC. You are the heart of the operation because without a group to produce the product, the organization would go under. You have the responsibility to coordinate and produce the product for delivery. The product involves an innovative "windmill" design which is cheaper, lighter, more portable, more flexible, and more aesthetically pleasing than other designs currently available in the marketplace. Your task is to build windmills within cost guidelines, according to specifications, within a prescribed time period, using predetermined materials.

For the purpose of this exercise, you are to organize your team, set production schedules, and build the windmills. Central Office has control over your budget and materials, as well as the specifications.

WINDSOCK, INC. has a total of 30 minutes (more if instructor assigns) to design an advertising campaign, design the windmill, and to produce the first windmill prototypes (your group's task) for delivery. Good luck to you all.

40. BUILDING BRIDGES*

PURPOSE:

1. To demonstrate the importance of intergroup coordination for organizational effectiveness.

2. To build awareness of the need for teamwork in completing a task.

3. To demonstrate the effects of competition on team efforts.

GROUP SIZE:

Any number of groups of 6-8 members.

TIME REQUIRED:

50-90 minutes.

ROOM ARRANGEMENTS:

Table space in a room large enough for each group to work separately without distracting other groups plus a room or waiting area for the construction specialists during the Design Phase.

MATERIALS:

_ 1 Basic Set of Tinkertoys and 1 ruler per group.

_ A stopwatch or watch with a second hand for each group.

_ A five pound weight (or object which weighs five pounds).

EXERCISE SCHEDULE:

1. (5 to 10 min.) After you have chosen your groups, read the Instructions for Participants. Keep in mind that you will be competing with other groups to design and construct a model bridge out of Tinkertoys under the following conditions:

   _ Designers may not participate in the actual construction of the bridge. They may observe the construction and redesign if necessary. They can only talk with the construction specialists or give advice if the group decides that they are willing to pay the consultation fee.

---

*By Douglas Austrom, Indiana University. Adapted from "Tinkertoy Bridge: Intergroup Competition" an exercise by Geoff Bellman from J. William Pfeiffer and John Jones (Eds.), A Handbook of Structured Experiences for Human Relations Training; Vol. III, San Diego, CA: University Associates, 1974. Additional modifications suggested by Joseph Gufreda. Used with permission.

– Construction specialists may only use one hand to build the model bridge. They must follow the design provided by the designers and must ask the designers to redesign it if necessary. If they do so, consultation/redesign fees will be assessed.

Within your group, decide who will be the observers (at least two), the designers (at least two), and the construction specialists (at least two). If you are chosen to be a construction specialist, adjourn to the "Union Hall" to wait for the designers to complete the design -- your instructor will tell you where it is. Read _only_ the instructions for the job you will be doing.

2. (15 to 25 min.) After the designers have read their instructions, they should start drawing the designs for their model bridge as well as estimate how much it will cost to construct. Observers begin timing the Design Phase for their group at this time. When a group completes the design of the model bridge and estimates its total costs, the observer records the group's design time and summons the group's construction specialists.

3. (10 to 15 min.) Construction begins on a group-by-group basis as soon as your group's designers complete the designs and the estimate. The observer also times this portion of the exercise. When you finish construction, the instructor will assess each bridge to determine if it meets specifications and supports the five pound weight. The observers complete the Estimate sheet for their group and post the following data:

   – Estimated costs
   – Actual costs
   – Difference between actual and estimated costs

4. (10 to 15 min.) Each team gives a one minute presentation on "who should be awarded the contract and why." The observers, subject to the veto of the instructor, will decide publicly which team is awarded the contract.

5. (10 to 25 min.) As a class, discuss how the exercise reflects actual work situations and the importance of interdepartmental coordination to effective organizational functioning. Participants and observers should comment briefly on the intragroup and intergroup dynamics they experienced and observed.

Building Bridges
Instructions for Participants

The State Highway Department has asked your company to design and construct a model of a new bridge across the White River. Several firms are also designing bridges for other locations. The Highway Department is going to build 20 bridges around the state and will award the remaining bridges to one of the competing companies. All the competing companies are building model bridges constructed of Tinkertoys. You want your team to win the contract.

The Highway Department will make its decision based on a number of factors including:

1. Minimum Specifications
   Length: At least 18"
   Height: At least 4"
   Width: At least 3"
   Strength: The model bridge must be able to support a five pound weight at its center.

2. Actual versus Estimated Cost
Completing construction of the model as close to the estimated cost is to your advantage.

3. Low Cost
This is naturally an important consideration. Labor rates and material costs will be available to your designers.

There are three main tasks facing your company.

1. Drawing the design.

2. Estimating the cost of designing and constructing the model bridge.

3. Constructing the model bridge.

Each company will be comprised of 2 observers and at least 2 designers and 2 construction specialists. Your first chore is to determine who will play which roles. The designers will be responsible for drawing two views of their design and for estimating how much it will cost to construct the model bridge. The construction specialists will only be able to use one hand to construct the bridge and they must follow the design provided by the designers.

Each group will be given a set of Tinkertoys.

Building Bridges
Instructions for Designers

Your task is to complete the following:

1. Draw two views of the bridge. The designs must be clear to the construction specialists, but they do not need to be exact.

2. On the sheet provided, estimate the costs of constructing the bridge including total design costs, construction costs, and material costs.

As you work, keep these constraints in mind:

1. Construction specialists will only be able to use one hand during the construction.

2. You will be assessed a penalty of $2,000 for each minute over or under your original time estimate. It is in your group's best interests to correctly anticipate construction time as well as how much time, if any, will be needed during the Construction Phase for consultation or redesign.

3. You are being timed by the observers. The sooner you complete your tasks, the lower your costs will be.

As soon as you have completed these tasks, submit your estimate sheet to your group's observer, and call your construction specialists to begin construction.

You are allowed to be present during the Construction Phase as observers only! The construction specialists may ask you to make design changes or to clarify the design. You may also initiate consultation with the construction specialists. But, if you consult with the construction specialists for any reason or make any design changes during construction, a consultation rate of $4,000 per minute with a minimum of $2,000 per consultation will be assessed by your group's observer.

Building Bridges

Estimate of Construction Costs

1. Material Costs

Items	Unit Price	#	Estimates Costs	Actual Costs
Wooden spools	$400 x	____	= ____	____
2 inch yellow rods	300 x	____	= ____	____
3.25 inch blue rods	400 x	____	= ____	____
5 inch red rods	500 x	____	= ____	____
7.5 inch green rods	600 x	____	= ____	____
Green panels	600 x	____	= ____	____
Yellow panels	400 x	____	= ____	____
Material Costs Subtotal			____	____

2. Labor Costs

	# or Min.		Estimated	Actual
Actual design time and cost	____ x	$3000 =	____	____
Designer consultation with construction specialists and/or redesign during construction	____ x	$4000 =	____	____
Estiamted construction time	____ x	$3000 =	____	____
Actual construction time	____ x	$3000 =	____	____
Penalty charges (Total number of minutes over or under estimate)	____ x	$2000 =	____	____
Labor Costs Subtotal			____	____

3. Total Costs (Materials + Labor)   ____   ____

4. Difference between estimated and actual total costs   ____   ____

Building Bridges

Instructions for Construction Specialists

Your task is to construct a model bridge.

Until the designers have completed their tasks, you will need to wait in the "Union Hall." Then you will be summoned by the observer to build a model bridge from the materials provided. During the construction, each member of the construction team may use only one hand.

The bridge must be faithful to the design provided to you by your designers. Only the designers may change the design of the bridge. If you feel the design is deficient (for example, it can not be assembled as drawn, or it will take too long to build, or it will not meet specifications), you may ask your designers to change the design. But, if you consult with the designers for any reason during the Construction Phase, a $4,000 per minute consultation/redesign fee will apply with a minimum of $2000 per consultation. Otherwise, the designers will be available during the construction phase as observers only.

Your task is to construct the bridge as quickly as possible. It is complete when your bridge matches the design and the instructor has inspected it and signed off.

Building Bridges

Instructions for Observers

Your task is to observe the group dynamics both within the subgroups and between the designers and construction specialists. Feel free to read the instructions for the designers and construction specialists so that you can better understand what is expected from them.

In addition to observing the group dynamics, you have the following specific chores:

1. Keep track of time. Record the times both phases start and are completed.

Design Phase	Starting time	_____
	Completion time	_____
Construction Phase	Starting time	_____
	Completion time	_____

2. Make sure that the designers complete the design and estimate sheets. When the designers have completed their tasks, summon the construction specialists.

3. Make sure that the designers and construction specialists do not talk to each other during the construction phase -- without the consultation time being billed at the specified rate.

4. Make sure that the completed bridge meets the minimum specifications.

5. Compute actual construction costs and compare them with the estimated costs.

Chapter 11   Leadership and Influence

41. LEADERSHIP STYLE INVENTORY[*]

PURPOSE:

To assess your leadership style.

GROUP SIZE:

Any number of groups of three to four members.

TIME REQUIRED:

15-30 minutes.

PREPARATION REQUIRED:

Complete and score "Leadership Inventory"

DIRECTIONS:

In order to get a better idea of what your leadership style is and how productive it would be, fill out the questionnaire below. If you are currently a manger or have been a manager, answer the questions considering "members" to be your subordinates. If you have never been a manger, think of situations when you were a leader in an organization and consider "members" to people working for you.

---

[*]Copyright 1988 by Dorothy Anne Marcic. Adapted with permission from Thomas Sergiovanni, Richard Metzcus and Larry Burden, "Toward a Particularistic Approach to Leadership Style: Some Findings;" <u>American Educational Research Journal</u>. Vol 6(1), January 1969, American Educational Research Assoc. Washington D.C.

Leadership Style

Response Choices for Each Item:
A. (always)   B. (often)   C. (occasionally)   D. (seldom)   E. (never)

	A	B	C	D	E
1. I would act as the spokesperson of the group.					
2. I would allow the members complete freedom in their work.					
3. I would encourage overtime work.					
4. I would permit the members to use their own judgment in solving problems					
5. I would encourage the use of uniform procedures.					
6. I would needle members for greater effort.					
7. I would stress being ahead of competing groups.					
8. I would let the members do their work the way they think best.					
9. I would speak as the representative of the group.					
10. I would be able to tolerate postponement and uncertainty.					
11. I would try out my ideas in the group.					
12. I would turn the members loose on a job, and let them go on it.					
13. I would work hard for a promotion.					
14. I would get swamped by details.					
15. I would speak for the group when visitors are present.					
16. I would be reluctant to allow the members any freedom of action.					
17. I would keep the work moving at a rapid pace.					
18. I wold let some members have authority that I should keep.					
19. I would settle conflicts when they occur in the group.					
20. I would allow the group a high degree of initiative.					

	A	B	C	D	E
21. I would represent the group at outside meetings.					
22. I would be willing to make changes.					
23. I would decide what will be done and how it will be done.					
24. I would trust the members to exercise good judgment.					
25. I would push for increased production.					
26. I would refuse to explain my actions.					
27. Things usually turn out as I predict.					
28. I would permit the group to set its own pace.					
29. I would assign group members to particular tasks.					
30. I would act without consulting the group.					
31. I would ask the members to work harder.					
32. I would schedule the work to be done.					
33. I would persuade others that my ideas are to their advantage.					
34. I would urge the group to beat its previous record.					
35. I would ask that group members follow standard rules and regulations.					

Score:

People oriented: Place a check mark behind the number if you answered either A or B to any of these questions.

Question #2 _____   10 _____   22 _____
        4 _____   12 _____   24 _____
        6 _____   18 _____   28 _____
        8 _____   20 _____

Place a check behind the number if you answered either D or E to any of these questions.
        14 _____   16 _____   26 _____   30 _____

Count your checks to get your total people-oriented score. _____

Task oriented: Place a check mark behind the number if you answered either A or B to any of these questions.

        3 _____   7 _____   11 _____   13 _____
       17 _____   25 _____   29 _____   31 _____
       34 _____

Place a check behind the number if you answer C or D to any of these questions.
        1 _____   5 _____   9 _____   15 _____
       19 _____   21 _____   23 _____   27 _____
       32 _____   33 _____   35 _____

Count your check marks to get your total task-oriented score. _____

	Range			Range	
People	0-7;		Task	0-10	You are not involved enough in either the task or the people.
People	0-7;		Task	10-20	You tend to be autocratic, a whip-snapper. You get the job done, but at a high emotional cost.
People	8-15;		Task	0-10	People are happy in their work, but sometimes at the expense of productivity.
People	8-15;		Task	10-20	People enjoy working for you and are productive. They naturally expend energy because they get positive reinforcement for doing a good job.

As a leader, most people tend to be more task-oriented or more people-oriented. Task-orientation is concerned with getting the job done, while people-orientation focuses on group interactions and the needs of individual workers.

Effective leaders, however, are able to use both styles, depending on the situation. There may be time when a rush job demands great attention placed on task completion. During a time of low morale, though, sensitivity to workers' problems would be more appropriate. The best managers are able to balance both task and people concerns. Therefore a high score on both would show this balance. Ultimately, you will gain respect, admiration and productivity out of your workers.

EXERCISE SCHEDULE:

1. (pre-class) Complete and score inventory.

2. (10-20 min.) In groups of four to six members, discuss group member's styles and implications for management and organizations.

3. (5-10 min.) Instructor will lead a discussion on leadership style.

42. WHAT'S THE BEST LEADERSHIP STYLE?
Vroom and Yetton's Model[*]

PURPOSE:

To show how situational leadership can work in practice.

GROUP SIZE:

Any number of groups of 5-8 members.

TIME REQUIRED:

30-50 minutes.

PREPARATION REQUIRED:

Read the "Background" below and decide which leadership style
is best for each of the three case studies.

RELATED TOPICS:

Decision-Making

BACKGROUND:

Decision-making is a vital part of being a manager. In recent years much has been written about
contingency or situational leadership styles. The research indicates there is no ONE best way to lead,
but rather variables in the situation indicate which style is most appropriate.

Vroom and Yetton have developed a normative model to show how to work this. It uses a
decision tree, answering a series of questions along the way. Similar models are used in medicine
and are called aprotocals or algorithms.

A New Look at Managerial Decision-Making
by Victor H. Vroom

Table I shows a set of alternative decision processes that we have employed in our research.
Each process is represented by a symbol (e.g., AI, CI,GII) that will be used as a convenient method
of referring to each process. The first letter in this symbol signifies the basic properties of the
process (A stands for autocratic; C for consultative; and G for group). The Roman numerals that
follow the first letter constitute variants on that process. Thus, AI represents the first variant on
an autocratic process, and AII the second variant.

_____

Table I
Types of Management Decision Styles

AI You solve the problem or make the decision yourself, using information to you at that time.

AII You obtain the necessary information from your subordinate(s) then decide on the solution to the problem yourself. You may or may not tell your subordinates what the problem is in getting the information from them. The role played by your subordinates in making the decision is clearly one of providing the necessary information to you, rather than generating or evaluating alternative solutions.

CI You share the problem with relevant subordinates individually, getting their ideas and suggestions without bringing them together as a group. Then you make the decision that may or may not reflect your subordinates' influence.

CII You share the problem with your subordinates as a group, collectively obtaining their ideas and suggestions. Then you make the decision that may or may not reflect your subordinates' influence.

GII You share a problem with your subordinates as a group. Together you generate and evaluate alternatives and attempt to reach agreement (consensus) on a solution. Your role is much like that of chairman. You do not try to influence the group to adopt to "your" solution and you are willing to accept and implement any solution that has the support of the entire group.

To aid in understanding the conceptual basis of the model, it is important to distinguish among three classes of outcomes that bear on the ultimate effectiveness of decisions. These are:

1) The quality or rationality of the decision.
2) The acceptance or commitment on the part of the subordinates to execute the decision effectively.
3) The amount of time required to make the decision.

We have found that managers can diagnose a situation quickly and accurately by answering this set of seven questions concerning it. But how can such responses generate a prescription concerning the most effective leadership style or decision process? What kind of normative model of participation in decision making can be built from this set of problem attributes? Figure 1 shows one such model expressed in the form of a decision tree.

Figure 1
DECISION MODEL

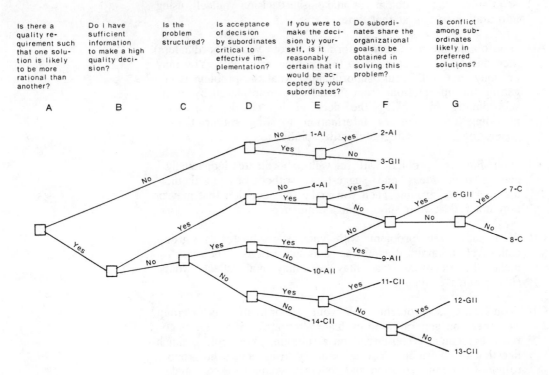

A. Is there a quality requirement such that one solution is likely to be more rational than another?

B. Do I have sufficient information to make a high quality decision?

C. Is the problem structured?

D. Is acceptance of decision by subordinates critical to effective implementation?

E. If you were to make the decision by yourself, is it reasonably certain that it would be accepted by your subordinates?

F. Do subordinates share the organizational goals to be obtained in solving this problem?

G. Is conflict among subordinates likely in preferred solutions?

CASE I

You are the senior manager for a group of ten highly educated engineers. Plans are now being finalized to build a newer and more suitable building, which you will move into within a few months.

All the groups members get along reasonably well, with only minor conflicts, most of which are solved in time. Everyone has been looking forward to the new building and talking about who will get which office an types of desks, etc. The best part, if seemed, was that the parking lot for the new building will make access much easier that it is now.

However, today you received the following memo from your boss.

> Due to irresoluble disagreements with the contractor and some recent disputes with the adjoining landowner over property lines, we will now have two parking lots. Lot number one will be in the previously planned place, right next to the building. Lot number two will be some distance away, approximately the length of two city blocks. YOur department has been assigned seven spaces in lot one and five spaces in lot two, since there are totally eleven including yourself. I trust you will make the fairest decision when allocating the parking spaces.

Which decision style do you use?

CASE II

You are the public relations manager for a software company which has just developed a new and revolutionary product. In fact, all indications are that this product will completely change the way people use computers.

The problem is how to market it, since the product is so vastly different, it is not clear that previous methods would work or not. There is considerable disagreement among your subordinates on what approach to use. Each of your five subordinates has been talking to different advertising agencies and each one has what he or she thinks is the absolute best advertising/marketing program.

Which decision style do you use?

CASE III

You are the manager in a large printing company. In the past few days several machines have been breaking down and causing decreased productivity. It has caused the workers to get more edgy and they have started yelling at one another, blaming each other for the problems. They are tired of the problems and want the machines to work at maximum like they used to.

Just now you have been handed the reports from the senior technician outlining the cause of the problems. This technician is quite competent and has always turned tin thorough reports previously. YOu must decide how to fix the machines.

Which style do you use?

EXERCISE SCHEDULE:

1. (5-10 min.) The instructor will discuss Vroom & Yetton's Managerial Decision Tree and divide the class into groups of 5-8 members.

2. (15-25 min.) Groups try to achieve consensus using Vroom & Yetton's model, on which leadership style is most appropriate for each of the four cases.

3. (10-15 min.) Each group reports on which leadership style it chose for Case I. After this the instructor reads Victor Vroom's choice of leadership style for this case. This is repeated for the other two cases.

43. WHAT TO DO WITH BOB AND NANCY?*

PURPOSE:

To determine styles of leadership which would be effective in a given situation.

GROUP SIZE:

Any number of groups of 4-8 members.

TIME REQUIRED:

40-60 minutes.

PREPARATION REQUIRED:

Read the Case Study below.

RELATED TOPICS:

Management of Diversity
Interpersonal Communication

WHAT TO DO WITH BOB AND NANCY?

Dave Simpson was sitting at his desk wondering how the devil to handle this situation. In Engineering School they don't tell you what to do when you think two of your key subordinates are having an affair! Dave knew a lot about the relative conducting properties of metals but what about the properties of people?

Dave was Engineering Manager of a division in a large corporation situated on the East Coast. The division was comprised of three engineering supervisors, five lead engineers and approximately 55 engineers (See Exhibit 1). The past two years had seen several reductions in manpower due to a temporary decline in the business base. The remaining men and women in the organization were "cream of the crop," all hard workers with a professional attitude about their jobs; any deadwood was long gone. The division had just won a large contract which would provide for long-term growth, but would also require a heavy workload until new people could be hired and trained. The work of the organization was highly technical, and required considerable sharing of ideas within and between the individual groups. This need for internal cooperation and support had been amplified because the organization was still understaffed.

Dave's previous secretary had transferred to an outplant location just before the new contract award, and it had taken a long time to find a suitable replacement. Because of a general shortage within the company, Dave had been forced to hire temporary help from a secretarial service. After

---

*By David L. Bradford. Reprinted with permission of Stanford University Graduate School of Business, (c) 1985 by the Board of Trustees of the Leland Stanford Junior University.

several months he found Nancy, and felt very fortunate to have located an experienced secretary from within the company. She was in her mid-thirties, attractive, had a pleasant disposition, and was very competent.

In the electronic design group was an enthusiastic, highly respected lead engineer named Bob. Bob and Dave had been close friends for several years, having started with the company at the same time. They shared several common interests, which had led to spending a fair amount of time together away from work.

Bob was struggling to get into management, and Dave's more rapid advancement had put a strain on the friendship. Dave had moved up from co-worker to being his boss and finally to being his boss's boss. Dave felt they could still be good friends at work, but he could not show Bob any favoritism. Bob understood the situation.

From Nancy's first day on the job, Bob began to hang around her desk. He would go out of his way to start conversations and draw her attention. This was not a surprise since Nancy was attractive and Bob had gained a reputation over the years as being a bit of a "wolf." He was always the first on the scene when an attractive new female joined the program.

Before long Bob and Nancy began eating lunch together. As time passed, the lunch dates became a regular routine, as did their trips together to the coffee machine. Their conversations during the working day also became more frequent. Dave felt slightly concerned about the wasted time, but since the quality and quantity of their work was not suffering in any measurable way, he did not say anything to either person. Furthermore, it was not unreasonable for Bob to be having numerous conversations with her since she had been instructed to provide typing and clerical support to the engineers whenever she had idle time. (Bob's section was temporarily looking for a secretary and the engineers were developing several new documents.)

After a few months Bob and Nancy introduced their spouses to each other and the two couples began to get together for an increasing number of social gatherings. Bob and Nancy continued their frequent lunch dates, now leaving the plant for lunch and occasionally returning late. This was not considered a major rule infraction, if the lateness was infrequent and if the time were made up in the long run. This tolerance policy was generally respected by all, including Bob and Nancy. On balance, the company seemed to be receiving at least a full week's work from both of them, since they often worked late.

What was also going on (but Dave didn't learn about until later) was that Bob and Nancy were calling each other on the phone during the work day; even though they worked in the same general area, just desks apart. They would wait until Dave had left the office, and then chat on the phone. However, Nancy's work performance was not visibly affected.

Of course, the internal grapevine was at work, and occasionally Dave would be asked about the situation between Bob and Nancy. "Do you know they've been seen having cocktails together in the evening?" "Did you know Nancy was having marital problems?" "Does Bob's wife know what's going on?"

It was apparent that Bob and Nancy were starting to have an affair, but how serious it was, and how long it would last, wasn't known. They were being very careful around Dave, and almost all of what Dave knew was based upon second and third-hand information and rumors. At this point, about four months after Nancy had started work, Dave did speak to Ron, Bob's supervisor, about it; but Ron was anxious to downplay the whole thing. He was willing to talk to Bob about the late lunches, but unwilling to discuss anything else. This seemed appropriate since, from the company's standpoint, employees' private lives were their own business. Ron was new to the organization and this factor contributed to his reluctance to discuss a delicate issue.

Dave decided not to confront Bob directly. If their relationship had been as close as it had been in years past, he might have spoken to Bob about the rumors going around, but during this period the friendship had further deteriorated. They were talking on a less personal level, and Bob was spending less off-hour time with old friends. Furthermore, Dave knew from previous discussions that Bob was particularly sensitive about private matters. "He probably wouldn't welcome my advice," thought Dave.

Dave did speak to Nancy about the need to be back in the office at the end of the lunch hour, but he had not made an issue out of it. Even though it was a definite annoyance when she was not there to answer the phone or type a memo, her performance had not declined. Dave certainly did not want to bring up the issue of an affair with Nancy. He imagined what might arise: tears, defensive denial (much of what Dave thought was going on would be difficult to substantiate if Nancy were to challenge his assessment), and even potential legal ramifications if the situation were handled improperly. Bob and Nancy could claim that their reputations or careers had been damaged. (Dave also didn't want to raise this issue with Personnel; it might permanently tarnish both of their records.)

During this same time frame there was a dramatic change in Bob's personal appearance. Instead of his usual coat-and-tie attire, he started wearing open-front shirts and a beaded necklace in an attempt to acquire the current "macho" look. Although perhaps acceptable in a Southern California business office, it certainly was out of place in the Northeast with the more conservative environment of the company. As a lead engineer, Bob directed, and often presented to management, the work of twelve other engineers. The custom was for all engineers and managers to wear a coat and tie especially since they might be called upon, with little notice, to meet with a customer or higher management. Even though Bob's attire was considered unprofessional, there was nothing in the company's written dress code requirement to forbid it.

Up to this point there had been no serious violation of company rules by either Bob or Nancy, although rules were being bent and tolerance policies abused. Then the situation took a turn for the worse while Dave was on a two-week company trip with Ron. Bob and Nancy used the opportunity to go out for a very long lunch. When they returned just before quitting time, George, one of the other supervisors, called Bob into his office and suggested that he "clean up his act." George told Bob that he was being foolish in chasing Nancy and that, among other things, he was jeopardizing his career opportunities with the company. Bob denied being anything more than friends with Nancy, and politely told George to stay out of his private affairs.

When Dave returned from his trip and heard of the incident, he told Ron to reprimand Bob and make it clear to him that "his actions are unacceptable, and that further long lunch periods will not be tolerated." Bob apologized, said he would make up the time, and that it wouldn't happen again.

Dave spoke to Nancy, and she also promised that there would be no more long lunches. But this was not the end of their noontime, outplant lunch dates and before long, Nancy's husband, Ted, got involved. Ted was a salesman for the company and worked in the same building. He began to drop by at lunchtime to question the engineers about Nancy's whereabouts. In addition he started calling Dave after work, wanting to know when Nancy had left, and expressing concern that she had not yet arrived home. This questioning was an unpleasant experience for everybody.

By now the entire organization was well aware of the irregular relationship, and was growing disrespectful of both Bob and Nancy. This was a difficult situation for the engineers. The attitudes of the organization had always been very professional, and the success of each group depended upon team-work and strong leadership from its lead engineer. Bob had been highly respected for his technical competence and ability to direct. In addition, the members of his group knew Bob's family, and had always considered him to be a good family man. Now this image had been destroyed. From a technical standpoint, Bob was still an excellent engineer and a vital resource on the new contract.

But with the group's declining respect, Bob was becoming less effective as a leader. Bob's own engineers felt very uncomfortable about the situation. They believed that Bob's real interests at work were more with Nancy than with them.

The situation had now deteriorated to the point where total organization effectiveness was being measurably affected. Something had to be done to remedy this situation. But what to do?

EXERCISE SCHEDULE:

1. (20-30 min.) In groups of 4-8, discuss what actions Dave should take.
2. (20-30 min.) Groups report their proposed strategies to the whole class.

Exhibit 1

WHAT TO DO WITH BOB AND NANCY

Table of Organization

ENGINEERING
MANAGER

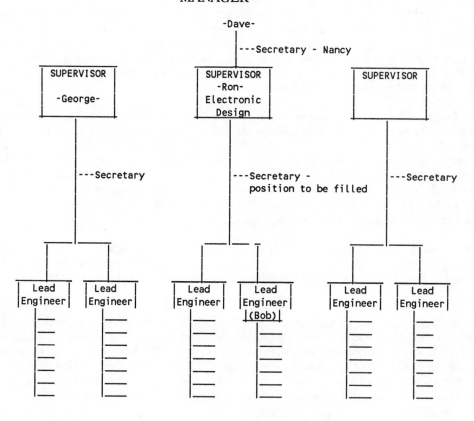

44. THE PRESIDENT'S DECISION: A ROLE PLAY*

PURPOSE:

To explore the effects of different types of leadership styles on group members.

GROUP SIZE:

Any number of persons.

TIME REQUIRED:

50-100 minutes.

ROOM ARRANGEMENT REQUIREMENTS:

Four chairs placed in a semi-circle in the front of the room.

RELATED TOPICS:

      Dynamics Within Groups
           Interpersonal Communications

EXERCISE SCHEDULE:

1. (5-10 minutes)
   a. Five persons are needed to play the roles. (When possible, role assignments for this case should be given before the meeting of the class in order to permit the participants to study the roles carefully.) Two participants play the role of John/Joan Ward, president of the company, and the other three are the vice-presidents: William/Wanda Carson, in charge of manufacturing and produce development, James/Jane Jackson, in charge of sales: and Russell/Rita Haney, in charge of personnel and industrial relations. Role descriptions are in the Appendix.

   b. The remaining persons in the class serve as observers.

   c. All group members read the Background Information. The instructor writes on newsprint or blackboard the name, position, age, and years with the company of all four participants.

   d. The participants study their roles so they can role play without referring to the written material. They do not read any role except their own.

   e. Observers read the Instruction for Observers.

---

   *Adapted from <u>The Role-Play Technique</u> by Norman R. F. Maier, Allen R. Solem and Ayesha Maier. Used with permission.

f. The instructor prepares the setting for the scene by planing a table and four chairs at the front of the room to represent the furniture in Ward's office. The table and one chair are for Ward's use and the other three chairs, arranged in a semicircle in front of Ward's desk, are for the vice-presidents. The furniture is arranged so that the observers are able to see the faces of all four role players.

2. (30-60 minutes)
   a. When all participants are ready, Ward I enters the office and sits at the desk. After a few moments, the vice-presidents enter, one at a time, and seat themselves so that Carson will be at Ward's left, with Jackson next to Carson, and Haney at the end, on Ward's right. Ward II remains in the hall.

   b. Ward I greets each person while entering and shows him/her the correct seat.

   c. When everyone is seated, Ward I begins the discussion.

   d. Fifteen to thirty minutes is usually needed for role playing.

   e. The leader is permitted to finish or ask for help whenever he wishes. If conflict develops and persists so that no progress is made after ten minutes, the role play is interrupted by the instructor and the problem is thrown open for general discussion. Role playing is resumed after the president feels he/she has gained enough hints to proceed.

   f. The scene is repeated with Ward II.

3. (15-30 minutes) DISCUSSION
   The instructor will lead a discussion on areas shown in the next sections.

   a. **Evaluation of the Solution**
      (1) Discuss the merits of the solution from the point of view of the future of the company and determine the extent of agreement among the observers. Compare the opinions of observers, vice-presidents, and Ward. In case these opinions differ, each role player introduces any relevant information that was given in that role to see if the new facts will alter the opinions of the observers.
      (2) Discuss the merits of the solution from the president's point of view.
      (3) What are Ward's prospects of being retained by the board of directors if the solution does not result in marked improvement?
      (4) Discuss the part the vice-presidents played in making the decision. Will they give Ward the support to retain his/her job?

   b. **Analysis of the Conference**
      (1) Did Ward give the vice-presidents an opportunity to help solve the real problem faced or were they given a somewhat different problem? Ward can describe why this situation caused him/her to act so.
      (2) Would Ward have given his/her side of the problem or confined the discussion to company matters as much as possible? Compare views of participants and observers.
      (3) Which participants persisted in discussing matters from their points of view? What could have been done to get everyone working together?

(4) How did the specialized information that different conferees possessed become integrated into the discussion? Was there an interest in getting facts or did Ward attempt to suppress facts?

(5) Stubbornness, aggression, and childish behavior indicate frustration. Enumerate the examples of these behaviors that were evidenced in the discussion and evaluate how they were handled.

c. **Discussion of Ward's Situation**

(1) How many observers would have taken the advice given by the vice-presidents (in this situation) had they played the part of Ward? How many would have declined the advice? List the arguments in favor of each position.

(2) What would happen if a president's decision was always the joint decision of the vice-presidents? Discuss the favorable and unfavorable aspects of such a philosophy of leadership.

BACKGROUND INFORMATION

The ABCO Electrical Manufacturing Company produces various part and subassemblies for radio, television, and other electronic industries. The factory is located in Philadelphia; there are sales offices in several of the eastern cities, in or near their major market area. During the Vietnam War, the company also operated a government-built plant in Kansas City which supplied equipment for military aircraft. However, this operation was abandoned when numerous military orders were cancelled; the plant was bought shortly thereafter by one of the large electronics manufacturing companies.

Two years ago, the company went through a major management reorganization, brought about by increasing losses in its operations and a steadily diminishing share of the market. The previous top management personnel were extremely conservative in their outlook and methods, and for many years had operated on a small share of the market as suppliers to the radio and broadcasting industries. During the Vietnam War, they made a good showing as a result of increased business and profits from military orders. For several years, there has been considerable growth in the electronic industry. At the same time, new problems have been created for the smaller producers, such as ABCO, by the unusually rapid technological developments and strong competition from the larger companies in the field.

The company's inability to compete for large-volume business has made it necessary to depend more and more on specialty orders. Although the unit profit margin on such orders is somewhat larger, the shifting demands of this type of market call for unusual flexibility in manufacturing processes and procedures and a highly alert, aggressive sales force in order to maintain demand for regular lines and push the sales of new products. Similarly, product development and engineering ingenuity are at a premium in order to meet competition, provide for economical changeover from one product to another, and achieve the quick solution of a variety of complex production problems. It is also necessary for production employees and foremen to adapt to frequent changes in jobs and methods without undue training or confusion.

It was the inability of the previous management to adapt to these changing conditions that led to the reorganization of the company and the installation of a new top management group. Following are the names of the present group of senior officers of the company, together with a summary of their previous background and experience:

John/Joan Ward, president of the company. Ward is forty-nine, has been with the company twelve years - first as an accountant, then as controller for six years - before being promoted to the present position two years ago. Ward has a college degree in accounting and is a CPA.

William/Wanda Carson, vice-president in charge of manufacturing and product development. Carson has an electrical engineering background and was hired fifteen years ago as a potential management person. Having progressed to general foreman of the night shift at the time, Carson was sent to Kansas City as superintendent. When the Kansas City plant was closed. Carson returned to Philadelphia as plant superintendent, and was promoted to the present position two years ago when Ward took over as president. Carson is forty-five years old.

James/Jane Jackson, vice-president in charge of sales. Jackson came to the company five years ago from the position of assistant sales manager for one of the divisions of a larger company. Jackson is the only holdover as vice-president from the previous management, having been brought in to set up a sales organization to attempt to recapture lost accounts and widen the market for company products. Jackson started in sales work from business administration school and is forty-six.

Russel/Rita Haney, vice-present, personnel and industrial relations, is thirty-nine. Haney was hired as personnel director for the Kansas City plant and then came to Philadelphia in a similar capacity. Previously, personnel functions had been the responsibility of the office manager. Haney remained as personnel director until a promotion to the vice-presidency one and one-half years ago.

INSTRUCTIONS FOR OBSERVERS

On the basis of what you already know about the ABCO Company and the four top executives, Ward, Carson, Jackson, and Haney, you probably have formed certain impressions about the situation. Most of the things you have learned so far are facts. However, you also know that these facts may be relatively unimportant except as background and that the attitudes, feelings, and personalities of these men, as well as their relationships with each other, may be more important. It is important to observe the feelings that are indicated and not be misled by the actual words spoken if you are to sense the developments as they occur in the role play. The following questions give you clues as to what to watch and listen for.

1. Observe how Ward opens the discussion. Does Ward seem at ease? Did he/she state a problem with all relevant facts for open discussion? Is Ward being open-minded about things?
2. What are Ward's reasons for calling this meeting? How do the other members react to Ward's views? To what extent does Ward accept their views? What evidence is there, if any, that Ward is defensive?
3. To what extent is this a problem-solving discussion? If not, why not? What do you think is the real problem here? What did Ward do to help or hinder the group?
4. Did any of the participants become stubborn? Why?
5. Note behaviors that indicate a member was holding back relevant information.
6. How acceptable is the decision to each of the members? Note behaviors that support your evaluation.
7. What evidence is there to indicate that fear or threat influenced the relationships of the various persons in the discussion?
8. What were the differences between Ward I and Ward II?

Chapter 12   **Managing the Boss**

45. MANAGING THE BOSS INVENTORY

PURPOSE:

To analyze factors in relationships with your present and previous bosses.

GROUP SIZE:

Any number of groups of 4-5 members.

PREPARATION REQUIRED:

Answer questions 1-3 and Part B.

TIME REQUIRED:

25-50 minutes

INTRODUCTION:

Most of the literature in management focuses on "downward" management while the relatively new area of Managing the Boss looks at "upward" management.

PART A: INVENTORY*

Complete the following inventory:

1. Make a list of all the "bosses" you have ever had in work situations. Include bosses from part-time jobs, summer jobs, and even professors with whom you worked closely.

_____   _____

_____   _____

_____   _____

_____   _____

_____   _____

_____   _____

2. Divide the names from above into three lists: those people with whom you had no difficulty, those with whom you had some problems, and those with whom you had severe problems.

NO PROBLEMS	SOME PROBLEMS	SEVERE PROBLEMS
_____	_____	_____
_____	_____	_____
_____	_____	_____
_____	_____	_____
_____	_____	_____
_____	_____	_____

3. Look for factors that might help explain why you have had some or severe problems with some bosses and not with others (or why you have always had no problems). For example, consider:

---

*By John P. Kotter. Used with permission of the author.

*The type of people involved: age, sex, personality, etc.
*The structure of your relationship with the people: how much and
 what type of power they had over you.
*The broader contexts: the kind of work involved, the type of
 organizations involved, etc. Think about it. Do you see any
 patterns...

regarding the type of people?

_____

_____

_____

_____

_____

_____

regarding the structure of the relationship?

_____

_____

_____

_____

_____

regarding the contexts?

_____

_____

_____

_____

_____

_____

PART B: Sentence Completions**

1. My boss and I get along best when...

2. The thing I like best about my boss is ...

3. The thing I like next best about my boss is...

4. The thing I like least about my boss is...

5. If I were my boss I would...

6. My boss could get more out of me by...

7. The reason I don't go all out for my boss is...

8. The thing I resent most about working for someone else is...

9. The thing about my boss that most upsets me is...

10. The changes I would make if I were boss are...

11. When I'm a boss I will never...

12. When I'm a boss I will never...

13. The thing I don't understand about my boss is...

14. The thing that irritates me about my boss is...

15. I wish my boss would...

16. All bosses are...

17. The ideal boss is...

**By Christopher Hegerty. Used with permission of the author.

PART C: DISCUSSION

1. (15-30 min.) In groups of 4-5, discuss responses for questions 1-3 and Part B.

2. (10-20 min.) Class Discussion

    1. Groups report main issues discussed to the whole class.

    2. What did you learn from this exercise about how to manage your boss more effectively?

46. THE MISBRANDED GOAT CASE AND ROLE PLAY*

PURPOSE:

To examine issues in Upward Management.

GROUP SIZE:

Any number of groups of 5-6 members.

TIME REQUIRED:

50-75 minutes.

PREPARATION REQUIRED:

Read the case below and answer the questions.

RELATED TOPICS:

Leadership
Interpersonal Communications

The Case

In March of 1976, I was approached by Fred Wilson, Director of Engineering of the Eastern Division of our parent company, about a job assignment that he hoped would interest me. Fred and I had never worked together but both knew of each other's characteristics and accomplishments. Everyone with whom I spoke knew Fred as brash, impersonal, demanding, and short-tempered. During our pre-job negotiations, Fred, who had been drafted for this division about one year ago, confided to me that Corporate had given him approval to do whatever was necessary to turn his division into a productive and efficient organization. He also explained that when he delved into the personnel statistics, he found that the group (with a few exceptions) had been formed with lower quartile people. In order to upgrade the group, he immediately acquired a few key upper quartile employees. Fred was offering me a new position reporting directly to him. His ultimate goal was to return to the Northwest division with me as his replacement in the East.

On my first work day, Fred informed me that there were three "dumb ***" engineering managers working for me that he wanted to replace as soon as possible. Because of my recent arrival, I begged off for 30 days so that I might become familiar with the division. Initially, I assumed that Fred was correct in the assessment of the three managers, but as time progressed, one of the three, Rae, appeared to differ from the other two. Rae responded instantly to requests made of her, accepted

---

*By David Bradford. Reprinted with permission of Stanford University Graduate School of Business. (c) 1983 by the Board of Trustees of the Leland Stanford Junior University. Used with permission.

any task that was put forth, and worked diligently to get good justifiable solutions. My concerns for the job and the people influenced me to apply more than normal amounts of time observing their work habits and performance. At meetings and in discussions with other organizations it became apparent that Rae had the respect and confidence of everyone on the program with the exception of Fred.

During lunch with Fred one day, I asked him to explain his reasons for wanting to replace the three. His concerns regarding the other two were understandable, but I pursued his opinions on Rae. Fred considered Rae worthless and that all of the problems seemed to originate from Rae's area. Her releases were usually late and/or incomplete; she lacked the answers to important questions; and she was continually asking for more people even though the manpower curve for the division was in the reducing mode.

After expressing myself very vividly, Fred tensely questioned my concerns about Rae. Listening to my observations, Fred became very upset. He ordered me to quit wasting time with Rae and to speed up the process of her replacement.

My next move was to check on Rae's background. Assessment of Rae's personnel folder revealed no negative statements. Actually, it was just the reverse. In her last 14 years of employment in our company she had had a variety of engineering and management assignments. In every case, Rae's capabilities in design, management and cooperation had been praised. This was later verified when I spoke to her previous supervisors.

Being thoroughly confused at this point, I decided to confront Rae. In the two-hour discussion that followed, Rae stated that Fred had informed her personally, prior to my arrival, that she was going to be fired. I asked Rae to explain her perception of Fred's reasoning. Her story concurred with Fred's. Her releases were late, even though she was working 40 to 50% overtime. She repeatedly requested additional personnel and her area was the major origin of problems. She also had difficulty answering some of Fred's questions related to the early parts of the program. But Rae also pointed out that she had been assigned her area of responsibility only six months prior to Fred's arrival. Since the program was over four years old, the design problems had been created by managers that Rae had replaced. However, each time that she had used this reasoning, Fred had become more and more irate. Rae also expressed the feeling that her work load was considerably greater than in other areas. I closed the discussion with the promise that I would continue to work the problem and that in my opinion the harassment was unjustified. I informed Rae that I appreciated the fine job that she was doing and requested that she continue her good performance.

Next I studied the work load in all areas, and found evidence confirming Rae's analysis. I then shuffled available manpower so that the capability was more evenly distributed. I explained to Fred that I had no plans to replace Rae and, in fact, thought that she was doing a creditable job. Fred became furious and made it quite clear that Rae's performance could reflect on me.

In the months that followed, Rae continued to do her tasks well. Her group started meeting schedules and eventually eliminated the need for overtime. However, Fred continued his relentless badgering. In meetings and in the group, he continued to try to embarrass Rae, especially when I was present. To my amazement Fred didn't apply the harassment to me. In fact he seemed to give me more and more freedom and responsibility as time went on.

Questions: What would you do about this problem?

How would you go about it?

EXERCISE SCHEDULE:

1. (Before Class) Read the case and answer the 2 questions.

2. (5-10 min.)   Divide into groups of 5-6 members.   Select one
   Fred (or Francine) per group.   Freds (or Francines) go into
   the hallway for instructions from the instructor.
   Freds/Francines read the role in the Appendix of this book.

   --Meanwhile, the other group members, who will play the
   subordinate, discuss their strategies.

3. (20-25 min.) Each   subordinate takes a turn trying to
   influence Fred/Francine. Wait until all are done before
   processing the role plays.

4. (10-20 min.)   Members give each other feedback on what was
   influential (and what was not).

5. (15-20 min.) The total class discusses what worked and what
   did not.

Chapter 13   **Organizational Culture and Socialization**

47. ORGANIZATIONAL CULTURE ASSESSMENT

PURPOSE:

OPTION 1: To identify campus norms students hold in common.

OPTION 2:   a. To diagnose organizational cultures in terms of corporate philosophy, valued performance, decision-making, reward system, communications, political system, etc.

   b. To classify several organizations using a modified version of the organizational culture typology of Deal and Kennedy (1982).

GROUP SIZE:

   Any number of groups of three to eight members.

TIME REQUIRED:

OPTION 1:   45 minutes in class

OPTION 2: 15-30 minutes advance preparation, several hours of preparation out of class, and one class period of at least 50 minutes for reporting and comparing findings are required.

PREPARATION REQUIRED:

OPTION 2: Read the "Introduction II" and "Corporate Culture Assessment Instrument" below.

RELATED TOPICS:

    Organization Structure
    Values
    Leadership

OPTION 1: Norms Exercise[*]

INTRODUCTION:

Every organization or social group has a set of norms that help to determine people's behavior. A norm is an unwritten rule for behavior in a group. When it is broken, negative feedback (negative comments, stares, sarcastic statements) is given.

EXERCISE SCHEDULE:

1. As an individual, write down all the norms you can think of now in the following areas:

Dress	Dating:
	Who? How often?
Studying	Inter-racial?
	Students/faculty?
Classroom Behavior	
Weekend activities	Eating in cafeteria

OPTION 2: Assessing Organizational Culture[**]

Organizational culture is the collection of relatively uniform and enduring beliefs, values, customs, traditions, and practices shared by the organizations' members and transmitted from one generation of employees to another. The expectations derived from culture create norms of acceptable behavior and ways of doing things in the organization. An organization's culture is analogous to an individual's personality. Like people, organizations can be described on trait continuum as conservative-experimenting, warm-cold, stable-dynamic, relaxed-tense, uncontrolled-controlled, practical-imaginative, etc. Culture influences the way members of the organization relate to each other as well as their relations with people outside the organization. Culture affects the kinds of goals the organization will pursue and how the organization will pursue them as well as how workers will be motivated to work toward the goals. The amount, direction, and openness of communication is influenced by organizational culture, as is the style of leadership exercised by supervisors in the organization. The use of rules, standard procedures, and close supervision versus the exercise of individual autonomy in job performance is a function of the organization's culture. Over time, heroes, myths, and rituals that perpetuate the values of the culture emerge and serve to demonstrate and emphasize the way things are done in the organization. Thus behaviors like innovating, decision-making, communicating, organizing, measuring success, and rewarding achievement may vary considerably from organization to organization and these differences are reflected in the organizational culture.

[**]By John E. Oliver. Used with permission.

Organizational culture can be diagnosed by observing the behavior of people at work, by interviewing people inside and outside the organization, and by questionnaires. In this exercise, you will be asked to investigate the culture of your university or organization, to compare your findings to those of other investigators, and to classify the organization into one of four types, or a combination of the four types, identified by previous research.

To diagnose the culture of your chosen organization, you may observe people's behavior, ask questions, and administer questionnaires. The following list of questions may be useful in conducting your diagnosis.

CORPORATE CULTURE ASSESSMENT INSTRUMENT***

	Ratings			
?? Don't Know	Not a Factor	Low--Done Infrequently, Little Recognition	Some Importance-in Regularity or Recognition	Important-Ingrained, Valued or Behavior Guide
1	2	3	4	5

A. Common Elements

1. Corporate philosophy, policy
Organization's tone or climate
"Who" we are and "what" we are trying to do and what we stand for
Clarity of corporate mission or objectives

2. Valued performance features and behaviors
Competitiveness, assertiveness, aggressiveness
Demonstrated company loyalty, act of organization commitment
"Macho," stoic, "hanging-in"
Productivity, performance ratings, workaholism
Control of resources, information
Valued departmental assignments

3. Decision making
Centralization vs. decentraliza.
Factors considered
Degree of support documentation
Scope of participation

4. Organization's reward system
Management by objectives, accomplishments
Performance appraisal ratings
Assessments of potential
Wage/salary increases, bonuses
Internal recognition (communications, ceremonials)

5. Sponsorship
"Adoption" by power figure
Expert guidance
Having a home department

6. Mentoring
Guidance/counseling by key person

7. Career ladders
Knowledge of valued routes
Qualifications to "enter" valued career routes
How to navigate valued routes

***From Elmer Burack, Creative Human Resource Planning and Application: A Strategic Approach. Englewood Cliffs, NJ: Prentice-Hall, 1988. Used with permission.

8. Social networking
   Acquaintance with key, power, or
   in-group figure(s) _____ _____ _____ _____ _____
   Part of recognized "old boy" or
   "old girl" network _____ _____ _____ _____ _____
   Support of "favored" charities _____ _____ _____ _____ _____
   Participation in selected sports/
   recreation activities _____ _____ _____ _____ _____

9. Dress, mannerisms, personal
   features, education
   Type of dress _____ _____ _____ _____ _____
   Posturing that is recognized/
   valued _____ _____ _____ _____ _____
   Knowing when to take a position
   or to "back off" (be flexible) _____ _____ _____ _____ _____
   Age, physical size _____ _____ _____ _____ _____
   Education: type of degree, school _____ _____ _____ _____ _____

10. Political system
    Knowledge of t he key "actors"
    and their areas of influence _____ _____ _____ _____ _____
    Who has the power and the bases
    for it _____ _____ _____ _____ _____
    How is power asserted, that is
    influence on decisions (e.g.,
    succession, recruiting, selec-
    tion) _____ _____ _____ _____ _____

B. Comprehensiveness and Social Integration
   1. Extent to which the "common ele-
      ments (A)" are identifiable by
      corporate leadership _____ _____ _____ _____

   2. Extent to which formal corporate
      communications feature regularly,
      "cultural" elements _____ _____ _____ _____ _____

   3. Extent to which informal corporate
      and organizational communications
      include culture elements _____ _____ _____ _____

   4. Consistency with which values and
      desired aspects of behavior have
      been transmitted to incoming and
      successive generations of managers
      and corporate leaders _____ _____ _____ _____ _____

   5. Extent to which "culture" elements
      are seen as working (adequately)
      well _____ _____ _____ _____

   6. Consistency with which elements
      of supervisory and managerial
      decision/behavioral patterns
      reflect "culture" (elements)--
      thereby, serving as models of
      behavior _____ _____ _____ _____ _____

EXERCISE SCHEDULE:

1. **15-30 minutes (at least one week in advance).**
   The group is divided into sub-groups of three to eight people. The "Introduction" and "Corporate Culture Assessment Instrument" is read and discussed.

2. Approximately three hours outside of class

   Participants must select an organization to diagnose. Depending on what the instructor assigns, it may be your university or it may be an organization in which a participant works or has worked.

   Participants try to answer the questions on the "Corporate Culture Assessment Instrument" by observing and questioning the members and clients of the organization. The answers are then used to classify the organization into one or a combination of the four types described on the "Organizational Culture Profiles."

3. (50 minutes)

   In class, the "Organizational Culture Profiles" is discussed and participants are asked to classify the organization culture that they studied into one or a combination of the four types. Each sub-group is allowed five minutes to discuss their culture and its classification giving examples to support their conclusions.

Discussion Questions:

1. What internal forces cause organizations to develop unique cultures?

2. What external(environmental) forces cause organizations to develop unique cultures?

3. How does organizational culture affect the behavior of individuals in the organization?

4. What are the dangers of organizational cultures?

5. How might organizational culture affect an organization's ability to change?

6. How might organizational culture affect personnel selection and promotion?

ORGANIZATIONAL CULTURE PROFILES****

Name of the culture	Driving	Outgoing	Specialist	Control
Type of risks that are assumed	High	Low	High	Low
Type of feedback from decisions	Fast	Fast	Slow	Slow
The ways survivors and/or heroes in this culture behave.	They have a tough attitude. They are individualistic. They can tolerate all-or nothing risks.	They are super sales-people. They often are friendly, hail-fellow-well-met types. They use a team approach to problem solving. They are non-superstitious.	They can endure long-term ambiguity. They always double check their decisions. They are technically competent. They have a strong respect for authority.	They are very cautious and protective of their own flank. They are orderly and punctual. They are good at attending to detail. They always follow established procedures.
Strengths of the personnel/culture	They can get things done in short order.	They are able to quickly produce a high volume of work.	They can generate high quality inventions and major scientific breakthroughs.	They bring order and system to the workplace.
Weaknesses of the personnel/culture	They do not learn from past mistakes. Everything tends to be short-term in orientation. The virtues of cooperation are ignored.	They look for quick-fix solutions. They have short-term time perspective and are more committed to action than to problem solving.	They are extremely slow in getting things done, are vulnerable to short-term economic fluctuations and often face cash-flow problems.	There is lots of red tape. Initiative is down-played. They work long hours.
Habits of the survivors and/or heroes	They dress in fashion. They live in "in" places. They like one-on-one sports such as tennis. They enjoy scoring points off one another in verbal interaction.	They avoid extremes in dress. They live in neighborhoods. They prefer team sports such football. They socialize together.	They dress according to their organizational rank. Their housing matches their hierarchical position. They like sports such as golf, in which the outcome is unclear until the end of the game.	They dress according to hierarchical rank. They live in apartments or no-frills homes. They enjoy process sports like jogging and swimming. They like discussing systems.

**** Source: Adapted from Terrence E. Deal and Allen A. Kennedy, Corporate Cultures: The Rites and Rituals of Corporate Life (Reading, MA: Addison-Wesley, 1982), Chapter 6.

| Typical kinds of organizations that use this culture. | Construction, cosmetics, television, radio, venture capitalism, management consulting. | Real estate, computer firms, auto distributors, door-to-door sales operations, retail stores, mass consumer sales. | Oil, aerospace, capital goods manufacturers, architectural firms, investment banks, mining and smelting firms, military | Banks, insurance companies, utilities, pharmaceuticals, financial-service organizations, many agencies of the government |

48. CAUGHT BETWEEN CORPORATE CULTURES

PURPOSE:

To analyze organization culture issues.

GROUP SIZE:

Any number of groups of 5-8 members.

TIME REQUIRED:

30-60 minutes.

PREPARATION REQUIRED:

Read "The Consolidated Life" case and answer questions.

RELATED TOPICS:

Leadership
Communication
Power

EXERCISE SCHEDULE:

1.   (Pre-class) Read case and answer questions.

2.   (15-30 min.) Groups discuss the five questions.

3.   (15-30 min.) The instructor leads a discussion on the case.

The Consolidated Life Case: Caught Between
Corporate Cultures*

PART I

It all started so positively. Three days after graduating with his degree in business administration, Mike Wilson started his first day at a prestigious insurance company - Consolidated Life. He worked in the Policy Issue Department. The work of the department was mostly clerical and did not require a high degree of technical knowledge. Given the repetitive and mundane nature of the work, the successful worker had to be consistent and willing to grind out paperwork.

---

*Reprinted by permission of the publisher from J. Weiss, M. Wahlstrom, and E. Marshall, "The Consolidated Life Case: Caught Between Corporate Cultures." <u>Journal of Management Case Studies</u>; 2, pp. 238-243. Copyright 1986 by Elsevier Science Publishing Co., Inc.

Rick Belkner was the division's vice-president, "the man in charge" at the time. Rick was an actuary by training, a technical professional whose leadership style was laissez-faire. He was described in the division as "the mirror of whomever was the strongest personality around him." It was also common knowledge that Rick made $60,000 a year while he spent his time doing crossword puzzles.

Mike was hired as a management trainee and promised a supervisory assignment within a year. However, because of a management reorganization, it was only six weeks before he was placed in charge of an eight-person unit.

The reorganization was intended to streamline workflow, upgrade and combine the clerical jobs, and make greater use of the computer system. It was a drastic departure from the old way of doing things and created a great deal of animosity and anxiety among the clerical staff.

Management realized that a flexible supervisory style was necessary to pull off the reorganization without immense turnover, so they gave their supervisors a free hand to run their units as they saw fit. Mike used this latitude to implement group meetings and training classes in his unit. In addition he assured all members raises if they worked hard to attain them. By working long hours, participating in the mundane tasks with his unit, and being flexible in his management style, he was able to increase productivity, reduce errors, and reduce lost time. Things improved so dramatically that he was noticed by upper management and earned a reputation as a "superstar" despite being viewed as free spirited and unorthodox. The feeling was that his loose, people-oriented management style could be tolerated because his results were excellent.

A Chance for Advancement. After a year, Mike received an offer from a different Consolidated Life division located across town. Mike was asked to manager an office in the marketing area. The pay was excellent and it offered an opportunity to turn around an office in disarray. The reorganization in his present division at Consolidated was almost complete and most of his mentors and friends in management had moved on to other jobs. Mike decided to accept the offer.

In his exit interview he was assured that if he ever wanted to return, a position would be made for him. It was clear that he was held in high regard by management and staff alike. A huge party was thrown to send him off.

The new job was satisfying for a short time but it became apparent to Mike that it did not have the long-term potential he was promised. After bringing on a new staff, computerizing the office, and auditing the books, he began looking for a position that would both challenge him and give him the autonomy he needed to be successful.

Eventually word got back to his former vice-president, Rick Belkner, at Consolidated Life that Make was looking for another job. Rick offered Mike a position with the same pay he was now receiving and control over a 14-person unit in his old division. After considering other options, Mike decided to return to his old division feeling that he would be able to progress steadily over the next several years.

Enter Jack Greely: Return Mike Wilson. Upon his return to Consolidated Life, Mike became aware of several changes that had taken place in the six months since his departure. The most important change was the hiring of a new divisional senior vice-president, Jack Greely. Jack had been given total authority to run the division. Rick Belkner now reported to Jack.

Jack's reputation was that he was tough but fair. It was necessary for people in Jack's division to do things his way and "get the work out."

Mike also found himself reporting to one of his former peers, Kathy Miller, who had been promoted to manager during the reorganization. Mike had always "hit it off" with Kathy and foresaw no problem in working with her.

After a week Mike realized the extent of the changes that had occurred. Gone was the loose, casual atmosphere that had marked his first tour in the division. Now, a stricter, task-oriented management doctrine was practiced. Morale of the supervisory staff had decreased to an alarming level. Jack Greely was the major topic of conversation in and around the division. People joked that MBO now meant "management by oppression."

Mike was greeted back with comments like "Welcome to prison" and "Why would you come back here? You must be desperate!" It seemed like everyone was looking for new jobs or transfers. Their lack of desire was reflected in the poor quality of work being done.

Mike's Idea: Supervisor's Forum. Mike felt that a change in the management style of his boss was necessary in order to improve a frustrating situation. Realizing that it would be difficult to affect his style directly, Mike requested permission from Rick Belkner to form a Supervisor's Forum for all the managers on Mike's level in the division. Mike explained that the purpose would be to enhance the exiting management-training program. The Forum would include weekly meetings, guest speakers, and discussions of topics relevant to the division and the industry. Mike thought the forum would show Greely that he was serious about both his job and improving morale in the division. Rick gave the O.K. for an initial meeting.

The meeting took palace and ten supervisors who were Mike's peers in the company eagerly took the opportunity to "Blue Sky" it. There was a euphoric attitude about the group as they drafted their statement of intent. It read as follows:

To: Rick Belkner
From: New Issue Services Supervisors
Subject: Supervisors' Forum

On Thursday, June 11, the Supervisors' Forum held its first meeting. The objective of the meeting was to identify common areas of concern among us and to determine topics that we might be interested in pursuing.

The first area addressed was the void that we perceive exists in the management-training program. As a result of conditions beyond anyone's control, many of us over the past year have held supervisory duties without the benefit of formal training or proper experience. Therefore, what we propose is that we utilize the Supervisors' Forum as a vehicle with which to enhance the existing management-training program. The areas that we hope to affect with this supplemental training are: a) morale/job satisfaction; b) quality of work and service; c) productivity; and d) management expertise as it relates to the life insurance industry. With these objectives in mind, we have outlined below a list of possible activities that we would like to pursue.

1.   Further utilization of the existing "in-house" training programs provided for manager trainees and supervisors, i.e., Introduction to Supervision, E.E.O., and Coaching and Counseling.

2.   A series of speakers from various sections in the company. This would help expose us to the technical aspects of their departments and their managerial style.

3.   Invitations to outside speakers to address the Forum on management topics such as managerial development, organizational structure and behavior, business policy, and the insurance industry. Suggested speakers could be area college professors, consultants, and state insurance officials.

4.   Outside training and visits to the field. This could include attendance at seminars concerning management theory and development relative to the insurance industry. Attached is a representative sample of a program we would like to have considered in the future.

In conclusion, we hope that this memo clearly illustrates what we are attempting to accomplish with this program. It is our hope that the above outline will be able to give the Forum credibility and establish it as an effective tool for all levels of management within New Issue. By supplementing our on-the-job training with a series of speakers and classes, we aim to develop prospective management personnel with a broad perspective of both the life insurance industry and management's role in it. Also, we would like to extend an invitation to the underwriters to attend any programs at which the topic of the speaker might be of interest to them.

cc: J. Greely
    Managers

The group felt the memo accurately and diplomatically stated their dissatisfaction with the current situation. However, they pondered what the results of their actions would be and what else they could have done.

PART II

An emergency management meeting was called by Rick Belkner at Jack Greely's request to address the "union" being formed by the supervisors. Four general managers, Rick Belkner, and Jack Greely were at that meeting. During the meeting it was suggested the Forum be disbanded to "put them in their place." However, Rick Belkner felt that if "guided" in the proper direction the Forum could die from lack of interest. His stance was adopted but it was common knowledge that Jack Greely was strongly opposed to the group and wanted its founders dealt with. His comment was "It's not a democracy and they're not a union. If they don't like it here, then they can leave." A campaign was directed by the managers to determine who the main authors of the memo were so they could be dealt with.

About this time, Mike's unit had made a mistake on a case, which Jack Greely was embarrassed to admit to his boss. This embarrassment was more than Jack Greely cared to take from Mike Wilson. At the managers staff meeting that day Jack stormed in and declared that the next supervisor to "screw up" was out the door. He would permit no more embarrassments of his division and repeated his earlier statement about "people leaving if they didn't like it here." It was clear to Mike and everyone else present that Mike Wilson was a marked man.

Mike had always been a loose, amiable supervisor. The major reason his units had been successful was the attention he paid to each individual and how they interacted with the group. He had a reputation for fairness, was seen as an excellent judge of personnel for new positions, and was noted for his ability to turn around people who had been in trouble. He motivated people through a dynamic, personable style and was noted for his general lack of regard for rules. He treated rules as obstacles to management and usually used his own discretion as to what was important. His office had a sign saying "Any fool can manage by rules. It takes an uncommon man to manage without any." It was an approach that flew in the face of company policy, but is had been overlooked in the past because of his results. However, because of Mike's actions with the Supervisor's Forum, he was not regarded as a thorn in the side, not a superstar, and his oddball style only made things worse.

Faced with the fact that he was rumored to be out the door, Mike sat down to appraise the situation.

PART III

Mike decided on the following course of action:

1. Keep the Forum alive but moderate its tone so it didn't step on Jack Greely's toes.

2. Don't panic. Simply outwork and outsmart the rest of the division. This plan included a massive retraining and remotivation of his personnel. He implemented weekly meetings, cross training with other divisions, and a lot of interpersonal "stroking" to motivate the group.

3. Evoke praise from vendors and customers through excellent service and direct that praise to Jack Greely.

The results after eight months were impressive. Mike's unit improved the speed of processing 60% and lowered errors 75%. His staff became the most highly trained in the division. Mike had a file of several letters to Jack Greely that praised the units excellent service. In addition, the Supervisor's Forum had grudgingly attained credibility, although the scope of activity was restricted. Mike had even improved to the point of submitting reports on time as a concession to management.

Mike was confident that the results would speak for themselves. However, one month before his scheduled promotion and one month after an excellent merit raise in recognition of his exceptional work record, he was called into his supervisor's, Kathy Miller's, office. She informed him that after long and careful consideration the decision had been made to deny his promotion because of his lack of attention to detail. This did not mean he was not a good supervisor, just that he needed to follow more instead of taking the lead. Mike was stunned and said so. But, before he said anything else, he asked to see Rick Belkner and Jack Greely the next day.

The Showdown. Sitting face to face with Rick and Jack, Mike asked if they agreed with the appraisal Kathy had discussed with him. They both said they did. When asked if any other supervisor surpassed his ability and results, each stated Mike was one of the best, if not **the best** they had. Then why, Mike asked, would they deny him a promotion when others of less ability were approved. The answer came from Jack: "It's nothing personal, but we just don't like you. We don't like your management style. You're an oddball. We can't run a division with ten supervisors all doing different things. What kind of business do you think we're running here? We need people who conform to our style and methods so we can measure their results objectively. There is no room for subjective interpretation. It's our feeling that if you really put your mind to it, you can be an excellent manager. It's just that you now create trouble and rock the boat. We don't need that. It doesn't matter if you're the best now, sooner or later as you go up the ladder, you will be forced to pay more attention to administrative duties and you won't handle them well. If we correct your bad habits now, we think you can go far."

Mike was shocked. He turned to face Rick and blurted out nervously, "You mean it doesn't matter what my results are? All that matters is how I do things?" Rick leaned back in his chair and said in a casual tone, "In so many words, Yes."

Mike left the office knowing that his career at Consolidated was over and immediately started looking for a new job. What had gone wrong?

EPILOGUE

After leaving Consolidated Life, Mike Wilson started his own insurance, sales and consulting firm, which specialized in providing corporate-risk managers with insurance protection and claims-settlement strategies. He works with a staff assistant and one other associate. After three years, sales averaged over $7 million annually, netting approximately $125,000 to $175,000 before taxes to Mike Wilson.

During a return visit to Consolidated Life, three years after his departure, Mike found Rick Belkner and Jack Greely still in charge of the division in which Mike had worked. the division's size had shrunk by 50 percent. All of the members of the old Supervisor's Forum had left. The reason for the decrease in the division's size was that computerization had removed many of the peoples' tasks.

DISCUSSION QUESTIONS

1. Describe the culture of Consolidated Life under Jack Greely.

2. What value conflicts existed between Wilson and Greely? Could these have been resolved?

3. Compare the leadership styles of Wilson and Greely. Which was most appropriate for the situation?

4. How could group dynamics help explain what happened in this case?

5. What were the power relationships between the major parties?

Chapter 14

Organization Design and Effectiveness

49. THE NASA SPACE SHUTTLE DISASTER: A CASE STUDY[*]

PURPOSE:

1.　　To understand some dynamics which led to organizational disasters.
2.　　To analyze the NASA experience using Bolman and Deal's Four Frame Model for Understanding and Managing Organizations.

GROUP SIZE:

Any number of group of 5 to 8 members.

TIME REQUIRED:

30-55 minutes.

PREPARATION:

1.　　Read Table 1 (end of the case) for a background on the Four Frame Model.
2.　　Read the NASA Case Study.

RELATED TOPICS:

Leadership
Dynamics Within Groups
Dynamics Between Groups

---

[*]Adapted from Robert Marx, Charles Stubbart, Virginia Traub, and Michael Cavanaugh, in the Journal of Management Case Studies, Vol. 3, 1987, pp. 300-318. Original source of material by Bolman, L. and T. Deal Modern Approaches to Understanding and Managing Organizations. San Francisco, Jossey-Besso, 1984.

EXERCISE SCHEDULE:

1.   (Pre-Class) Read "Background on the Four Frames Model" and the NASA Case Study.

2.   (15-25 minutes) The instructor announces, "Your groups will serve as consultants to NASA, since the Rogers Commission (appointed by the President to investigate the shuttle disaster) was largely made up of rocket scientists and engineers and did not ask all of the important questions necessary to get at the true problems of NASA. Read the philosophies of each of the four consulting firms and decide as a group which firm should get the contract with NASA."

Groups then rank order the four consulting firms, with "1" most preferred and "4" least preferred.

3.   (15-30 minutes) The instructor leads a discussion on how the Four Frames Model can be used to analyze the NASA shuttle disaster.

THE CONSULTING FIRMS

1. Structor Associates   A structural approach to organizations. "We design management systems to meet tomorrow's needs."

2. Humanotics   A human resource approach to organizations. "We emphasize people in high tech."

3. The Luyd Group (pronounced Lloyd) (line up your ducks)   A political approach to organizations. "Carving coalitions for creative causes.

4. Northstar   A symbolic approach to organizations "Pointing the way with symbols since 1903."

Structor Associates

This consulting firm has been highly successful in solving problems in some of our nation's most prestigious and powerful public and private organizations. The key to their success has been a focus on structure. The staff of Structor Associates believe the primary goals of a smoothly running organization is to have clear goals and established policies and lines of authority that will lead to reaching or surpassing those goals. "The key thing is structure," stated one Structor executive recently. "When you have the right structure and the people understand it, the organization will function as it is supposed to. A Structor consultant stated that, "If the right procedures are in place at NASA, things will work. You don't need to worry about pressure from Congress or personalities in the system. Let's design a NASA where engineers can engineer, managers can mange, and astronauts fly."

Humanotics

This consulting firm has been highly successful in solving problems in some of our nation's most prestigious and powerful public and private organizations. The key to their success has been a focus on people. Humanotics feels that organizations are basically made up of people. When the organization is responsive to their needs and supports their goals you can **count** on their loyalty and commitment. They believe that management that doesn't communicate effectively and "really listen" to their employees is risking the creation of a disenchanted and unmotivated workforce, where problems lie simmering just beneath the surface and company support is for show. One Humanotics consultant said, "The good old days where NASA was really a tightly knit family of people who talked straight to one another, and cared about each other is gone. Once Webb left morale dropped and bureaucracy has crept in. People don't come first any more at NASA and it took the explosion of Challenger to make this public."

The Luyd Group

This consulting firm has been highly successful in solving problems in some of our nation's most prestigious and powerful public and private organizations. The key to their success has been a focus on political realities. The Luyd group believes that all organizations are coalitions of various interest groups, each having its own agenda. There are not enough resources to give everyone what he/she wants so those who can anticipate and manage these inevitable conflicts will survive while the others will become extinct. The Luyd group has not only helped organizations handle internal political issues that can sap an organization of its vitality, but has helped organizations become more cohesive internally thus enabling them to compete for scarce resources more effectively in the marketplace.

The Luyd group helps organizations negotiate differences and reach reasonable compromises while at the same time teaching them how to "line up your ducks." One Luyd representative put it this way: "NASA got creamed by the politics in D.C. They said launch, launch, launch, while cutting back their funds. That led to a lot of infighting over safety issues and manned/unmanned space flights and split the teams. You can bet no heads in Congress are being chopped off by this disaster. The people on the hill know how to protect themselves."

Northstar

This consulting firm has been highly successful in solving problems in some of our nation's most prestigious and powerful public and private organizations. The key to their success has been a focus on the symbols and culture of an organization. Northstar believes that organizations have unique identities like people. They have stories, history, and rituals. Really getting to know the essence of an organization is crucial if you want to help it grow and change. You can't really learn much from an annual report to understand the essence of an organization. Northstar believes that the saga is always unfolding and changing and that new symbols and heroes and villains are being added to the legacy of the past. What is needed is a shared vision, meanings, that bond people together and help them overcome obstacles, and create a sense of mission. A Northstar consultant stated that after Apollo landed on the moon, Kennedy's vision had been realized and the drama was over. The image of space pioneers cavorting on the moon in their high tech version of covered wagons had given way to the less glamorous image of space lab assistants who were forced to rely on gimmicks, such as flying foreigners, minorities, senators, and civilians to gain national attention. "NASA has lost its magic. It can't make it on technology alone. There has to be a special feeling there, a commitment, a leader with vision, a '90's version of JFK."

Ranking

After reading the perspectives of these four companies indicate which company you think should get the NASA contract. Please rank order your most preferred company "1" and the rest of the companies in declining order to "4" for your least preferred.

Rank

_____ Structor Associates
_____ Humanotics
_____ The LUYD Group
_____ Northstar

THE CASE STUDY

NASA: A FUNCTIONAL ANALYSIS

<u>NASA - The Organization</u>

Officially NASA is an agency of the Executive branch, under the control of the President, who directs space policy and appoints NASA's head administrator. Congress sets spending limits and can specify projects to be undertaken. The head administrator has several important tasks, including drawing up proposals and making decisions on future programs, resolving high-level personnel problems,and selling NASA to Congress and the U.S. public. Assistant administrators head various support functions and programs. During the Apollo program, and in the early days of the shuttle, astronauts, who had an appreciation of operations and flight safety, were regularly promoted to management. By the 1980s, this had stopped. NASA has nine field centers, each with its own special mission in support of the overall NASA effort. Private contractors work with, and report to, the field centers.

NASA has undergone several reorganizations in order to meet changing goals. A 1961 reorganization was made to develop a stronger headquarters team that could coordinate efforts among the field centers. In 1963, NASA decentralized to better meet the "man-on-the-moon" goal. After a tragic fire took the lives of three astronauts, organizational changes in 1967 created a centralized structure that could integrate decision making and increase emphasis on safety. Another reorganization occurred in 1983 when the shuttle program was reclassified from "developmental" to "operational."

CONSTITUENCIES. From the very beginning, many people feared that NASA would become more political and less scientific. Although it still has a highly scientific orientation, the goals and polices of the agency have been dictated by political considerations. Whether NASA must answer primarily to the Executive branch, Congress, or some other constituency is always a matter of debate. According to veteran observers of NASA, "NASA is a child of Congress, rather than that of the executive branch" (Hirsch and Trento, 1973, p. 126). On the other hand, former NASA Administrator James Beggs saw space-program support as a matter of "the mood of the country and a question of priorities" (Sky and Telescope, 1982, p. 333).

Without a doubt, each President set the tone for much of NASA's activities. It was during the Kennedy-Johnson administrators that NASA received its greatest support. In the post-Apollo days, NASA, fueled by the overwhelming technological success of its moon landings, pushed for manned space flight to Mars. One observer described NASA as "an organism that was more responsive to its own internal technological momentum than to externally developed objectives" (Logsdon, 1983, p. 86). The Nixon administration favored more practical goals. And politicians, who controlled matters of budget and set policy, pushed for a program with tangible benefits to science, the economy, and national security.

President Reagan's 1982 policy consisted of two priorities: maintaining U.S. leadership in space, and expanding private-sector involvement and investment. A less publicized policy was the increasing involvement of the Department of Defense and use of the space program for national defense. After three years of lobbying on the part of those supporting a space station, Reagan, in his 1984 State of the Union address, set a goal of an orbiting space station within ten years. Administrator Beggs' push to make the shuttle "operational" may have been in part politically motivated; he recognized this was a necessary step in garnering support for the permanent, manned space station. Many people in NASA supported this goal. So did commercial private enterprise.

Furthermore, the contracting companies who performed 80-90% of NASA's design and development work had active trade associations and lobbying efforts to promote their interests. With the shuttle in an "operational" state and the potential development of the manned space station, NASA was no longer its own customer. It now had to serve the needs of private industry. IN short, there was a close-knit network between NASA, Congress, the Department of Defense, and private industry.

PUBLIC RELATIONS. With so many different constituencies, NASA had always been acutely aware of the value of public relations and image. In its earliest days, NASA was particularly concerned with maintaining secrecy. The Kennedy administration felt that openness was a better approach to provide a counter attack to Soviet propaganda and secrecy. It was also a way of getting the most mileage out of the image of the U.S. as the underdog, steadily maintaining its effort to "catch up." The press was eager for involvement in the space program. The knew it made good copy -- spaceships, astronaut heroes, patriotism, and American know-how. Engineers were "scientists" and words like "enhance" and "update" replaced the verb "improve." "Integrity" now described machines, and the press became members of an exclusive space-age fraternity.

The merits of manned versus unmanned space flight had been a continuing debate within and outside of NASA. Manned flights were criticized for being expensive, dangerous, and largely unnecessary, particularly in light of improving robotics and computer capabilities. Proponents countered that the intelligence and versatility that on-board humans brought to space missions could not be duplicated by any machine. Even more important was the use of manned missions to win support and bolster enthusiasm of both NASA personnel and the general public.

If anything represented the public's pride in the national space program, it was the original seven Mercury astronauts. They were the nation's "champions" at the same time they were the All-American boys next door. But as the number of astronauts and the size of missions increased, it became harder for the public to keep track of and identify with astronauts. Until the first manned moon flights, a rigid pecking order among the astronauts kept scientist and engineer astronauts on the ground while former fighter and test pilots were selected for moon missions.

Post-Apollo astronauts were selected for their capabilities as scientists. Racial and gender barriers were broken with the selection of female, black, and Asian astronauts. As NASA's programs became increasingly commercialized, it was difficult to retain the astronaut's pioneering and heroic image. Christa McAuliffe, selected as the first teacher in space, represented a new orientation toward the astronaut. The image of the fearless daredevil was no longer appropriate. Instead, outer space belonged to all and now the astronaut was Everyman and Everywoman.

SUCCESSES AND FAILURES. Even some of the most disastrous events in the agency's history were viewed as at least partial successes by NASA personnel. Prior to 1961, there were many rocket failures. In 1959, seven out of 17 launches failed. NASA saw these as necessary learning experiences, but there was much public criticism of their cost and delay.

By many accounts, however, the 1967 Apollo tragedy was an accident that should not have happened. In January 1967, during "routine" testing, a flash fire broke out in the command module, killing the three astronauts on board. The NASA review board acknowledged insufficient attention to crew safety. Some aspects of the investigation were suppressed by NASA and later revealed by a Congressional inquiry. Among the Congressional findings were "overconfidence" and "complacency" on the part of NASA and a lack of concern on the part of the prime contractor. A more critical review of the incident characterized Congressional findings as "ambiguous" and asserted that because of its close ties with NASA, Congress was reluctant to do anything that would implicate itself. The critique alleged that "sloppy workmanship and slipshod quality" had been with the program all along.

Despite "official" stringent safety standards, the agency was more concerned with meeting deadlines than with safety issues. NASA used this tragedy to its best advantage. Invoking the memory of the dead, they stressed the importance of getting on with the program because that's what the astronaut would have wanted. In spite of this setback, Kennedy's challenge to land a man on the moon was met.

The lives of three other astronauts were seriously endangered during the Apollo 13 mission. While enroute to the moon, the capsule's main oxygen tank exploded. Anderson, NASA's official biographer, believed that technology saved the day. The system contained sufficient flexibility and depth to permit the astronauts to ride safely back to earth. A review board investigating the incident had another perspective. They attributed the accident to a number of human errors and lack of proper monitoring and testing by NASA personnel and concluded that "the lessons of the Apollo 104 (fire) had not been fully applied" (Hirsch and Trento, 1973, p. 121).

Technical problems and failures with various Skylab and Shuttle missions called for the massive round-the-clock efforts by ground personnel and astronauts. Once again, failures became successes where problems were solved with "human ingenuity and courage" (Anderson, 1981, p. 83).

FINANCES AND BUDGET. In terms of both budget and employment, NASA enjoyed its greatest power in the mid 1960s with the buildup of the man-on-moon effort. Funding decreased steadily over the next ten years, as the nation turned its attention and priorities to other matters. Although funding improved with the shuttle, inflation-adjusted figures show little increase, and the watchword has been fiscal restraint.

NASA -- Life on the Inside

DECISION MAKING. Decisions had to be made about the agency's overall goals. But NASA could not be a good decision maker because "government policy is based on partisan and interest group politics instead of an business or technological grounds" (Goldman, 1985, pp. 48-49).

Decision making and problem solving around technical issues were accomplished by creating consensus. For example, one of Apollo's early tasks was to plan the mechanics of putting a man ont he moon. A number of options were possible. A group of engineers came up with the idea of a lunar orbiter-lander combination. They spent two years refining the idea, arguing their case before various NASA groups, and they even went "out of channels" directly to NASA's general manager. Their idea gradually won adherents and was adopted.

In mid-1968, with the Apollo program seriously behind schedule, the head of the Manned Space Flight Center, George Low, decided that the scope of each mission should be broadened. Specifically, he believed the Apollo 8 mission should orbit the moon rather than the earth, as originally planned. This represented a bold new step in the Apollo program. He presented his idea to Robert Gilruth, the head of the space task group, who responded enthusiastically. Next they polled the senior project managers, who agreed that all current problems appeared to be solvable in time for the launch deadline. Within just a few months, the mission was reconfigured for its newly established goal.

By the mid-1980s, NASA administrators and engineers made a distinction between engineering and program management decisions. This represented a change from years past. An engineer who had been with NASA since 1960 said (Bazell, 1986, p. 12):

At the beginning, all the decisions were made at the lowest possible level. We worked together toward one goal. It was simply inconceivable that one person could have thought something was wrong -- particularly if it was dangerous -- and everyone else not know about it.

Another engineer echoed this perspective: "People making the decisions are getting farther and farther away from the people who get their hands dirty" (Bazell, 1986, p. 14).

A CHANGING ORGANIZATION. What was clear was that NASA had changed in many ways over the past 25 years; in other ways it remained the same.

NASA at the start faced many challenges on many fronts dealing with rapid expansion and coordination of activities: leapfrogging the Soviets, dealing with the Executive branch and Congress, creating an environment good for scientific and technological creativity. The task was not merely to provide technical resources but also technical management so that a government-industry-university team could be built. The entire organization had to be geared toward flexibility to improve quality and reliability as the problems of space exploration were better understood. The emphasis was on avoiding "quick fixes" so that many small changes did not eventually add up to serious problems. The crash-program atmosphere of intense effort demanded by the program and by Kennedy's end-of-the-decade deadline was not without personal costs (divorces, heart attacks, and suicides) among NASA personnel.

At its 25th anniversary in 1983, NASA was facing a variety of issues, some of them new to the agency: commercialization of space activity; competition with Europe, Japan, and the Soviet Union; working closely with government military and civilian agencies as well as developing private-sector space activities; and meeting customer commitments. While the shuttle program had changed NASA's mandate, its field organizations retained their scientific and engineering orientations. Although this was appropriate for the Apollo era, observers felt this was currently causing problems for the agency.

Even before this time, NASA had shown resistance to certain changes. IN 1973, one observer noted that there were difficulties associated with increasing the professional female and nonwhite staff and that the "overwhelming white domination of NASA is making it an increasingly conspicuous and embarrassing anomaly among government agencies" (Holden, 1973). Although NASA had hired a black woman for a top post in the agency's Affirmative Action department, the political realities of the Nixon administration made it a token gesture. She was dismissed for not fitting into the bureaucracy, but some felt her dismissal was precipitated by her refusal to play Nixon-era politics. It is not clear how much had changed by the mid-1980s, for in 1986 Robert Bazell described NASA insiders as a homogeneous group -- white males in their fifties, career men with NASA or its contractors.

A 1979 shuttle management review team, headed by USAF General James Abrahmson, called for changes in management structure and philosophy. Some of the team's findings included the following:

> The near-term potential for unanticipated technical problems, schedule slippage and cost growth is high and appropriate reserves should be included in all aspects of program planning.

> There has been a lack of adequate long-range planning. . . . Emphasis has been on the current fiscal year, with only secondary attention to succeeding years. . . . Long range planning has not been performed to the extent required for a program as complex as the shuttle.

> . . . The successive program changes and associated up and down expenditure rates have resulted in experienced contractor and subcontractor personnel being terminated. Recent and current aerospace industry demand for such personnel is such that experienced people do not remain available, resulting in the employment of inexperienced personnel at a cost to overall efficient performance. This constitutes a major cause of concern, especially for the production phase of the program.

> . . . The space transportation system associate administrator (or Level 1 management) has, through an ever increasing personal participation in program activities, became the de facto program director . . . during the course of the fact finding, it became apparent that there was a broad and detailed involvement of Level 1 on technical issues with lesser attention given to cost and schedule.

In the effort to live with funding limitations while still progressing acceptably toward completion, shuttle management has generally set up work schedules that demanded more performance than could be delivered.

Members of the shuttle management review team also mentioned that NASA managers felt the way to keep shuttle costs down was to set up high work performance goals. One NASA manager said (Covault, 1979, pp. 20-21):

If we hadn't done it this way we could never have converted this thundering herd of Apolloites to more reasonable people. This program would have cost $10-$12 billion with the same philosophies we had in Apollo, and then there wouldn't have been any shuttle program.

A concern for costs persisted as the shuttle project progressed. Hans M. Mark, a NASA deputy administrator, reported that, "It is very unlikely that it will be possible to control costs of operations if the developmental attitudes that prevail at Johnson Space Center dominate after the shuttle becomes operational" (Covault, 1981, p. 13).

Despite a changing orientation toward the space program by the administration, many at NASA viewed the shuttle as another Apollo program. Therefore certain considerations, such as technical simplicity, minimizing operational costs, and meeting development schedules were seen by NASA people as less important than the technological development of the shuttle.

Heretofore, NASA had run with a single-flight focus. But because of the pressures of military needs and commercialization of shuttle flights, the program began to include several flights at various stages of readiness. It was becoming difficult to meet the flight schedule and maintain the overall efficiency of the system. By 1986, the schedule allowed for less than one month between flights. Furthermore, certain attitudes persisted from the resource-rich days of Apollo. There was still an inclination toward "can do" spontaneity in responding to crises and technological challenges and a very positive approach to problem solving. This type of enthusiasm was very costly at a time when the shuttle program required nurturing resources. The agency had an established tradition of flexibility, frequently changing shuttle plans as different needs and priorities of its commercial customers arose. These frequent and sometimes last-minute changes were a further drain on resources.

Tight schedules had to be balanced with cost constraints, and NASA contractors had rules governing employee overtime. Some required clearance for overtime in excess of 20 hours per week. Approval was frequently granted. For example, two contractors with employees working at Kennedy Space Center reported the 20-hour limit was exceeded about 5,000 times from October 1985 through January 1986.

During this era of multiple launches, it was necessary for key NASA and contractor personnel-skilled technicians and managers to log 72-hour work weeks and 12-hour days for weeks on end. One team leader worked consecutive work weeks of 60 hours, 96.5 hours, 94 hours, and 81 hours in January 1986. Given this unrelenting pace, it is not surprising that the likelihood for human error increased in early January 1986, when a group of technicians at Kennedy Space Center, working 12-hour shifts, repeatedly misinterpreted fuel-system error messages and made faulty decisions during previous shuttle launch preparations. The mission was scrubbed just 31 seconds before takeoff when an insufficient supply of liquid oxygen in the shuttle's fuel tank triggered alarms. A subsequent investigation attributed the launch abort to human error produced by fatigue. Human safety issues may have taken a back seat to cost considerations, as key personnel were pushed beyond their limits of endurance.

Much of NASA's current staff joined the organization in the Apollo build-up days of the early 1960s. Some were still in mid-career and interested in taking on technological challenges. The changed emphasis to cost and schedule constraints prompted these talented and motivated individuals to leave the organization. However, according to John Pennington, NASA's Director of Human Resources, surveys indicated high motivation and morale and low turnover in the organization (Pennington, 1986).

Nevertheless, the motivation for many of NASA's personnel was still the excitement and challenge of manned missions, large space systems, and interplanetary exploration. Despite the inbred staff of the space program, there was no consensus on what the program's goals should be. For many who remembered the effort and accomplishments of Apollo, there was a growing "return to the moon" movement; others favored focus on a suborbital manned space station. Some people in NASA believed it should become an operational organization, others felt it should remain an R&D agency.

Overall, the lack of a clear mission and the seemingly conflicting roles created difficulties for the agency. There was a tendency at some of the field centers to solve problems in-house rather than pass them up the hierarchy. NASA project managers at some of the centers felt isolated from headquarters and more accountable to their field centers. Conflicting goals, roles, and expectations produced an almost schizoid character. There was difficulty transferring an Apollo-era mood to shuttle realities, in switching from shuttle to routine operations, and in moving from an organi dominated by scientists and engineers to one dominated by bureaucrats and administrators.

FLIGHT READINESS AND SAFETY. Much of NASA's decision making was structured around flight readiness and safety issues. Planning for a shuttle flight began 12-18 months before a shuttle lifted off the pad. The Shuttle Flight Readiness Review was a complicated process. Flights required careful coordination among thousands of contractors, subcontractors, and three space centers (Kennedy, Marshall, and Johnson). Besides obvious concerns about the ability of the rocket to fly, officials allocated cargo space, trained the crew, designed a flight plan, scheduled space activities and experiments, and programmed dozens of computers. Literally hundreds of decisions were involved in a shuttle launch. Therefore, NASA had evolved a "Japanese" style of management: disagreements "bubbled up" the hierarchy until somebody resolved them.

The flight design process was the central concern in flight preparation. In this process, NASA officials and scientist set the flight objectives and laid out a detailed schedule of flight activities from launch until landing. Four field centers reported the Space Flight Program: Kennedy (launches), Johnson, Marshall (vehicle design and development), and the National Space Technology Laboratories. The planning went through several steps as outlined below.

Level 4. Level 4 was initiated by a formal directive from the NASA Associate Director of Space Flight. The burden was on contractors at the various space centers (who performed the bulk of the design and development and all of the manufacturing) to certify in writing that their components met the necessary standards.

Level 3. After all certifications were received the decision making moved down to Level 3. At Level 3, the project managers for the Orbiter, solid rocket booster, and external tank and main engines at Johnson, Kennedy, and Marshall made official presentations to their respective Center Directors. Each review verified the readiness of launch support elements.

Level 2. Next came the Preflight Readiness Review at Level 2 at Johnson Space Center. In the Level 2 review, each shuttle program element certified that it had satisfactorily completed the manufacture, assembly, tests, and checks on shuttle equipment. The manager of the National Space Transportation Program presided.

Level 1. The reviews culminated with Level 1. Under the direction of the Associate Administrator for Space Flight, the Flight Readiness Review at Level 1 checked previous planning activities, and a Mission Management Team was established.

Mission Management Team. This team takes over management 48 hours before the launch and continues until the shuttle had landed and been secured. This team met 24 hours before the planned launch to take care of unsatisfied requirements, to assess weather forecasts, and to discuss any anomalies. The Mission Management Team encouraged officials at lower levels to report any new problems or difficulties.

The director of the Shuttle Project Office reported to the Director of the Marshall Space Center. But the readiness review process mainly took place outside the normal chain of command. The levels of the Readiness Review paralleled and overlapped the levels of the formal management structure.

NASA's Safety, Reliability and Quality Assurance Program came under the duties of the Chief Engineer at NASA headquarters. Out of a staff of 20, one person spent 25% of his time, and another spent 10%, on safety. At the various centers, the personnel who developed the shuttle hardware were also responsible for related safety issues. Components were engineered to meet stringent specifications, and they were tested. In 1980, NASA appointed a special committee to study the flight worthiness of the entire shuttle system.

Safety issues often cropped up at various levels of the Readiness Review. Flights had to meet 28 specific criteria before the countdown could begin. Participants mulled over technical specifications, interpretation of test results, and what constituted an adequate margin for safety. Those systems that had no back-up and which might bring about the loss of the vehicle and life were called "critical" and received special attention. In addition, the Flight Readiness Review procedure included official procedures for waiving nonconforming components or systems in the interests of flexibility, expedience, or extenuating circumstances.

SHUTTLE FLIGHT PROCEDURES: CHALLENGER FLIGHT 51-L

May 1985. Crew training begins.

August 20, 1985. NASA conducts a Preflight Readiness Review. They discuss the crew, storage, engineering status, photo and TV requirements, the Teacher-in-Space program and the launch window.

December 13, 1985. Associate Administrator for Space Flight (Moore) schedules Flight Readiness Review for January 15, 1986.

January 9, 1986. Morton Thiokol (MTI) certifies solid rocket booster flight readiness (Level 4). This is the first stage where equipment problems can delay a launch. The O-rings are a known problem, but MTI and NASA personnel do not believe they are serious enough to stop launch.

January 14, 1986. After weeks of preparation, including a dress rehearsal and a mock firing of the main engines, Kennedy Center Director Richard Smith convenes the Preflight Readiness Review meeting (Level 2) and sets the schedule for Level 1/Mission Management Team meetings. Over 100 participants from Kennedy, Marshall, Johnson, Lockheed, and various subcontractors discuss what time of day to launch, conditions for viewing Halley's comet, excessive cargo weight, and the schedule of crew activities. No problems with the solid rocket booster were identified. Kennedy Center Director Smith signs launch-readiness certificate.

January 15, 1986. NASA associate administrator Moore chairs Flight Readiness Review Meeting (Level 1). A video teleconference links NASA flight centers to Cape Kennedy. All systems are reviewed in detail, from engineering through flight responsibilities. They decide, "Go."

January 22, 1986. NASA officials are worried about dust storms in Dakar, the main emergency landing site. A shuttle can't go up unless it has a safe place to land if something goes wrong. Countdown is reset for January 26 at 9:30 a.m.

January 25, 1986. 11 a.m. EST. Level 1 team meets again. All unresolved flight readiness review items were reported closed. But rainstorms prompt officials to postpone until the 27th.

January 27, 1986. 12:36 p.m. Mission Management Teach scrubs launch because of high winds and overcast at launch site. Rain can damage the shuttle's heat-resistant tiles. Problems with a sticky bolt cause a 90-minute delay in the astronauts' disembarking from the orbiter. Team resets launch for 9:38 a.m., January 28.

2:00 p.m. Mission Management Team meets again. Because weather forecasts predict temperatures in low 20s, someone raises concerns about cold weather effects on launch facility water drains, fire suppression system, and water trays. They decide to activate heaters on the shuttle.

2:30 p.m. in Utah. Morton Thiokol engineers in Wasatch, Utah, hearing about forecast cold temperatures, discuss possible effects of cold weather predicted for January 28 on solid rocket booster (see Figure 4 for MT1 organization.)

5:45 p.m. First teleconference between NASA Level 3 personnel at Kennedy (Lovingood) and Marshall (Reinartz) and Thiokol personnel in Utah. Morton Thiokol officials express reservations about effects of temperatures on O-rings. They postpone launch until noon or afternoon of 28th. Lovingood proposes going to Level 2 (Aldrich) if MT1 stands by no-launch recommendation at second teleconference set for 8:15.

8:45 p.m. Second teleconference between MT1 Utah (six members), Kennedy (Reinartz, Mulloy, McDonald -- MT1 liaison), and Marshall (Hardy, Lovingood, et al.). A technical discussion of O-ring problems and tests. Problems with the O-rings had a long history. One MT1 vice-president of engineering (Lund) says not to fly 51-L until temperature exceeds 53^0F. Another MT1 engineer Boisjoly presents charts and tables about problem. Mulloy asks MT1 vice-president Kilminster for recommendation. Kilminster says he cannot recommend launch. Reinartz, Mulloy, and Hardy challenge MT1 conclusions, asking for hard data to support Boisjoly's conjectures. Hardy says he is "appalled" by the recommendation. Mulloy says, "Do you want us to wait until April to launch?"

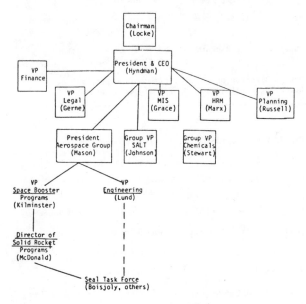

Figure 4

Kilminster asks for time to caucus. Later, Mr Boisjoly remarks, "This was a meeting where the determination was to launch, and it was up to us to prove beyond a shadow of a doubt that it was not safe to do so. . . usually it is exactly opposite that." Mulloy says, "There was no violation of launch commit criteria . . . [there] were 27 full-scale tests of the O-rings damage tolerances. . . we had experience with this problems" (see Figure 5).

10:30 p.m. to 11:00 p.m. at Kennedy. McDonald, Mulloy, Reinartz, Buchanan, and Houston discuss whether to delay. Mulloy says that one of MT1's data change the rationale from previous successful flights.

11:00 p.m. Second teleconference continues. The MT1 officials say that O-rings are a concern but data are not conclusive against launch. Kilminster recommends launching. NASA asks MT1 to put recommendation in writing.

11:15 p.m. to 11:30 p.m. at Kennedy. McDonald strongly argues for delay, says he would not like to answer to board of inquiry. Mulloy says that the temperature of the fuel in the booster will still meet the Minimum Launch Criteria. Reinartz and Mulloy tell McDonald that it is not his decision, that his concerns are noted and will be passed on. (See Figure 5 for summary of disputants.)

11:30 p.m. to 12:00 a.m. Teleconference at Kennedy. Mulloy, Reinartz, and Aldrich discuss icing in launch area and recovery ships' activities. The O-rings are not mentioned.

NASA TOP MANAGEMENT	POSITION	ACTION (INACTION)
1. Jesse Moore	Associate Administrator for space flight	Made decision to launch 51L did not know of no-go recommendations
2. Arnold Aldrich	Shuttle Manager at Johnson	Knew only Rockwell reservations
MARSHALL CENTER		
1. William Lucas	Director	Outside launch chain of command
2. Stanley Reinartz	Mgr., Shuttle Projects	Did not tell superiors about Thiokol reservations
3. Lawrence Mulloy	Chief of Solid Rockets	Did not accept Thiokol engineer's doubts
4. George Hardy	Deputy Director of Space Engineering	Did not accept Thiokol engineer's doubts
MORTON THIOKOL		
1. Jerald Mason	Senior Vice President	Asked for decision
2. Joseph Kilminster	V.P. for Boosters	Signed "go" memo
3. Robert Lund	V.P. for Engineering	Persuaded to OK launch recommendation
4. Allan MacDonald	Director of Solid Rockets	At Kennedy - opposed launch
5. Rogert Boisjoly	Head of Seals Task Force	Worried about low temp.
6. Arnold Thompson	Engineer	Opposed launch
7. Brian Russell	Engineer	Opposed launch

FIGURE 5. Main players at NASA, Marshall Center, and Morton Thiokol. *Source: Rogers Commission Report* (1986).

Figure 5

January 28, 1986. 1:30 a.m. to 3:00 a.m. at Kennedy. The Ice Crew reports large quantities of ice on pad B. The spacecraft can be damaged by chunks of ice that can be hurled about during the turbulent rocket ignition.

5:00 a.m. at Kennedy. Mulloy tells Lucas of MT1 concerns over temperature and resolution and shows the recommendations written by MT1.

7:00 a.m. to 9:00 a.m. at Kennedy. The clear morning sky formed what glider pilots call a "blue bowl." Winds dwindled to 9 mph. During the night temperatures fell to 27^0F. The ice crew measures temperatures at 25^0F on the right-hand solid rocket booster, 8^0F on the left. They are not concerned as there are no Launch Commit Criteria relating to temperatures on rocket surfaces.

8:00 a.m. at Kennedy. Lovingood tells Deputy Director of Marshall (Lee) about previous discussions with MT1.

9:00 a.m. at Kennedy. MIssion Management Team meets with Level 1 and 2 managers, project managers, and others. The ice conditions on launch pad are discussed, but not the O-ring issue.

10:30 a.m. at Kennedy. The ice crew reports to the Mission Management Team that ice is still left on booster.

11:18 a.m. A Rockwell engineer in California watching the ice team over closed-circuit television telephones the Cape to advise a delay because of the ice. Kennedy Center Director Smith, advised by the ice team that there is little risk, permits the countdown to continue.

11:29 a.m. Inside Challenger's flight deck (about the size of a 747), Commander Scobee and pilot Smith run through their elaborate checklists. The orbiter's main computer, supported by four backup computers, scans data from 2,000 sensors. If it detects a problem, it will shut down the entire system. In June 1984, the computer aborted four seconds before the rocket ignition. This time it doesn't.

11:30 a.m. Thousands of motorists pull off highways to face toward the ocean.

11:37 a.m. The launch platform is flooded by powerful streams of water from 7-foot pipes to dampen the lift-off sound levels, which could damage the crafty's underside.

11:38 a.m. Flight 51-L is launched. Two rust-colored external fuel tanks, each 154 feet high, carrying 143,351 gallons of liquid oxygen and 385,265 gallons of liquid hydrogen power the rocket. They will burn until the fuel runs out.

11:39 a.m. Everything looked like it was supposed to look. As one MT1 engineer watched the rocket lift off the pad into a bright Florida sky he thought, "Gee, it's gonna be all right. It's a piece of cake . . . we made it."

References

Bolman, Lee and Terry Deal. Modern Approaches to Understanding and Managing Organizations.. San Francisco: Jossey-Bass, 1984.

(For other references see Journal of Management Case Studies)

TABLE I

The Four Frame Model

The Structural Perspective

The structural perspective is based on a set of core assumptions:

1. Organizations exist primarily to accomplish established goals.
2. For any organization, there is a structure appropriate to the goals, the environment, the technology, and the participants.
3. Organizations work most effectively when environmental turbulence and the personal preferences of participants are constrained by norms of rationality.
4. Specialization permits higher levels of individual expertise and performance.
5. Coordination and control are accomplished best through the exercise of authority and impersonal rulers.
6. Structures can be systematically designed and implemented.
7. Organizational problems usually reflect an inappropriate structure and can be resolved through redesign and reorganization.

The Human Resource Approach

1. Organizations exist to serve **human needs** (and humans do not exist to serve organizational needs).
2. Organizations and people need each other. Organizations need the ideas, energy, and talent that people provide, while people need the careers, salaries, and work opportunities that organizations provide.
3. When the fit between the individual and the organization is poor, one or both will suffer: The individual will be exploited or will seek to exploit the organization or both.
4. When the fit is good between the individual and the organization, both benefit: Humans are able to do meaningful and satisfying work while providing the resources the organization needs to accomplish its mission.

The Political Approach

The political frame views organizations as "alive and screaming" political arenas that house a complex variety of individuals and interest groups. Five propositions summarize the political perspective:

1. Most of the important decisions in organizations involve the allocation of scarce resources.
2. Organizations are coalitions composed of a number of individuals and interest groups (for example, hierarchal levels, departments, professional groups, ethnic groups).
3. Individuals and interest groups differ in their values, preferences, beliefs, information, and perceptions of reality. Such differences are usually enduring and change slowly if at all.
4. Organizational goals and decisions emerge from ongoing processes of bargaining, negotiation, and jockeying for position among individuals and groups.
5. Because of scarce resources and enduring differences, power and conflict are central features of organizational life.

The Symbolic Approach

1.   What is most important about any event is not what happened but the meaning of what happened.
2.   The meaning of an event is determined not simply by what happened but by the ways that humans interpret what happened.
3.   Many of the most significant events and processes in organizations are substantially ambiguous or uncertain, it is often difficult or impossible to know what happened, why it happened, or what will happen next.
4.   Ambiguity and uncertainty undermine rational approaches to analysis, problem solving, and decision making.
5.   When faced with uncertainty and ambiguity, humans create **symbols** to reduce the ambiguity, **resolve** confusion, **increase** predictability, and provide direction. Events themselves may remain illogical, random, fluid, and meaningless, but human symbols make them meaningful. Improvements come through symbol, myth and magic.

From Lee Bolman and Terry Deal's Modern Approaches to Understanding and Managing Organizations, as referenced earlier.

50. HOSPITAL DEPARTMENTAL CONSOLIDATION[*]

PURPOSE:

To apply concepts of Organizational Design through a hospital case study.

GROUP SIZE:

Any number

TIME REQUIRED:

30-35 minutes

PREPARATION REQUIRED:

Read the Hospital Case below

RELATED TOPICS:

Decision-Making
Goal Setting

EXERCISE SCHEDULE:

Step 1. Read the following Hospital Case.

Janet Johns is the Administrator of Suburban Memorial Hospital, a 275-bed hospital in a upper class suburb located in the western states.

Mrs. Johns recently asked the new Assistant Administrator, Sam Donalds, to investigate whether a consolidation of the EKG, Pulmonary Function and Cardio-Pulmonary Rehabilitation departments would result in a significant savings to the hospital.

BACKGROUND

The three departments do basically the same types of patient tests. As medicine has progressed, there has been a movement away from static (at rest) testing to dynamic (in-motion) testing. Dynamic testing is used in the EKG Department for tests on the heart, in the Pulmonary Function Department for lung tests and in the Cardio-Pulmonary Rehabilitation Department for both heart and lung.

At present there is a duplication of services and equipment among the three departments at Suburban Memorial. In addition, three separate technicians are employed as well as three different part-time physicians who work on a percentage basis, according to the volume of work.

---

[*]By Dorothy Marcic and Richard C. Housley. Copyright 1988.

The EKG and Pulmonary Function Departments make a significant contribution to Suburban's revenue. The contribution margin of Pulmonary Function has been 80% (for every $100 earned, the hospital spends only $20 to earn it) and that of EKG has been 60%.

Revenues for each department have been:

DEPARTMENT	ANNUAL REVENUE	CONTRIBUTION MARGIN
EKG	$360,000	60%
Pulmonary Function	520,000	80%
Cardio-Pulmonary (new department, less than one year)	80,000	unknown

The total annual revenue of Suburban Memorial is $16.1 million and the net income is $1.3 million. Mr. Donalds has calculated that a departmental consolidation could initially save the hospital $100,000 by selling duplicated equipment. In addition, the annual savings would amount to:

$ 44,000	personnel costs (fewer technicians needed, etc.)
15,000	ordering and supplies reduction (no duplication, less ordering)
125,000	reduced physician fees (only one physician would be needed
16,00	plant and facilities (can lease out space not needed after consolidation)
$200,000	Total

Therefore, the annual savings, in essence additional revenue, would be $200,000 in addition to the initial $100,000 for the selling of equipment.

Physicians

Dr. Bartl, head of Pulmonary Function, is responsible for 80% of the pulmonary admissions to the hospital and about 4.7% of the total admissions. He is an extremely popular physician, attracting respiratory cases from well outside the normal service area of Suburban Memorial.

Dr. Neuman, head of EKG, controls 20% of the hospital's cardiac/internal medicine cases. She admits about 30% of the hospital's patients.

Finally, the head of the new Cardio-Pulmonary Rehabilitation Department, Dr. Hermann, controls 100% of those cases which at this point represent a negligible percentage of the hospital's patient revenue.

All three physicians have more or less equal support from the medical staff.

Ms. Johns is wondering what to do about the physicians, if she decides to go through with the consolidation. One of the three physicians would have to be chosen (with a new reimbursement contract) to head this new department, or perhaps a new, salaried physician could be brought in. The combined workload would still be less than full-time.

However, Ms. Johns sees several problems with either of those two alternatives. First of all, the physicians who would become "excluded" from this new department might become resentful and start admitting their out-of-service-area patients to other hospitals. Ms. Johns and Mr. Donalds have estimated a 25% probability that the three physicians woud do so, which would mean a possible loss to the hospital of 15% of these physicians' admissions.

Ms. Johns has asked Mr. Donalds to prepare a report of the situation, including his recommendations, which will be discussed at the next management council meeting.

Step 2. (15-20 mins.)   In groups of four to six members, discuss the following questions:

    a. If you were Mr. Donalds, what would you recommend?
Prepare the type of report Ms. Johns has asked for,
as if it were going to be presented to the management
council.

    b. Assuming the council votes for consolidation, prepare
another report outlining your recommended strategy,
which would result in the least amount of alienation
and maximum cooperation.

    c. Which organization design theorists would back up and
which would disagree with your proposal?

Step 3. (15 mins.) Group Discussion

    As a total class, discuss the responses to the questions in Step 2.

51. CASTLE BUILDING[*]

PURPOSE:

To design an organization, given certain parameters.

GROUP SIZE:

Any number of groups of six to eight persons.

TIME REQUIRED:

50-75 minutes.

MATERIALS NEEDED:

Newsprint and markers.

RELATED TOPICS:

Leadership
Goal Setting
Intragroup Dynamics

BACKGROUND:

Your group is one of three product-development teams working within the research and development division of the GTM(General Turret and Moat) Corporation. GTM has decided to enter new markets by expanding the product line to include fully designed and produced castles, rather than selling components to other companies, as it has in the past.

Each of the three teams has been asked to design a castle for the company to produce and sell. Given limited resources, the company cannot put more than one design on the market. Therefore, the company will have to decide which of the three designs it will use, discarding the other two designs.

Your task is to develop and design a castle. You will have forty-five minutes to produce a finished product. At the end of this period, several typical consumers, picked by scientific sampling techniques, will judge which is the best design. Before the consumers make their choice, each group will have one to two minutes to make a sales presentation.

---

[*] Adapted from <u>Organizational Behavior in Action</u> by William Morris and Marshall Sashkin. St. Paul: West Publishing Co., 1976. Used with permission.

EXERCISE SCHEDULE:

1.   (5 minutes) Each group is designated either #1, #2, or #3. Members read <u>only</u> one
     memorandum, the appropriate one for their group. One (or two for larger groups)
     observers selected for each group. Observers read their materials.

2.   (10 minutes) Groups design their organization in order to complete goal.

3.   (15-20 minutes) Each group designs its own castle and draws it on newsprint.

4.   (5-10 minutes) "Typical consumers" (may be observers or others) tour building locations
     and hear sales pitches. Judges caucus to determine winner.

5.   (10-15 minutes) Groups meet again and write up what was the central goal statement of
     the group. Also write organization chart on newsprint with goal written beneath. These
     are posted around the room.

6.   (5-15 minutes) Instructor leads a class discussion on how the different memos affected
     organization design. Which design seemed most effective for this task?

<u>Option 2</u>
     Your instructor may allow more time and actually have you <u>build</u> the castles.

CASTLE BUILDING

MEMORANDUM

TO: PROJECT TEAM #1

FROM: Edward Grimsbsy Bullhouse III
          Chief Executive Officer
          General Turret and Moat Corporation

SUBJECT: Development of new castle product

     In order to perform effectively and to develop a useful product for our firm, I have decided that
_____ will serve as manager of the product development team #1. It is
_____ responsibility to see that the team develops a useful and feasible product,
and I hope that all of you will cooperate with _____ in this effort.

CASTLE BUILDING

MEMORANDUM

TO: PROJECT TEAM #2

FROM: Edward Grimsbsy Bullhouse III
         Chief Executive Officer
         General Turret and Moat Corporation

SUBJECT: Development of new castle product

In order to perform effectively and to develop a useful product for our firm, I am asking that you select one of your team to serve as manager of product development team #2. I trust that you will also determine and select any committees, task forces, subgroups, etc. that are needed in order to perform your job.

CASTLE BUILDING

MEMORANDUM

TO: PROJECT TEAM #3

FROM: Edward Grimsbsy Bullhouse III
        Chief Executive Officer
        General Turret and Moat Corporation

SUBJECT: Development of new castle product

In order to perform effectively and to develop a useful product for our firm, I am asking that each of you put forth your maximum effort. I trust that you will provide us with a worthwhile product that can contribute to the profits of the firm.

Observer's Guide

During the course of the building period, observe what is happening within your particular group. Specifically, you should look for the following things:

1. What was the reaction of the group to the memorandum?

2. What was the basic structure of the group?

3. To what degree did people specialize and work on the same particular part of the overall task? How did this specialization come about?

4. Who was(were) the leader(s) of the group? How was leadership determined? How effective was the leadership in helping the group to perform its task?

5. Were there any specific patterns of communication among members of the group, or did everyone talk with everyone else?

6. How were important decisions made? Did you see conflicts or were decisions made cooperatively and with compromise?

7. Other general observations:

After the session, be prepared to discuss your observation with the entire group.

52. WORDS-IN-SENTENCES COMPANY

PURPOSE:

To design an organization for a particular task and carry through to production; to compare design elements with effectiveness.

GROUP SIZE:

Any number of groups of 6-14 persons.

TIME REQUIRED:

50-85 minutes.

RELATED TOPICS:

Dynamics within Groups
Work Motivation

BACKGROUND:

You are a small company that manufactures words and then packages them in meaningful English-language sentences. Market research has established that sentences of at least three words but not more than six words are in demand. Therefore, packaging, distribution, and sales should be set up for three- to six-word sentences.

The "words-in-sentences" industry is highly competitive; several new firms have recently entered what appears to be an expanding market. Since raw materials, technology, and pricing are all standard for the industry, your ability to compete depends on two factors: (1) volume and (2) quality.

TASK

Your group must design and participate in running a WIS company. You should design your organization to be as efficient as possible during each ten-minutes production run. After the first production run, you will have an opportunity to reorganize your company if you want.

RAW MATERIALS

For each production run you will be given a "raw material word or phrase." The letters found in the word or phrase serve as the raw materials available to produce new words in sentences. For example, if the raw material words is "organization," you could produce the words and sentence: "Nat ran to a zoo."

PRODUCTION STANDARDS

There are several rules that have to be followed in producing "words-in-sentences." If these rules are not followed, your output will not meet production specifications and will not pass quality-control inspection.

1.   The same letter may appear only as often in a manufactured words as it appears in the raw material word or phrase; for example, "organization" has **two o's**. Thus "zoo" is legitimate, but not "zoonosis." It has too many o's and s's.
2.   Raw material letters can be used again in different manufactured words.
3.   A manufactured word may be used only once in a sentence and in only one sentence during a production run; if a word - for example, "a" - is used once in a sentence, it is out of stock.
4.   A new word may not be made by adding "s" to form the plural of an already used manufactured word.
5.   A word is defined by its spelling, not its meaning.
6.   Nonsense words or nonsense sentences are unacceptable.
7.   All words must be in the English language.
8.   Names and places are acceptable.
9.   Slang is not acceptable.

MEASURING PERFORMANCE

The output of your WIS company is measured by the <u>total number of acceptable words</u> that are packaged in sentences. The sentences must be legible, listed on no more than two sheets of paper, and handed to the Quality Control Review Board at the completion of each production run.

DELIVERY

Delivery must be made to the Quality Control Review Board thirty seconds after the end of each production run, or else all points are lost.

QUALITY CONTROL

If any word in a sentence does not meet the standards set forth above, all the words in the sentence will be rejected. The Quality Control Review Board (composed of one member from each company) is the final arbiter of acceptability. In the event of a tie vote on the Review board, a coin toss will determine the outcome.

EXERCISE SCHEDULE:

1.   (2-5 minutes) Form groups, organizations and assign workplaces. Groups should have between six to fourteen members (if there are more than 11-12 persons in a group, assign one or two observers). Each group is a company.

2.   (5 minutes) Read "Background" and ask the instructor about any points which need clarification.

3.   (7-15 minutes) Design your organization using as many members as you see fit to produce your "word-in-sentences." You may want to consider the following:
   a.   What is your objective?
   b.   What type of task and environment do you have?
   c.   What technology would work here?
   d.   What type of division of labor is effective?

Assign one member of your group to serve on the Quality Review Board. This person may also take part in production runs.

4.   (7-10 minutes) Production Run 1. The instructor will hand each WIS company a sheet with a raw material word or phrase. When the instructor announces "Begin production," you are to manufacture as many words as possible and package them in sentences for delivery to the Quality Control Review Board. You will have ten minutes. When the instructor announces "Stop production," you will have thirty seconds to deliver your output to the Quality Control Review Board. Output received after thirty seconds does not meet the delivery schedule and will not be counted.

5.   (5-10 minutes) Quality Review Board meets and evaluates output. While that is going on, groups discuss what happened during the previous production run.

6.   (5-10 minutes) Companies evaluate performance and type of organization. Groups may choose to restructure and reorganize for the next production run.

7.   (7-10 minutes) Production run #2 -- same as #1.

8.   (5-10 minutes) Quality Review Board evaluates output while groups draw their organization Charts (for runs #1 and #2) on the board.

9.   (7-15 minutes) Instructor leads discussion of exercise as a whole, answering the following questions.
   a.   What were the companies scores for runs #1 and #2?
   b.   What type of structure did the "winning" company have? Did it reorganize for run #2?
   c.   What type of task was there? technology? environment?
   d.   What would Joan Woodward, Lawrence and Lorsch, or Burns and Stalker say about WIS Company organization?

53. SOCIOTECHNICAL SYSTEMS*

PURPOSE:

To learn to integrate the social as well as technical systems in an organization.

GROUP SIZE:

Three teams or organizations of members.

TIME REQUIRED:

50-95 minutes.

PREPARATION REQUIRED:

Read the "Background" section below.

MATERIALS:

150-300 business size envelopes
> The amount of material will depend on your budget, but the higher numbers are recommended.

150-300 sheets of 8 1/2 x 11 red paper
> The colors are not important, but there should be some contrast among the three. University copy centers often have scrap printed materials which may be obtained at no charge if arrangements are made far enough in advance.

150-300 sheets of 8 1/2 x 11 blue paper
150-300 sheets of 8 1/2 x 11 yellow paper
30-60 rubber bands
3-12 manual staplers (loaded)
1 electric stapler (loaded) -- optional

ROOM ARRANGEMENT REQUIREMENTS:

3 tables or work areas

BACKGROUND:

Sociotechnical Systems (STS) a term originated by the research group at the Tavistock Institute in London, represents a specific application for General Systems Theory in work settings. It narrows the broad focus of General Systems Theory to the interface between two organizational subsystems: social/human and technical. Cooper and Foster (1971, p. 467) provide the following definition:
> The concept of the sociotechnical system is based on the simple fact that any production system requires both a technology -- machinery, plant layout, raw materials -- and a work-relationship structure that relates the human operators both to the technology and to each other. The

---

*Adapted from Karen Brown, "Integrating Sociotechnical Systems into the Organizational Behavior Curriculum: Discussion and Class Exercise," OBTR, Vol. XII(1), 1987-88, pp. 35-48. Used with permission.

technology makes demands and places limits on the type of work structure possible, while the work structure itself has social and psychological properties that generate their own unique requirements with regard to the task to be done.

According to Cummings and Srivasta (1977, p. 49), the term "social system" refers to "...a relationship between people who interact with each other in a given environment for the basic purpose of achieving an agreed-upon task or goal." They suggest that this may include human-human interaction, as well as human-environment interaction. These authors go on to describe the technological system as consisting of "...the tools, techniques and methods of doing that are employed for task performance." They emphasize the importance of not just viewing technology in terms of tangibles such as tools and machinery, and they advocate including abstract factors such as procedures, ideas, and methods of production as well.

Sociotechnical Systems Principles

Cherus (1978) has systematized the writings of others in the field of sociotechnical systems to develop a list of principles for this paradigm. These are named and described (briefly) below.

Principle 1: Compatibility. The process of system design must be compatible with its objectives. That is, if an organization is to be prepared to continuously adapt to its environment, it must make full use of the creative capacities of its members through participation.

Principle 2: Minimal Critical Specification. This implies that organizations should specify as little as possible about how tasks should be performed and who should perform them. Instead, organizations should specify what is to be done without designing jobs so specifically as to rule out creative options for meeting objectives.

Principle 3: The Sociotechnical Criterion. Variances, or unplanned events that affect outcomes, should be controlled as closely as possible to their point of origin. Examples might include machine maintenance being performed by the person who uses the machine, or quality inspection being performed by the person producing the goods.

Principle 4: The Multifunctional Principle - Organism vs. Mechanism. Organizations will be more adaptive to changing demands imposed by the environment if they avoid fractionating the tasks of elements (e.g., members). Instead, elements should be capable of a range of functions which may be used and combined in various ways over time. For example, an organization that employs a rigid assembly line with narrowly-defined tasks will find it difficult to adapt quickly to a market-driven change in product lines.

Principle 5: Boundary Location. Here, Cherus suggests that intra-organizational boundaries based on technology are likely to be simple for a manager to control, but are less likely than other forms to be efficient. Division of a job shop by machine-type, for example, results in clusters of like-technology (e.g., lathes) performing portions of many jobs in large batches. These batches of partially completed jobs move rather sluggishly through the system because of all the time they must spend waiting for other batches of jobs to be processed within each of a series of technology clusters. The alternative, which is exemplified by "group technology" and "just-in-time" manufacturing, involves creating boundaries based on time. That is, certain operations tend to occur in sequence, so the technologies required may be grouped together into small, responsive clusters.

Principle 6: Information Flow. This principle is an important adjunct to Principle 3, regarding proximity of control. It suggests that information systems should provide information initially to those who are in the best position to act upon it (i.e., those who control the variance). For example, feedback about production quality or quantity should be first (and frequently) made available to those at the operating level. Cherus (1978, p. 68) indicates that most information systems provide operating performance data to top levels first, inciting "...top management to intervene in the conduct of operations for which their subordinates are and should be responsible."

Principle 7: Support Congruence. According to Cherus (1978), "support" includes pay systems, selection, training, conflict resolution, measurement of work, performance evaluation, timekeeping, leave allocation, promotion, and separation. Principle 7 advocates consistency between these systems and the organization's design and general philosophy. Specifically, if an organization is to employ the "team" approach advocated by STS, then all of the aforementioned systems should be congruent with that design. For example, an individual incentive pay system, or promotion based on individual output, would be counter-productive in a team-based structure.

Principle 8: Design and Human Values. This principle has to do with quality of work life. It suggests that QWL for members is an important responsibility of the organization. Each member of an organization may define QWL somewhat differently, but in general, jobs should be designed so that they are reasonably demanding, and provide opportunities for leaning, decision making, and recognition. Additionally, they should meet an individual's needs for relating one's job to one's social life, and perceiving the job as moving one toward a desirable future (Cherus, 1978).

Principle 9: Incompletion. This final principle emphasizes that organization design, involving the simultaneous consideration of social/behavioral and technical systems, is an ongoing process. Evaluation and review must continue indefinitely.

OBJECTIVE:

You will be a member of one of three teams whose job it will be to accomplish a simple production task. This will entail gathering, stapling, and folding three-page packets of paper, then stuffing them into envelopes and sealing them. The exercise allows teams to determine the layout and production process they will use. TEams will compete with each other to complete the production task in the shortest time. The subsequent class discussion will focus on the reasons for differences in team performance. Both the social system and the technical system will emerge as important determinants of productivity.

EXERCISE SCHEDULE:

1. (5-10 min.) Instructor explains exercise, groups are created and members read relevant roles.

2. (10-15 min.) Team planning on layout and process.

3. (20-40 min.) Performing the production task. Time depends on the amount of material used.

4. (5 min.) Students fill out the two questionnaires at the end of the exercise.

5. (10-25 min.) The instructor will lead a group discussion ont he exercise, looking at how individual groups performed.
    a. Which team finished the task first? Why?
    b. What did you observe about productivity rates at the beginning of the operation compared to the? (Items 6 and 7 from Team Performance Data.)
    c. Did the teams' initial estimates of sub-task times (e.g., stapling, folding) differ from actual task times? If so, how did teams respond?
    d. Was the team with the electric stapler (if applicable) more efficient than the others?
    e. How did team members feel as they performed the production task? What about boredom and fatigue?

f.   How would task configuration influence the way in which an incentive-based compensation system was designed?

g.   How did team members feel about having their work inspected for quality?

Questionnaire results

a.   What appears to be the most important determinant of productivity? Do the observers agree with the team member's ratings?

b.   Is this response what you expected?

Instructions for All Team Members

Four members of your team will be performing a "production" task. Your team's first assignment is to select those four individuals. Remaining team members will participate in the planning process, but once production begins, they will act as observers, filling the roles specified under "Instructions for Observers." The task to be performed by the four production workers is as follows:

Your team will receive the following materials: stapler(s), staples, rubber banks, three stacks of colored paper, and envelopes.

Use all of the paper at your work station to form as many three-page packets as you can. The colors must be in the same sequence for every packet that you complete. Staple each packet of three pages in the upper left-hand corner, then fold the packet to fit an envelope. Stuff each packet into an envelope. Seal each envelope. Count envelopes into stacks of five and put a rubber band around each stack. You will be competing with the other two teams to see who can complete the entire task in the shortest time.

The work may be structured in any way your team decides. You will have five to ten minutes outside the classroom to discuss the technique you will employ. Do not begin setting up your process until you have been instructed to do so.

Instructions for Observers

Each team member who will not serve as a production worker will serve in one of the following roles:

Methods Analyst. Observe and describe the methods used by your team. Pay attention to division of labor, "bottlenecks," idle time, team work, etc.

Industrial Engineer. Time team members performing individual tasks, as well as keeping track of total time elapsed for completing the entire task. Keep records for summarization on the Team Performance Data Sheet. (This individual should have a watch with a second-hand.)

Quality Assurance Inspector. Ensure that quality standards are met. Any products not meeting standards will be redone. Before the team begins work, introduce yourself. Ask the team if they have any questions about your expectations.

Rover. Observe all three teams and compare their methods.

References

Brown, K.A. & T.R. Mitchell (in pres). "Performance Obstacles for Direct and Indirect Labor in High Technology Manufacturing. International Journal of Production Research.

Cherus, A.B. "The Principles of Sociotechnical Design." Sociotechnical Systems: A Source Book W. A. Pasmore and J.J. Sherwood (eds.). LaJolla, CA: University Associates, pp. 61-71.

Cooper, R., and M. Foster. "Sociotechnical Systems." American Psychologist, 26, 1971, pp. 467-474.

Cummings, T.G. and S. Srivasta. Management of Work: A Sociotechnical Systems Approach. Kent, Ohio: Comparative Administration Research Institute, Kent State University Press, 1977.

Hackman, J.R. and G.R. Oldhamn. "Motivation Through the Design of Work: A Test of a Theory." Organizational Behavior and Human Performance, 18, 1976, pp. 250-279.

Huse, E.F. and T.G. Cummings. Organizational Development and Change. 3rd ed. St. Paul: West Publishing, 1985.

Kast, F.E. and J.E. Rosenzweiz. Organization and Management. 4th ed. New York: McGraw Hill, 1985.

Kotter. Organizational Dynamics: Diagnosis and Intervention. Reading: Addison-Wesley.

"Management Discovers the Human Side of Automation." Business Week: September 29, 1986, pp. 70-75.

Pasmore, W.A. and J.J. Sherwood (eds.). Sociotechnical Systems: A Sourcebook. LaJolla, CA: University Associates, 1978.

Pasmore, W.A., C. Francis, J. Haldeman, and A. Shani. "Sociotechnical Systems: A North American Reflection on Empirical Studies of the Seventies." Human Relations, 35, 1982 pp. 1179-1204.

Rousseau, D.M. Technological Differences in Job Characteristics, Employee Satisfaction, and Motivation: A Synthesis of Job Design Research and Socio-technical Systems Theory." Organizational Behavior and Human Performance, 19, 1977, pp. 18-42.

Sasser, W.E. et al. Teacher's Manual to Accompany Cases in Operations Management Analysis and Action. Homewood, IL: Richard D. Irwin. 1982.

Schonberger, R.J. Japanese Manufacturing Techniques. New York: The Free Press, 1982.

Susman, G.I. Autonomy at Work: A Sociotechnical Analysis of Participative Management. New York: Praeger, 1976.

Trist, E.L. "On Sociotechnical Systems." Sociotechnical Systems: A Sourcebook. Eds. W. A. Pasmore and J. J. Sherwood. La Jolla, CA: University Associates, 1978, pp. 43-57.

Trist, E.J. and K. W. Bamforth. "Some Social and Psychological Consequences of Longwall Method of Coal-getting." Human Relations, 4, 1951, pp. 3-38.

Van Bertalanffy, L. General System Theory: Foundations, Development, Applications. New York: Braziller, 1968.

Questionnaire 1
Team Performance Data Sheet

Overall Productivity Measures	Team 1	Team 2	Team 3
1. Total number of envelopes completed	_____	_____	_____
2. Total set-up time	_____	_____	_____
3. Total operating time	_____	_____	_____
4. Grand total time	_____	_____	_____
5. Total envelopes/minute =			

Additional Measures

	Team 1	Team 2	Team 3
6. Number of envelopes completed per minute during the first minutes of operation	_____	_____	_____
7. Number of envelopes completed per minute during one of the last minutes of operation	_____	_____	_____

Questionnaire 2
Production Exercise Questionnaire

Team # _____ Date _____ Envelopes/minute _____

(a) To what extent do you feel that individual motivation played a role in determining the output rate of your group?

1	2	3	4	5	6	7
Not at all			To a moderate extent			To a very great extent

(b) To what extent do you feel that individual abilities played a role in determining the output rate of your group?

1	2	3	4	5	6	7
Not at all			To a moderate extent			To a very great extent

(c) To what extent do you feel that the way you laid out your task determined the output rate of your group?

1	2	3	4	5	6	7
Not at all			To a moderate extent			To a very great extent

(d) To what extent do you feel that the technology available to you determined the rate of output for your group?

1	2	3	4	5	6	7
Not at all			To a moderate extent			To a very great extent

Chapter 15

Management of Diversity

54. SEX ROLE STEREOTYPES

PURPOSE:

To explore attitudes toward sex role stereotypes.

GROUP SIZE:

Any number of mixed sex groups of 6 to 10 members.

TIME REQUIRED:

35-50 minutes.

PREPARATION REQUIRED:

Complete the Opinion Questionnaire before class.

RELATED TOPICS:

Interpersonal Relationships

EXERCISE SCHEDULE:

1. (Before Class) Fill out the following questionnaire.

2. (20-30 min.) In mixed-sex groups of 6-10 members, discuss the responses to the questions.

3. (15-20 min.) Class Discussion.

The instructor will lead a discussion on the exercise, with the groups and the class as a whole, identifying those items for which there was the most agreement and the most disagreement.

SEX ROLES OPINION QUESTIONNAIRE

Fill out the following questionnaire. It consists of a series of opinions or statements that deal largely with women and working and masculinity issues. You are asked to carefully read each statement and to indicate next to each the extent to which you agree or disagree with the view expressed. Please circle the letter next to each statement which most accurately reflects your personal opinions or beliefs. For each statement select one of four answers:

Strongly Agree (A)   Disagree (d)
Agree (a)   Strongly Disagree (D)

SECTION I: WOMEN AND WORK*

Please consider each statement separately from the others and try to make some response to every statement.

A a d <u>D</u>   1. I think that it is unnecessary for women to go outside of the home to find challenge because there is plenty of challenge for women in child rearing and in running a home.

A a d D   2. I believe that when a husband and wife both work it is important that the husband make the larger salary.

A a <u>d</u> D   3. I believe that women experience physical and emotional changes throughout the month that make them less suitable for positions of responsibility than men.

A <u>a</u> d D   4. I believe that women with children should not work outside of the home.

A a d D   5. One reason women do not get along with male co-workers or move ahead as fast in the organization is that they don't converse about sports.

A a d <u>D</u>   6. I would rather not work for a woman.

<u>A</u> a d D   7. The popular belief that women are too emotional for high level positions is a fallacy.

A <u>a</u> d D   8. A woman would be a liability on a construction crew because she couldn't contribute her fair share.

A a d <u>D</u>   9. Even when she is paying her own way a woman should let the man she is with handle the money.

A <u>a</u> d D   10. I believe that the women's liberation movement will probably help women more than hurt them.

A <u>a</u> d D   11. I believe that hiring single women into management trainee positions represents a poor investment for an organization.

---

*Adapted from Gerald D. Klein and Kathryn B. Klein from "Surfacing Student Sexism and Raising Consciousness Through The Use of an Opinion Questionnaire," <u>Exchange</u>, Vol. 4(1), 1979, p. 45. Used with permission.

A a d <u>D</u>   12. I think that married women who are eager to leave the home and enter the world of work full-time don't realize how easy they have it.

<u>A</u> a d D   13. Women possess the aggressiveness and decisiveness necessary for leadership positions.

SECTION II: MASCULINITY[**]

A a d <u>D</u>   14. It is a bit embarrassing for a man to have a job that is usually filled by a woman, such as secretary, nurse, or hairdresser.

A a d <u>D</u>   15. It annoys me a little to see a man sitting with his legs crossed like a woman.

<u>A</u> a d D   16. I might find it a little silly or embarrassing if a male friend of mine cried over a sad love scene in a movie.

A a d <u>D</u>   17. Success in his work has to be a man's central goal in this life.

A <u>a</u> d D   18. It's much more important in life for a man to be liked than for him to be financially successful.

A a <u>d</u> D   19. A young man should aim for a high-paying career, even if it doesn't interest him quite as much as other kinds of work that don't pay well.

A <u>a</u> d D   20. It's important for a man to always be up on all current events including sports that are reported in the newspapers.

A <u>a</u> d D   21. A business man should be tough enough to fire an employee who is hurting the company, even if the employee has been sick and has personal problems.

A <u>a</u> d D   22. I admire the kind of athlete who will stay in the game, even when he has an injury that is causing him some pain.

<u>A</u> a d D   23. Men have just as much right to a paternity leave as women do to maternity leave.

A <u>a</u> d D   24. A man must always be cool and calm and think rationally, even during a disaster or a personal tragedy.

[**]Adapted from Robert Brannon. Reprinted by permission from <u>Beyond Sex Roles</u> by Alice Sargent; Copyright 1985 by West Publishing Company. pp. 110-115.

References

Brannon, R., and S. Junio. "A Scale for Measuring Attitudes About Masculinity." Journal <u>Supplementary Abstract Service: Catalog of Selected Documents in Psychology</u>, in press.

Brannon, R. "The Male Sex Role: Our Culture's Blueprint for Manhood, and What It's Done For Us Lately." <u>The Forty-Nine Percent Majority: The Male Sex Role</u>, Ed. D. David and B. Brannon. Reading, MA: Addison-Wesley, 1976.

55. MANAGERIAL DECISION-MAKING[*]

PURPOSE:

1. To practice making decisions in a managerial setting.

2. To explore organizational problems resulting from male/female differences.

GROUP SIZE:

Any number of mixed sex groups of 4 to 6 members.

TIME REQUIRED:

50-70 minutes.

PREPARATION REQUIRED:

1. Read the "Background" and "Introduction" below.
2. Read the memoranda (there are 6 cases).
3. Complete the "Response Sheet."

RELATED TOPICS:

Decision-Making

BACKGROUND:

In the course of a busy workday, the typical manager is faced with a variety of decisions involving the behavior of other people. Some of these decisions involve personnel actions such as selection, promotion, training, and discipline. Other decisions involve more subtle questions of interpersonal influence, such as the choice of a leadership style or a motivational approach, or the resolution of various kinds of personal problems.

Although decisions of this sort must often be made under time pressures and on the basis of limited information, they have an important cumulative effect on managerial performance.

You will find the questions framed as a series of "in-basket" organizational problems that could arise during the course of a normal workday. This approach has the advantage of greater realism than simply explaining situations. It asks you to assume a specific managerial role and to treat each questionnaire item as if it were a separate memo or letter in your in-basket, giving your evaluations and decisions. There are six "cases" for you to consider.

---

[*]Adapted from Dianne McKinney Kellogg, Duncan Spelman and Marcy Crary from "Introducing Women in Management Issues in an OB Course." The Organizational Behavior Teaching Review, Vol. 9 (3), 1984-1985, pp. 83-95. Used with permission.

INTRODUCTION:

Try to put yourself in the following situation. You are the executive vice president at Miller Clothing Company, which manufactures several lines of men's apparel and employs a work force of about 5,000. Recently, the decision was made to expand operations and put into production a new line of clothing and men's furnishings for casual living. In order to implement this expansion, the "Bennett Division" has been created and a new factory has been constructed.

You have been put in charge of the start-up phase of this new operation. Your major responsibility is to act as troubleshooter, resolving the daily problems and conflicts associated with a new operation of this sort. The president of the company has asked you to take complete charge, making your own decisions to the greatest extent possible. "Be decisive and I'll back you to the hilt - as long as you are right," he urged.

You are to assume the role of the executive vice president and to go through the contents of this questionnaire, treating each item as if it were a separate memo or letter in your "in-basket," and indicating on the Response Sheet how you would evaluate and handle each situation.

EXERCISE SCHEDULE:

Step 1. Read the following memoranda and complete the "Response Sheet" before class.

Case 1

MEMORANDUM

TO: FROM:
Executive Vice President   Richard Bell,
                                   Accounting Manager

SUBJECT:
Request for Leave of Absence

Ruth Brown, an accountant in the main office, has requested one month's leave beginning next week. She has already taken her vacation this year. She wants the leave in order to take care of her three young children. The day care arrangements the Browns had made for the period covered by the request suddenly fell through, and they have been unable to make other arrangements satisfying their high standards. Ruth's husband is principal of the junior high school and he cannot possibly get time off during the next month.

The problem is that Ruth is the only person experienced in handling the "cost" section in the accounting department. We would either have to transfer an accountant with the same experience from the Richardson Division or else train a replacement for only one month's work. I have urged Ruth to reconsider this request, but she insists on going ahead with it.

I have also checked with the legal department and we do not have to hold the position open for Ruth if she insists on taking the whole month off.

I would appreciate it if you could give me your decision on this as soon as possible.

Case 2

MEMORANDUM

TO:
Executive Vice President

FROM:
Joseph Schmidt,
Computer Operations

As you know, Ronald Cooper is a computer operator in my section. He has played a key role in computerizing our inventory system. Recently, Ronald's wife was offered a very attractive managerial position with a large retail organization on the West Coast. They are seriously considering the move. I told Ronald that he has a very bright future with our organization and it would be a shame for him to pull out just as we are expanding our operations. I sure would hate to lose him now. What do you think we should do about the situation?

Case 3

MEMORANDUM

TO:
Executive Vice President

FROM:
Mark Taylor-
Corporate Personnel Office

SUBJECT:
Promotion of Margaret Adams

We are at the point where we must make a decision on the promotion of Margaret Adams of our personnel staff. Margaret is one of the most competent employees in the corporate personnel office, and I am convinced that she is capable of handling even more responsibility as Bennett Division Personnel Director. However, I am not altogether certain that she is willing to subordinate time with her family to time on the job, to the extent that may be required with Bennett. I have had the opportunity to explore with her the general problem of family versus job, and she strongly believes in a healthy balance between them. She believes that she should very rarely stay late at the office or participate in weekend meetings.

She believes that her first duty is to her family, and that she should manage her time accordingly. This viewpoint has not affected her performance in the past, but it could be a problem in the more demanding position as head of personnel with the Bennett Division.

What do you think we should do?

Case 4

MEMORANDUM

TO:
Executive Vice President

FROM:
Judy Garrison, Marketing
Staff, Bennett Division

I appreciate the discussion we had the other evening. It was comforting to learn that the problem I am having with my husband is not unusual in managerial ranks. I have taken your suggestion and written up a recent conversation between me and my husband, for your use in your human-relations seminar in Chicago.   This is, of course, with the understanding that the source of this case will not be revealed to anyone.

I would really appreciate it if you would let me know how you think this situation should be resolved. I'll also be looking forward to hearing from you about the discussion in Chicago.

I have entitled the attached case "The cocktail party."

The cocktail party.

Jack and Judy Garrison have been married three years.   Judy is an aspiring business executive and Jack is a very successful free-lance writer.   Below is a part of their conversation after attending a cocktail party at the home of an executive in Judy's division.

JACK: Oh boy, what a bunch of creeps. Do we have to go to these parties honey?

JUDY: Jack, honey, you know we have to. These things mean a lot to me. Tonight I had a chance to talk with Mr. Wilson. On the job it would take a week to get an appointment with him. I was able to get across two good ideas I had about our new sales campaign, and I think he was listening.

JACK: Is Wilson that fat slob who works in marketing, the one with the dull wife? I spent ten minutes with her and I nearly died! She's too much. Judy, the people there tonight were so dull I could have cried. Why did I major in English Lit, anyhow? I prefer to talk with people who know what is going on in the world, not a bunch of half-wits whose main interests are their new cars and spoiled kids. I tried to talk to one guy about Virginia Woolf and he didn't even know who she was. These people are incredible. Do we have to go to another cocktail party again next week? I'd like to see "Look Back in Anger" instead. I've got the tickets. One of my husbandly duties is to give you culture. What an uncouth bunch in the business world.

JUDY: One of my wifely ambitions is to get ahead in the business world. You know that these parties are required for bright junior executives coming up in the organization. And I'm a bright junior executive. If we don't go, who knows which of the other junior execs will get to Wilson with their good ideas.

JACK: Can't you relax and work a 40-hour week? That's what they pay you for.

JUDY: I guess I'm too ambitious to relax.

JACK: I'd still like to go to the play. At least we could think about real problems.

JUDY: And I'd be mediocre, lower-management nobody for the rest of my career.

JACK: I want you to be a success, Judy. But the idea of spending more evenings talking to idiots is too much!

Case 5

MEMORANDUM TO: Executive Vice President - CONFIDENTIAL

FROM: Frank Williams, Controller

I would like to get your advice on a matter of great sensitivity involving one of the junior executives in our organization.   It has been brought to my attention by an unimpeachable source that Roger Holman, Assistant Comptroller in my division, is having an affair with a prominent young playgirl. I understand it has reached the point where any day now Roger's wife will publicly denounce the

young playgirl as a homewrecker. I have been reluctant to bring this up, but I know that Roger's marital problems will hurt his work. I would appreciate any advice you could give me on this.
Case 6

MEMORANDUM

TO: FROM:
Executive Vice President   Production Manager

SUBJECT: Conference for Production Supervisors

I am pleased that we have the opportunity to send a representative to the Dunbar conference on production supervision. I know from personal experience that it is a high-quality conference, and it has developed such a favorable reputation in this area that it is considered an important form of recognition for those who are selected to attend.

I have reviewed our supervisory staff quite carefully and have narrowed the choice down to two people, both of whom I feel are qualified to attend. Unfortunately, we can send only one person, and I will leave the final selection up to you, depending on what you feel we want to emphasize. The two candidates are John Elms and Susan Adams.

Susan Adams is supervisor of knitting unit A. She is 25, married, and has no children.   She has been employed by our company for three years. She is a college graduate with a general business degree, and we consider her to have good potential for higher-level positions.

John Elms is supervisor of knitting unit B. He is 43, married, and has two teen-age children. He has been employed by our company for 20 years.   He is a high school graduate. He has been a steady, conscientious employee, advancing gradually from a helper's job to his present position, which may be as high as he will be able to go, judging from our assessment of the information in his file. Selection for this conference would mean a lot to John.

RESPONSE SHEET

1. How appropriate is it for Ruth to request a leave of absence?

Highly Inappropriate	Moderately Inappropriate	Slightly Inappropriate
____	____	____

Slightly Appropriate	Moderately Appropriate	Highly Appropriate
____	____	____

Would you grant the leave (without pay)?

_____ Yes   _____ No

My rationale is:

_____

_____

2. Please evaluate each of the following courses of action that Schmidt might take to influence Ronald Cooper's decision, checking either yes or no for EACH alternative.

Yes   No

a.___ ___   Try to convince Ronald to remain with the organization.

b.___ ___   Don't try to influence Ronald

c.___ ___   Offer a raise as an incentive to stay

d.___ ___   Find an attractive position in the organizations for Ronald's wife.

My rationale is:

_____

_____

_____

3. Which of the following three actions would you recommend?

a.____   Do not promote Margaret.

b.____   Try to persuade Margaret to make a commitment before going ahead with the promotion

c.____   Promote Margaret based on past performance

My rationale is:_____

_____

_____

4. Which of the following alternatives would you recommend to the Garrisons?

a. ____   Jack should go to parties and stop making it an issue

b. ____   Judy should attend parties alone

c. ____   Judy should stop attending parties

My rationale is:_____

_____

_____

5.   Evaluate each of the following methods of dealing with this situation, checking either yes or no for EACH alternative.

Yes   No

a.___   ___   Confront Roger--tell him that he better terminate the affair or he will be fired

b.___   ___   Advise Roger to see a marriage counselor before it is too late

c.___   ___   Do nothing unless Roger brings it up

My rationale is:_____

_____

_____

6.   Please indicate which candidate you would send to the conference.

a. _____   John   b. _____   Susan

My rationale is:_____

_____

_____

Step 2.   (30-50 mins.)   In mixed sex groups of 4-6 members, discuss your answers to the Response Sheet and the following questions:

Case 1:   Why are people more inclined to give a leave of absence for childcare to a woman than to a man?   What can managers do to moderate their own bias in this area?   Will the time ever come when men will feel as comfortable as women in asking for such a special consideration?   What would the long term costs and benefits be to the company of granting such a request?

Case 2:   Why would people be more inclined to persuade a male to stay than a female, even if it could result in the loss of a valuable employee?   To what extent should a company try to persuade an employee to stay if his or her spouse has an attractive offer in another city?   What else could a company do to convince an employee to stay?   How would or could dual career couples decide which career takes precedence at any given time?

Case 3:   Why would people be more accepting of a man putting family first than a woman?   To what extent should promotion decisions be based on guesses about future performance?   loyalty?   values and priorities of the employee?   Does Margaret represent the manager of the future?   If so, what will the costs and benefits be to the organizations such managers work for?   What are your priorities and values regarding family vs. career?

Case 4: Why is the issue of participation in work-related social gatherings different for women than it is for men:
Is this changing? To what extent is a spouse responsible for attending work-related social gatherings? How important are social gatherings to a person's career?

Case 5: Why would people be less likely to talk with a man about being involved in an affair than with a woman? How involved should companies get in the private lives of their employees? Should the boss's values about such behavior be a factor in whether or not to become involved?

Case 6: To what extent was the factor of age rather than sex a determinant of which employee was sent to the conference? In those cases where the younger employee was sent, why would people be more likely to choose the male than the female? What factors should a manager take into account when selecting an employee for training?

Step 3. (20 mins.) Class Discussion

The instructor will lead a discussion focusing on the main issues brought out in each case.

56. BECOMING A MINORITY: BEING EXPOSED TO CULTURAL DIVERSITY[*]

PURPOSE:

1. To become exposed to cultural or ethnic differences.
2. To examine your feelings resulting from being a minority.

GROUP SIZE:

Any number.

TIME REQUIRED:

Guidelines for Minority Exercise done outside of class.
In-class discussion - 35-45 minutes.

PREPARATION REQUIRED:

Complete "The Assignment".

RELATED TOPICS:

Interpersonal Communication
Interpersonal Relationships
Perception
Learning

INTRODUCTION:

Because we are moving into more of a cosmopolitan world, it is important to understand and appreciate people's backgrounds which are different from your own. This is supported by continuing demands from both the business and academic communities to educate our students to become sensitive to foreign cultures, to become aware of and open to different value systems, and to develop an understanding of the social aspects of a pluralistic society (Neureiter, 1984; Nanus, 1984, Pollock, Bartol, Sherony, and Carnahan, 1983).

[*]By Renate R. Mai-Dalton. In The Organization Behavior Teaching Review, Vol. 9(3), 1984-85, pp.76-82. Used with permission.

EXERCISE SCHEDULE:

PART A - Guidelines for Minority Exercise

The following assignment exposes you to a new situation, requires you carefully to observe your surroundings, and asks you both to describe what <u>you</u> felt and what <u>other</u> individuals might feel to have you among them.

Your task is to go by yourself (you may not take anyone with you) to a place where you have not been before and to observe what you see. Then, from this experience, write a two-page paper that reports on the following:

1. Date and address of where the experience took place.
2. Length of time that you were there.
3. Brief description of the setting.
4. Your reaction to the situation in terms of your behavior and feelings.
5. The reaction of the other individuals toward you.
6. What this experience teaches you about being different from others in your environment.
7. How such an experience might influence your development if you were to live or work in such a setting all your life.
8. Concluding comments about the experience.

Whenever possible, relate your experience to the literature that we have covered in the course.

To give you some ideas about possible places to visit, below are examples of previous students' choices:

a. Protestants visited a Catholic service and vice versa.
b. Caucasians visited Black churches, and student organizations.
c. A student went to a Japanese birthday party.
d. A student visited a Croatian wedding.
e. Students went to the School for the Deaf or the School for the Blind.
f. White-collar workers went to a blue-collar cafeteria.
g. A student visited a body building club.
h. A younger student visited a nursing home.
i. A female student went to a car auction with predominantly male customers.
j. A student sat in the Faculty Lounge.

There are, of course, many other possibilities. Think of situations that you have often wondered about and want to get to know. Do not choose a setting where you would feel like an intruder into someone's privacy. If in doubt, telephone ahead and inquire if your presence is acceptable to the group. Only choose a setting that you sincerely want to learn about. This will avoid your feeling of being an "undercover agent." Instead, your sincere wish to learn about a group, different from your own, will maintain your integrity and will justify your visit.

One word of caution: Use your good judgment. Do not place yourself into a situation that is physically dangerous to you. We shall discuss in class what you might have learned from this exercise.

PART B - General Class Discussion

1. (5 min.)   After completing the papers, during class you will be divided into groups of 4-7 members according to where you visited. Examples of possible group compositions are students who have visited:

    a. similar religious services (e.g., Catholic, Jewish, Protestant)
    b. different racial groups
    c. physically and/or mentally handicapped groups
    d. different ethnic groups

2. (15-20 min.) Groups discuss what they have experienced and record:

    a. similarities and
    b. differences of the experiences,
    c. advantages and
    d. disadvantages of the exercise.

3. (15-20 min.) Total class discussion.

    Each group reports on its conclusions of 2, a-d, above.

57. FREIDA MAE JONES: RACISM IN ORGANIZATIONS*

PURPOSE:

To examine issues of racism in organizations.

GROUP SIZE:

Any number of group of 5-8 members.

TIME REQUIRED:

30-50 minutes.

PREPARATION REQUIRED:

Read "Freida Mae Jones" and answer the questions.

RELATED TOPICS:

Interpersonal Communication
Leadership
Women in Management

EXERCISE SCHEDULE:

1. (Pre-Class) Read the case and answer the questions.

2. (15-20 minutes) Groups discuss the questions.

3. (15-30 minutes) The instructor leads a discussion on the case.

BACKGROUND:

Freida Mae Jones was born in her grandmother's Georgia farmhouse on June 1, 1949. She was the sixth of George and Ella Jones' ten children. Mr. and Mrs. Jones moved to New York City when Freida was four because they felt that the educational and career opportunities for their children would be better in the North. With the help of some cousins, they settled in a five-room apartment in the Bronx. George worked as a janitor at Lincoln Memorial Hospital, and Ella was a part-time housekeeper in a nearby neighborhood. George and Ella were conservative, strict parents. They kept a close watch on their children's activities and demanded they be home by a certain hour. The Joneses believed that because they were black, the children would have to perform and behave better than their peers to be successful. They believed that their children's education would be the most important factor in their success as adults.

Freida entered Memorial High School, a racially integrated public school, in September 1963. Seventy percent of the student body was caucasian, 20 percent black, and 10 percent hispanic. About 60 percent of the graduates went on to college. Of this 60 percent, 4 percent were black and hispanic and all were male. In the middle of her senior year, Freida was the top student in her class. Following school regulations, Freida met with her guidance counselor to discuss her plans upon graduation. The counselor advised her to consider training in a "practical" field such as housekeeping, cooking, or sewing, so that she could find a job.

George and Ella Jones were furious when Freida told them what the counselor had advised. Ella said, "Don't they see what they are doing. Freida is the top-rated student in her whole class and they are telling her to become a manual worker. She showed that she has a fine mind and can work better than any of her classmates and still she is told not to become anybody in this world. It's really not any different in the North than back home in Georgia, except that they don't try to hide it down South. They want her to throw away her fine mind because she is a black girl and not a white boy. I'm going to go up to her school tomorrow and talk to the principal."

As a result of Mrs. Jones' visit to the principal, Freida was assisted in applying to ten Eastern colleges, each of which offered her full scholarships. In September 1966, Freida entered Werbley College, an exclusive private women's college in Massachusetts. In 1970, Freida graduated summa cum laude in history. She decided to return to New York to teach grade school in the city's public school system. Freida was unable to obtain a full-time position, so she substituted. She also enrolled as a part-time student in Columbia University's Graduate School of Education. In 1975 she had attained her Master of Arts degree in Teaching from Columbia but could not find a permanent teaching job. New York City was laying off teachers and had instituted a hiring freeze because of the city's financial problems.

Feeling frustrated about her future as a teacher, Freida decided to get an MBA. She thought that there was more opportunity in business than in education. Churchill Business School, a small, prestigious school located in upstate New York, accepted Freida into its MBA program.

Freida completed her MBA in 1977 and accepted an entry-level position at the Industrialist World Bank of Boston in a fast-track management development program. The three-year program introduced her to all facets of bank operations, from telling to loan training and operations management. She was rotated to branch offices throughout New England. After completing the program she became an assistant manager for branch operations in the West Springfield branch office.

During her second year in the program, Freida had met James Walker, a black doctoral student in business administration at the University of Massachusetts. Her assignment to West Springfield precipitated their decision to get married. They originally anticipated that they would marry when James finished his doctorate and could move to Boston. Instead, they decided he would pursue a job in the Springfield-Hartford area.

Freida was not only the first black but also the first woman to hold an executive position in the West Springfield branch office. Throughout the training program Freida felt somewhat uneasy although she did very well. There were six other blacks in the program, five men and one woman, and she found support and comfort in sharing her feelings with them. The group spent much of their free time together. Freida had hoped that she would be located near one or more of the group when she went out into the "real world." She felt that although she was able to share her feelings about work with James, he did not have the full appreciation or understanding of her co-workers. However, the nearest group member was located one hundred miles away.

Freida's boss in Springfield was Stan Luboda, a fifty-five-year-old native New Englander. Freida felt that he treated her differently than he did the other trainees. He always tried to help her and took a lot of time (too much, according to freida) explaining things to her. Freida felt that he was treating her like a child and not a like an intelligent and able professional.

"I'm really getting frustrated and angry about what is happening at the bank," Freida said to her husband. "The people don't even realize it, but their prejudice comes through all the time. I fell as if I have to fight all the time just to start off even. Luboda gives Paul Cohen more responsibility than me and we both started at the same time, with the same amount of training. He's meeting customers alone and Luboda has accompanied me to each meeting I've had with a customer."

"I run into the same thing at school," said James. "The people don't even know that they are doing it. The other day I met with a professor on my dissertation committee. I've known and worked with him for over three years. He said he wanted to talk with me about a memo he had received. I asked him what it was about and he said that the records office wanted to know about my absence during the spring semester. He said that I had to sing some forms. He had me confused with Martin Jordan, another black student. Then he realized that it wasn't me, but Jordan he wanted. All I could think was that we all must look alike to him. I was angry. Maybe it was an honest mistake on his part, but whenever something like that happens, and it happens often, it gets me really angry."

"Something like that happened to me," said Freida. "I was using the copy machine, and Luboda's secretary was talking to someone in the hall. She had just gotten a haircut and was saying that her hair was now like Freida's - short and kinky - and that she would have to talk to me about how to take care of it. Luckily, my back was to her. I bit my lip and went on with my business. Maybe she was trying to be cute, because I know she saw me standing there, but comments like that are not cute, they are racist."

"I don't know what to do," said James. "I try to keep things in perspective. Unless people interfere with my progress, I try to let it slide. I only have so much energy and it doesn't make sense to waste it on people who don't matter. But that doesn't make it any easier to function in a racist environment. People don't realize that they are being racist. But a lot of times their expectations of black people or women, or whatever, are different because of skin color or gender. They expect you to be different, although if you were to ask them they would say that they don't. In fact, they would be highly offended if you implied that they were racist or sexist. They don't see themselves that way."

"Luboda is interfering with my progress," said Freida. "The kinds of experiences I have now will have a direct effect on my career advancement. If decisions are being made because I am black or a woman, then they are racially and sexually biased. It's the same kind of attitude that the guidance counselor had when I was in high school, although not as blatant."

In September 1980, Freida decided to speak to Luboda about his treatment of her. She met with him in his office. "Mr. Luboda, there is something that I would like to discuss with you, and I feel a little uncomfortable because I'm not sure how you will respond to what I am going to say."

"I want you to feel that you can trust me," said Luboda. "I am anxious to help you in any way I can."

"I feel that you treat me differently than you treat the other people around here," said Freida. "I feel that you are overcautious with me, that you always try to help me, and never let me do anything on my own."

"I always try to help the new people around here." answered Luboda. "I'm not treating you any differently than I treat any other person. I think that you are being a little too sensitive. Do you think that I treat you differently because you are black?"

"The thought had occurred to me," said Freida. "Paul Cohen started here the same time that I did and he has much more responsibility than I do." (Cohen was already handling accounts on his own, while Freida had not yet been given that responsibility.)

"Freida, I know you are not a naive person," said Luboda. "You know the way the world works. There are some things which need to be taken more slowly than others. There are some assignments for which Cohen has been given more responsibility than you, and there are some assignment for which you are given more responsibility that Cohen. I try to put you where you do the most good."

"What you are saying is that Cohen gets the more visible, customer contact assignments and I get the behind-the-scenes running of the operation assignments," said Freida. "I'm not naive, but I'm also not stupid either. Your decisions are unfair. Cohen's career will advance more quickly than mine because of the assignments that he gets."

"Freida, that is not true," said Luboda. "Your career will not be hurt because you are getting different responsibilities than Cohen. You both need the different kinds of experiences you are getting. And you have to face the reality of the banking business. We are in a conservative business. When we speak to customers we need to gain their confidence, and we put the best people for the job in the positions to achieve that end. If we don't get their confidence they can go down the street to our competitors and do business with them. Their services are no different than ours. It's competitive business in which you need every edge you have. It's going to take time for people to change some of their attitudes about whom they borrow money from or where they put their money. I can't change the way people feel. I am running a business, but believe me I won't make any decisions that are detrimental to you or to the bank. There is an important place for you here at the bank. Remember, you have to use your skills to the best advantage of the bank as well as your career."

"So what you are saying is that all things being equal, except my gender and my race, that Cohen will get different treatment than me in terms of assignments," said Freida.

"You're making it sound like I am making a racist and sexist decision," said Luboda. "I'm making a business decision utilizing the resources at my disposal and the market situation in which I must operate. You know exactly what I am talking about. What would you do if you were in my position?"

QUESTIONS FOR DISCUSSION

1. Briefly summarize the case. What were Freida's concerns?

2. When Freida approached her manager, Mr. Luboda, he denied that he treated her unfairly. He suggested that she was too sensitive to the racial issue. Was Mr. Luboda being defensive or, was Freida highly sensitive to this issue? Support your position.

3. Were Freida's concerns justified? Why or why not?

4. What were Mr. Luboda's concerns? How do you evaluate his actions in light of those concerns?

5. Were Mr. Luboda's actions illegal under Title VII of the 1964 Civil Rights Act? Why or why not?

6. Suppose Freida had benefitted from Mr. Luboda's actions (e.g., by gaining more accounts). How would that change your evaluation of the case?

7. If you were in Mr. Luboda's position what would you do differently, given the conservative nature of the bank's clients?

8. If you were Freida, how would you have approached Mr. Luboda? What could she have done to be more persuasive?

58. THE OWL: CROSS-CULTURAL SENSITIVITY[*]

PURPOSE:

To experience and understand how cultural values influence behavior and relationships.

GROUP SIZE:

Any number of groups of five to seven members.

TIME REQUIRED:

45-65 minutes.

PREPARATION REQUIRED:

In a previous class session, roles need to be assigned: three X-ians and two Americans per group. Larger classes may have one - two observers per group. X-ians must meet for about an hour prior to class to prepare for the role-playing. Americans meet for no more than 15 minutes before the role play begins.

ROOM ARRANGEMENT REQUIREMENTS:

Circles of five chairs set up in various places around the room.

EXERCISE SCHEDULE:

1. (Pre-class) X-ians, Americans and observers roles are assigned. Each group reads only its role sheet. Observers read both role sheets.

2. (15 minutes) X-ians take their places in groups of chairs and wait for American couple to arrive. Then the conversation begins.

3. (5 minutes) The instructor signals time up and the American couple leaves the room while X-ians remain.

4. (5 minutes) The Americans return and ask the questions. X-ians give a "yes" or "no" reply.

5. (20-40 minute) The instructor will lead a discussion on the exercise covering the following areas:
   a. Which groups get a "yes"? Which ones a "no"?
   b. What were the reasons for the "success" or "failure"?
   c. What did the Americans understand about Culture X?
   d. How does this exercise relate to stereotyping?

---

[*] Adapted from Theodore Gochenour in Beyond Experience. Published by Experiment Press. Used with permission.

ROLE SHEETS FOR "THE OWL"

<u>BRIEFING SHEET #1</u> -- To be read **ONLY** by X-ians.

You are a member of Country X, an ancient land of high culture, which has, in the course of the centuries, tended to develop along somewhat isolationist lines. X-ians has a deep and complete acceptance of a way of life which no outside influence has altered in any appreciable way for many years, due to the sense of perfection and harmony of life which each X-ian derives from her/his culture.

In Country X, **women** are the natural leaders, administrators, heads of households, principal artistic creators, owners of wealth through whom inheritance functions, and rulers of the State. **Men** rarely work outside the home, where they keep house, cook, mind children, etc., and then only in menial positions where heavy labor is required. Among X-ian women, education is important, with a high percentage going on to the university level. Among men, there is little interest and no encouragement to go beyond basic literacy. In all respects, women know themselves to be superior to men, and are acknowledged to be superior by the men, both in individual attitudes and as expressed institutionally. There is a well-known expression, for example, which goes, "Don't send a man on a woman's errand."

Knowing much of the outside world -- and rendered somewhat uncomfortable by what they know of male-female relationships in many other countries -- X-ians have tended to withdraw into themselves. In Country X, marriage is between two women, forming what is known as the Bond. The two women (the Bond) then may wish to receive jointly a man into their household, for purposes of creating children, for tending the home, etc. Two women in the Bond are equal in all respects, jointly agree in all decisions, mutually have responsibility for a man, should he be affiliated with them. Relating to a Bond, a man is legally regarded as an entity, having protection from the Bond. The man is considered "cherished" by the Bond. The women are "married"; his relationship is to the Bond, whereby he is "cherished." A state of being "cherished" is considered very desirable among men.

The artistic powers of X-ian women are famous, particularly in having developed the design and care of gardens into a unique art form. In Country X, the Queen's Garden is open once a year on her birthday to the women of the country (no men allowed) in celebration of the natural processes of growth and rebirth. No foreigners have been able, so far, to observe this Queen's Garden Festival, though there is no law to the contrary which would prevent it from happening.

X-ians share with some cultures of the world a marked discomfort with prolonged eye contact. They, of course, look at another person with brief, polite glances when they are in conversation, but do not hold another person's eyes with their own. In Country X, one is very careful not to "stare," since it is very impolite, and considered to be the worst kind of aggressiveness.

You are an X-ian Bond, Ms Alef and Ms. Beh, with your Cherished Man Peh. Ms. Alef holds an important position in the Ministry of Foreign Affairs, as Directress of Cultural Affairs. Ms. Beh holds a position also in the Ministry of Foreign Affairs, as Special Assistant to the Minister. Both women are distantly related to the Queen. Cherished Man Peh has been taken along by the two women of the Bond on one of their official trips outside Country X. The three of you are now in a restaurant in Athens, and have been spotted by an American couple whom you have met once before but do not know very well.

When speaking with the Americans, you must limit your vocabulary to words of only one or two syllables. The purposes for this are: (1) your native language is that of Country X, and thus it is quite natural for you to be limited in your command of English, and (2) by making you conscious of your language, it is an easy way to prevent a use of vocabulary and concepts which people rarely use except as sociologists and anthropologists.

This American couple will attempt to gain your help in getting permission to observe the next Queen's Garden Festival. They will talk with you for about fifteen minutes. At that time, on some pretext, the American couple will excuse themselves for a few minutes, then return to the three of you. At that time they will ask you for your help.

You must decide whether to say "yes" or "no." There are three things to consider. Basically, you should decide "yes" if, in your judgement, the Americans have shown cultural sensitivity to what X-ians like. This means looking for three main things:

1. The American woman must be the one asking for permission, and she must ask the X-ian Bond (not Peh). The men in the role play (both the American man and Peh) must not be involved in the request.
2. You must decide how thoughtful the Americans have been about your limitations in use of English. They should not just rattle on, when it is obvious by your speech that you may not understand them very well. If they show sensitivity in this, it will be one factor toward saying "yes."
3. The Americans must also show sensitivity to your customs in eye-contact. If they continue to "stare" at you during the conversation (and the request), then your answer would be "no."

BRIEFING SET #2 - to be read **ONLY** by the Americans
  You are two Americans, male and female, both of you well-known journalists.

Both of you have M.A.'s in Journalism from recognized schools, and have spent several years in international travel and reporting on political, cultural and artistic subjects in a number of countries.

Never at a lost to detect a possible "story," you are pleased to encounter three people in a restaurant in Athens whom you have met once before briefly. You do not remember their names, but do remember that they are from Country X, a rather exotic and unusual place not often visited by foreigners. Country X is one of those places in the world about which there are more legends than facts. It is know, however, to be a society with highly developed arts, literature and gardens (which are apparently some kind of art form); with an atmosphere of being inaccessible and not too interested in getting into the world tourism business. One of the intriguing things about which speculation sometimes appears in the Sunday Supplements is the X-ian Queen's Garden Festival, which takes place apparently once a year, and which no one has ever visited or photographed. To do so, especially to be the firs, would be a true journalistic "coup."

In this exercise, you will approach the X-ians at their restaurant table and ask to join them. Talk with them for about 15 minutes. Then, find a pretext and leave the table for one or two minutes and decide together what would be the best way to approach your real subject: can you get permission to observe the next Queen's Garden Festival and do a story with pictures?

Try not to let your conversation run on too long. After you return from your two or three minutes of conferring, make your request to the X-ians. You will get a "yes" or "no" answer. At that point, the exercise is over, and you then excuse yourselves again and leave.

Chapter 16   Power and Politics

59. POWER QUESTIONNAIRE AND EXERCISE

PURPOSE:

1. To measure levels of empowerment.
2. To apply French and Raven's power model.

GROUP SIZE:

Any number of groups of 5-8 members

TIME REQUIRED:

50-80 minutes

PREPARATION REQUIRED:

Complete Part A, steps 1 and 2

RELATED TOPICS:

Assertiveness
Dynamics Within Groups
Interpersonal Relationships

EXERCISE SCHEDULE:

PART A - Questionnaire

1. Complete and score Empowerment Instrument and fill out checklists under "Empowerment" section.

2. Read the analysis of scoring.

3. (5-10 minutes) Discussion.

   The instructor will lead a discussion on empowerment of individuals and how it is impacted by organizations.

EMPOWERMENT INSTRUMENT[*]

Check either A or B to indicate how you usually are in these situations:

1. If someone disagrees with me in a class or a meeting, I
   a. immediately back down
   b. explain my position further
2. When I have an idea for a project I
   a. typically take a great deal of time to start it
   b. get going on it fairly quickly
3. If my boss or teacher tells me to do something which I think is wrong I
   a. do it anyway, telling myself he or she is "the boss"
   b. ask for clarification and explain my position
4. When a complicated problem arises, I usually tell myself
   a. I can take care of it
   b. I will not be able to solve it
5. When I am around people of higher authority, I often
   a. feel intimidated and defer to them
   b. enjoy meeting important people
6. As I awake in the morning, I usually feel
   a. alert and ready to conquer almost anything
   b. tired and have a hard time getting myself motivated
7. During an argument I
   a. Put a great deal of energy into "winning"
   b. Try to listen to the other side and see if we have any points of agreement
8. When I meet new people I
   a. Always wonder what they are "really" up to
   b. Try to learn what they are about and give them the benefit of the doubt until they prove otherwise
9. During the day I often
   a. criticize myself on what I am doing or thinking
   b. think positive thoughts about myself

---

10. When someone else does a great job I
    a. find myself picking apart that person and looking for
       faults
    b. often give a sincere compliment
11. When I am working in a group, I try to
    a. do a better job than the others
    b. help the group function more effectively
12. If someone pays me a compliment I typically
    a. try not to appear boastful and I downplay to compliment
    b. respond with a positive "thank you" or similar response
13. I like to be around people who
    a. challenge me and make me question what I do
    b. give me respect
14. In love relationships I prefer the other person
    a. have his/her own selected interests
    b. do pretty much what I do
15. During a crisis I try to
    a. resolve the problem
    b. find someone to blame
16. After seeing a movie with friends I
    a. wait to see what they say before I decide whether I
       liked it
    b. am ready to talk about my reactions right away
17. When work deadlines a approaching I typically
    a. get flustered and worry about completion
    b. buckle down and work until the job is done
18. If a job comes up I am interested in I
    a. go for it and apply
    b. tell myself I am not qualified enough
19. When someone treats me unkindly or unfairly I
    a. try to rectify the situation
    b. tell other people about the injustice
20. If a difficult conflict situation or problem arises, I
    a. try not to think about it, hoping it will resolve itself
    b. look at various options and may ask others for advice
       before I figure out what to do

SCORING:

Score one point for each of the following circled:

1b, 2b, 3b, 4a, 5b, 6a, 7b, 8b, 9b, 10b, 11b, 12b, 13a, 14a, 15a, 16b, 17b, 18a, 19a, 20b.

ANALYSIS OF SCORING

16-20 -   You are a take-charge person and generally make the most of
            opportunities. When others tell you something cannot be done, you may
            take this as a challenge and do it anyway. You see the world as an
            oyster with many pearls to harvest.

11-15 -   You try hard, but sometimes your negative attitude prevents you from
            getting involved in produtive projects. Many times you take responsibility,
            but there are situations where you look to others to take care of
            problems.

0-10 -   You complain too much and are usually focused on the "worst case
                 scenario." To you the world is controlled by fate and no matter what you
                 do it seems to get you nowhere, so you let other people develop
                 opportunities. You need to start seeing the positive qualities in yourself
                 and in others and see yourself as the "master of your fate."

EMPOWERMENT

A word that is more tuned into the teamwork concept is empowerment, since it does not assume
dominance over others. Empowerment means that you feel more able to reach your goals and work
with those around you. All of us can remember times when we felt extremely powerless and
dependent. We hate situations that make us feel we are returning to that state. Along with a feeling
of empowerment comes a sense of mastery over the tasks at hand and a sense of future success in
interpersonal relationships.

Most of us can think of times when we felt on top of the world. Whatever was at hand, we
could manage it. We could tough it out. That's what it feels like to be empowered.

Empowerment comes from the inside. It comes from self-confidence, liking yourself, and
determination to get the job done. These are quality that you can develop.

If you feel that your self-confidence is low, you can work on that. One way is to give yourself
affirmations, to notice what is good about yourself. For a start, list below the ten thing you like best
about yourself.

1.
2.
3.
4.
5.
6.
7.
8.
9.
10.

Did you find that hard to do? If I'd asked you to list ten things you <u>didn't</u> like about yourself,
you probably would have had an easier time. That just shows how used we are to looking at
ourselves negatively. And that only chips away at our self esteem and lessens our personal power.

Keep reminding yourself of your good qualities. It's not bragging or boasting, it's just
appreciating yourself. And unless you like yourself, you're not going to be able to like other people,
either.

People who feel secure within themselves and empowered have less need to dominate others and
can cooperate more easily. Below is an exercise to help you understand under what conditions you
feel powerful or powerless. Complete the sentences and then re-read your answers, do you notice
patterns?

While doing this inventory, keep your frame of mind in the work place. It will be natural for
some of you to focus on your personal relationships. You'll have a chance to do that in a later
chapter. For now, though, think of your co-workers when you fill in the statements below.

Answer the following questions/statements.

1. I feel powerless when_____.

2. I feel powerful when_____.

3. People I hold the most power or control over are _____.

4. People who exert the most power or control over me are _____

_____.

5. I feel intimidated when _____.

6. I am intimidating when_____.

7. It's easy for me to cooperate with _____(names) and

when _____.

8. I'm afraid of cooperation because _____.

9. I don't trust _____(names) because _____

_____.

10. It's easy for me to trust _____(names) because _____

_____.

11. Trust breaks down when_____.

12. I need to be careful around _____(names).

13. I can encourage cooperation by_____.

14. I become insecure when_____.

15. I feel confident and secure when _____.

List five things you can do to strengthen your own empowerment.
     1.
     2.
     3.
     4.
     5.

If you are a manager, list four things you can do in your organization to increase trust and help your subordinates to feel more empowered.
     1.
     2.
     3.
     4.

Although cooperation is generally very important in the workplace, it also can be dangerous at times. When you're working in a hostile, distrustful environment, or interacting with a manipulative person, trying to cooperate will probably mean that you will be taken advantage of. In those cases you need to make some hard choices on whether you will stay in that job or not.

One organization had a lot of back-biting, and lies were spoken about people who weren't part of the central clique. In this environment it would be foolish to be honest and open with people because the clique would take advantage of you.

If you find yourself in a situation like that, you have three choices; one is to live with it the way it is, and make the best of it. Try not to store up a lot of resentment because it will only eat away at your own self-esteem and your own productivity.

Choice number two is to prove to the people in power that you are competent and trustworthy. That may take some time and determination.

Choice number three is to get a job elsewhere. Many people believe that they have no other career options where they live. Don't limit yourself. Maybe your job is the only one of its kind available there; then maybe it's time to start considering moving or a career change. An excellent book to read on this is What Color Is Your Parachute by Richard Booles. It helps you to look at what positive qualities and abilities you have and to discover where those might best fit.

PART B - An Exercise in Social Power[**]

EXERCISE SCHEDULE:

1. (5 mins.) Divide the class into 5 groups of equal size, each
   of which is assigned one of the French and Raven power bases.

2. (10-15 mins.) Read the following case and prepare an actual influence plan using the type of power that has been assigned to your group. When finished with your planning, select one member to play the role of instructor. Then, also choose from your own or another group a "student" who is to be the recipient of the "instructor's" attempt.

   You are an instructor in a college class and have become aware that a potentially good student is repeatedly absent from class and sometimes unprepared when he is there. He seems to be satisfied with the grade he is getting, but you would like to see him attend regularly, be better prepared, and thus do better in the class. You even feel that the student might get really turned on to pursuing a career in this field, which is an exciting one for you. You are respected and liked by your students, and it kind of irritates you that this person treats your dedicated teaching with such a cavalier attitude. You want to influence the student to start attending class regularly.

3. (15-30 mins.) Role-Playing

   a. Each group role-plays its influence plan, going in the following order--punishment, reward, referent, legitimate, expert.

   b. During the role-plays, members in other groups should think of yourselves as the student being influenced. Fill out the "Reaction to Influence Questionnaire" at the end of the exercise for each role-play, including your own.

[**]Adapted from Gib Akin from Exchange, Vol. 3(4), 1978, pp. 38-39. Used with permission.

Reaction to Influence Questionnaire

Role Play #1

1. Type of power used (mark one)

   Punishment - ability to influence because of
   capacity to coerce or punish

   Reward - ability to influence because of
   potential reward

   Referent - comes from admiration and liking

   Legitimate - stems from formal position in
   organization

   Expert - comes from superior knowledge or ability
   to get things done or image of it

   Information - because of having information
   others want

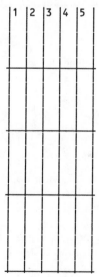

Role Plays

1	2	3	4	5

Fill in the number of each of the scales below which indicated in the grid
the best statement completion for you. That is, think of yourself on the
receiving end of the influence attempt described and record your own
reaction.

1	2	3	4	5

2. As a result of influence attempt I will....

   definitely not comply   definitely comply
       1   2   3   4   5

3. Any change that does come about will be....

       temporary   long lasting
           1   2   3   4   5

4. My own personal reaction is...

       resistant   acceptant
           1   2   3   4   5

5. As a result of this influence attempt my relationship with the professor will probably be...

           worse   better
           1   2   3   4   5

4. (5 mins.) Tabulate the results of the questionnaire within your group. For each role-play
   determine how many people thought the power used was punishment, reward, etc., then add
   up each member score for item 2 doing the same for items 3, 4, and 5.

5. Group Discussion (10-15 mins.)

   a. As a total class discuss which influence strategy is the most effective in compliance,
      long-lasting effect, acceptable attitude, and enhanced relationship.

   b. What are the likely side effects of each type of influence strategy?

60. A SIMPLE BUT POWERFUL POWER SIMULATION*

PURPOSE:

To understand some of the power dynamics in organizations at every level--from the individual to the systematic.

GROUP SIZE:

24-90 people

TIME REQUIRED:

60-90 minutes, or more if time permit.

MATERIALS:

Each student brings a dollar bill to class

ROOM ARRANGEMENT REQUIREMENTS:

A room large enough to accommodate two work groups and enough space in a hallway or corridor for a third group.

RELATED TOPICS:

Interpersonal Communications
Organizational Design

EXERCISE SCHEDULE:

PART A - Simulation

1. (5 mins.) Students turn in a dollar bill to the teacher and are divided into three groups based on criteria given by the instructor, assigned to their work places, and instructed to read the rules and tasks below.

2. (5 mins.) The money is divided to giving two-thirds of it to the top group, one-third to the middle, and none to the bottom.

3. (30-55 min.) Groups go to their assigned work places and complete their tasks.

---

*By Lee Bolman and Terrence E. Deal from <u>Exchange</u>, Vol. 4(3), 1979, pp. 38-42. Used with permission.

Rules:

a. Members of the top group are free to enter the space of either of the other groups and to communicate whatever they wish, whenever they wish. Members of the middle group may enter the space of the lower group whenever they wish but must request permission to enter the top group's space (which the top group can refuse). Members of the lower group may not disturb the top group in any way unless specifically invited by the top. The lower group does have the right to knock on the door of the middle group and request permission to communicate with them (which can also be refused).

b. The members of the top group have the authority to make any change in the rules that they wish, at any time, with or without notice.

Tasks:

a. <u>Top Group</u>: To be responsible for the overall effectiveness and learning from the simulation, and to decide how to use its money.

b. <u>Middle Group</u>: To assist the Top Group in providing for the overall welfare of the organization, and to decide how to use its money.

c. <u>Bottom Group</u>: To identify its resources and to decide how best to provide for learning and the overall effectiveness of the organization.

PART B - Group Discussion

1. (10-15 mins.) Each of the three groups chooses two representatives to go to the front of the class and discuss the following questions with the instructor.
    a. What can we learn about power from this experience? Does it remind us of events we have seen in other organizations?

    b. What did each of us learn individually? How did we think about what power is? Were we satisfied with the amount of power we had? How did we try to exercise or to gain more power?

2. (15-25 min.)
    a. Discuss what occurred within and between the three groups.
    b. What were the in-group, out-group dynamics?
    c. How did trust and mistrust figure into the simulation?
    d. What does this exercise say about structural injustice?
    e. What were some differences of being in the top group versus being in the bottom one?

61. THE VISIBILITY/CREDIBILITY INVENTORY*

PURPOSE:

To measure visibility and credibility in groups.

GROUP SIZE:

Any number of groups of 2-8 members.

TIME REQUIRED:

25-40 minutes.

PREPARATION REQUIRED:

Complete and score the inventory prior to class.

RELATED TOPICS:

Dynamics within Groups
Interpersonal Conversation

EXERCISE SCHEDULE:

1. (Pre-class) Complete and score the inventory prior to class. This takes about 20 minutes.

2. (10-15 minutes) Instructor gives a presentation on the theory behind the visibility/credibility inventory.

3. (15-25 minutes) Form groups of 2-8. Members share and discuss their positions on the matrix, considering implications of these positions, and provide feedback about perceptions of behavior.

---

* Adapted from Brendan Reddy and Gil Williams and reprinted from William Pfeiffer and John Jones, The 1988 Annual Handbook for Group Facilitators, pp. 115-125. Used with permission.

THE VISIBILITY/CREDIBILITY INVENTORY

Instructions:

Completing this instrument will give you an opportunity to learn about your power and influence in your group or team. Please answer each question candidly, recognizing that there are no right/wrong, good/bad answers. Base your responses on your initial reaction to your actual behavior, **not** what you wish your behavior to be. Circle one of the numbers next to each statement to indicate the degree to which that statement is true for you or is descriptive of you.

	Strongly Disagree (Very Unlike Me) 1	Disagree (Unlike Me) 2	Slightly Disagree (Somewhat Unlike Me) 3	Neither Agree nor Disagree (Neither Like nor Unlike Me) 4	Slightly Agree (Somewhat Like Me) 5	Agree (Like Me) 6	Strongly Agree (Very Like Me) 7
1. I am usually one of the more vocal members of the group.	1	2	3	4	5	6	7
2. I frequently volunteer to lead the group.	1	2	3	4	5	6	7
3. People in the group usually listen to what I have to say.	1	2	3	4	5	6	7
4. I frequently find myself on "center stage."	1	2	3	4	5	6	7
5. I am able to influence the decisions that the group makes.	1	2	3	4	5	6	7
6. People often seek me out for advice.	1	2	3	4	5	6	7
7. I feel that I am trusted by the group.	1	2	3	4	5	6	7
8. I enjoy the role of being "up-front."	1	2	3	4	5	6	7
9. My opinion is usually held in high regard by group members.	1	2	3	4	5	6	7
10. I am often reluctant to lead the group.	1	2	3	4	5	6	7
11. I receive much recognition for my ideas and contributions.	1	2	3	4	5	6	7
12. I have a reputation for being believable.	1	2	3	4	5	6	7
13. Group members typically influence what I have to say in the group.	1	2	3	4	5	6	7
14. I would rather lead the group than be a participant.	1	2	3	4	5	6	7
15. I do not like being the limelight and avoid it whenever possible.	1	2	3	4	5	6	7
16. My ideas are usually implemented.	1	2	3	4	5	6	7
17. Group members frequently ask for my opinions and input.	1	2	3	4	5	6	7

	1	2	3	4	5	6	7
	Strongly Disagree (Very Unlike Me) 1	Disagree (Unlike Me) 2	Slightly Disagree (Somewhat Unlike Me) 3	Neither Agree nor Disagree (Neither Like nor Unlike Me) 4	Slightly Agree (Somewhat Like Me) 5	Agree (Like Me) 6	Strongly Agree (Very Like Me) 7

18. I take the initiative in the group and am usually one of the first to speak out. 1 2 3 4 5 6 7

19. I usually volunteer my thoughts and ideas without hesitation. 1 2 3 4 5 6 7

20. I seem to blend into a crowd at parties. 1 2 3 4 5 6 7

21. During meetings I am alone in presenting my own point of view. 1 2 3 4 5 6 7

22. I wait to be asked for my opinion in meetings. 1 2 3 4 5 6 7

23. People seek out my advice. 1 2 3 4 5 6 7

24. During meetings my point of view is not joined by others. 1 2 3 4 5 6 7

25. People check with others about the advice I give to them. 1 2 3 4 5 6 7

26. I ask questions just to have something to say. 1 2 3 4 5 6 7

27. I often find myself in the role of scribe during meetings. 1 2 3 4 5 6 7

28. Group members usually "check out" data I give them. 1 2 3 4 5 6 7

29. Group members view me as an expert in my field. 1 2 3 4 5 6 7

30. I am in a highly visible race, ethnic, or gender group (for example, a woman in a predominantly male organization). 1 2 3 4 5 6 7

31. I am often asked to work at organizational levels higher than my own. 1 2 3 4 5 6 7

32. Group members usually consult me about important matters before they make a decision. 1 2 3 4 5 6 7

33. I try to dress well and/or differently from members of my group. 1 2 3 4 5 6 7

34. I usually try to sit at the head of the conference table at meetings. 1 2 3 4 5 6 7

35. Group members often refer to me in their statements. 1 2 3 4 5 6 7

	Strongly Disagree (Very Unlike Me) 1	Disagree (Unlike Me) 2	Slightly Disagree (Somewhat Unlike Me) 3	Neither Agree nor Disagree (Neither Like nor Unlike Me) 4	Slightly Agree (Somewhat Like Me) 5	Agree (Like Me) 6	Strongly Agree (Very Like Me) 7

36. I speak loudly during meetings. 1 2 3 4 5 6 7

37. I have noticed that group members often look at me even when not talking directly to me. 1 2 3 4 5 6 7

38. I stand when I have something important to say. 1 2 3 4 5 6 7

39. Sometimes I think group members do not know I am present. 1 2 3 4 5 6 7

40. I am emotional when I speak. 1 2 3 4 5 6 7

41. Following my absence from the group, I am not asked to explain where I was. 1 2 3 4 5 6 7

42. The word "wisdom" has been used in reference to me. 1 2 3 4 5 6 7

43. Group members come to me for gossip but not for "substance." 1 2 3 4 5 6 7

44. I seem to have the "ear" of the group. 1 2 3 4 5 6 7

45. I am very influential in my group. 1 2 3 4 5 6 7

46. I clown around with group members. 1 2 3 4 5 6 7

47. Group members do not like me to disagree with them. 1 2 3 4 5 6 7

48. I jump right into whatever conflict the group members are dealing with. 1 2 3 4 5 6 7

49. I like telling jokes and humorous stories in the group. 1 2 3 4 5 6 7

50. My contributions to the group are not very important. 1 2 3 4 5 6 7

THE VISIBILITY/CREDIBILITY INVENTORY
SCORING SHEET

Instructions:

Transfer the number you circled for each item onto the appropriate blank on this scoring sheet. Then add each column of numbers and write its total in blank provided.

	Visibility		Credibility	
Item Number	**My Score**	**Item Number**	**My Score**	
1.	_____	3.	_____	
2.	_____	5.	_____	
4.	_____	6.	_____	
8.	_____	7.	_____	
10.	_____ *	9.	_____	
14.	_____	11.	_____	
15.	_____ *	12.	_____	
18.	_____	13.	_____ *	
19.	_____	16.	_____	
20.	_____ *	17.	_____	
22.	_____ *	21.	_____ *	
26.	_____	23.	_____	
27.	_____	24.	_____ *	
30.	_____	25.	_____ *	
33.	_____	28.	_____ *	
34.	_____	29.	_____	
36.	_____	31.	_____	
38.	_____	32.	_____	
39.	_____ *	35.	_____	
40.	_____	37.	_____	
41.	_____ *	42.	_____	
43.	_____	44.	_____	
46.	_____	45.	_____	
48.	_____	47.	_____	
49.	_____	50.	_____ *	
Total	_____	Total	_____	

*Reverse-score item. Change your score according to the following scale and write the corrected number in the blank.

1 = 7   2 = 6   3 = 5   4 = 4   5 = 3   6 = 2   7 = 1

THE VISIBILITY/CREDIBILITY INVENTORY
PROFILE SHEET

Name _____   Date _____

Instructions:

Plot your position on the matrix below by finding the square at which your Visibility score and your Credibility score intersect.   For example, if your Visibility score is 90 and your Credibility score is 120, find where 90 on the horizontal axis and 120 on the vertical axis intersect.   Mark the spot by shading in that square.

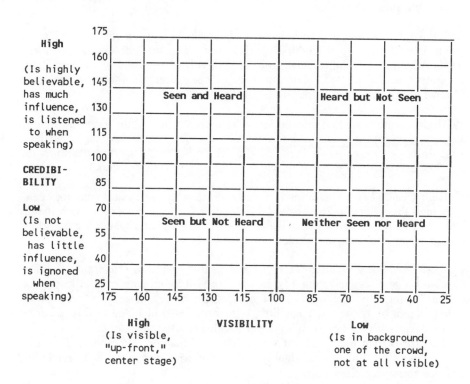

THEORETICAL FRAMEWORK

The concept of power is important in organizational and group dynamics. However, behaviors called "power moves" or "plays" are often misinterpreted. In fact, most group members are not aware of the ways in which they use power and influence among themselves. Consequently, the authors have developed an instrument that assists group members in understanding their own and one another's functioning with regard to power within the group.

This instrument is based on two of the primary components of power: visibility and credibility. Visibility results from those behaviors that permit a person to be "up-front" and physically visible; the focus is on the person's **visible, external attributes**. Credibility results from those behaviors that give a person influence so that he or she is believed - and believed in - by others; the focus is on the person's **credible internal attributes.**

These two components are interactive, and an individual's behavior in a group can be rated along a visibility continuum as well as along a credibility continuum. The two continua thus form a matrix (see Figure 1) on which the individual's position with regard to visibility and credibility within a particular group can be plotted. For purposes of discussion, we focus on the more extreme or "pure" types that the matrix helps to identify.

1. **High Visibility/High Credibility.** People who fall in Quadrant I are both "seen and heard." They exhibit behaviors that permit them to be physically seen by others as well as to have influence on others. In large organizations these people are typically the upwardly mobile and young leaders, and they are often referred to as"water walkers" and "fast trackers."

2. **Low Visibility/High Credibility.** Quadrant II locates those who are "heard but not seen." These people are "behind-the-scenes" influences who are content to have power but wish to stay out of the limelight. In this quadrant is included the "sage" or the opinion leader whose sound input is sought before major decisions are made.

3. **High Visibility/Low Credibility.** Those "seen but not heard" reside in Quadrant III. This quadrant houses a wide range of organizational types who are visible but who have little credibility or influence. One of these people is the resident "gossip"; he or she may be well-known among colleagues but cannot be trusted and has little influence. Also included in this quadrant is the "yes man," who derives his or her visibility from another source, usually the boss. Also, it is unfortunately the case that in this quadrant we find tokens, that is, women and minorities whose gender, race, or position makes them highly visible but who have very little credibility because the formal power resides elsewhere.

4. **Low Visibility/Low Credibility.** In Quadrant IV we find those who are "neither seen nor heard." For whatever reasons, Quadrant IV people prefer or are placed in positions that offer little credibility or visibility. Although they may do their work, they rarely move up in the organization. Most often they remain unknown or are passed over.

Chapter 17   Conflict Management and Assertiveness

62. BORDER DISPUTE*

PURPOSE:

To develop both competitive and collaborative behavior.

GROUP SIZE:

Any number of dyads.

TIME REQUIRED:

50 minutes minimum, 90 minutes preferable.

PREPARATION REQUIRED:

Read the "Background" below.

RELATED TOPICS:

Dynamics within groups
Dynamics between groups

BACKGROUND:

---

*By Gary Whitney. Used with permission.

Situation

There are two developing countries, Arak and Barkan, who have an unresolved border dispute. The result has been continuous squabbling over resource rights and political jurisdiction. The two countries have come together for one last chance at solving the dispute through negotiation. A failure to resolve the border dispute at this last conference will result in war between the two countries. To prevent war, the conference must end with a treaty agreed upon and signed in its entirety.

Background

You have been selected to represent your country at this conference because of your patriotism and grasp of the perilous situation which confronts your country. The future welfare of your country is at stake, and your countrymen are depending upon you to bring about a favorable and honorable solution to the dispute.

Negotiation

The negotiation is scheduled to last thirty minutes. As each minute of the negotiation passes, both of the countries are involved in a costly defense buildup for the possibility of war. If no agreement is reached after thirty minutes, then war will break out.

Treaty

A treaty form is in the appendix. Complete all the necessary information. The negotiation is not over until the treaty is complete and signed by both negotiators. The treaty must include all details of the agreement.

The Disputed Region

The region is 50 miles wide and 180 miles long and divided into two areas of contention. The region is bounded in the north by Arak and in the south by Barkan. The Blue Ocean borders the region on the west and the country Cordan borders the region in the east. The two areas of dispute are:

Area I: Coastal Valley and Mountains

The history of Area I is tumultous. Many small wars between Arak and Barkan have been waged over this area in the last 100 years because of its rich agricultural and natural resource potential. The area has been alternately owned by Arak and Barkan and as a result the area is populated by both Arakians and Barkanians. In addition to the valley near the coast, there is a mountainous region with peaks from 3000 to 6000 feet high which is heavily forested but sparsely inhabited.

The people who live in Area I have no particular allegiance to either Barkan or Arak, but they do have a strong allegiance to their township. For this reason, the townships shown on the map cannot be subdivided in any way. Presently, Area I is occupied by a United Nations peacekeeping force pending settlement of the negotiations between the two countries.

Area II: Desert Region

This is an arid, uninhabited region. The average annual rainfall is two inches and that comes in one or two storms in the winter.

EXERCISE SCHEDULE:

Step 1. (5 min.) Read the "Top Secret" Negotiation Information document. See the Appendix for this document and read only the one which applies to your country (i.e., Arak or Barkan).

Step 2. (30 min.) The teacher will assign you a partner that is from the other country. You must negotiate a solution with your partner.

Step 3. (5 min.)

    a. Use treaty form in the Appendix to record your agreement.

    b. Use scoring protocol in the Appendix to measure the quality of your agreement.

Step 4. (10-30 min.) Questions for Discussion

    a. How did your definition of the situation affect your behavior?

    b. Did running short of time influence your negotiation tactics?

    c. Can you be perceptive enough and flexible enough to recognize different kinds of issues and act appropriately?

    d. What is the risk of sharing information during negotiations?

    e. Would the outcome be different if you had collaborated on Area II before discussing Area I?

    f. Can you see the parallels between these negotiations and "real world" negotiations? (e.g., in labor negotiations, wage is usually a competitive issue while job enrichment is a potentially collaborative issue.)

63. ASSERTIVE BEHAVIOR INVENTORY AND ROLE PLAYS*

PURPOSE:

To assess your level of assertiveness and to practice using assertive skills.

GROUP SIZE:

Any number of groups of 4-6 members.

TIME REQUIRED:

20-75 minutes.

PREPARATION REQUIRED:

1. Complete the Assertive Inventory.
2. Read the "Background" for Part B and fill in the passive, aggressive and assertive responses after each situation.

RELATED TOPICS:

Interpersonal Communication

PART A - THE INVENTORY

This is an instrument for measuring your assertiveness.

Assertive Inventory

For the questions below, use the following scale:
        5 if behavior almost always occurs
        4 if behavior generally occurs
        3 if behavior sometimes occurs
        2 if behavior rarely occurs
        1 if behavior never occurs

Areas of Assertiveness[**]

A. Expressing Positive Feelings

_____1. I give compliments easily and sincerely.

_____2. I can tell people that I care about them.

*_____3. I usually feel critical towards others.

*_____4. I can think of more negative characteristics of myself than I can positive.

_____5. I tell teachers when I like a course.

*_____6. It's hard for me to tell my parents and family how much I love them.

B. Expressing Negative Feelings

_____7. If I get defective merchandise from a store, I can return it easily.

_____8. If my food comes differently than I ordered, I send it back.

_____9. I can disagree with people.

*_____10. If there is something I don't like about a course, I usually don't say anything to the teacher, but I complain to other students.

*_____11. If a family member of a close friend's is annoying me, I usually pretend not to be bothered.

*_____12. I smile even when I am not happy.

*_____13. I find it difficult to negotiate prices for purchases, services, or repairs.

*_____14. When people cut in line in front of me, I usually let them.

[**]Some ideas adapted from Pamela Butler, <u>Self-Assertion for Women</u>. New York: Harper & Row, 1981. Used with permission.

C. Setting Limits

*____15. I have a hard time saying "no."

*____16. I get involved in activities merely because someone I know asked me to.

*____17. If I get invited somewhere and do not want to go, I usually make up a story and beg off.

____18. I can say sincerely to people "No thanks, I am not interested."

____19. I know how much I can handle and am careful not to take on too much.

D. Self-Initiative

____20. I think of new projects or activities and then do them.

____21. I can ask a member of the opposite sex for dates.

*____22. I feel left out because not many people invite me places.

____23. I easily initiate conversations with new people.

*____24. I have a difficult time meeting new people.

Total Score _____

*indicates reverse scoring:
   1 if behavior almost always occurs
   2 if behavior generally occurs
   3 if behavior sometimes occurs
   4 if behavior rarely occurs
   5 if behavior never occurs

INTERPRETATION***

100-120   You always stand up for yourself and take initiative, but you may "overdo" it at times and be aggressive. You may need to practice letting others take charge at times and not always saying everything negative that comes to mind.

  61-99   You are probably quite assertive and use appropriate behaviors. You do not often "overdo" it, so you are rarely aggressive and you also usually stand up for your rights, but are respectful of other people at the same time.

24-60   You are too passive and let other people make decisions for you and/or control your life. You need to try not to please others so often and take more initiative in relationships.

_____

   ***This inventory is not validated and only should be used to give a general sense of your level of assertiveness.

PART B - ROLE PLAYS****

Background: The theory of assertiveness includes three styles of behavior: passive, aggressive and assertive as explained below.

1.   Passive - Passive people generally do not stand up for their rights; they easily let others take advantage of them; they underreact to situations, often responding too little and too late. Other qualities of the passive person include a quiet voice, little or no eye contact, few gestures, and frequency of agreeing with others' opinions. In addition, they tend to be under responsible. For example, a passive woman may say "let's go to dinner wherever you want, I don't care." But then at the restaurant she is now saying "this place is terrible, the food is awful; why did you bring me here?" She can easily complain because she was not responsible for the decision.

2.   Aggressive - Aggressive people do stand up for their rights, but they don't care who gets in their way; they overreact to situations, often too quickly; they are most concerned about not being taken advantage of without worrying about the other person's rights. In addition, they tend to have loud voices, too much eye contact, and they invade other people's body space. They are also over-responsible, i.e., they make decisions for other people, answer someone else's questions and make plans for their friends. Of course, they genuinely believe they are doing these to help other people.

3.   Assertive - Assertive people stand up for their own rights and at the same time are sensitive to other people's rights. They respond with the appropriate amount of behavior at the appropriate time. So, if someone says, "Can't you be too assertive?," by definition, the response would be "how can you be too appropriate?" What they usually mean to ask is "Can't you be too aggressive?," and the answer to that is yes. Assertive people can negotiate solutions to problems with one goal being the enhancement of the relationship.

Directions:

1.   Read the three situations on the next page and fill in the passive, aggressive and assertive response for each one.

Situation #1

   You have just received your yearly evaluation, and you find your boss has given you a "satisfactory" rating. This seems quite unfair to you, because you have worked extremely hard during the last year and have surpassed a number of your co-workers several times. You have made an appointment with your boss to discuss this matter. What do you say?

Passive -

Aggressive -

_____

****With the collaboration of Maxine Rossman.

Assertive -

Situation #2

One of your subordinates, the Director of Sales, has been overspending on his/her voucher limit. Department heads are allowed to spend up to $750 without your approval, but the Director of Sales frequently spends more than that without clearing it with you. The sales department has been doing well in the past year, but also has been overspending its total budget. You have called the Director of Sales into your office. What do you say?

Passive -

Aggressive -

Assertive -

Situation #3

Your hard-working and generally efficient secretary has recently been bringing in resumes and cover letters to type for her unemployed husband who lost his job six weeks ago. This has caused the regular work to be backlogged somewhat. You have been concerned about this for several weeks but have been hesitant to bring this up because she frequently does personal favors for you such as buying presents for your spouse and children, typing letters to personal friends, and picking up clothes from the cleaners. You have called your secretary into your office. What do you say?

Passive -

Aggressive -

Assertive -

2. Role Plays: in groups of 4-6 members. (You may do one or more of the role plays).

    a. (10-20 min.) Situation #1
        1. Assign one person to be the boss, then other members to play passive subordinate, aggressive subordinate and assertive subordinate.
        2. "Passive" subordinate interacts with boss.
        3. "Aggressive" subordinate interacts with boss.
        4. "Assertive" subordinate interacts with boss.

Other members of the group not participating in the immediate role play should act as observers, giving feedback on whether the actors were really passive, aggressive, or assertive. Look particularly at eye contact, gestures, posture, voice, etc.

Your instructor may choose to have some volunteers from each group role play in front of the class.

    b. (10-20 min.) Situation #2
        1. Assign one person to be subordinate. Others are assigned to be passive boss, aggressive boss and assertive boss.
        2. The three bosses interact, one at a time, with the boss. Follow the same format as in Situation #1.

    c. (10-20 min.) Situation #3
        1. Assign one person to be the secretary. Three other members are then assigned as passive boss, aggressive boss and assertive boss.
        2. The three bosses interact, one at a time, with the secretary. Follow same format as in Situation #1.

3. (10-15 min.) Class Discussion

As a class, answer the following questions:

a. Which of the behavior styles (passive, aggressive, assertive) was most effective in solving the problems?

b. Which of the three behavior styles do you think is used most in conflict situations?

c. Why isn't the assertive mode used more often?

64. THE UGLI ORANGE ROLE PLAY[*]

PURPOSE:

To practice negotiation skills in a conflict situation.

GROUP SIZE:

Any number of groups with three members.

TIME REQUIRED:

30 to 40 minutes.

RELATED TOPICS:

Interpersonal Communication

EXERCISE SCHEDULE:

1.   (5 min.) Form groups of three members. One person will be Dr. Roland, one will be Dr. Jones and the third will be an observer.

2.   (5 min.) Roland and Jones read only their own roles, while the observer reads both (roles are in the Appendix).

3.   (10 min.) Instructor announces: "I am Mr./Ms. Cardoza. The owner of the remaining Ugli oranges. My fruit-export firm is based in South America. My country does not have diplomatic relations with your country, although we do have strong trade relations."

Groups spend about 10 minutes meeting with the other firm's representative and decide on a course of action. Be prepared to answer the following questions:

1.   What do you plan to do?
2.   If you want to buy the oranges, what price will you offer?
3.   To whom and how will the oranges be delivered?

4.   (5-10 min.) Observers report the solutions reached. Groups describe decision-making process used.

5.   (5-10 min.) The instructor will lead a discussion on the exercise addressing the following questions:
      a.   Which groups had the most trust? How did that influence behavior?
      b.   Which groups shared more information? Why?
      c.   How are trust and disclosure important in negotiations?

---

[*]By Robert J. House, University of Toronto. Used with permission.

ROLE OF "DR. JONES"

You are Dr. John W. Jones, a biological research scientist employed by a pharmaceutical firm. You have recently developed a synthetic chemical useful for curing and preventing Rudosen. Rudosen is a disease contracted by pregnant women. If not caught in the first four weeks of pregnancy, the disease causes serious brain, eye, and ear damage to the unborn child. recently there has been an outbreak of Rudosen in your state, and several thousand women have contracted the disease. You have found, with volunteer patients, that your recently developed synthetic serum cures Rudosen in its early stages. Unfortunately, the serum is made from the juice of the Ugli orange, which is a very rare fruit. Only a small quantity (approximately 4,000) of these oranges were produced last season. No additional Ugli oranges will be available until next season, which will be too late to cure the present Rudosen victims.

You've demonstrated that your synthetic serum is in no way harmful to pregnant women. Consequently, there are no side effects. The Food and Drug Administration has approved of the production and distribution of the serum as a cure for Rudosen. Unfortunately, the present outbreak was unexpected, and your firm had not planned on having the compound serum available for six months. Your firm holds the patent on the synthetic serum, and it is expected to be a highly profitable product when it is generally available to the public.

You have recently been informed on good evidence that Mr. R. H. Cardoza, a South American fruit exporter, is in possession of 3,000 Ugli oranges in good condition. If you could obtain the juice of all 3,000 you would be able to both cure present victims and provide sufficient innoculation for the remaining pregnant women in the state. No other state currently has a Rudosen threat.

You have recently been informed that Dr. P. W. Roland is also urgently seeking Ugli oranges and is also aware of Mr. Cardoza's possession of the 3,000 available. Dr. Roland is employed by a competing pharmaceutical firm. He has been working on biological warfare research for the past several years. There is a great deal of industrial espionage in the pharmaceutical industry. Over the past several years, Dr. Roland's firm and yours have sued each other for infringement of patent rights and espionage law violations several times.

You've been authorized by your firm to approach Mr. Cardoza to purchase 3,000 Ugli oranges. You have been told he will sell them to the highest bidder. Your firm has authorized you to bid as high as $250,000 to obtain the juice of the 4,000 available oranges.

ROLE OF "DR. ROLAND"

You are Dr. P. W. Roland. You work as a research biologist for a pharmaceutical firm. The firm is under contract with the government to do research on methods to combat enemy uses of biological warfare.

Recently several World War II experimental nerve gas bombs were moved from the United States to a small island just off the U.S. coast in the Pacific. In the process of transporting them, two of the bombs developed a leak. The leak is presently controlled by government scientists, who believe that the gas will permeate the bomb chambers within two weeks. They know of no method of preventing the gas from getting into the atmosphere and spreading to other islands, and very likely to the West Coast as well. If this occurs, it is likely that several thousand people will incur serious brain damage or die.

You've developed a synthetic vapor that will neutralize the nerve gas if it is injected into the bomb chamber before the gas leaks out. The vapor is made with a chemical taken from the rind of the Ugli orange, a very rare fruit. Unfortunately, only 4,000 of these oranges were produced this season.

You've been informed on good evidence, that a Mr. R. H. Cardoza, a fruit exporter in South America, is in possession of 3,000 Ugli oranges. The chemicals from the rinds of all 3,000 oranges would be sufficient to neutralize the gas if the serum is developed and injected efficiently. You have also been informed that the rinds of these oranges are in good condition.

You have also been informed that Dr. J. W. Jones is also urgently seeking purchase of Ugli oranges, and he is aware of Mr. Cardoza's possession of the 3,000 available. Dr. Jones works for a firm with which your firm is highly competitive. There is a great deal of industrial espionage in the pharmaceutical industry. Over the years, your firm and Dr. Jones' have sued each other for violations of industrial espionage laws and infringement of patent rights several times. Litigation on two suits is still in process.

The federal government has asked your firm for assistance. You've been authorized by your firm to approach Mr. Cardoza to purchase 3,000 Ugli oranges. You have been told he will sell them to the highest bidder. Your firm has authorized you to bid as high as $250,000 to obtain the rind of the oranges.

Before approaching Dr. Cardoza, you have decided to talk to Dr. Jones to influence him so that he will not prevent you from purchasing the oranges.

Chapter 18   **Work Stress**

65. STUDENT STRESS MANAGEMENT

PURPOSE:

   To assess the stress level in your life.

GROUP SIZE:

   Any number of groups of 3 to 4 members.

TIME REQUIRED:

   20-35 minutes.

PREPARATION REQUIRED:

   Complete Stress Assessment before class.

EXERCISE SCHEDULE:

1. (pre-class) Fill out and score Stress Assessment.

2. (10-20 minutes) In groups of 3-4 members, discuss responses and total scores of the inventories.

3. (10-15 minutes) The instructor leads a discussion and stress and stress management.

Personal Stress Assessment Inventory--Student Edition[*]

1.   Predisposition.[**]
     Our typical behavior lies somewhere along the line described at the right and left of each
     10-point scale below. Please underline circle the number for each item below to most closely
     describe your customary behavior.

a.   I often feel impatient   1 2 3 4 5 6 7 8 9 10   I seldom feel impatient
     behind slow-poke drivers.   behind slow-poke drivers.

b.   I seldom speak in a loud   1 2 3 4 5 6 7 8 9 10   I often speak in a loud
     voice or use expressive   voice or use expressive
     gestures.   gestures.

c.   I am seldom more precise   1 2 3 4 5 6 7 8 9 10   I am often more precise
     about details than others   about details than others
     are.   are.

d.   I seldom arrive early for   1 2 3 4 5 6 7 8 9 10   I often arrive early for
     appointments.   appointments.

e.   I often get annoyed when   1 2 3 4 5 6 7 8 9 10   I seldom get annoyed when
     I must wait in line.   I must wait in line.

f.   I seldom do several   1 2 3 4 5 6 7 8 9 10   I often do several things
     things simultaneously.   simultaneously.

g.   While involved in one   1 2 3 4 5 6 7 8 9 10   While involved in one task,
     task, I often think ahead   I seldom think ahead to the
     to the next task.   the next task.

h.   I seldom experience annoying 1 2 3 4 5 6 7 8 9 10   I often experience annoying
     or irritating situations.   or irritating situations.

i.   I often have enough time   1 2 3 4 5 6 7 8 9 10   I seldom have enough time for
     for personal errands.   personal errands.

j.   I hear others out fully   1 2 3 4 5 6 7 8 9 10   I anticipate what others will
     without finishing a thought   say and will finish a thought
     for them.   for them.

k.   I often hurry, even when   1 2 3 4 5 6 7 8 9 10   I seldom hurry when I have
     I have plenty of time.   plenty of time.

l.   I seldom eat rapidly.   1 2 3 4 5 6 7 8 9 10   I often eat rapidly.

m.   I often push myself,   1 2 3 4 5 6 7 8 9 10   I seldom push myself when
     even when tired.   I feel tired.

n.   I seldom feel hard-   1 2 3 4 5 6 7 8 9 10   I often feel hard-driving
     driving and competitive.   and competitive.

o.   I often compare my per-   1 2 3 4 5 6 7 8 9 10   I seldom compare my perfor-
     formance with others.   mance with others.

---

[*]By Herbert S. Kindler, Ph.D. Center for Management Effectiveness, P.O. Box 1202, Pacific
Palisades, CA 90272. Used with permission.

[**]Adapted from Type A Behavior and Your Heart by Meyer Friedman and Ray Rosenman,
Fawcett Crest, 1974. Used with Permission.

p. I often feel I haven't   1 2 3 4 5 6 7 8 9 10   I seldom feel I haven't met all
    met all my goals in a day.   my goals in a day.

q. I prefer respect for what 1 2 3 4 5 6 7 8 9 10   I prefer respect for who I am.
    I have achieved.

r. I seldom compare my per-   1 2 3 4 5 6 7 8 9 10   I often compare my performance
    formance to some standard.   to some standard.

s. I often keep my feelings   1 2 3 4 5 6 7 8 9 10   I seldom keep my feelings to
    to myself.   myself.

t. I play to win or excel.   1 2 3 4 5 6 7 8 9 10   I play to relax or have fun.

2. Intermittent Sources of Stress.***

For each of the events that occurred during the <u>past twelve months or so</u>, indicate your emotional impact score (i.e., write in a number from "1" low impact, to "10" major impact). Impact may be positive or negative; scoring only reflects magnitude. "Emotional Impact" is the force that tends to disturb your emotional balance or equilibrium, or the energy you require to get back to "feeling normal." <u>Only score events that occurred</u> - skip items that did not occur during the past 12 months, or that don't apply.

Emotional Impact
   Score

_____   a. I received one or more grades that were unexpected.

_____   b. I wasn't adequately prepared for an assignment or exam.

_____   c. The registration process or its results were frustrating.

_____   d. I made a presentation in class or for an outside activity.

_____   e. I transferred to a new major, department or school.

_____   f. I changed my residence.

_____   g. I achieved a scholastic honor or received other special recognition.

_____   h. I had to complete an unreasonable assignment, or meet a tight
                       deadline, or had too many exams scheduled closely together.

_____   i. I was reprimanded or put on probation.

_____   j. I dropped a course after investing time to master it.

_____   k. I protested a grade I received, or argued with an
                       instructor, teaching assistant or administrator.

_____   l. I got into, or failed to get into, the graduate or professional
                       school I preferred.

***Suggested by "The Social Readjustment Rating Scale," by T. H. Holmes. <u>Journal of Psychosomatic Research</u>, 1967, pp. 213-218. Used with permission.

_____ m. A close friend or family member went through a crisis (such as an accident, illness, divorce or death).

_____ n. I felt really high or low in an intimate relationship.

_____ o. I had an accident or illness, or a chemical dependency problem.

_____ p. I changed smoking, drinking or eating habits.

_____ q. A close friend graduated, transferred or quit school.

_____ r. An important source of income was interrupted, reduced or ended.

_____ s. I was accepted or denied acceptance into a fraternity, sorority, club, activity or team.

If not covered above, add on two emotionally unsettling events or experiences that occurred during the past year or so, and were intermittent in nature. These may be positive or negative such as: a blind date, visit from your parents, seeing someone cheat on an exam, marriage, pregnancy, litigation, car breaking down, etc.

Emotional Impact
    Score

_____ t. _____

_____ u. _____

_____ Total for emotional impact score (a. - u.).

3. Ongoing Sources of Stress

For each of the events that occurred during the past month or so indicate your emotional impact score ("1" low impact, to "10" major impact). After you have assessed the emotional impact (for example, assume you judged a "6" impact), then place the 6 in either column A or B, whichever is applicable. Alternatively, you may divide your score between Columns A and B (for example, scoring "4" in column A, and "2" in column B). Only score events that occurred--skip items that didn't occur or aren't applicable.

Emotional Impact Score	
Events Beyond My Power To Change	Events Within My Power To Change
COLUMN A	COLUMN B
_____	_____
_____	_____
_____	_____
_____	_____
_____	_____
_____	_____
_____	_____
_____	_____
_____	_____
_____	_____
_____	_____
_____	_____
_____	_____
_____	_____
_____	_____
_____	_____
_____	_____
_____	_____
_____	_____
_____	_____
_____	_____

a. My course load or study requirements feel excessive.

b. I find some instructors boring, or I feel inadequately challenged.

c. I haven't enough quiet for study, or have too many distractions.

d. My outside commitments conflict with school work.

e. My class schedule creates problems.

d. My outside commitments conflict with school work.

e. My class schedule creates problems.

f. I feel too much peer or parent pressure.

g. I question what value I get from going to school.

h. My procrastination or cramming create excessive pressure.

i. I have continuing problems with one or more teachers, teaching assistants or the administration.

j. I am uncertain about my career objectives, or future plans.

k. I don't find school socially rewarding, or my standards and preferences conflict with other activities.

l. I miss social support from a relationship, family or roommate.

m. I don't have adequate privacy.

n. My budget is too tight.

o. Transportation creates problems for me (.e.g., parking, commuting, mobility).

p. I am concerned with security on or off campus.

q. Getting the kind of food I prefer is a problem.

r. I don't have easy access to my preferred forms of recreation

s. School facilities, such as the library, health care, or the computer center are inadequate.

t. I feel self-conscious about a personal problem (such as weight, pimples, social ease).

Emotional Impact Score	
Events Beyond My Power To Change	Events Within My Power To Change
COLUMN A	COLUMN B
_____	_____
_____	_____

If not covered above, add on two emotionally unsettling events that occurred during the past month or so (positive or negative).

u. _____

v. _____

Total for Emotional Impact Score:

    Column A _____   Column B _____

4.   Interpreting Your Inventory Scores.

Your scores highlight areas of your life that may be contributing to excessive stress. Should you decide to make changes in your lifestyle, workstyle, diet or exercise patterns, start with a medical checkup.

a. Predisposition: Scoring Key

Insert your answers in Columns 1 and 2. Subtract each Column 2 number from 11 and write in your answer in Column 3. Total Columns 1 and 3.

Column 1	Column 2	Column 3
b. _____	11- _____ a.	= _____
c. _____	11- _____ e.	= _____
d. _____	11- _____ g.	= _____
i. _____	11- _____ o.	= _____
j. _____	11- _____ p.	= _____
l. _____	11- _____ q.	= _____
n. _____	11- _____ s.	= _____
r. _____	11- _____ t.	= _____

TOTAL
COLUMN 1 _____

TOTAL
COLUMN 3 _____

GRAND
TOTAL _____ DIVIDED BY 20 =
(Column 1 + Column 3)

YOUR
PREDISPOSITION
SCORE

Scores above 7.0 reflect "Type A" behavior. Type A behavior is exhibited by persons who are compulsive about time, strive with single-minded dedication to achieve specific quantitative goals, seek approval from others, and see life as a serious competitive game in which they intend to be "winners." While this behavior may have short-term benefits, in the long run it tends to undermine one's health. In fact, research has shown "Type A's" have a much greater risk of dying from a heart attack than "Type B's" do. Scores may be reduced by consciously giving up some control and risking more spontaneity; learning to relax without guilt into more creative hobbies and pure leisure; and focusing more on the quality of one's relationships.

b. **Sources of Stress/Stressors:**

Intermittent Sources of Stress include those life changes that demand and drain energy as one attempts to adjust and restore balance. Scores higher than 50 for stressors suggest attention to finding ways of better pacing with more spacing of future changes.

Ongoing Sources of Stress manifest as the daily "wear and tear" one experiences. Total scores of over 50 suggest the need for more active confrontation and dealing with these ongoing irritants. Where Column A scores "Beyond My Power to Change" are appreciably higher than Column B scores "Within My Power to Change," one may want to take more responsibility for events in one's life in order to feel less helpless and "victimized." Scores below 10 indicate opportunities for growth by being more adventuresome.

c. Overall Stress Factor:

CALCULATING YOUR OVERALL STRESS FACTOR

Predisposition Score   _____[1]

Emotional Impact Score-Inter-   _____
mittent Sources of Stress

Emotional Impact Score-Ongoing
Sources of Stress
   Column A (from page 325)   _____
   Column B (from page 325)   _____

TOTAL SOURCES OF STRESS
(Add the preceding 3 numbers)   _____[2]

OVERALL STRESS FACTOR = [1] x [2]
[1] _____ x [2] _____

= | _____ |
Your Overall Stress Factor

If this number exceeds 700 or so, you should review the high component scores to consider where stress level reductions seem appropriate and feasible.

5. Managing Stress Effectively

Your and Your Stress Source

Intermittent Sources of Stress

When a change occurs in your life, whether self-initiated or not, your equilibrium is disturbed. The energy your require to restore your balance, or homeostasis, reflects the stress level induced by change. Energy absorbed in the process of regaining harmony is not available for other purposes, such as protecting you from illness and accident.

If you are experiencing excessive stress from too many concurrent changes in your work or personal life, be especially kind to yourself, slow your pace, and avoid strenuous effort. Where feasible, defer new commitments or try to space them out over time.

Ongoing Sources of Stress

If you are experiencing excessive stress from enduring a number of abrasive or hostile life events, three overlapping strategies are available to you: (1) You can leave the situation (e.g., change jobs to get away from smog that has become a health hazard for you.); (2) You can attempt to change the situation (e.g., Speak to your teacher when you feel he or she has treated you unfairly; speak with another group member whose performance is concerning you.): (3) Change your own behavior (e.g., Procrastinate less; say "no" more.).

While multiple changes divert energy, adapting to day-in-and-day-out irritation drains it. The cost of excessive adaptation sustained over time is higher risk of illness, lower satisfaction, and impaired effectiveness. In addition to considering the three strategies outlined, also consider asking friends for their help and emotional support.

66. SUPPORT SYSTEMS AND SELF CARE

PURPOSE:

To learn about developing support systems and methods for self-care.

GROUP SIZE:

Any number of groups of 3 to 4 members.

TIME REQUIRED:

25-40 Minutes

PREPARATION REQUIRED:

Complete Exhibit 1, the Support Systems Model in Part B
and the lists in Part C.

EXERCISE SCHEDULE:

1. (pre-class) Complete the inventories.

2. (15-20 minutes) Groups of 3-4 discuss responses and how well each person
   does with support systems and self-care.

3. (10-20 minutes) The instructor leads a discussion on support systems
   and self-care.

PART A: Successful Executives: How Independent American Folklore Values the Notion of
         Independence[*]

   Our heroes--like Franklin Delano Roosevelt, Dwight David Eisenhower, and Lee Iacocca -
- are individuals who appear larger than life. Yet, while they appear individualistic and independent,
such people actually depend on a host of others in their public and private lives.
   Consequently, they achieve success while not being torn apart by the accompanying demands and
stresses. Their attachments to many people through their public and private support networks enable
them to sustain success and manage heavy demands and stresses with a minimum of distress. They
recognize their own limitations and form relationships that enable them to transcend those limits.
Those who are not able to extend themselves in this way may suffer from problems rooted in
separation anxiety that inhibit them from forming healthy attachments to other people.

   In light of these observations executives pursuing success should ask themselves two questions:
(1) Is forming healthy attachments with other people an integral part of my behavior? and (2) Is
separation anxiety a personal problem that poses a health risk to me?   Below is a list of ten
questions. Answer each one.

---

[*]By Jonathan D. Quick, Debra L. Nelson and James Campbell Quick from Academy of
Management Executive, Vol. 1(2), May 1987, 139-45.

Exhibit 1

Forming Healthy Attachments: A Questionnaire

	Yes	No
1. Do you make a strong effort to work alone and in a solitary fashion?	_____	_____
2. Is your work the single most important aspect of your life?	_____	_____
3. Do you regularly and easily spend time with other people during the work day?	_____	_____
4. Do you have a healthy, happy home life?	_____	_____
5. Do you have one or two major nonwork interests?	_____	_____
6. Do you trust at least two other people to have your best interests at heart?	_____	_____
7. Do you think you are the only one who can do a job right?	_____	_____
8. Do you avoid depending on other people because you feel crowded by close relationships?	_____	_____
9. Can you easily ask for help when you need it?	_____	_____
10. Are you frequently suspicious of other people's motives and intentions?	_____	_____

What is Success?

Success has no universal definition, yet it is a goal all executives are expected to pursue. Every occupation and profession has its own culturally derived criteria -- often unwritten -- to serve as the yardsticks of success. For many executives, money and financial wealth may be the key criteria. For still others, it may be progress toward some ideal contained in a philosophical or religious set of beliefs. American corporate culture strictly measures success by upward mobility, defined as increasing wealth, income, and occupational stature. There are, of course, variations. For example, to the president of one of the country's ten leading real estate firms, success means satisfying the needs of each and every customer.

Presidents, board chairmen, and chief executive officers are leaders with strong self-images. The self-image is the way an executive views himself at a particular time. It incorporates strengths, talents, and abilities as well as limitations and shortcomings.

One's self-image operates in conjunction with an ego ideal, which is the way an executive defines personal success. The ego ideal is a partially conscious element of the executive's psychological makeup. It is the ideal self the executive is striving to become.

There is inevitably a dynamic tension between one's self-image and one's ego ideal. This tension provides much of the impetus for an executive's efforts and striving. The tension can never be fully released for the healthy executive because the self-image and ego ideal change over time and never converge. As the gap between the self-image and ego ideal narrows -- the result of the executive's successful efforts -- the ego ideal is modified to serve again as a new goal and road map. The elusive ego ideal can therefore never be reached.

Healthy executives with strong, positive self-images and ego ideals allow themselves to serve as role models for developing executives. Yet they have the capacity to allow those followers freedom of action. That is, they allow a follower to behave independently so long as the follower's behavior complements and supplements their own. They punish those whose behavior directly conflicts with their ego ideal and definition of success, painful as that may be. Rather than being megalomaniacs, these healthy executives recognize their competencies and extend themselves through their followers. The ego ideal serves as the guide for this process.

An executive pursues an ego ideal through some combination of drive, ability, and support from other people. While innate drive and ability can bring an executive success, they alone may not be able to sustain him or her in the face of the demands and stresses that accompany success.

Driving Ambition

Some executives achieve success by combining their natural talents with driving ambition. But in the process they can become overextended and vulnerable by failing to develop the supportive relationships that would allow them to maintain their success. An unfortunate example of this type of executive is Alvin Feldman, president of Continental Airlines, who committed suicide in 1981. Eli Black of United Brands did likewise in 1975, and Vernon Watson of Walston & Company preceded Black in 1964. Problems and poor reactions of a less extreme nature also characterize leaders who become overextended.

A case in point is T. Woodrow Wilson. Wilson is known to have had great ambition and a warm and influential public presence, but he felt very little interest in self-examination and was not comfortable in most relationships. Wilson was also a complex, contradictory person with a narrow range of interests and a "one track" mind. His personal attributes and driving ambition helped him gain substantial success as president of Princeton and President of the United States. However, his tenure was scarred by failures.

Wilson's failures were ones of relationships, not ability or drive. In attempting to install the quad system at Princeton, he relied heavily on his own power and judgment, failing to develop support from various constituencies and exhibiting substantial rigidity. This pattern of isolation and rigidity in a situation that called for flexibility and responsiveness was repeated during his campaign for the League of Nations at the end of his term as President in 1919. He assembled a very partisan and ineffective Peach Commission to herald his "cause" and failed to do the essential political lobbying to make the League of Nations a strong reality. It was precisely when he needed the most support that he exhibited rigidity that interfered with his development of that support. Wilson had sufficient driving ambition and ability to achieve the success he sought, but he lacked the capacity to develop supportive relationships that would have enabled him to sustain and enjoy his success.

Consider the case of Lee Iacocca. Throughout his career Iacocca has coupled his drive and ability with the support of a variety of talented people. This was evident with the Fairlane Committee, which he assembled to develop the Mustang while he was a new vice-president at Ford. It was also evident with the management team he assembled to rebuild Chrysler. In Iacocca: An Autobiography, he writes:

> I was the general in the war to save Chrysler. But I sure didn't do it alone. What I'm most proud of is the coalition I was able to put together. It shows what cooperation can do for you in hard times.

His natural abilities, a strong personal support network, and his diversified management team prevented him from caving in under stress and demands that would have meant failure for many other men and women.

While Iacocca's experiences may be a dramatic illustration, there is little doubt that the pursuit of success involves an assortment of demands and stresses. Clearly, the notion of "stress" is often interpreted pejoratively and viewed as an experience to be avoided. This is unfortunate because stress is an inevitable consequence of the demands an executive experiences in work and at home. Some people even believe that successful individuals are not supposed to "have" stress. This creates a potentially destructive double bind for successful executives: It can encourage them to deny the adverse effects of stress on their health and well-being. Only when one consciously acknowledges the demands and stress he or she feels can action be taken to manage either.

Managing Stress

Some executives are more effective than others at managing stress. Consider an illustration of poor management exhibited by the president of a small, private college in the Southwest. Several years ago when the NCAA instituted its new playoff system, members of the faculty approached him about the conflict between the playoff schedule and final exams. They pressed him to exclude the college's football team from any playoff games on the grounds that participation would conflict with the academic goals of the college. The president, a former literature professor, went along with the request immediately. He informed the trustees and alumni board of his administrative decision and released a brief pres notice about it -- all without consulting the athletic director, football coach, or players. Reacting to a faculty demand in a way that was compatible with all personal values but failing to consult all affected constituencies, he overlooked the relatedness of all organizational life.

Quite understandably, the athletic director, coach, and players were upset, particularly in light of the commitments the coach had made to his players during recruitment. In addition, certain alumni factions were very upset. After much internal conflict at the university, the president reversed his original, hard-line decision and arrived at a patchwork solution: The team would play during the first three playoff seasons -- after which all current students would have graduated -- and then the college would drop out. This solution did not really satisfy the coach, faculty or alumni. Groups of alumni continued writing angry and provocative letters for nearly a year to the president and the alumni newspaper. Several players and the coach had bad feelings for more than a year.

Much of this stress could have been averted had the president originally taken boarder initiative. His reactive action in the face of the faculty demand illustrates that problems can arise when an executive in a stressful situation does not collaborate with all affected constituencies in formulating an appropriate and effective response to a demand.

The president and chief executive officer of a leading international oil-field service corporation responded much differently to a very stressful situation. From 1978 through early 1982, his company experienced remarkable growth and expansion. The corporation doubled its dollar volume revenue, becoming a half-billion-dollar corporation, and expanded to 9,000 employees worldwide. Capital budgets of $150 million to $200 million were set. However, after the second quarter of 1982 the dramatic downturn in the industry occurred, and by 1984 the company had returned to its 1978 level of activity. This meant the company had to reduce the workforce to roughly 5,000 while slashing capital budgets to the $40 million $50 million range.

Both the growth years and the contraction years were stressful for the CEO and company, but the CEO's response to these dramatic changes was neither reactive nor panicky. In an effort to meet the needs of all constituencies -- including shareholders, employees, suppliers, and customers -- he formulated a response that took two forms, one active and one passive. On the one hand, he acted in a slow, deliberate, and methodical manner to gather information and make critical decisions. He describes his behavior very aptly: "Don't overreact to first reports of serious problems. Be patient.

Seek additional information from other sources before arriving at a full appraisal of the situation." Through direct action and decision making, he maintained an active dialogue with all affected constituencies. He never withdrew to make solitary decisions but also was never hesitant to act decisively when the situation dictated such an action.

On the other hand, this CEO was quite capable of seeing the limits of his ability to act and was able to respond positively, -- which meant neither hopelessly or helplessly -- when it was appropriate. For example, he often trusted his subordinates to act effectively on his behalf in dealing with the company's problems. Their abilities, talents, and knowledge complemented his own.

A Leap of Faith

The oil company's CEO was capable of a leap of faith in responding to stressful situations. It is essential for any executive to take such a leap of faith at times because it is not possible for an executive to deal personally with all his or her work demands. Harold Geneen, Chairman of the Board at ITT, has been quoted as saying, "If I had enough arms and legs and time, I would do it all myself. (Allen, p. 13)   But every executive has limits. Reaching one's limits often results in uncertainty, anxiety, and stress. an executive in this position can frantically lash out at the limitation and struggle to overcome it alone, **or** can take a leap of faith and trust others to do what he or she cannot because of time, ability, knowledge, or skill limitations. A reasoned leap of faith, however, involves careful personnel selection, delegation, and honest communication.

Personnel Selection

Successful executives do not select key managers at random; they develop mechanisms for careful, systematic personnel selection. While this does not eliminate the risk that depending on another person entails, it does define and minimize those risks. In building his management team at Chrysler, Iacocca carefully reviewed his personal "black books" developed over the years at Ford, which contained detailed information about the careers of hundreds of Ford executives and managers. After a systematic review of his needs at Chrysler and the special talents of various executives in his books, he chose executives who had particular strengths and competencies that would supplement and complement his own. The president of one of the largest health-care operating companies in the world selects his subordinates in a similar fashion. He chooses men and women he believes are **more** capable than he is -- that is, men and women with talents, skills, or knowledge he doesn't possess. By doing so, he builds a team of executives who are most able to help him achieve his objectives. His own self-confidence ensures that he will not be threatened or frightened by the competence and ability of others. A less secure executive would be too threatened to select the best people.

A naval flag rank officer stationed at the glass house in Washington, D.C. echoes the importance of a talented, capable support staff: "Surround yourself with very competent, capable people... Make sure that they are the best performers that you can get... that they are the best qualified and the best experienced."

The president of the real estate firm mentioned earlier identifies effective personnel selection and training as key factors that keep her firm among the country's top ten residential real estate companies. By selecting agents who are best equipped in drive and interpersonal skills to render excellent service, she assures that customer needs are met. Selection of support staff is also critical, and is undertaken with great care. Her capable, motivated staff have helped her identify industry trends over the past 25 years, which has enabled the firm to stay on the leading edge. In fact, her firm was one of the first, if not the first, to offer corporate relocation services 20 years ago.

Personnel selection is important not only in building a permanent staff, but also in solving particularly difficult or complex problems. While the oil company CEO relied heavily on his subordinates and his board of directors, he also was not hesitant to solicit the specialized knowledge of outside experts to reduce his oil-field service operations. He depended on an assortment of individuals in dealing with his company's difficult problems, yet he took full responsibility for organizing and integrating their efforts and contributions.

Delegation Involves Faith

Unless a chief executive is able to depend on and have faith in the managers recruited, he or she will never delegate work effectively. And the interdependence required in corporate life makes delegation an absolute necessity. As the health-care executive says, "In a large corporation I really think you can't operate by yourself." Once this executive has selected people with particular expertise, he then turns them loose to work quite independently. His organization is very decentralized, and he strongly resists establishing many controls, believing that such centralization inhibits the natural ability of good executives and managers.

The oil company CEO operates in a very similar fashion. He considers it essential to get out of the way of his subordinates once he has given them an assignment, reasoning that involvement would be seen as interference. He is not disinterested in his subordinates' work -- he makes himself available to deal with problems and questions -- but his primary initiative is to delegate the assignment. After that he is primarily a respondent to his personnel as they resolve problems to complete the assignment.

Effective delegation is particularly difficult for an executive who has not established a secure, distinct identity because he or she is not able to trust other people. An executive who has a distinct identity does not depend on other individuals to provide him or her with identity and definition. Such executives know how to rely on themselves **and others**, which is an essential prerequisite to effective delegation.

Honest Communication

The leap of faith executives take in depending on others involves honest communication. The oil company CEO says he places a particularly high value on honest communication and exhibits little tolerance for a lack of honesty or integrity in work relations. In his words, "Speak and act honestly at all times.... (This does not eliminate the need for diplomacy, tact, and silence at times.)" Without fundamental, honest communication, it is difficult to get a firm grasp on problems, dilemmas, and circumstances. The lack of honest communication increases uncertainty and confusion in the work environment, especially for the chief executive.

An important feature of honest communication is the ability to listen to the truth, as told by various constituencies. The health-care executive spends a great deal of time in direct communication with a wide variety of people. He estimates that he spends as much as 70% of his time listening to subordinates, colleagues, and other constituencies. He allows the speaker full expression in order to obtain a clear, accurate sense of the individual's circumstances and/or problems. If his subordinates have problems, he helps them resolve them or obtain resources, expertise, or personnel who can help.

Is Work Their Life?

There are executives whose self-concepts are based on their work. Their identity seems directly related to work. Certainly the very stressful circumstances faced by Lee Iacocca and the oil company president led to periods in which work was an all-consuming emotional drain. For the successful executive who is effective in managing the stress a job entails, however, work will not be the basis of his or her identity -- at least not the primary one. The successful executive does not require other people, objects, or activities to give him or her a sense of identity; instead an identity emerges from within that person. The successful executive does, however, acknowledge his or her dependence on others in successfully executing a job.

The oil company executive is a good illustration here. He communicates with his behavior and department a personal sense of security. And while his work is important to him, it is not overly important. He says, "I can truthfully look you in the eye and say that my work is not the most important thing in my life. It is very important, but it's not the most important thing. To me, my family, my friend, my church, my personal enjoyment of life are actually more important to me than my job." These other aspects give this executive's life balance and wholeness, which is a great source of strength, particularly in stressful times.

The health-care professional's experience is quite similar. His religious faith and his family are very important aspects of his life. His work is very important, but it is not **the** life most important thing. "to me, my religious faith has always been, for as long as I can remember, the motivating factor in my life," he says. "And it has always given me a great sense of comfort. I know, for instance, if I fail at anything I am doing, I'm going to succeed in the **most important part of** my life."

These successful executives are not independent in the traditional sense of the world, but are self-sufficient because they have their own distinct identity. How does this distinct identity develop? How do they deal with the psychological issues of dependence and independence? How are they able to act both independently and dependently at the same time? How are they both separated form the world and yet an integral, involved part of it?

Attachment, Separation Anxiety, and Self Reliance

Attachment
Much of the stress of life grows out of one's feeling of separateness from the world. One of the most natural ways of combating the stress of separateness is through attachment behavior. This pattern of behavior is first exhibited when a child psychologically and physically bonds with the mother, but it becomes generalized to include other people during adolescence and adulthood. One forms a natural, healthy attachment with another person not necessarily when he or she is physically present, but when one has psychological access to that person. Most adults establish comfortable operating rules that ensure access to key people in their lives. The healthiest attachments are ones that have reciprocity and balance. People with whom one forms healthy attachments offer protection from stress by providing information, emotional comfort, feedback and suggestions, and/or defense against the demand or person causing the stress.

Separation Anxiety
The absence or inaccessibility of key attachment figures early in life causes intense anxiety and distress. If this experience occurs frequently and intensely enough, a person's natural ability to seek and form relationships may not develop completely. the result is fear and separation anxiety, which causes people to withdraw prematurely from significant relationships in time of stress or need. People who suffer from separation anxiety problems frequently become angry in response to their own pain over unsatisfied emotional needs. Were it not for the separation anxiety problem, they would be able to form the necessary attachments to meet those emotional needs.

An illustration of an executive who suffers substantial problems with separation anxiety is the chairman of a large commercial bank. He has a very authoritarian and highly directive management style in all of his working relationships, often instructing subordinates with a shaking, pointed index finger and an angry voice. He goes to unusual lengths to avoid depending on others, maintaining a withdrawn and aloof posture with managers and staff in the bank. In addition to typing all of his own memos and failing to confide in either staff or colleagues, he periodically causes conflict by involving himself in details rather than leaving them to others. For example, the chairman frequently interferes with his loan department by directing that certain pet loans be made while others be turned down. His decisions in these cases are not based on the bank's guidelines, but on individual whims and personal preferences that are never clear to his loan officers. His behavior communicates a lack of trust in his loan officers and creates an uncertain and unpredictable atmosphere for them. This chairman exhibits overly individualistic behavior, which signals that he has not achieved a satisfactory ability to form necessary attachments with other people.

Self-Reliance

The John Wayne myth in our culture, which extols the rugged individualist, has some serious limitations that can pose a health risk for the executive who subscribes to it. What is important to note here is the critical difference between independence, as it is often defined, and self-reliance. The self-reliant executive is able to (1) rely comfortably on other people when the demands of the situation warrant such reliance and (2) identify the demands and circumstances that make such reliance appropriate. In general, it is most appropriate for an executive to rely on others when his or her own limitations -- or time, energy, ability, or knowledge -- are reached.

The healthy self-reliant person is also able to reciprocate by being a source of security and strength for others. Thus, as situations and circumstances change, the healthy executive is able to exhibit role reversals, alternately being a source of strength and turning to others for strength. Self-reliance is an important form of responsible behavior. Specifically, it means accepting responsibility for oneself. This involves knowing that one can in fact rely on others or, in other words, having confidence that an attachment figure will be available in time of need. This knowledge and confidence evolve slowly during the early years as the personality develops. People with separation anxiety problems have not developed this self-reliance and self-confidence. This does not mean they cannot develop it; in fact, they **can** develop it.

What to Look For

Executives who are not successfully self-reliant and who experience separation anxiety problems will **not necessarily** have problems with stress. They are, however, at risk because of their difficulty in responding to their need for other people when their own limits are tested. Executives can benefit by observing those who work for them to identify individuals who might have problems coping with stressful situations. They also should examine themselves.

Turn back to your answers to the questions. A "No" for Questions 1, 2, 7, 8, and 10 and a "Yes" for Questions 3, 4, 5, 6, and 9 suggest that you are a successfully self-reliant person. If your answers are the reverse, you may need to learn how to become more self-reliant. Observing those with whom you work and listening to their dialogue will give you clues as to how they might answer these questions and how successful they are in achieving self-reliance.

Observing Other Executives

As a senior executive, you may be concerned about whether your subordinates have problems with separation anxiety and self-reliant behavior. If your subordinates are not self-reliant, you should be aware that they may not respond well in stressful situations and may have difficulty asking for help in such situations. They may be more vulnerable to break down under severe or prolonged stress. Such was the case for Alvin Feldman. During his presidency, Continental Airlines faced a long strike by flight attendants, a hijack incident, and a rough takeover campaign by a competitor. One of Feldman's colleagues remarked that Feldman felt alone with the responsibility and carried this singular responsibility too far. The demands of the industry and his own difficulties in responding or seeking support no doubt contributed to his suicide.

Executives who lack balanced and diversified interpersonal relationships are potential time bonds that need careful attention. They should not be given excessive responsibilities, nor should they be exposed to highly stressful situations. Encouraging those managers to cultivate relationships of various sorts and helping them resolve internal obstacles to this effort will be invaluable to them in their career and life. In addition to putting themselves at risk, those executives create stress and strain for those around them. They react to internal needs and feelings triggered by a particular stressor or demand instead of formulating constructive courses of action with clearly identified consequences and outcomes. They do not recognize the truth about themselves -- their limitations, strengths, and needs.

Observing Oneself

If an executive is not self-reliant, he or she cannot become self-reliant alone. Because attachment and separation are interpersonal issues, interpersonal work is needed to achieve healthy self-reliance. A strong, supportive father figure or mentor in the work environment or a competent counselor may help an executive become self-reliant. The task involves confronting old conflicts and at the same time developing new skills.

It is a difficult task because an executive who has separation anxiety problems will have a reflex action that will encourage him or her to avoid close personal and professional working relationships. Keep in mind that this may be a faulty reflex action. It can become a particular problem when an executive assumes a new position or relocates to a new living environment, situations in which it is important to cultivate the various relationships essential to meeting new demands, challenges, and stresses. Without a conscious effort to cultivate such relationships, the executive with an unresolved separation anxiety problem may slide into a need deficit from which it is sometimes difficult to recover.

Successfully self-reliant executives **do not** face fewer demands in life than do executives who are less self-reliant. In fact, they may even accept **more** demands and challenges. But they are able to manage the demands and stresses they do experience more effectively because they understand their own limits and the professional and personal networks essential to complement and supplement their natural abilities. In this way they are able to sustain the success they pursue and achieve.

References

Allen, Steven A. "International Telephone and Telegraph(A)." Harvard Business School Case (9-472-007/Rev. 10/80).

Iacocca, Lee. Iaccoca: An Autobiography. Toronto: Bantom Books, 1984.

Levinson, Harry and Stuart Rosenthal. CEO: Corporate Leadership in Action. New York: Basic Books, 1984.

Quick, James C. and Jonathan D. Quick. Organizational Stress and PreventiveManagement. New York: McGraw-Hill Book Company, 1984.

PART B: Support Systems[**]

Fill in as many of the boxes as you can with names of people who are supportive of you in the ways indicated.

	Personal	Professional/ School
Challenger: Someone who tells you when you are doing something wrong.		
Questioner: Someone who probes your motives or forces you to think through plans		
Comforter: Someone who listens when you are upset		
Celebrator: Someone to whom you can "toot your horn"		

PART C: Self Care[***]

One of the most important steps in self-care is to truly accept that it is legitimate to take care of yourself. You <u>must</u> take care of yourself. You are in transition, making changes, adding to your store of knowledge. Some thoughts and feelings that you have not experienced over a long time might be coming into your awareness. This is a vulnerable time. Do not deny this: you have done that long enough. Taking care of yourself might involve taking breaks, moving slowly, as well as thinking over the differences between what you feel, what you think, and how you behave. Taking care of yourself also means giving yourself permission to set new priorities. Your first priority right now can be to take care of your recovery - not the recovery of your family.

Be gentle with yourself. Remember you are growing. Success is beginning to take steps forward. Complement yourself for starting a new path. Give to yourself. It's time to learn. Start with small steps, scheduling activities and time with people who will nourish you. Surround yourself with people, who can understand and who care about you. That in itself may be a new behavior.

[**]Adapted from Janice Eddy, President of Janice Eddy, Inc. Business Consultants. Used with permission.

[***]Adapted from Herbert Gravitz and Juli Bowden, "Self Care," <u>Guide to Recovery</u>. Simon and Schuster, 1985.

Self-Esteem and Self-Care****

Ten Things I like about myself:

1.

2.

3.

4.

5.

6.

7.

8.

9.

10.

Recent "fun" experiences:

1.

2.

3.

4.

How I take care of myself:

1.

2.

3.

4.

Goals to have fun and take care of myself:

1.

2.

3.

4.

5.

Chapter 19   **Career Planning and Development**

67. PROFESSIONAL SKILLS ASSESSMENT[*]

PURPOSE:

To assess your professional skills.

GROUP SIZE:

Any number of groups of two to three members.

TIME REQUIRED:

Discussion: 30-50 minutes.

PREPARATION REQUIRED:

1. Read the "Introduction" below.
2. Complete the Professional Skills Assessment Questionnaire before class.

MATERIALS:

15 pieces of paper or 15 index cards.

RELATED TOPICS:

Goal Setting

---

[*]By Fernando Bartolome and Diane McKinney Kellogg. Used with permission.

INTRODUCTION:

Any job you have or career you choose should provide for you an opportunity for both success and enjoyment. The following instrument is designed to help you identify the professional skills which you both enjoy using and have in the past had some success using.

Discovering these skills can be important to your future planning. A career built not only on your strengths, but on the strengths (or skills) you enjoy using is a career that can promise you greater satisfaction.

The following process for identifying the professional skills you both use successfully and enjoy using is an enlightening one. Have fun with it!

EXERCISE SCHEDULE:

PART A - (15-30 min.--do before class)

1. Think about achievements in your life since you graduated from high school. Remember that an achievement is defined as a task or activity that you completed which you both enjoyed and excelled at. As a task or activity it should be somewhat specific and discrete. For example, becoming more self-confident is certainly an accomplishment, but using your self-confidence to negotiate a raise would be an achievement. It can be in a work or non-work setting. Other people may or may not have recognized it as an achievement, but to you it was a successful and enjoyable undertaking.

    On 15 different pieces of paper or index cards, list the 15 most prominent achievements. If you get stuck, leave them for awhile, but do return to complete 15. (If you list more, feel free to do so.)

    Sort the 15 achievements in descending order from most important to least.

    List the first 10 achievements in the 10 columns on the next three pages of this book.

    Taking each achievement, one at a time, go down the column of the 14 Professional Skills listed and check each of those you used in completing that particular achievement.

    After completing this process for all ten achievements, total the check-marks across and record in the Skill Total column the total number of times you checked each professional skill.

    To summarize your findings, list the seven professional skills you checked most often (in rank order from most to least) under "SUMMARY." These are the skills you most enjoy using, and perhaps are most motivated to use.

Write on top of each column a single word
or phrase to describe each achievement.

QUESTIONNAIRE	1	2	3	4	5	6	7	8	9	10	Skill Total
1. <u>Analytical Skills</u> Comparing, evaluating and understanding complex pro- <u>blems or situations.</u>											
2. <u>Interpersonal Communication</u> <u>Skills</u> Speaking with clarity, addressing both thoughts and feelings, clarifying misunderstandings, and listening effectively, through use of questions, reflecting skills, and attention to non-verbal <u>cues.</u>											
3. <u>Making Presentations</u> Presenting ideas to groups of people, with attention to audience response as well as effectively structuring presentation <u>of information.</u>											
4. <u>Writing Skills</u> Writing with clarity, conciseness, good logic, with appropriate attention <u>to creativity if called for.</u>											
5. <u>Manipulating Data and</u> <u>Numbers</u> Processing information and numbers skillfully, plan- ning and administering budgets, preparing <u>statistical reports.</u>											
6. <u>Entrepreneural Skills and</u> <u>Innovation</u> Recognizing and seizing opportunities for new ideas or products, creating new services or processes or <u>products.</u>											
7. <u>Leading and Managing Others</u> Inspiring others, assessing other's abilities, dele- gating effectively, moti- vating others to achieve a set of goals, setting <u>priorities.</u>											

Write on top of each column a single word
or phrase to describe each achievement.

QUESTIONNAIRE, Cont'd.

	1	2	3	4	5	6	7	8	9	10	Skill Total
8. **Learning Skills** Grasping new information quickly, using common sense to deal with new situations, using feedback from others to increase my effectiveness											
9. **Team Membership Skills** Working well on committees, incorporating a variety of perspectives toward a common goal.											
10. **Human Conflict Resolution Skills** Dealing with differences of personality and/or opinion, confronting others effectively, taking responsibility for my "share" of the conflict.											
11. **Developing, Helping, Teaching, Training Others** Encouraging, guiding, and evaluating others; explaining and/or demonstrating new ideas or skills, creating an environment for learning and growth.											
12. **Technical Competence** Demonstrating skill in specific functional areas; i.e., engineering, marketing, financial analysis or whatever.											

Add below any additional skills that you saw manifested in your accomplishments.

	1	2	3	4	5	6	7	8	9	10	
13.											
14.											
15.											

SUMMARY:

MOTIVATED SKILLS

List the 7 professional skills you have most often used (from most to least).

1.

2.

3.

4.

5.

6.

7.

PART B - (20 minutes--before class)

Complete "Analyzing Your Current Job Against Your Ideal" if you are currently or recently employed. This will help you analyze the extent to which your current or recent job gives you the opportunity to use the Professional Skills you most enjoy using.

ANALYZING YOUR CURRENT JOB AGAINST YOUR IDEAL

1. Assuming your list of seven skills accurately reflects the skills
   you would most enjoy using, you might consider this to be a list
   of skills you would have the opportunity to use in your ideal job.
   List the seven skills in column A below, adding others which you
   feel belong there.

   In column B evaluate the extent to which you use each skill in
   doing your current job. Use this scale:

There are plenty	7 6 5 4 3 2 1	No opportunities
of opportunities to		to use this
use this skill		skill at all

   In column C evaluate the extent to which you could realistically
   reshape your current job to give you more opportunities to use
   this skill. Use this scale:

Extremely easy to	7 6 5 4 3 2 1	Impossible to
add to my current		add to my
job		current job

2. If your present job is too far away from your ideal, and too difficult to reshape, begin thinking about other jobs which might come closer to your ideal job--providing more opportunities for you to do the things you do well and enjoy!

(A) Skills I Enjoy Using	(B) Opportunities for Using This Skill in my Job	(C) Potential for Reshaping my Job
1.		
2.		
3.		
4.		
5.		
6.		
7.		
8.		
9.		
10.		

PART C - Discussion

(Steps 1, 2, and 3, 20-30 min.)

1. In groups of 2 to 3 discuss the responses on the questionnaire and the table. You may exchange questionnaires, compare results and help each other analyze findings.

2. What is the most important thing you learned about yourself from this exercise?

3. For which career areas would your skills be appropriate?

4. (15-20 min.) The instructor will lead a class discussion covering the areas of skill assessment and goal setting.

68. MARRIAGE/CAREER EXPECTATION QUESTIONNAIRE*

PURPOSE:

To explore career and marriage expectations.

GROUP SIZE:

Any number of groups of 4 to 6 members.

TIME REQUIRED:

30-45 minutes.

PREPARATION REQUIRED:

Complete one of the questionnaires
before class.

RELATED TOPICS:

Interpersonal Communication

EXERCISE SCHEDULE:

1. (20-30 min.) Meet in mixed-sex groups of 4 to 6 members,
   and discuss responses.

   Questions: a. Which items had the most disagreement?
                   b. What was learned about your career and
                       marriage expectations?

2. (10-15 min.) Groups will report to the whole class on items
   of most disagreement.

MARRIAGE CAREER EXPECTATION INVENTORY
FEMALE FORM

Strongly Agree   Neutral   Strongly Disagree
   1   2   3   4   5

_____ 1. It will be preferable for my husband to have at least as much or more education than I do.

_____ 2. I expect to fully develop my career and for my husband to encourage me.

_____ 3. If I am not employed, I will do all the housework; if I am employed, I will expect my husband to help somewhat.

_____ 4. I expect to stay home full-time with our children.

_____ 5. It is preferable for my husband to make most of the financial decisions, regardless of whether (and how much) income I would bring to the household.

_____ 6. Weekends will be time for my husband to relax, watch TV, etc., and I will strive to keep distractions (i.e., visitors, children) to a minimum for him.

_____ 7. Substitute mothers can do an excellent job and will take care of our children while I work.

_____ 8. I expect to have the major responsibility of raising our children, regardless of whether I am employed or not.

_____ 9. If there is a disagreement which we cannot resolve, I think the wife should most often give in to the husband.

_____ 10. I expect to take some vacations either a) by myself, or b) with my husband, but no children.

_____ 11. I may not want children, since I want to develop my career.

_____ 12. I expect to be able to continue my education if I wish, even if we have children.

_____ 13. I expect to be able to go out in the evening with my friends.

_____ 14. Yard work and fix-it tasks will mainly be done by my husband.

_____ 15. If my husband gets an excellent job offer elsewhere, I will expect to pick up and move to the new place. Therefore, his career will be more important than mine.

_____ 16. I expect that my husband will at some times have to put his career before our family, but I will not.

MARRIAGE/CAREER EXPECTATION INVENTORY
MALE FORM

| Strongly Agree | | Neutral | | Strongly Disagree |
| 1 | 2 | 3 | 4 | 5 |

_____ 1. It will be preferable for me to have at least as much or more education than my wife.

_____ 2. I expect my wife to fully develop her career and I will encourage her.

_____ 3. If my wife is not employed, I will expect her to do all the housework; if she is employed I will help somewhat.

_____ 4. I expect my wife to stay home full-time with our children.

_____ 5. It is preferable for me to make most of the financial decisions, regardless of whether (and how much) income is brought to the household by my wife.

_____ 6. Weekends will be time for me to relax, watch TV, etc., and I expect my wife to keep distractions (i.e., visitors, children) to a minimum for me.

_____ 7. Substitute mothers can do an excellent job and will take care of our children while my wife works.

_____ 8. I expect my wife to have the major responsibility for raising our children, regardless of whether she is employed or not.

_____ 9. If there is a disagreement which we cannot resolve, I think the wife should most often give in to the husband.

_____ 10. I expect to take some vacations either a) by myself, or b) with my wife, but no children.

_____ 11. We may not want children since I expect my wife to develop her career.

_____ 12. I expect my wife to be able to continue her education if she wishes, even if we have children.

_____ 13. I expect my wife to go out in the evening with her friends, as I do with mine.

_____ 14. Yard work and fix-it tasks will mainly be done by me.

_____ 15. If I get an excellent job offer elsewhere, I will expect my wife to pick up and move to the new place. Therefore, my career will be more important than hers.

_____ 16. I expect at some times to put my career before our family, but my wife will not.

69. CAREER COUNSELING*

PURPOSE:

1. To practice career counseling skills.
2. To learn to build trust in a superior-subordinate relationship.
3. To learn how to collect information in a trust-enhancing manner.

GROUP SIZE:

Any number of dyads.

TIME REQUIRED:

50-70 minutes.

RELATED TOPICS:

Dynamics within Groups
Interpersonal Communication

EXERCISE SCHEDULE:

1. (5-10 min.) Instructor gives a background on the importance of "knowing the subordinates."

2. (5 min.) Class divides into dyads. Each person should pair with someone known <u>less well</u>. Dyad members decide who will be superior and who will be subordinate.

3. For the superior:
"You will have 20 minutes to get to know your subordinate. You will want to know that person's skills and experience, interests and aspirations, undeveloped abilities, things that person does well and not so well."

"You hired this employee about a month ago (so you are not selling that person into taking a job). However, you were under severe time pressure and even though this individual was the strongest candidate, you didn't get a chance to know that person as fully as you wanted to. Now that things have settled down a bit, you have set up this meeting to really get to know your subordinate."

---

*Adapted from David K. Bradford, "An Exercise on Career Counseling." <u>Organizational Behavior Teaching Review</u>, Vol. XI (2), 1986-87, pp. 114-116. Used with permission.

For the subordinate:
"First of all, be yourself. That is, don't make up information. But there is a difference between 'telling the truth' and 'telling the **whole** truth.' You know that every boss says 'I want to get to know you' but how will that person use this information? - will it be for you or against you?

"In terms of how open and honest to be, take your cue from your superior. Just because he/she smiles, doesn't mean that you automatically will fully self-disclose, warts and all. If your superior does things that makes you feel safe opening up, do so. If not, just say what you feel comfortable telling."

3. (15-20 min.) Dyads meet.

4. (5 min.) After the meeting, dyads have a new assignment.
    For the superior:
    "On the basis of what you have heard, think of a job that would really motivate and excite your subordinate. Don't worry about salary; pay attention to the characteristics of the job."

    "There is only one restriction; you **cannot** use a job that the subordinate told you would really turn him/her on."

    For the subordinate:
    "Write down what your superior did that made you want to fully open up and disclose. Also write down what your superior did that kept you closed (or made you even more guarded)."

5. (5 min.) In each dyad, the boss tells the subordinate the selected job. The subordinate indicates the extent to which the boss was on target using the scale below:

"Totally Missed it"		"O.K."		"Really Hit it"
1	2	3	4	5

    The instructor gets a frequency distribution form the subordinates.

6. (5-10 min.) The subordinates give the superior feedback on (a) what he/she did that led to full self-disclosure, and (b) what the superior did that caused the subordinate to feel guarded.

7. (10-15 min.) The instructor leads a discussion and writes down responses to (a) and (b) above on the board.

Chapter 20 Organization Development and Change

70. FORCE FIELD ANALYSIS

PURPOSE:

To apply Lewin's Force Field Analysis Model to a problem in your life.

GROUP SIZE:

Any number of groups of 3-4.

TIME REQUIRED:

40-45 minutes.

PREPARATION REQUIRED:

Read the "Introduction".

INTRODUCTION:

A Force-Field Analysis is one way to assess what is happening in an organization. This concept reflects the forces, driving and restraining, at work at a particular time. It helps to assess organizational strengths and to select forces to add or remove in order to create change. The theory of change suggested by Kurt Lewin, who developed the force field analysis, is that while driving forces may be more easily affected, shifting them could increase opposition (tension and/or conflict) within the organization and add restraining forces. Therefore, it may be more effective to remove restraining forces to create change.

The use of the force-field analysis will demonstrate the range of forces pressing on an organization at a particular time. This analysis can increase the organization's optimism that it is possible to strategize and plan for change.

Example--Trying to increase student participation in Student Government.

```
        Driving Forces                        Restraining Forces

   More money allocated             <--- High emphasis on grades--
   for Student Govt. activities.         a need to study more.
                    ----->
                                     <--- Other activities, cultural,
   Better publicity and public            social, sports--divert
   relations programs for   ----->        interest.
   Student Government.
                                     <--- Not much public relations
                                           work in the past.
   Student Government representa-
   tives to to classes and explain   <--- Students do not see Student
   positive effects of student             Government as effective or
   govt. decisions.        ----->          helping them get a job.


   Special Career programs offered
   for Student Govt. participants.
                    ----->
   _____|_____
                          Present
                          balance
                          point
```

EXERCISE SCHEDULE:

1. (10-15 min.) Complete the Problem Analysis section and fill in the   model.

2. (20 min.) In groups of 3-4, discuss the driving and restraining forces in each person's problem.

3. (10 min.) Class discussion

   a. Why is it useful to break a problem situation up into driving and restraining forces?
   b. Would the model be used any differently whether applied to an individual or organizational problem?

Problem Analysis.

1. Describe the problem in a few words.

2. A list of forces driving toward change would include:
    a.
    b.
    c.
    d.
    e.
    f.

3. A list of forces restraining change would include:
    a.
    b.
    c.
    d.
    e.
    f.

4. Put the driving and restraining forces of the problem on the
    force-field analysis below, according to their degree of
    impact on change.

FORCE FIELD ANALYSIS

_____Driving Forces   Restraining Forces_____

------------------------ >   < -------------------------------

low extreme--_____|_____high extreme--
try to avoid   try to attain
                        present
                      balance point

71. AN ANCIENT TALE*

PURPOSE:

To analyze issues of organization, boundary, membership and responsibility for change.

GROUP SIZE:

Any number of groups of three to four members.

TIME REQUIRED:

35 to 40 minutes.

PREPARATION REQUIRED:

Read the "Introduction" below and complete Part A.

INTRODUCTION:

To understand, analyze, and improve organizations, we must carefully think through the issue of who is responsible for what activities in different organizational settings. Often we hold responsible someone who has no control over the outcome, or we fail to teach or train someone who could make the vital difference.

To explore this issue, the following exercise could be conducted on either an individual or group basis. It provides an opportunity to see how different individuals assign responsibility for an event. It is also a good opportunity to discuss the concept of organizational boundaries (what is the organization, who is in or out, etc.)

PART A - Case Study

You should read the short story and respond quickly to the first three questions. Then take a little more time on questions four through six. The results, criteria, and implications could then be discussed in groups.

> Long ago in an ancient kingdom there lived a princess who was very young and very beautiful. The princess, recently married, lived in a large and luxurious castle with her husband, a powerful and wealthy lord. The young princess was not content, however, to sit and eat strawberries by herself while her husband took frequent and long journeys to neighboring kingdoms. She felt neglected and soon became quite unhappy. One day, while she was alone in the castle gardens, a handsome vagabond rode out of the forest bordering the castle. He spied the beautiful princess, quickly won her heart, and carried her away with him.

---

*By J.B. Ritchie and Paul Thompson Reprinted by permission from Organization and People: Readings, Cases and Exercises in Organizational Behavior. Copyright 1980 by West Publishing, pp. 68-70. All rights reserved.

Following a day of dalliance, the young princess found herself ruthlessly abandoned by the vagabond. She then discovered that the only way back to the castle led through the bewitched forest of the wicked sorcerer. 'Fearing to venture into the forest unaccompanied, she sought out her kind and wise godfather. She explained her plight, begged forgiveness of the godfather, and asked his assistance in returning home before her husband returned. The godfather, however, surprised and shocked at her behavior, refused forgiveness and denied her any assistance. Discouraged but still determined, the princess disguised her identity and sought the help of the most noble of all the kingdom's knights. After hearing the sad story, the knight pledged his unfailing aid--for a modest fee. But alas, the princess had no money and the knight rode away to save other damsels.

The beautiful princess had no one else from whom she might seek help, and decided to brave the great peril alone. She followed the safest path she knew, but when she was almost through the forest, the wicked sorcerer spied her and caused her to be devoured by the fire-breathing dragon.

1. Who was inside the organization and who was outside? Where were the boundaries?

2. Who is most responsible for the death of the beautiful princess?

3. Who is next most responsible? Least responsible?

4. What is your criterion for the above decisions?

5. What interventions would you suggest to prevent a recurrence?

6. What are the implications for <u>organizational development and change</u>?

	Most Responsible	Next Most Responsible	Least Responsible
Princess			
Husband			
Vagabond			
Godfather			
Knight			
Sorcerer			

Check one character in each column.

PART B: GROUP DISCUSSION

1. (20 min.) In groups of 3-4 discuss your answers.

2. (15-20 min.) Report to the whole class.

72. ORGANIZATIONAL ASSESSMENT OF CAMPUS*

PURPOSE:

To apply organizational development concepts.

GROUP SIZE:

Any number of groups of 4-8 members.

TIME REQUIRED:

40-60 minutes.

INTRODUCTION:

One of the first steps in organization development is doing an organizational assessment to evaluate the strengths and weaknesses of the organization. You and your team have been hired as a consulting group by the university to assess the strengths and weaknesses of the university. You are to collect data from your group members in these five areas:

1. Academics and scholarly environment.
2. Quality of teaching on campus.
3. Campus social life.
4. Cultural events on campus.
5. Management by the university administration.

After you have gathered the data, evaluate the strengths and weaknesses and make recommendations for intervention. These recommendations must be very specific so the university administration could implement them tomorrow without any more explanation. Avoid saying things like, "teachers need to lecture better." Be specific by saying things such as, "we found 10% of the teachers didn't talk loud enough in class" or "50% of them get off the subject too frequently."

EXERCISE SCHEDULE:

1. (15-25 min.) Groups form and evaluate strengths and weaknesses of university, using Campus Profile Assessment. Prepare recommendations for interactions.

2. (15-20 min.) Each group presents its strengths, weaknesses, recommendations.

3. (10-15 min.) Instructor leads a discussion on organization development concepts applied on campus.

Project Option
Instead of an in class exercise, this may be assigned as a project. Each group would go and "collect" data from students, faculty and administrators and present the data analysis to the class along with recommended interactions.
Optional: The instructor may assign a paper to be done in conjunction with the presentation.

Campus Profile and Assessment

I. <u>Academics</u>

Not True   1   2   3   4   5   Very True

    1 2 3 4 5 1. There is a wide range of courses to choose from.

    1 2 3 4 5 2. Classroom standards are too easy.

    1 2 3 4 5 3. The library is adequate.

    1 2 3 4 5 4. Textbooks are helpful.

II. <u>Teachers</u>

    1 2 3 4 5 1. Teachers here are committed to quality instruction.

    1 2 3 4 5 2. We have a high quality faculty.

III. <u>Social</u>

    1 2 3 4 5 1. Students are friendly to one another.

    1 2 3 4 5 2. It's difficulty to make friends.

    1 2 3 4 5 3. Faculty get involved in student activities.

    1 2 3 4 5 4. Too much energy goes into drinking and goofing off.

IV. <u>Cultural Events</u>

    1 2 3 4 5 1. There are ample activities on campus.

    1 2 3 4 5 2. Student activities are boring.

    1 2 3 4 5 3. The administration places on high value on student activities.

    1 2 3 4 5 4. Too much emphasis is placed on sports.

    1 2 3 4 5 5. We need more "cultural" activities.

V. <u>Organizational/Management</u>

    1 2 3 4 5 1. Decision-making is shared at all levels of the organization.

    1 2 3 4 5 2. There is unity and cohesiveness between departments and units.

    1 2 3 4 5 3. Too many departmental clashes hamper the organization's effectiveness.

    1 2 3 4 5 4. Students have a say in many decisions.

    1 2 3 4 5 5. The budgeting process seems fair.

    1 2 3 4 5 6. Recruiting and staffing are handled thoughtfully with student needs in mind.

Identify Organizations Strengths

1. In Academics:

2. In Teaching:

3. In Social:

4. In Cultural Activities:

5. In Campus Management:

Identify Organizations Weaknesses

1. In Academics:

2. In Teaching:

3. In Social:

4. In Cultural Activities:

5. In Campus Management:

What Interventions (in each of the five areas) would you recommend to resolve weaknesses and build on strengths?

1. In Academics: a.

              b.

2. In Teaching: a.

              b.

3. In Social: a.

              b.

4. In Cultural Activities: a.

                b.

5. In Campus Management: a.

                b.

Chapter 21   **Developing Creativity**

73. CREATIVITY AND LEFT/RIGHT BRAIN THINKING[*]

PURPOSE:

    1. To measure different aspects of creativity.
    2. To examine differences in left and right brain thinking.

GROUP SIZE:

    Any number.

TIME REQUIRED:

    20-30 minutes.

PREPARATION REQUIRED:

    1. Complete and score the Creativity Inventory.
    2. Read "Left/Right Brian Thinking."

RELATED TOPICS:

    Learning and Reinforcement

---

[*] Adapted from Eugene Raudsepp. From <u>How Creative Are You?</u> New York: G. P. Putnam, 1981, pp. 18-20, 23-39 and 103-138. Used with permission.

EXERCISE SCHEDULE:

1. (Pre-Class) Complete and score the creativity inventory and read the left-right brain background and decide whether you are more left or right brain oriented.

2. (20-30 minutes) The instructor will lead a group discussion on the importance of creativity in a modern society and the characteristics of the creative individual. Also, answer the following questions.
   a. In what situations is creativity most useful?
   b. How can you enhance your own creativity?
   c. Are there times when creativity may be a hinderance?
   d. Who "fits in" better: a creative or non-creative person? Why?

INTRODUCTION:

We are now confronting an accelerating rate of change in new technologies, socio-economic trends, and new attitudes and values. The "enervating eighties" promise to bring us, among other problems and challenges: (1) economic uncertainty, (2) rising costs, (3) scarcity of resources, (4) sharper competition, (5) a greater influence of international events in domestic affairs, (6) quicker paced demographic changes, (7) rising consumer discontent, (8) greater emphasis on the quality of work life, (9) the specter of more government regulation, and (10) growing employee discontent with the corporate world of work.

To cope with the uncertainty and complexity that these and other new situations, challenges and problems present, everyone needs to become more creative, imaginative and resourceful. The crucial question is, are you creative enough to meet tomorrow's challenges?

INVENTORY
ATTITUDES TOWARDS WORK

A = Agree   B = In-between or Don't Know   C = Disagree

1. I place relatively greater values on rewards such as salary and status than on "job interest" and "challenge." _____
2. I always work with a great deal of certainty that I'm following the correct procedures for solving a particular problem. _____
3. I like work that has regular hours. _____
4. One of my primary concerns is to discover the kind of work that would be most natural for me to do, most inclusive of and challenging to all my capacities. _____
5. I prefer specific instructions to those which leave many details optional. _____
6. I concentrate harder than most people on whatever interests me. _____
7. I usually work things out for myself rather than get someone to show me. _____
8. I apply myself longer and harder in the absence of external pressure than do most people. _____
9. I seldom get behind in my work. _____
10. I don't enjoy tackling a job that might involve many unknown difficulties. _____
11. I seldom begin work on a problem that I can only dimly sense and not yet express. _____
12. I am more inclined to derive my major satisfactions from people than from my work. _____
13. I don't mind routine work if I have to do it. _____
14. I sometimes get so involved with a new idea that I forget to do the things I ought to be doing. _____
15. I regard myself more as a "specialist" than a "generalist." _____

PROBLEM SOLVING BEHAVIORS

16. I prefer tackling problems for which there are precise answers. _____

17. When a certain approach to a problem doesn't work, I can easily drop it.
18. Intuitive hunches are unreliable guides in problem-solving. _____
19. I have never felt very inspired. _____
20. I don't like to ask questions that show ignorance. _____
21. I get irritated when somebody interrupts me when I'm working on something I really enjoy. _____
22. I often get my best ideas when doing nothing in particular. _____
23. Ideas often run through my head preventing sleep. _____
24. In evaluating information, the source of it is more important to me than the content. _____
25. I feel that a logical step-by-step method is best for solving problems. _____
26. People who are willing to entertain "crackpot" ideas are impractical. _____
27. Complex problems and situations have no appeal to me. _____
28. I have vivid imagery. _____
29. I cannot get excited about ideas that may never lead to anything. _____
30. Daydreaming has provided the impetus for many of my more important projects. _____

INTERESTS

31. If I were a college professor, I would rather teach fact courses than those involving theory. _____
32. I sometimes "get lost" in the library for hours on end, just browsing and looking at interesting books. _____
33. I have broader interests and am more widely informed than are most people of equal intelligence and educational background. _____
34. I have many hobbies. _____
35. I can learn more from self-instruction than through taking courses. _____
36. I like hobbies that involve collecting things. _____

PERSONALITY DIMENSIONS

37. I always consider carefully the consequences of each of my actions.
38. People often say that I'm somewhat absent-minded. _____
39. I keep my things well organized. _____

40. I like to stick my neck out even if it is not well warranted. _____
41. I resent things being uncertain and unpredictable. _____
42. The room in which I work is quite cluttered and messy. _____

SCORING KEY

ATTITUDES TOWARDS WORK

	A	B	C
1.	-1	0	+1
2.	0	+1	0
3.	0	+1	0
4.	+2	0	-2
5.	-1	0	+1
6.	+2	0	-2
7.	+1	+2	0
8.	+1	0	-1
9.	-1	0	+1
10.	-1	0	+1
11.	-1	0	+1
12.	-1	0	+1
13.	0	+1	+2
14.	+1	0	-1
15.	-1	0	+1

INTERESTS

	A	B	C
31.	-1	0	+1
32.	+1	0	-1
33.	+2	0	-2
34.	+1	0	-1
35.	+1	0	-1
36.	-1	0	+1

PERSONALITY DIMENSIONS

37.	-1	0	+1
38.	+1	0	-1
39.	-1	0	+1
40.	+1	0	-1
41.	-1	0	+1
42.	+1	0	-1

PROBLEM SOLVING BEHAVIORS

	A	B	C
16.	-1	0	+1
17.	+1	0	-1
18.	-2	0	+2
19.	-2	0	+2
20.	-1	0	+1
21.	+1	0	-1
22.	+1	0	-1
23.	+1	+2	0
24.	-2	0	+2
25.	-2	0	+2
26.	-1	0	+1
27.	-1	0	+1
28.	+1	0	-1
29.	-1	0	+1
30.	+2	0	-2

YOUR TOTAL SCORE

43	-	54	Especially Creative
27	-	42	Very Creative
12	-	26	Above Average
5	-	11	Average
-2	-	-4	Below Average
-38	-	-3	Non Creative

3. Characteristics of the Creative Person.

    a. <u>Fluency</u> - the ability to generate and juggle a large number of ideas when confronting a problem.

    b. <u>Flexibility</u> - the ability to explore a wide variety of approaches to the problem and to adapt quickly when necessary.

    c. <u>Sensitivity to Problems</u> - can see the challenges that have escaped the attention of others.

    d. <u>Originality</u> - thoughts not jammed up with stereotypes and can think of more unique solutions.

    e. <u>Curiosity</u> - high imagination, fantasy-making and interest beyond one's own specialization (intellectually restless).

    f. <u>Openness to Feelings and the Unconscious</u> - more energy common, more impulsive and more responsive to emotions.

    g. <u>Motivation</u> - a strong desire to create.

    h. <u>Persistence and Concentration</u> - enormous capacity for taking pains in the face of difficulties and frustrations.

    i. <u>Ability to Think in Images</u> - (thought visions)

    j. <u>Tolerance of Ambiguity</u> - open to the intricate, confusing and paradoxical qualities of most situations.

    k. <u>Background of Fundamental Knowledge</u> - generalists vs specialists.

CHARACTERISTICS OF LEFT/RIGHT BRAIN THINKERS

The left hemisphere (in our culture the more dominant and "overdeveloped") specializes in overbal and numerical information processed sequentially in a linear fashion. It is the active, verbal, logical, rational and analytic part of our brain. The right hemisphere is associated primarily with those activities we consider to be creative. It is the intuitive, experimental, nonverbal part of our brain and it deals in images and holistic, relational grasping of complex configurations and structures. It creates metaphors, analogies and new combinations of ideas. The following gives a more detailed comparison of the Left/Right Brain functions and modes.

LEFT MODE	RIGHT MODE
Logical, analytical, sequential, linear--drawing conclusions based on logical order of things; figuring things out in a sequential order, step-by-step, part-by-part, one element after another in an ordered way; proceeding in terms of linked thoughts, one idea directly following another, leading to a convergent conclusion; going from premises to conclusions in a series of orderly, logical steps. Utilizing precise, exact connotations--right/wrong, yes/no, etc.	Intuitive, holistic, gestalt, utilizing intuitive non-linear feeling of how things fit, belong or go together, making leaps of insight based on hunches, feelings, incomplete data, patterns, imagery; perceiving through pattern recognition and spatial references where things are in relation to other things and how parts connect to form wholes, holographic percep- tion and recognition of overall patterns, configura- tions, complex relationships --all at once, simultaneously, multiple processing of infor- mation-- arriving at conclu- sions without proceeding through logical, inter- mediary steps.
Convergent thinking--one con- clusion or alternative, one meaning.	Divergent thinking--many con- clusions or alternatives, many meanings.
Rational--basing conclusions on facts and reason.	Nonrational--does not require basis of reason or facts.
Conscious processing.	Subconscious or preconscious processing.
Literal meaning.	Metaphorical/analogical mean- ing--perceiving likeness between disparate things, grasp- ing of metaphoric likenesses.
Verbal, semantic--language, speech, counting, naming, reading.	Nonverbal use of imagery.
Realistic thinking--strong reality orientation	Fantasy, reverie, daydreaming
Dominant (usually)	Nondominant (quiet)
Linear time--keeping track of time, sequencing one thing after another.	Timelessness, nontemporal-- without sense of time.
Mathematical, scientific	Artistic, musical, symbolic
Directed	Free, associational, tolerant of ambiguity
Judgmental, evaluative	Nonjudgmental, noncritical-- willing to suspend judgment.

In current discussions about the differentiation between the mental processing of the two hemispheres of the brain, the tendency is to "overvalue" the creative capabilities of the right hemisphere. It seems highly probable, however, that what we should aim at is the utilization and

hemisphere. It seems highly probable, however, that what we should aim at is the utilization and education of the "whole brain," the double-dominant mode. What occurs in creative thinking and problem solving is an oscillating, iterative, switching back and forth type of processing, and sometimes even a "synchronous," or simultaneous usage of both hemispheres, rather than an exclusive or predominant emphasis on the right hemisphere.

REFERENCES

Agor, Weston H. Intuitive Management: Integrating Left and Right Brian Management Skills. Englewood Cliffs, N.J.: Prentice Hall, 1984.

Mintzberg, Henry. "Planning on the Left Side and Managing on the Right Side." Harvard Business Review, July-August, 1976, pp. 49-58.

Taggert, William and Daniel Robey. "Minds and Managers: On the Dual Nature of Human Information Processing and Management." Academy of Management Review, 6 (2), 1981, pp. 187-195.

74. MANAGEMENT IN THE YEAR 2005*

PURPOSE:

To use creative thinking for looking at the future.

GROUP SIZE:

Any number of groups of three to four members.

TIME REQUIRED:

30-50 minutes.

PREPARATION REQUIRED:

Read the "Introduction" below and complete Step 1 before class.

RELATED TOPICS:

Decision-Making, Goal Setting

INTRODUCTION:

In about 10 years we will celebrate a change of decades. This century which has witnesses so much change will give way to the 21st century and a future world in which most of us will still be active as managers or management educators. What kind of world will we be managing?

There are four possible scenarios which can be used to help prepare us for the future world we will be managing. In order to develop these alternative scenarios it is a useful exercise to first re-examine the changes over the last 15 years in order to be able to make some predictions about the next 15 years.

What have we witnessed over the last 15 years that can help us predict the next 15? The following list examines some of the high points of our recent past:

1. People's values and concerns change.
2. Physical resource constraints.
3. Unstable and disruptive economic conditions.
4. Political shifts and re-alignments.
5. Growth of OD, QOWL and similar programs.
6. Technological development: computerization and machines replacing labor.
7. Continuous shifts to service and government sector employment.
8. Entry of women in workforce and increasing acceptance and involvement of minorities.
9. Industrial and population shifts to sun-belt.
10. Possible pendulum shift - sensation we are on the verge of some major turn of events provokes questions about which way the world is going. Today's liberals are thinking and the conservatives are acting and the results are obvious.

---

*Adapted from Kenneth L. Murrell, Department of Management, University of West Florida, Pensacola, FL. Used with permission.

The four alternative scenarios are as follows:

A. Continuous increase in change and rate of change with significant shifts in underlying values and perceptions of life.

B. A return to the more conservative political and economic philosophies of the past and an effort to find what made American great.

C. The occurrence of a dramatic event like a major war or a realignment of the international political and/or economic environment.

D. Some mix of all the scenarios above with increasingly large pockets of sub cultures able to exist simultaneously with each other but not without increasing conflict.

EXERCISE SCHEDULE:

1. The management response to each possible future scenario is based on being prepared and being able to understand what is going on. In each of the four possible scenarios develop a list of recommended management actions. In other words, for each scenario, what should management be planning to do and what skills will be necessary in order to operate effectively in this new environment. Also, rank order the four scenarios, with one being your most likely candidate to occur.

    Scenario A - Continuous change

    Scenario B - A return to conservatism

    Scenario C - The dramatic event

    Scenario D - A mix of everything

    Use the Scenario Building Worksheet which follows:

2. (20-30 min.) In groups of three to four members, discuss your recommended management actions and rank in order the four scenarios, with "1" being the most likely to occur.

3. (10-20 min.) Class discussion.
    Discuss the scenarios and also rank order them again as a class.

Scenario Building Worksheet

Rank*	What should management plan to do under each scenario?	What skills are necessary to operate an organization in these new environments?
Scenario A Continuous Change		
Scenario B Return to Conservatism		
Scenario C The dramatic Event		
Scenario D Mix of Everything		

*Rank order where "1" is most likely; "4" is least likely.

75. TOLERANCE FOR AMBIGUITY*

PURPOSE:

To measure level of tolerance for ambiguity.

GROUP SIZE:

Any number.

TIME REQUIRED:

15-20 minutes.

PREPARATION REQUIRED:

Complete and score the inventory.

BACKGROUND:

Literature on creativity and innovation suggest that tolerance for ambiguity is correlated with higher levels of creativity. Complete the inventory below and then compare with the norms.

Tolerance for Ambiguity Survey Form

Please read each of the following statements carefully. Then rate each of them in terms of the extent to which you either agree or disagree with the statement using the following scale:

Completely Disagree	Neither Agree Nor Disagree	Completely Agree

| 1 | 2 | 3 | 4 | 5 | 6 | 7 |

Place the number which best describes your degree of agreement or disagreement in the blank to the left of each statement.

_____ 1. An expert who doesn't come up with a definite answer probably doesn't know too much.

_____ 2. I would like to live in a foreign country for a while.

_____ 3. The sooner we all acquire similar values and ideals the better.

_____ 4. A good teacher is one who makes you wonder about your way of looking at things.

_____ 5. I like parties where I know most of the people more than ones where all or most of the people are complete strangers.

_____ 6. Teachers or supervisors who hand out vague assignments give a change for one to show initiative and originality.

---

*Adapted from Paul Nutt. Used with permission.

_____ 7. A person who leads an even, regular life in which few surprises or unexpected happenings arise, really has a lot to be grateful for.

_____ 8. Many of our most important decisions are based upon insufficient information.

_____ 9. There is really no such thing as a problem that can't be solved.

_____ 10. People who fit their lives to a schedule probably miss most of the joy of living.

_____ 11. A good job is one where what is to be done and how it is to be done are always clear.

_____ 12. It is more fun to tackle a complicated problem than to solve a simple one.

_____ 13. In the long run, it is possible to get more done by tackling small, simple problems rather than large and complicated ones.

_____ 14. Often the most interesting and stimulating people are those who don't mind being different and original.

_____ 15. What we are used to is always preferable to what is unfamiliar.

Norms Using the Tolerance of Ambiguity Scale

Source: The Tolerance For Ambiguity Scale

Basis: The survey asks 16 questions about personal and work oriented situations with ambiguity. You were asked to rate each situation on a scale form one (tolerant) to seven (intolerant). (Alternating questions have the response scale reversed.) The index scores the items. A perfectly tolerant person would score 16 and perfectly intolerant person 112. Scores between 20 and 80 are reported with means of 45. The responses to the even numbered questions with 7 minus the score are added to the response for the odd numbered questions.

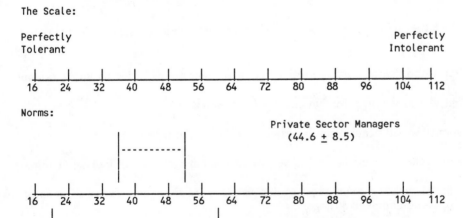

Data From: Nutt, P.C. "The Tolerance for Ambiguity and Decision Making." The Ohio State University College of Business Working Paper Series, WP88-291, March 1988.

Chapter 22

Current Issues in Management

76. WINDELL HOLMES: AIDS IN THE WORKPLACE

PURPOSE:

To discuss worker's rights in organizations.

GROUP SIZE:

Any number of groups of 5 to 7 members.

TIME REQUIRED:

40 to 50 minutes.

PREPARATION REQUIRED:

Read the case and answer the questions.

RELATED TOPICS:

Ethics and Values
Dynamics with Groups
Leadership

EXERCISE SCHEDULE:

1.   (pre-class) Read the case and answer the questions.
2.   (20 to 30 min.) Groups discuss questions.
3.   (20 min.) Instructor leads a class discussion.

Windell Holmes: AIDS Incident[*]

Assume that you are the General Manager of a direct sales firm. As you are working at your desk, three employees from the telemarketing department barge into your office. They are visibly upset. According to the workers a new employee, Windell, is an active homosexual who has Acquired Immune Deficiency Syndrome (AIDS). It seems that the previous afternoon, one of the three employees was visiting a friend at the hospital. As he was leaving, he saw Windell coming out of a small building at the far end of the hospital parking lot, several hundred feet away. Windell got in his car and drove off. Curious, the co-worker walked over to the building. A small sign indicated that it was the hospital's AIDS outpatient clinic. Since you didn't see the incident, you are not sure whether it was Windell or not. However, the employee is convinced that the man was Windell; upon arriving at work he told the story to his two friends.

The three workers want you to fire Windell, or at least to segregate him from the other workers. Because people who work different shifts in the telemarketing department share telephones and computer terminals, they were concerned that Windell might cough on a telephone receiver or sweat on a terminal keyboard and an employee who used that equipment later might acquire AIDS. Further, the workers claim that although he is a fine worker, Windell has a reputation for being clumsy, and recently cut himself while trying to peel an orange. Because they fear that they might come in contact with Windell's body fluids (e.g. blood), the workers feel the risk of infection is quite high.

Questions for Discussion

1. What will you tell this group of workers? What if they refuse to work with him or call a "wildcat strike?"
2. Will you investigate the workers' story? If so, how will you do this?
3. Will you talk to Windell? What difference will it make if he admits to having AIDS?
4. How will you balance the interests of those employees with the disease with the interests of those who do not wish to be exposed to the possibility of infection?
5. What sort of personnel policy will you devise for dealing with AIDS in the workplace? Will you refuse to hire those with AIDS? Will you fire (or segregate) those with AIDS? Will you test every employee for the HIV-III antibodies that suggest the presence of the virus and causes AIDS? Will you exclude AIDS patients from your medical plan? What exactly will your personnel policy contain?

---

[*]This exercise was prepared by William H. Ross, University of Wisconsin-La Crosse. Although this scenario is fictional, it is similar to many actual situations such as those described in J. Aberth's "AIDS in the Workplace." Management Review, 74, (12), December 1985, pp. 49-51. Used with permission.

77. JERRY'S PERFORMANCE APPRAISAL: ALCOHOLISM AND WORKERS*

PURPOSE:

To explore behavioral problems of workers.

GROUP SIZE:

Any number of groups of 5 to 7 members.

TIME REQUIRED:

40 to 50 minutes.

PREPARATION REQUIRED:

Read the case and answer the questions.

RELATED TOPICS:

Leadership
Work Motivation

EXERCISE SCHEDULE

1. (Pre-class) Read the case and answer the questions.
2. (20 to 30 min.) Groups discuss questions.
3. (20 min.) Instructor leads a class discussion.

Jerry's Performance Appraisal

Mr. Burke, the Vice-President of Marketing, leaned back in his chair. He was trying to decide what performance evaluation to give to Jerry, a middle-level manager.

"Jerry is a great guy," he though. "He's a real 'go-getter.' He comes into the office at 6:30 every morning -- long before anyone else. He does take two-hour lunches, but he seems to get the job done. Why two years ago, his department was the most productive of all the departments in the entire organization!"

"I think I particularly like his management style. He's an efficient delegator. His staff members seem to work together as a team. Why, sometimes I think the team seems to run itself."

The more he thought about Jerry, the less impressed Mr. Burke was. "Lately, his productivity has fallen off a bit. It took him six weeks to get the Baxter report to me. He should have had that done in three. And he seems to get 'colds' a lot. He is rarely absent but he sometimes leaves early. Maybe that nagging cold could account for his drop in productivity. Maybe he should take a few days off and get over it, rather than plugging away when he isn't 100%.

---

*This exercise was prepared by William H. Ross, University of Wisconsin-La Crosse. Used with permission.

"Also, I wish he'd be a bit more sociable. He keeps to himself quit a bit these days, working with the office door shut. It seems to promote rivalry with the other managers. I believe they think he is "too good for them." Ralph even acted like he was jealous! He said that I shouldn't have given Jerry the Baiter project because he wouldn't do a good job. Well, Ralph was right; the report <u>was</u> late. But the work was in top form. I particularly enjoyed his presentation to Baiter. Quite entertaining! He was also a riot at Baiter's dinner party. That should be good for insuring Baiter's account for the next five years at least! I think the other managers could learn something from Jerry; I wish they wouldn't be do jealous!"

"One point I will have to make when I conduct the performance appraisal feedback session with Jerry is that he needs to take better notes at meetings. I don't think he pays attention. At our meeting last Monday, I promised him some projected sales figures for the Northeastern U.S. region. When he got the information Tuesday morning he called me to ask why I had sent it. That wasn't an isolated incident. There have been several times when he hasn't remembered that we even had a meeting! He really does need to develop a system for keeping track of important information. The poor man has just got too much on his mind. He forgets too many things."

Performance Evaluation

Rater's name: Name of person being rated:

        <u>Jim Burke</u>   <u>Jerry Strand</u>

Position: <u>V-P Marketing</u>   <u>Director, Sales</u>

Instructions: Please assess this worker's overall performance:

```
|-----|-----|-----|-----|-----|-----|
 1     2     3     4     5     6     7
poor             average       outstanding
```

Comments and Explanation of rating:

Signature: _____(Rater)   _____(Ratee)

Questions for Discussion:

1. What are Jerry's strengths in his performance? What are his weaknesses? What seems to be the cause(s) of his weak areas of performance? What solutions do you suggest?

2. What should Mr. Burke tell Jerry when conducting his performance appraisal review?

3. Suppose that this firm used Management by Objectives (MBO). What objectives should Mr. Burke seek to set with Jerry.

4. To what extent should "political" considerations (e.g., giving a good evaluation may increase Jerry's chance of receiving a promotion) play a part in how Mr. Burke completes the evaluation form?

78. THE RAMBUSCH COMPANY: GAY WORKERS

PURPOSE:

To explore issues of discrimination of gay employees.

GROUP SIZE:

Any number of groups of 5-8 members.

TIME REQUIRED:

45-60 minutes.

PREPARATION REQUIRED:

Read "The Rambusch Company" and answer the questions.

RELATED TOPICS:

Interpersonal relationships

EXERCISE SCHEDULE:

1.   (Pre-class) Read the case and answer the questions.

2.   (20-25 minutes) Groups discuss answers to questions.

3.   (25-35 minutes) Instructor leads a discussion on the case.

THE RAMBUSCH COMPANY[*]

Louis Dashman had been working at The Rambusch Company for eight weeks, having had accepted the position of Operations Manager in January 1978. He was thirty two years old, and had finished his BBA from Churchill Business School in June 1973. Dashman's first position was with Stenson-Forsgren, and R&D Company, where he gained extensive experience in computer design and construction. He came to Rambusch because of the potential career and financial opportunities it offered him. His long run goals was to be come a corporate executive.

The Rambusch Company, Inc. manufactured a wide range of products associated with the computer world. The firm started in 1966 with the intense growth of the computer and computer components industry. A major breakthrough came for Rambusch in its fourth year of operations when it gained a contract with Zerom, one of the largest computer design and manufacturing firms in the world. Since then the firm had been expanding, its latest step had been into the office equipment field (or "office of the future," as Business Week labeled it). Its largest recent contract had been with the Department of the Navy for specialized office equipment, designing and producing entire office systems including copiers, word-processors, data storage and the like. The Navy contract was negotiated after two years of experimenting, testing and bidding. At present, the contract was

---

[*]Copyright 1981 by Martin R. Moser, Ph.D., Associate Professor of Management, College of Management, University of Lowell, Lowell, MA 01854.

on a nine month trial basis. If accepted beyond this trial period, it will mean approximately $650,000 annually for Rambusch for at least four years running.

Rambusch products are designed and manufactured in Western Massachusetts. Two plants in Turners Falls, one in Sunderland, and a fourth in Greenfield. In 1976 the central office moved to Deerfield in order to be more centrally located between the four manufacturing units. This also allowed the Turner Falls plants some badly needed expansion space made possible by the evacuation of the executive offices.

Gilbert Winston was the Vice-President for The Rambusch Company. Winston was forty four years old, twice divorced and currently single. He was a dapper, well dressed and very flamboyant man. He had an MBA from the University of Massachusetts, and his work was very efficient. He began at Rambusch in 1967, at the lowest management level, and worked his way up through the ranks. Some said his pull in certain places finally helped Rambusch get the Navy contract, but nobody knew for sure.

Pearly Anderson had been the Operations Manager before Dashman. During his job interview, Winston said to Dashman "You will probably hear rumors about how Pearly left Rambusch because of a personality clash between he and I. Pearly left because Dillman Corp. offered him almost twice the salary he was getting here, and also for some personal reasons which I am not at liberty to discuss with you. A lot of people around here don't like me. It has nothing to do with the quality of my work or the way I treat my subordinates. It's a matter of my style. It seems to offend people that I am not exactly as they think I should be. They are all curious about my personal life and what I do in my spare time. But as far as I am concerned, that's none of anybody's business except my own.I want to be straight with you and also give you my perspective about what it would be like to work here. People will want a lot of information about me from you because you will be working for me. They will not be satisfied with purely work related information. This can be a hard situation to deal with, because unless you give them what they want they isolate you. But ont he other hand, there is great opportunity here at Rambusch. Our contract with the Navy is just the beginning. I am quite sure that we will get the four year contract. Let's just say my intuition is very good. And there are a lot more potential government contracts on the horizon. Rambusch will be growing larger and probably within the next few years. But that's between me and you, and if anyone asks me how I know, I'll say I never said a thing!"

Winston was correct about the employees at Rambusch not liking him. During Dashman's first few weeks on the job more people spoke to him about Winston that about work. Jack Kozenski was a line supervisor who reported directly to Dashman. Kozenski was a Polish immigrant and a survivor of Auschwitz. He was very intense, drawn and austere person, prone to occasional out bursts of temper. He work thick, steel-rimmed glasses which made Dashman feel as if Kozenski was looking straight through him. Self-make and self-educated, Kozenski began with Rambusch as a maintenance man in 1966; he was married and had seven children. One day during a conversation with Dashman, Kozenski said, "I have a cousin like Winston. We never understood him. He never married, but became a successful lawyer. Always dressed sharp. When he was a young boy he never played with the other boys. He read and played his piano. But he is smart, a good lawyer, and he makes a lot of money."

Preston Johnson was one of five foremen on Kozenski's line. He was twenty nine years old, originally from New Orleans, and was the first black employee at Rambusch. He had been with the company for six years, did very high quality work and was well liked throughout the organization. He was currently going to night school to complete his college degree. Dashman was at the Sunderland plant when Johnston said to him, "I want to give you some advice. Play your cards close to your vest. People around here let their imagination get the best of them. That was the reason Pearly left. He thought that everyone was talking about him because he worked so close with Winston. Truth is, he was right. What people should be doing is judging people by the work that they do, not by the color of their skin or what they do in their own time. But people talk, and they imagine. I just wanted to let you know what you are in for."

When the employees talked about Winston, Dashman tried not to listen. He made a contract with himself that he was at Rambusch to work hard, and that he wouldn't get involved in petty office politics. Besides in the eight weeks he had been working at the company, Winston had been extremely helpful in phasing him into the work process. Winston had been open and straight forward with him, and Dashman felt, at least so far, he was an excellent person to work for.

Dashman's first priority was to establish himself at Rambusch. He like Western Massachusetts and would be happy to settle here. His fiance, Anne Weston, also like the area. She would be finished with her doctoral studies in two years and there were many schools in the area where she could teach. Anne wanted to be out of the city. She was born in Boston and had been in New York for the past seven years. They both wanted to restore an old New England farmhouse. The opportunity to work at Rambusch fit into Dashman's plans, and if Winston's comments about the future at the company were true, he felt he might have found the almost perfect opportunity.

Since the work that Rambusch was doing for the Navy was so specialized there was a need for a lot of personal contact. Winston made frequent trips to Washington, D.C. to discuss engineering and design issues. He usually made these trips alone, but in July he asked Dashman to accompany him. "I want to let you know that I am aware of the excellent work you have been doing in your six months with the company. I think that it is important that you get more involved with my contacts in D.C., and also to get some experience in playing the government contracts game. The future of Rambusch is in these government contracts. I've been working on my sources in D.C. for over ten years and it's starting to pay off. We are at the stage where it's becoming too much for me to handle alone, and I would like to get you involved. We will go down to Washington next Monday and return on Thursday. Get things in order so that you can get away for a few days."

Dashman was fascinated by the way Winston worked in Washington. Winston seemed to know everybody at the Department of the Navy, and at a meeting with a Vice-Admiral, it was confirmed that the four year contract had been awarded to Rambusch. Both men return to Massachusetts in very good spirits.

In September Winston and Dashman made another trip to Washington to meet with officials from the Department of Defense. The Defense Department representatives were interested in getting a bid from Rambusch on a contract for advanced office systems. The dollar value of the contract was twice as large as the Navy contract. The meeting with the Defense Department officials was very informative, and Rambusch, under the guidance of Winston, submitted a proposal in October. In January 1980, a five year pact, worth approximately $1,200,000 per year, was awarded to the Rambusch Company by the Department of the Defense.

Winston and Dashman celebrated their success by going to lunch at Judy's the most expensive restaurant in Western Massachusetts. "I've also been informed by the Chairman of the Board of Rambusch that I am going to be promoted," said Winston. "President Jameson is going to retire in March, and the Board unanimously voted for me to be his successor. I've also got approval to hire an assistant to help me work on obtaining and managing the government contracts for the company. I would like to promote you to that position. You will also be involved in shaping the expansion plans of the company, as well as recruiting and hiring new people."

Dashman was delighted. "I'm overwhelmed. I don't know what to say. It's an incredible opportunity for me."

"There are some other things that you need to know before you decide whether or not you will take the promotion," said Winston, "I've been waiting for this opportunity for some time now. I've made a very important decision that has to do with my personal life. It might affect you if you decide to accept the promotion, or even if you decide to stay at Rambusch. I'm telling you this now because I like and respect you and I want you to be informed. I am a member of a gay political action group. The members of this group are all professional people, men and women who are respected community members. They include lawyers, business people, doctors, a political leader, a judge and so on. We have decided to hold a news conference and to openly declare our alternative sex preference. The group has been waiting for my promotion, which I had anticipated. We're not sure how this will affect our professional lives, but we all believe the time has come for us to stop hiding and to openly acknowledge who we are. This is an important step for all of us. I told Pearly Anderson about this decision, and that is one of the reason he went to Dillman. I'm telling you now because I want to give you some time to think it over. We will hold our news conference in March after I have signed my new contract as President of Rambusch. As you know, the business is very secure for the next five years. You have the opportunity to gain invaluable experience in this new position as well as to profit financially. The news conference might attract a lot of attention. To my knowledge, this is the first time an organized effort like this has ever been done. It might also blow over without any really hullabaloo. In any case I'd like to know what your decision is in one week."

Dashman decided to seek the advice of a former professor about his available courses of action: "I have to be pleased at the career opportunities open to me in the new job, and the obvious growth potential of the company. Yet, I wonder if the military people will be as persuaded by Winston once he announces his new status. They seem to have a decided distaste for people like him and may quietly cut him off after he comes out in the open. Should I try to persuade Winston to forget this group of people he is associated with, or at least not come out in the open like he plans? On the other hand, maybe if he is going to blow himself out of the water with this nutty scheme of his I should stick around and if he fails I will be ready to move up and take over in a strong managerial position. I have already established myself favorably with the Navy and the Defense people, and if I assure them that I am straight and not one of Winston's crowd will they hand onto the contracts and renew them on my ability rather than Winston? I also have some concern about my reputation inside the company. Perhaps I should quietly talk to the important people inside the firm and let them know that I am not next to Winston in any personal way, and that my contracts are purely professional. But then they may not believe me. I may even be worrying too much about the effect of this thing, and it will all go away without creating more than a temporary sensation, and I will have worried for nothing. I understand that gay rights is on the rise and there are many states and cities where gay rights laws are in effect, and a federal bill has been submitted. But then I have to remember that we aren't located in a big city like San Francisco or New York, and Western Massachusetts is quite provincial. What do you think would be the best course for me?"

The professor, a gray hired gentlemen tamped the tobacco in his pipe. "As I understand it you are wondering whether you should accept the promotion."

Questions for Discussion

1. Briefly trace Louis Dashman's career with the Rambusch Company. How had he gradually become more involved with Gilbert Winston?

2. What is the major decision facing Louis? What are his options?

3. What factors should Louis consider when making his choice?

4. What are the arguments for accepting Gilbert Winston's offer?

5. What are the arguments for not accepting Gilbert Winston's offer?

6. How should Louis Dashman decide? Why?

7.   Should a person's off-the-job behavior be considered when evaluating an employee if their performance is satisfactory? What if the firm loses business as a result, even if the employee's individual performance is satisfactory?

8.   Should Dashman try to talk Winston out of "going public"? Why or why not?

9.   Should Dashman "expose" Gilbert Winston after both are promoted?

10.   Louis Dashman had heard rumors about Gilbert Winston ever since he went to work at Rambusch. He chose to ignore the rumors and to work hard instead. If you were Louis would you have kept quite? Contributed to the rumors? Confronted Winston over the rumors? or done something else entirely? What are the advantages of your recommended course of action?

79. DYSFUNCTIONAL FAMILIES AND DYSFUNCTIONAL ORGANIZATIONS[*]

PURPOSE:

To learn which behaviors we bring from our family or origin to the workplace.

GROUP SIZE:

Any number of groups of 3-4 members.

TIME REQUIRED:

35-60 minutes.

PREPARATION REQUIRED:

1. Complete the Family Genogram.
2. Complete the Family Role Sheet.

RELATED TOPICS:

Interpersonal relationships

BACKGROUND:

Much attention has been paid to issues of US companies losing the technological edge to the Germans and the Japanese, to declining rates of productivity by workers, loss of the so-called "work ethic" by the younger generation, and the difficulties in motivating employees. Millions of dollars have been spent on organizational analysis and training programs to overcome these problems.

One area receiving almost no attention is the relationship between dysfunctional families and dysfunctional organizations. In other words, people from dysfunctional families go on to create and reinforce dysfunctional organizations. The same "rules" apply in both cases:

1. Don't talk
2. Don't trust/don't risk
3. Don't feel

Whether in a family or organization, any person trying to break one of the rules (and therefore attempting to make the system healthier) is punished by the leaders (or parents) and other members (siblings). In such an environment, morale and productivity would usually be greatly reduced.

The norm in both dysfunctional families and organizations is co-dependent behavior, which includes frozen feelings, denial, lack of honesty, perfectionism, workaholism, hidden aggression in the forms of collusion and procrastination, and rigid behavior norms. Such systems tend to become "closed" and discourage interaction with outsiders. Most organizational members do not question the rules and risk behaviors because they are all too familiar. According to one estimate, between 80-95% of families are dysfunctional, which means most of us are accustomed to the norms of a dysfunctional system and fit adequately into a dysfunctional organization.

Members of dysfunctional families (sometimes, but not always, from alcoholic families) often fall into certain roles, as shown below (Wegscheider-Cruse, 1987, p. 43):

---

[*]Copyright 1988 by Dorothy A. Marcic. All rights reserved.

The characteristics -- traits, feelings and behaviors of Children of Alcoholics

The name of the game or the mode of survival.	What you see or visible traits. Outside behavior.	What you don't see, or the inside story. Feelings.	What he/she represents to the family & why they play along.	As an adult without help, this is very possible.	As an adult with help, this is also very possible.
THE FAMILY HERO or SUPER KID.	"The little mother" "The little man of the family." Always does what's right, over achiever, over responsible, needs everyone's approval. Not much fun.	Hurt, inadequate, confusion, guilt, fear, low self-esteem. Progressive disease, so never can do enough.	Provides self-worth to the family, someone to be proud of.	Workaholic, never wrong, marry a dependent person, need to control & manipulate, compulsive, can't say no, can't fail.	Competent, organized, responsible, make good managers. Becomes successful and healthy.
THE SCAPEGOAT or PROBLEM KID.	Hostility & defiance, withdrawn & sullen, gets negative attention, troublemaker.	Hurt & abandoned, anger & rejection, feels totally inadequate & no/low self-worth.	Take the heat, "see what he's done -- "Leave me alone.	Alcoholic/addict, unplanned pregnancy. cops & prisons. TROUBLE. Legal trouble.	Recovery, has courage, good under pressure, can see reality, can help others. Can take risks.
THE LOST CHILD.	Loner, day dreamer, solitary (alone rewards, i.e., food), withdrawn, drifts & floats through life not missed for days, quiet, shy & ignored.	Unimportant, not allowed to have feelings, loneliness, hurt & abandoned, defeated and given up. Fear.	Relief, at least one kid no one worries about.	Indecisive, no test, little fun, stays the same, alone or promiscuous, dies early, can't say NO.	Independent, talented & creative. Imaginative, assertive & resourceful.
THE MASCOT or FAMILY CLOWN.	Supercute, immature, and anything for a laugh or attention, fragile and needful of protection, hyperactive, short attention span, leaning disabilities, anxious.	Low self-esteem, terror, lonely, inadequate & unimportant.	Comic relief, fun & humor.	Compulsive clown, lampshade on head, etc. Can't handle stress, marry a "hero," always on verge of hysterics.	Charming host & person, good with company, quick wit, good sense of humor, independent, helpful.

FAMILY GENOGRAM

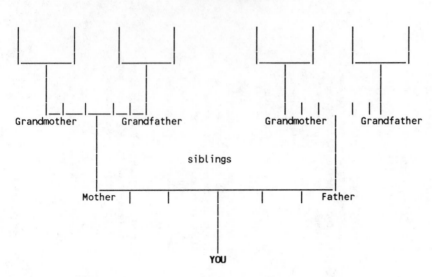

Grandmother   Grandfather   Grandmother   Grandfather

siblings

Mother   Father

YOU

Directions:
1. Fill in appropriate names for siblings, aunts/uncles, grandparents, etc.
2. Indicate, by the following marks, whether a person had/was:

    # Alcohol or drug abuse
    ^ Other addiction, i.e., workaholism, gambling, sports, etc.
    * Abuser-perpetrator of sexual abuse, battered, emotional abuser
    + Victim -- of sexual, physical or emotional abuse

YOUR FAMILY OF ORIGIN

"Rules" in your family
1.

2.

3.

4.

Examples:
1. Don't be angry
2. Don't be selfish
3. It's OK to make mistakes
4. Pick up your own mess
5. Don't talk back

YOUR WORKPLACE

"Rules" in your workplace
1.

2.

3.

Examples:
1. Don't contradict boss
2. Give honest feedback
3. Don't rock the boat

What behaviors do I bring from my family of origin which:

1. Are dysfunctional in my work environment?
    a.

    b.

    d.

2. Help me perform positively/effectively in my work environment?
    a.

    b.

    c.

FAMILY ROLE SHEET

Directions: Fill in names of people in boxes to show which roles you have seen in both family and work environments:

Role	Family	Present or Previous Work Situations
Super-Kid		
Scapegoat		
Lost Child		
Mascot		

EXERCISE SCHEDULE:
1. (Pre-class) Complete "Family Genogram" and "Family Role Sheet"
2. (10-15 min) Instructor gives background on dysfunctional families and relationship to organizations.
3. (15-25 min.) Groups of 3-4 members discuss genograms and role sheets.
4. (10-20 min.) Instructor leads a discussion with the whole class.

Reference

Wegscheider-cruse, Sharon. Choicemaking. Pompano Beach, FL: Health Communications, 1987.

80. CHASTITY CHASTEEN: A CASE OF SEXUAL HARASSMENT*

PURPOSE:

1. To identify various forms of sexually harassing conduct that may create a hostile and intimidating work enviroment inviolation of Title VII.

2. To provoke discussion of the legal and organizational consequences of sexual harassment upon the victim, the perpetrators, and the employer.

3. To stimulate discussion of management strategies that can be developed to reduce the likelihood of sexual harassment charges (and the costly and damaging lawsuits they engender).

4. To suggest proper management responses to sexual harassment claims.

GROUP SIZE:

Any number of groups of 5-8 members.

TIME REQUIRED:

50 - 70 minutes.

PREPARATION REQUIRED:

Read the case study and the case background information and answer the case questions before class.

RELATED TOPICS:

Decision-Making

EXERCISE SCHEDULE:

1. (Pre-Class) Read the case and background and answer the questions.

2. (20-30 minutes) In groups of 5-8 members, discuss the questions students prepared before class.

3. (15-20 minutes) Groups report on the major points of their discussions to the whole class.

4. (15-20 minutes) The instructor broadens the discussion beyond the case to focus on the legal and organizational consequences of both blatant and subtle forms of sexual harassment.

---

*Copyright 1988 by Susan L. Willey. Used with permission.

Chastity Chasteen: A Case of Sexual Harassment

Roberta Collins began working for Ace Life and Casualty Insurance Co. of America (Ace) in May 1983 upon her graduation from State University with a marketing major and a finance major. The job was ideal for both professional and personal reasons. After she completed a brief, but intensive, training program, Ace made Roberta an assistant sales representative in their Butler office. Her fiance', Tom Chasteen, was already employed by a food distributor in Butler, and her assignment there enabled the couple to marry at Thanksgiving.

Roberta soon established herself as a competent insurance agent. She received high performance appraisals from her supervisor at the end of her probationary period and again at the end of her first year with Ace. Her evaluations noted her professional handling of claims, her excellent reports, and her high sales. In both February and May of 1984,in fact, Roberta sold more life insurance than the other three more experienced agents in the Butler office.

Roberta became pregnant with twins that summer. She maintained her vigorous work schedule, including frequent evening meetings with prospective clients, until January 1985 when her doctor advised her to slow down. Ace was understanding and accomodating; they permitted Roberta to reduce her hours and to cease traveling. Even so, the twins were born seven weeks prematurely and required several weeks of intensive care at Butler Memorial Hospital. In May, Roberta returned to work part-time and by the end of June, had resumed her position full time.

Tom, however, could adjust neither to the pressure of fatherhood nor to Roberta's dual role as careerwoman and mother - she seemed to have time and energy only for her job and the twins, none for him. In August, Tom moved out and three weeks before the second anniversary in November 1985, he filed for divorce.

When the divorce became final, Roberta asked for and received a transfer to Ace's regional office in Metropolis. Faced with the prospect of supporting two young children alone, she hoped that her strong sales skills would enable her to advance within the company and earn a better income. Roberta Chasteen (she continued using her married name, despite the divorce) found the working enviroment in Metropolis substantially different than that in Butler. The regional manager set a tone that upset her. He repeatedly offered her a ride home form work her first week on the job. When she refused, he called her "Chastity Chasteen," a nickname that her co-workers began using. Although she didn't consider herself puritanical, Roberta found herself offended by the atmosphere at work, particularly in the employee lounge. There many of the male employees told off-color jokes, passed around vulgar cartoons and looked at <u>Penthouse</u> and <u>Playboy</u> during their breaks. A coffee can used as an ashtray in the lounge was labeled a "butt can" and had pictures of clothed buttocks taped around it. The sexual atmosphere was not confined to the lounge, however. A few of the salesmen sent her occasional memoranda on what she considered to be lewd memo paper. One pad, entitled a "Scratch" pad, showed a hand scratching a buttock. Another was imprinted "A day without sex is like a day without sunshine." A co-worker once showed her a coconut carved to resemble a monkey that he kept on a shelf in his office. When he pulled open the lid, a replica of an erect penis was inside.

More offensive than these events, however, were the office affairs, typically between upper level managers and their female secretaries. One supervisor and his secretary frequently took lunch breaks that lasted all afternoon. Others began "happy hour" at lunch, and continued drinking after they returned to work. After hours office parties were also frequent. The first (and only) party Roberta attended was the 1986 Christmas party. Again, the regional director showed her unwanted attention. While several employees watched, he cornered Roberta near the bar, untied her sweater and attempted to kiss her. She left immediately. The next day she found a Snow White and the Seven Dwarfs poster taped to the wall behind her desk. "Chastity" was written on the side of the poster with an arrow pointing to Snow White. She complained to her supervisor who told her to "loosen up" and enjoy the "relaxed and friendly atmosphere" at Ace. Another female sales representative, in whom Roberta had confided, reminded her that as a single parent, she could not afford to lose her job.

Despite the fact that Roberta found it hard to concentrate on her work with so much drinking and sexual involvement among the Ace staff, her sales figures did not suffer. Roberta worked longer hours, and more of them on the road visiting clients. By mid-1987, she had led the office in life insurance sales twice and had brought in more new clients than any other agent in the Metropolis office. Thus, her performance appraisal in October came as a devastating shock. Her supervisor evaluated her performance as only satisfactory and denied her a requested promotion. She overheard some office gossip that one secretary, who had accompanied another supervisor to a hotel in the city (where they had reportedly spent the night discussing theology) received a perfect score on her performance appraisal, a cash award and her second promotion in a single year. Another female insurance sales agent, who had been involved in a sexual relationship with the regional manager for some time, likewise received a promotion and a bonus. Roberta became convinced that the performance appraisal system was being used both to reward mistresses and to retaliate against those who opposed the misconduct and refused to participate.

After the performance appraisal, Roberta sought a transfer to another Ace office. She did not tell her supervisor that her reason was to escape the pervasive sexual atmosphere at Ace, and the request was denied. Afraid to quit her job, Roberta continued working for Ace, but her sales plummetted. She began having nightmares and frequent headaches. She became moody and depressed, lost considerable weight, and experienced difficulty concentrating. Two months ago, she sought counseling with a psychologist who diagnosed her condition as "post-traumatic stress disorder." Upon the advice of her counselor, Roberta took the issue to her supervisor a final time. She told him that she considered herself a victim of sexual harassment because of the enviroment at Ace where those who submitted to sexual advances by their superiors received preferential treatment. She told him that if the harassment did not stop, she would see an attorney about filing a sex discrimination lawsuit.

You are Roberta's supervisor. After she left your office, you consulted your Ace employee handbook, which contains the policy statement reprinted in the Appendix. You have also made an appointment with the Ace attorney for early next week. Her secretary provided you with relevant provisions of the state Human Rights Act and the Official EEOC Guidelines defining sexual harassment. These provisions are also reprinted for you in the Appendix.

Questions for Discussion

1. Does Roberta have a valid complaint against Ace for creating and/or condoning an "intimidating, hostile or offensive working enviroment" that adversely affected her because of her sex?

2. As Roberta's supervisor, how should you respond to her complaint? Since the director of the regional office sets the tone that has created this allegedly hostile enviroment, should you confront the director? (With what possible consequences?) investigate her allegations? inform a company official at the national office?

3. Assuming that Ace has been informed that Roberta may file a sex discrimination lawsuit, what can the company do to avert such a suit? or to reduce its liability should one be filed?

4. What strategies should management adopt to prevent the development of a sexually harassing workplace atmosphere?

5.   What are the consequences of sexual harassment upon the victim (Roberta)? Upon other employees who may not even perceive themselves as victims of illegal sex discrimination (e.g. the female employees who submitted to the advances presumably in exchange for favored treatment)? Upon the employer?

CASE BACKGROUND INFORMATION

COMPANY HANDBOOK

Policy Statement: Harassment of Employees

It is the intent of the Ace Life and Casualty Insurance Co. of America to provide a working enviroment for all employees which is free of harassment and discriminatory intimidation whether based on race, religion, sex, age, national origin, handicap, or veteran status, consistent with the State Human Rights Act, Stat. Section 363.01, Subd. 10.

This company will not condone, permit nor tolerate harassment in any manner whatsoever. Persons engaged in such harassment may be subject to discipline and discharge.

STATE HUMAN RIGHTS ACT

State Stat. Section 363.01, Subd. 10a. Sexual harassment includes "unwelcome sexual advances, requests for sexual favors, sexually motivated physical conduct or other verbal or physical contact or communication of a sexual nature when ... that conduct or communication has the purpose or effect of substantially interfering with an individual's employment ... or creating an intimidating, hostile or offensive employment ... enviroment.

OFFICIAL EEOC GUIDELINES

The Equal Employment Opportunity Commission (EEOC) has issued official guidelines which define sexual harassment as a form of sex discrimination under Title VII of the Civil Rights Act of 1964. They are:

Section 1604.11 Sexual Harassment

a) Harassment on the basis of sex is a violation of Sec. 703 of Title VII. Unwelcome sexual advances, requests for sexual favors and other verbal or physical conduct of a sexual nature constitute sexual harassment when (1) submission to such conduct is made either explicitly or implicitly a term or condition of an individual's employment, (2) submission to or rejection of such conduct by an individual is used as the basis for employment decisions affecting such individual, or (3) such conduct has the purpose or effect of unreasonably interfering with an individual's work performance or creating an intimidating, hostile or offensive working enviroment.

b) In determining whether alleged conduct constitutes sexual harassment, the Commission will look at the record as a whole and at the totality of the circumstances, such as the nature of the sexual advances and the context in which the alleged incidents occurred. The determination of the legality of a particular action will be made from the facts, on a case by case basis.

c) Applying general Title VII principles, an employer, employment agency, joint apprenticeship committee or labor organization (hereinafter collectively referred to as "employer") is responsible for its acts and those of its agents and supervisory employees with respect to sexual harassment regardless of whether the specific acts complained of were authorized or even forbidden by the employer and regardless of whether the employer knew or should have known of their occurrence. The Commission will examine the circumstances of the particular employment relationship and the job functions performed by the individual in either a supervisory or agency capacity.

Appendices

INSTRUCTIONS TO NEW GROUPS[*]

This sheet is for new class groups. Its purpose is to (1) explain why groups are used as a part of the learning process, and (2) to identify the steps group members must take in order to work effectively together.

Businesses are formed around tasks which are too large for one person to carry out. Consequently, it is necessary for businesspeople to master the skills needed in working together. Many students who have not held positions of responsibility in business believe that these skills are easily mastered. However, students seldom have had to cope with the kinds of situations which businesspeople do. People in business commonly must deal with "people" situations involving leadership, exercise of power and authority, motivation, face-to-face work skills, persuasion, communication, empathy, work group effectiveness, management of conflict, ambiguity, establishing relations with superiors, politics, and networks. We know that when a person takes on a position of responsibility in business, his or her appreciation and need for skills in working with others rises <u>dramatically</u>.

A primary purpose for using groups in class is to provide students with the opportunity to learn and practice "people" skills involved in working on a common task.

Many students are reluctant to join groups. The most commonly given reason is that they have been in groups before which have not worked well. Many students cite instances of past groups before which have not worked well. Many people wound up doing all the work, while the rest did nothing. If the failures of these groups are analyzed, virtually all can be traced to one of two causes. The <u>first</u> is that the group was given insufficient power over outcomes important to its members. In many courses groups are not given the authority to allocate group scores to members, and cannot hire or fire members. Consequently, they are unable to motivate group members to carry out the group's work. The <u>second</u> is that the group did have control over important rewards, but failed

---

[*]By John Bigelow. Used with permission.

to exercise this power effectively. For example, groups always have control over the social approval and acceptance which members give to others in the group. In many groups, however, approval and acceptance is not given to members for good performance. Again, even when a group has control over score allocation and hiring and firing, it may back off from using this power.

Let's look now at how these two causes for group failure can be avoided.

Control over important rewards. Many students have had the experience of being assigned to a group project, with no say as to who was to be in the group or how scores earned by the group are to be distributed. A group of this design is an invitation to disaster, since some students are quick to realize they don't have to do anything; since everyone gets the same grade, they can rely on the more concerned students in the group to carry them. Sometimes a low performing member can be brought around by pressure from others, but often low performing members don't care very much how they are regarded by others. This has led to intense resentment by many group members, and failure of others to learn anything from the group project.

In the class you are now in, groups may have control over at least three types of member rewards. The first is the scores which members receive upon completion of a group assignment. Groups are expected to allocate earned points to members in proportion to their contribution to the assignment. The second reward is membership. Groups may recruit new members or discharge current members who are not meeting their standards. Similarly, an individual may move out of a group if it does not meet his or her standards (NOTE: if any changes in membership are being considered, contact the instructor for procedures). The third reward is approval and acceptance of members by the group. It is very important for many people to feel they are accepted by their group and that they are seen as doing good work.

Taking responsibility. In order for a group to work, members must not only have power over important rewards -- they must also use this power to motivate group members. It is all too common for a beginning group to start out with some statement like, "we're all equals here -- we know everyone will do their share". This is an invitation to disaster. Very often it is discovered later that someone is not pulling his or her share of the load. If explicit expectations had not been set, it then becomes difficult either to penalize this person for not performing, or to avoid penalizing the other group members who are hurt by the low performer.

In order for a group to be effective, members must receive important rewards only when they are performing up to expectations. While this is easy to say, it takes some work to realize it in practice. The following guidelines are recommended during the course of their group life:

1. Take time at the start to find out about who the people in your group are: what they are looking for and the resources they bring to your group.

2. Involve everyone in group decisions which affect them. Don't let people sit back and let others do the deciding. Involvement in making decisions is an important way of involving people in carrying them out.

3. Develop clear expectations as to what people need to do to stay in the group and to get their share of group rewards. Don't wait until people screw up to set these expectations.

4. When delegating work to individuals, be triple sure you have the means to pull their work back together again into an integrated group product. Usually, assigning someone to edit the pieces is not enough.

5. Don't assume that agreement at the start of the course will carry through to the end. Be ready to renegotiate as the group develops.

APPENDIX B

ORGANIZATIONAL BEHAVIOR SKILLS ASSESSMENT SURVEY[*]

PURPOSE:

To relate course concepts with personal experience

TIME REQUIRED:

30 minutes

Part I - Fill out the following table.

Briefly describe a situation where you were involved in the described activities.

ACTIVITY - describe in several sentences	POSITIVE - describe a situaton where you observed someone else do this in a positive manner.	NEGATIVE - describe when you observed it applied with negative consequences.	Chapter in text where discussed
Had AUTHORITY or POWER over someone else.			
CONFORMED to a group norm			
Had a CONFLICT with someone			
Helped someone to CHANGE			
MOTIVATED someone to work harder--got someone interested in something.			
WORKED IN A GROUP			
You were a LEADER for a group of people.			
Had a COMMUNICATION problem			

ACTIVITY - describe in several sentences	POSITIVE - describe a situaton where you observed some-one else do this in a positive manner.	NEGATIVE - describe when you observed it applied with negative consequences.	Chapter in text where discussed
Involved in an ETHICAL dilemma--did not know which course of action was right.			
Planned for your CAREER			
Involved in ISSUES relating to racism, male/female con-flicts, cross-cultural interactions.			

PART II - Using your textbook, find which chapter or chapters deal with each of the twelve items.

PART III - In groups of 4-5 reach a consensus on which chapters fit each topic and be prepared to present this to the class.

APPENDIX C

10 CASE DISCUSSION RULES[*]

1. Each remark must follow in some way from the last comment offered. Listen to what is being said and build on it.

2. Attempt to relate the case to your readings and what you have learned in class. Don't just speak from experience but connect your remarks to theory or the concepts of the course.

3. Only one person should speak at a time. Obviously it's more difficult to pay full attention to 2 or 3 people at once.

4. Control your personal evaluations of each other and use your intellect to try to understand what as well as why a person is saying what he or she is saying.

5. Attempt to build consensus on a conclusion or solution which reflects the best thinking of the group as a whole and not just an individual's view.

6. Practice active listening skills and if you need more information to understand what someone is saying ask for it. It's your responsibility to understand, so if you don't, then ask for help.

7. When speaking put your ideas in a logical form and be sure you are understood. Help the listeners understand your message by making sense (logic) of it for them.

8. Avoid excessive rhetoric or preaching, the professor does enough of that; try to stick to the facts of the case.

9. If you have to make assumptions about the case because there is not enough information, then state and support your assumptions clearly.

10. Test and evaluate what you have learned from the case. Share these learnings with others; it may help us all learn more.

---

[*]By Kenneth Murrell. Department of Management, University of West Florida, Pensacola, FL. Used with permission.

APPENDIX D

JUNG'S PERSONALITY TYPOLOGY[*]

Theory of Personality

Jung's personality typology, as operationalized in the Myers-Briggs Type Indicator, provides the theoretical basis for some of the exercises in chapter 2. Jung observed that people's behavior, rather than being individually unique, fit into patterns, and that much of the seemingly random differences in human behavior are actually orderly and consistent, being explained by differences in psychological attitudes and functions. These differences were termed preferences, because people actually prefer one type of functioning over another (Myers, 1962).

Two of these preferences concern the persons attitude toward the world. It can be one of extraversion or introversion.

The introvert is interested in exploring and analyzing the inner world and is introspective, withdrawn, very preoccupied with her own thoughts and reflections and tending to be distrustful (Jung, 1971). What is happening inside the introvert's head is much more interesting that what is outside; the inner world is rich, fascinating, and engrossing. Therefore, the introvert seems to be in continuous retreat from the outer world, holding aloof from external happenings, feeling lonely and lost in large gatherings. This type may often appear awkward and inhibited because the best qualities are kept only for a few close people. Mistrust and self-will characterize the introvert; however, this apprehensiveness of the objective world is not due to fear but because the outer world seems negative, demanding, and overpowering. The introvert's best work is done by self-initiative without interference from others and not influenced by majority views or public opinion. In work situations, introverted managers tend to "like quiet for concentration, be careful with details, like to think a lot before they act, and work contentedly alone" (Myer, 1962).

The extravert, on the other hand, is characterized by an interest in the outer world, by responsiveness to and a willing and ready acceptance of external events, by desire to influence and be influenced by events, a need to join in, the capacity to endure, the actual enjoyment of all kinds of noise and bustle, by a constant attention to environment, the cultivation of friends and acquaintances (none too carefully selected), and, finally, by the great importance associated with the image one projects and therefore a strong tendency to make a show of oneself. As a result, the extravert's philosophy and morals tend to be highly collective with a strong streak of altruism, while moral misgivings result when "other people know." At work, extraverted managers "like variety and action, tend to be faster," "dislike complicated procedures," are often impatient with long, slow jobs, are interested in the results of their job, often act quickly (sometimes without thinking), and usually "communicate well" (Myers, 1962).

No one is a "pure" type. We are all in a state of balance between extraversion (E) and introversion (I), using one type more naturally and more frequently. Earlier research indicates a disproprotionate number of extraverted managers. Since a manager is often required to work with and through other people, some extraversion would be useful. But too much can be counterproductive, with the real threat of getting "sucked" into external demands and becoming completely lost in them as well as losing identify and becoming submerged in conformist herd psychology.

Psychological Functions

Jung described four psychological functions which exist along two continua; the perception dimension, with sensing at one end and the intuition at the other; and the judgement dimension, with thinking at one end and feeling at the other. According to Jung, one of these four functions will tend to dominate the personality of the individual. For example, a person may be a

---

sensation-thinking, an intuition-thinking, a sensation-feeling, or an intuition-feeling type. No one is a "pure" type, but we all strive to achieve a state of balance.

The perception dimension of sensation vs. intuition relates to the ways in which a person becomes aware of ideas, facts, occurrences. When using sensing, perception occurs literally through the use of the five senses (Jung, 1971). As a result, this type is very much present-oriented, interested in practical matters, and prefers things to be orderly, precise, and unambiguous. They typically work steadily, like established routine, seldom make errors of fact, and rarely trust their inspirations (Myers, 1962).

Perceiving by intuition, alternatively, cannot be traced back to a conscious sensory experience but rather it is a sub-conscious process, with ideas or hunches coming "out of the blue," yielding the hidden possibilities of a situation. The intuitive is future-oriented (Myers, 1962), always looking ahead and inspiring others with innovations. By the time everyone else catches up, the intuitive is off on another idea. In fact, the intuitive finds it difficult to tolerate performance of routine tasks; as soon as one is mastered, another is started. Intuitives also "like solving new problems, work in bursts of energy, frequently jump to conclusions, are impatient with complicated situations, dislike taking time for precision, and follow their inspirations, good or bad" (Myers, 1962, p. 50).

Just as there are two ways of perceiving the world, there are two ways of making judgments about one's perceptions; namely, by thinking or by feeling. Thinking is a logical and analytical process, searching for the impersonal, true vs. false, correct vs. incorrect. Principles are more important to the thinker than are people (Myers, 1962), and the thinker often has a difficult time adapting to situations which cannot be understood intellectually (Jung, 1971). Other characteristics of this type are: they "are relatively unemotional and uninterested in people's feelings, may hurt people's feelings without knowing it, like analysis and putting things into logical order, can get along without harmony, need to be treated fairly, are able to reprimand people or fire them when necessary, and may seem hard-hearted" (Myers, 1962, p. 80).

Alternatively, feeling is a personal, subjective process, seeking a good vs. bad or like vs. dislike judgment. Whereas thinking occurs using objective criteria, feeling occurs on the basis of personal values and, in this sense, is different from emotion since feeling judgments are mental evaluations and not emotional reactions. The feeling type lives according to such subjective judgments based on a value system which is either related to society's values, as in the case of the extravert, or personal values, as in the introvert.

Dominant Process

The remaining preference determines which function is the principal or dominant one, i.e., whether perceiving or judging is the primary mode. For instance, when a person follows explanations open-mindedly, then perception (P) is being used; if, on the other hand, one's mind is rather quickly made up as to agreement or disagreement, then judgment (J) is preferred.

A fundamental difference in these two preferences is manifested in terms of which process is turned off or ignored. In order for judging to take place, perception must stop; all the facts are in, so a decision can be made. On the other hand, in order for perception to continue, judgments are put off for the time being as there is not enough data, new developments may occur.

Basically, the preference shows the difference between the perceptive types who live their lives as opposed to the judging types who run theirs. Each type is useful, but works better if the person can switch to the other mode when necessary. For a pure perceptive type is like a ship with all sail and no rudder, while a pure judging type is all form and no content (Myers, 1962).

As mentioned above, the perception-judgment (P-J) preference determines the principal function. For instance, an ST who prefers perceiving would have sensation, that is, the perceiving function, as his principal functions. The principal function of an NF who prefers judging would be feeling, the judging function.

However, in the case of the introvert, the dominant process is turned inward and his auxiliary or secondary function is shown to the world. Hence, the best side is kept for self or very close friends. The M-B indicator measures the principal function that is used on the outside world, in the case of the introvert, this is actually the auxiliary function.

Shadow Side

The unconscious and less developed side of a person's personality Jung calls the "shadow side." For example, if a person is primarily a thinking type, the shadow will be feeling, will compensate, at times, for the thinking process, and it may show itself at unexpected times. (Jung, 1971).

Perception-Judgment Combinations

The four functional types are a means to comprehend the world. Sensation tells us something exists, thinking tells us what that something is, feeling enables us to make value judgments on this object, and intuition gives us the ability to see the inherent possibilities (Mann, et al, 1968).

In each person one of the perception dimensions and one of the judgment dimensions are favored, so that we all prefer one of the following: 1) sensation with thinking; 2) intuition with thinking; 3) sensation with feeling; or 4) intuition with feeling.

Sensation with Thinking (ST).

This type is usually practical, impersonal and down-to-earth, being interested in facts, data, and statistics and wanting everything to be orderly, precise and unambiguous. The ST's tend to value efficiency, production, and clear lines of authority. In problem solving, the ST analyzes the facts through step-by-step logic, focusing on short-term problems and using standard procedures to find solutions (Hellriegel and Slocum, 1975).

Intuition with Thinking (NT).

NT's are inventive and concept-oriented and are likely to see the possibilities in a situation through impersonal analysis; though sometimes their conceptualizations confuse the other types. Flow charts, graphs, PERT, etc., all are tools that NT's feel comfortable with. These people are innovators of new ideas, frequently spark enthusiasm in others, and when solving problems, will often rely on hunches which they attempt to analyze later.

Sensation with Feeling (SF).

Individuals who are SF's tend to be practical, yet also sociable and gregarious. Like the ST's they are interested in facts, but SF's are more interested in facts about people; and they too, dislike ambiguity. SF's would strive to create an open, trusting environment where people care for one another and communicate well (Kilmann, 1975).

Although concerned with people's welfare, SF's have no time or inclination for global reflections on problems, but rather look at small aspects of problems and try to solve these (Hellriegel and Slocum, 1975).

Intuition with Feeling (NF).

Creativity, imagination, and personal warmth are valued by the NF, who is enthusiastic and insightful, generally seeing possibilities in and for people. Their goals are proud and general, often encompassing world problems. Their ideal organization is a decentralized one that has no strict hierarchy, few rules, policies and procedures, and encourages flexibility and open communication (Kilmann, 1975). It is very important to NF's to be committed to organizational goals. They may seem to be "dreamers" when solving problems, since theirs is, at times, an idealistic view of the world and its difficulties; but they are persistent and committed (Hellriegel and Slocum, 1975).

To summarize, then, Jung's Personality Typology is shown in Figure 1.

FIGURE 1

JUNG'S PERSONALITY TYPOLOGY (THE FOUR PREFERENCES)--AS OPERATIONALIZED BY MYERS AND BRIGGS

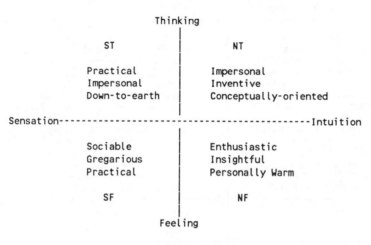

REFERENCES

Hellriegel, Don, and John W. Slocum, Jr. "Managerial Problem-Solving Styles." <u>Business Horizons</u>, December, 1975, pp. 29-37.

Jung, Carl. <u>Psychological Types</u>. Princeton, New Jersey: Princeton University Press, 1971.

Mann, Harriett, Miriam Siegler, and Humphrey Osmond. "The Many Worlds of Time." <u>Journal of Analytical Psychology</u>, 13, 1 (1968), 33-56.

Myers, Isabel B. <u>The Myers-Briggs Type Indicator Manual</u>. Princeton, New Jersey: Education Testing Service, 1962.

Kilmann, "Stories Managers Tell: A New Tool for Organizational Problem Solving," <u>Management Review</u> (July 1975) pp. 18-28.

EFFECTS OF THE COMBINATION OF ALL FOUR PREFERENCES IN YOUNG PEOPLE[**]
SENSING TYPES

WITH THINKING	WITH FEELING
ISTJ Serious, quiet, earn success by concentration and thoroughness. Practical, orderly, matter-of-fact, logical, realistic and dependable. See to it that everything is well organized. Take responsibility. Make up their own minds as to what should be accomplished and work toward it steadily, regardless of protests or distractions. Live their outer life more with thinking, inner more with sensing.	**ISFJ** Quiet, friendly, responsible and conscientious. Work devotedly to meet their obligations and serve their friends and school. Thorough, painstaking, accurate. May need time to master technical subjects, as their interests are not often technical. Patient with detail and routine. Loyal, considerate, concerned with how other people feel. Live their outer life more with feeling, inner more with sensing.
ISTP Cool onlookers, quiet, reserved, observing and analyzing life with detached curiosity and unexpected flashes of original humor. Usually interested in impersonal principles, cause and effect, or how and why mechanical things work. Exert themselves no more than they think necessary, because any waste of energy would be inefficient. Live their outer life more with sensing, inner more with thinking.	**ISFP** Retiring, quietly friendly, sensitive, modest about their abilities. Shun disagreements, do not force their opinions or values on others. Usually do not care to lead but are often loyal followers. May be rather relaxed about assignments or getting things done, because they enjoy the present moment and do not want to spoil it by undue haste or exertion. Live their outer life more with sensing, inner more with feeling.
ESTP Matter-of-fact, do not worry or hurry, enjoy whatever comes along. Tend to like mechanical things and sports, with friends on the side. May be a bit blunt or insensitive. Can do math or science when they see the need. Dislike long explanations. Are best with real things that can be worked, handled, taken apart or put back together. Live their outer life more with sensing, inner more with thinking.	**ESFP** Outgoing, easygoing, accepting, friendly, fond of a good time. Like sports and making things. Know what's going on and join in eagerly. Find remembering facts easier than mastering theories. Are best in situations that need sound common sense and practical ability with people as well as with things. Live their outer life more with sensing, inner more with feeling.
ESTJ Practical realists, matter-of-fact, with a natural head for business or mechanics. Not interested in subjects they see no use for, but can apply themselves when necessary. Like to organize and run activities. Tend to run things well, especially if they remember to consider other people's feelings and points of view when making their decisions. Live their outer life more with thinking, inner more with sensing.	**ESFJ** Warm-hearted, talkative, popular, conscientious, born cooperators, active committee members. Always doing something nice for someone. Work best with plenty of encouragement and praise. Little interest in abstract thinking or technical subjects. Main interest is in things that directly and visibly affect people's lives. Live their outer life more with feeling, inner more with sensing.

(Rows are labeled: INTROVERTS — JUDGING, PERCEPTIVE; EXTRAVERTS — PERCEPTIVE, JUDGING)

[**]Reprinted by permission of the publisher from Manual for the Myers-Briggs Type Indicator by Isabel Briggs Myers, (c) 1962 by Consulting Psychologists Press.

INTUITIVES

WITH FEELING	WITH THINKING
INFJ	**INTJ**
Succeed by perseverance, originality and desire to do whatever is needed or wanted. Put their best efforts into their work. Quietly forceful, conscientious, concerned for others. Respected for their firm principles. Likely to be honored and followed for their clear convictions as to how best to serve the common good. Live their outer life more with feeling, inner more with intuition.	Have original minds and great drive which they use only for their own purposes. In fields that appeal to them they have a fine power to organize a job and carry it through with or without help. Skeptical, critical, independent, determined, often stubborn. Must learn to yield less important points in order to win the most important. Live their outer life more with thinking, inner more with intuition.
INFP	**INTP**
Full of enthusiasms and loyalties, but seldom talk of these until they know you well. Care about learning, ideas, language, and independent projects of their own. Apt to be on yearbook staff, perhaps as editor. Tend to undertake too much, then somehow get it done. Friendly, but often too absorbed in what they are doing to be sociable or notice much. Live their outer life more with intuition, inner more with feeling.	Quiet, reserved, brilliant in exams, especially in theoretical or scientific subjects. Logical to the point of hair-splitting. Interested mainly in ideas, with little liking for parties or small talk. Tend to have very sharply defined interests. Need to choose careers where some strong interest of theirs can be used and useful. Live their outer life more with intuition, inner more with thinking.
ENFP	**ENTP**
Warmly enthusiastic, high-spirited, ingenious, imaginative. Able to do almost anything that interests them. Quick with a solution for any difficulty and ready to help anyone with a problem. Often rely on their ability to improvise instead of preparing in advance. Can always find compelling reasons for whatever they want. Live their outer life more with intuition, inner more with feeling.	Quick, ingenious, good at many things. Stimulating company, alert and outspoken, argue for fun on either side of a question. Resourceful in solving new and challenging problems, but may neglect routine assignments. Turn to one new interest after another. Can always find logical reasons for whatever they want. Live their outer life more with intuition, inner more with thinking.
ENFJ	**ENTJ**
Responsive and responsible. Feel real concern for what others think and want, and try to handle things with due regard for other people's feelings. Can present a proposal or lead a group discussion with ease and tact. Sociable, popular, active in school affairs, but put time enough on their studies to do good work. Live their outer life more with feeling, inner more with intuition.	Hearty, frank, able in studies, leaders in activities. Usually good in anything that requires reasoning and intelligent talk, such as public speaking. Are well-informed and keep adding to their fund of knowledge. May sometimes be more positive and confident than their experience in an area warrants. Live their outer life more with thinking, inner more with intuition.

INTROVERTS
JUDGING / JUDGING
PERCEPTIVE

PERCEPTIVE / EXTRAVERTS
PERCEPTIVE / JUDGING

APPENDIX E

WHAT IS THE MOST IMPORTANT FEATURE OF AN IDEAL JOB

AUBURN FRESHMEN

ISTJ	ISFJ A Stable and Secure Future	INFJ Use My Special Abilities	INTJ Be Creative and Original
ISTP A Stable and Secure Future	ISFP	INFP Be Creative and Original	INTP Use My Special Abilities Earn a Lot of Money
ESTP	ESFP A Stable and Secure Future	ENFP Be Creative and Original	ENTP Be Creative and Original
ESTJ A Stable and Secure Future	ESFJ Be of Service to Others	ENFJ Use My Special Abilities	ENTJ

APPENDIX F

NON-DIRECTIVE INTERVIEWING

Non-Directive Interviewing[*]

Nondirective interviewing is based on the work of Carl Rogers. (some call it active listening) and is best used when you are listening to someone talk about an issue which has an emotional component. It basically means that you respond to the feelings behind the words of what the person really means. Managers can use the technique when dealing with an upset subordinate (or boss, for that matter), helping a colleague solve his problem, etc. Like any other tool, it is effective only under certain conditions. For example, nondirective interviewing is not best used when there is a technical problem to solve, or in emergency situations.

What is Non-Directive Interviewing?

This method differs from the popular view of problem solving in that no solution to a problem is supplied and no advice is given. Rather, the interviewer stimulates others to uncover their problems themselves and to decide their own courses of action. A person is more likely to act upon a solution worked out personally because it is more acceptable. Giving advice, asking questions, making a diagnosis, and supplying the solution characterize the directive approach. Volunteered advice is notoriously unproductive; even people who ask for it seldom are pleased or moved to act by what they hear.

Non-Directive Skills

Active Listening - Listeners must demonstrate their desire to understand through their behavior and through their acceptance of the person, as well as of the person's statement. If interviewers indicate doubt, surprise, disagreement, or criticism, they are acting as judge or critic; if they express agreement, pity, or even sympathy, they are acting as supporter. Judging stimulates defensive behavior; offering support stimulates dependent behavior.

The active listener's behavior includes a posture indicative of attention, a friendly facial expression, patience, and acceptance of pauses. Certain vocal expressions may rightly be included under listening. These include such expressions as "Uh-huh," "I see," "I understand," and "Do you want to tell me about that?" Even if directly asked to express an opinion, an interviewer can avoid entering into a discussion by saying, "Would you like to tell me how you feel about it?" or "I think it is best for you to tell me about it."

Accepting Feelings - This means a sensitivity to the other person's feelings and avoidance of evaluation of those feelings. If a person expressing hostile feelings is told by a supervisor that he or she is reacting unjustly, the employee may feel judged and rejected and become defensive. If the supervisor gives advice before understanding the person's true problem, the advice may be inappropriate and unacceptable. Nevertheless, hostile and childish feelings may require more than permissive listening; in this case, they can be accepted and verbalized by the counseling supervisor without either agreeing or disagreeing with them. Examples of verbal acceptance of feelings are:

*You must have been very upset to have walked out of his office like that.
*I can see that your feelings were hurt badly by that incident.
*I can see you were badly upset by my criticism of the job you did.

---

[*]Adapted from Psychology in Industrial Organizations by Norman R. Maier and Gertrude Casselman Verser, Houghton-Mifflin, 1982, pp. 487-495.

<u>Reflecting Feelings</u> - The method of reflecting feelings is analogous to the interviewer serving as a <u>selective</u> mirror. The interviewer mirrors or restates some parts of the conversation and allows other parts to pass. Facts, incidents, justifications, details of arguments and reasons, the chronology and geography of events are relatively unimportant, but how the person feels about any of these things is important. These feelings must be reflected so they can be seen in a different setting. In learning to reflect feelings, the following points should be observed.

1. Restate the other person's expressed feelings in your own words rather than mimicking or parroting the original words.

2. Preface reflected remarks, at first, with "You feel...," "You think...," "It seems to you that...," "It sometimes appears to you that...," and so on. Later in the interview, you can dispense with such prefatory phrases.

3. Formulate reflected remarks as statements, not as questions. Try to speak quietly and slowly, and with a neutral emotional tone.

4. Wait out pauses. Long pauses often enable a person to say things that are difficlt to admit. Inexperienced interviewers often are embarrassed by pauses and make distracting remarks to fill them.

5. When many feelings are expressed, as in a long speech, only the last feeling area expressed should be reflected.

6. In reflecting another person's state of mind, any indication of approval or disapproval should be avoided. It is important to refrain from questioning, probing, blaming, interpreting, giving advice, persuading, reassuring, and giving sympathy.

7. Diagnoses should be avoided. A diagnosis is an interviewer's interpretation of why the disturbed person feels that way and leads to biased listening.

8. It is almost always safe to assume that what initially is presented as the problem is not the central one.

Values and Assumptions About People

1. A belief that individuals are basically responsible for themselves and a willingness to let them keep that responsibility.

2. A belief that people are capable of solving their problems once interfering obstacles are removed and that most people basically want to do the right thing.

3. An appreciation of the fact that every solution to life's problems must conform with a person's values and beliefs, and that individuals know their own feelings and aspirations better than an outsider does.

4. The development of an acceptant attitude is crucial because a person will bring out hidden feelings only when confident of being understood and not judged. A permissive atmosphere is necessary if a person is to express absurd, unconventional, contradictory, or hateful feelings.

5.   A profound respect for the importance of feelings in learning to live a full life. In most situations, people are asked to justify or give reasons for their opinions. Innocent remarks such as "I don't like that person," "I don't feel comfortable there," or even "I don't like olives" are met with the question "Why?" and a person who cannot supply good reasons may be judged as biased or not too bright. Since feelings are so often misunderstood, they frequently are withheld. The interviewer must respect the dignity of feelings, no matter how unreasonable they at first appear, in order to help another person express them.

APPENDIX G

GIVING AND RECEIVING FEEDBACK

Effective and Ineffective Feedback Behaviors[*]

Effective Feedback	Ineffective Feedback
1	Describes the behavior which led to the feedback: "You are finishing my sentences for me."	Uses evaluative/judgmental statements: "You're being rude." Or generalized ones: "You're trying to control the conversation."
2	Comes as soon as appropriate after the behavior - immediately if possible, later if events make that (something more important going on, you need time to "cool down," the person has other feedback etc.)	Is delayed, saved up, and "dumped." Also know as "gunny-sacking" or ambushing. The more time that passes, the "safer" it is necessary to give the feedback. Induces guilt and anger in the receiver, because after time has passed there's usually not much she or he can do about it. to deal with,
3	Is direct, from sender to receiver.	Indirect: ricochetted ("Tom, how do you feel when Jim cracks his knuckles?) - also known as "let's you and him fight."
4	Is "owned" by the sender, who uses "I messages" and takes responsibility for his or her thoughts, feelings, reactions.	"Ownership" is transferred to "people." "the book," "upper management," everybody," "we," etc.
5	Includes the sender's real feelings about the behavior, insofar as they are relevant to the feedback: "I get frustrated when I'm trying to make a point and you keep finishing my sentences."	Feelings are concealed, denied, misrepresented, distorted. One way to do this is to "transfer ownership" (see #4). Another way is to smuggle the feelings into the interaction by being sarcastic, sulking, competing to see who's "right," etc. Other indicators: speculations on the receiver's intentions, motivations, or psychological "problems": "You're trying to drive me nuts": "You're just trying to see how much you can get away with": You have a need to get even with the world."
6	Is checked for clarity, to ensure that the receiver fully understands conveyed. "Do you understand what I mean when I say you seem to be sending me a double message?"	Not checked. Sender either assumes clarity or - fairly often - is not **interested** in what's being whether receiver understands fully: "Stop interrupting me with "Yes, buts!"

---

[*]Reprinted with permission from NTL Institute, "Giving and Receiving Feedback; It Will Never Be Easy, But It Can Be Better," by Larry Porter, pp. 43-44, Reading Book for Human Relations Training, edited by Lawrence Porter and Bernard Mohr, Copyright 1982.

7   Asks relevant questions which seek information (has a problem-solving quality), with the receiver knowing information is sought and having a clear sense that the sender does not know the answer.

Asks questions which are really statements ("?Do you think I'm going to let you get away with that?") or which sound like why the traps ("How many times have you been late this wee?") Experts at the "question game" can easily combine the two ("How do you think that makes me feel? or "Do you behave that way at home too?")**

8   Is solicited or at least to some extent desired by the receiver.***

Is imposed on the receiver, often for her or his "own good."

9   Refers to behaviors about which the do something. ("I wish you'd stop interrupting me."), if wants to.

Refers to behaviors over which the receiv-receiver can er has little or not control, if she or he is to remain authentic: "I wish you'd   she or he laugh   at my jokes."

10   Affirms the receiver's existence and worth by acknowledging his or have the reactions she or he has, whatever they may being willing to work through issues in a game-free way.

Denies or discounts the receiver by using statistics, abstractions, averages: by re- her "right" to fusing to accept his/her feelings: "Oh, you're just being paranoid." "Come on!   be, and by You're over-reacting." "You're not really as angry as you say you are."****

Most people can make significant improvements in the feedback skills by not asking **any questions!

***Since the condition doesn't exist all that often you may wonder how you can ever give feedback. Keep two things in mind (1) Not all the criteria have to be met all the time; and (2) If you have to **impose** it on the recipient, it's likely to be helpful to the process if you'll keep that in mind and take it into ac count as you interact.

****These may be accurate interpretations, of course, but the sender is not likely to "reach" the receiver by being "right" in these instances in some significant human interactions there are often more important things than being that kind of "right."

APPENDIX H

"WHAT TO OBSERVE IN A GROUP"*

Group Observation Table

Behavior in the group can be seen from the point of view of what its purpose or function seems to be. When a member says something, is he primarily trying to get the group task accomplished (task), to improve or patch up some relationships among members (maintenance), or to meet some personal need or goal without regard to the group's problems (self-oriented)?

Description of Behavior	Names of Individuals Observed				
Task: - Types of behavior relevant to the group's task fulfillment					
1) Initiator - proposes tasks or goals. defines a problem; suggests ways to solve problems					
2) Information or opinion seeker - asks for facts, ideas, or suggestions; seeks relevant information about group concern; solicits expressions of values.					
3) Information or opinion giver-offers facts; states belief or opinion.					
4) Clarifyer and Elaborator - interprets ideas or suggestions; clears up confusions; defines terms; indicates alternatives and issues for the group.					
5) Summarizer - pulls together related ideas; restates suggestions; offers a decision or conclusion for acceptance or rejection.					
6) Consensus Tester - asks to see whether the group is nearing a decision; sends up a trial balloon to test a possible conclusion.					
Maintenance - types of behavior relevant to the groups remaining in good working order, having a good task work climate, and good relationships which permit maximum use of member resources.					

---

*Adapted from Edgar H. Schein. From Readings Book for Human Relations Training, 1979 edition. Copyright by NTL Institute. Used with permission.

Description of Behavior	Names of Individuals Observed				
1) Harmonizer - mediates differences; relieves tension in conflict situations; gets people to explore differ ences.					
2) Gatekeeper - keeps communication open; facilitates the participation of others; suggests procedures for sharing information.					
3) Encourager - friendly and responsive to others; offers praise; accepts others' points of view.					
4) Compromiser - when own idea is involved in conflict, offers compromise and admits error; maintains group cohesion.					
5) Standard Setter and Tester - tests whether group is satisfied with its procedures; points out explicit or implicit norms to test.					
Self-Oriented - behavior that interferes with group work.					
1) Aggressor - attacks; deflates, uses sarcasm.					
2) Blocker - resists beyond reason; prevents group movement by using hidden items.					
3) Dominator - interrupts; asserts authority; over-participates to the point of interference with others.					
4) Avoider - prevents group from facing controversy; stays off subject to avoid commitment.					
5) Abandoner - makes obvious display of lack of involvement.					

QUESTIONS

1. Who talks the most?
2. Who talks the least?
3. Who is listened to the most?
4. Who is listened to the least?
5. Who is the informal leader? (Look for the person who is looked at most when members speak.)
6. Leadership style?   autocratic   _____
                        democratic   _____
                        laissez-faire   _____
7. How is conflict resolved?

8. Are there any subgroups?
9. Are members withdrawn? What happened?
10. What are the group's norms? (i.e., voting or discussion, joking, interrupting, etc.)
11. How is expertise established and used?

APPENDIX I

ANALYSIS OF TEAM OR GROUP EFFECTIVENESS
GOALS AND DIRECTION[*]

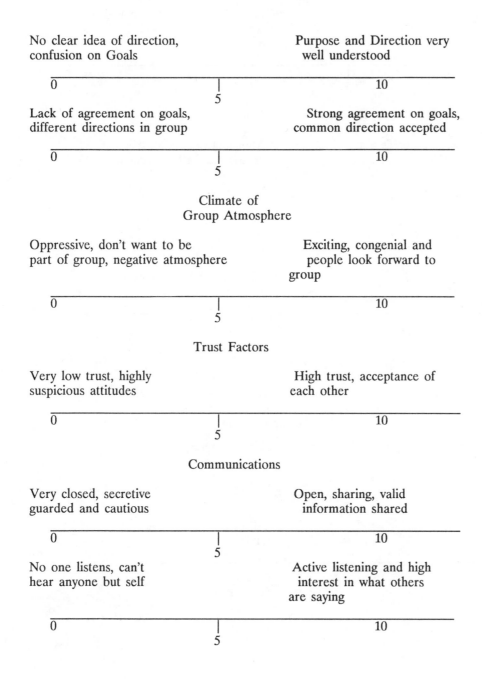

No clear idea of direction,
confusion on Goals

Purpose and Direction very
well understood

0 | 10
                                         5

Lack of agreement on goals,
different directions in group

Strong agreement on goals,
common direction accepted

0 | 10
                                         5

Climate of
Group Atmosphere

Oppressive, don't want to be
part of group, negative atmosphere

Exciting, congenial and
people look forward to
group

0 | 10
                                         5

Trust Factors

Very low trust, highly
suspicious attitudes

High trust, acceptance of
each other

0 | 10
                                         5

Communications

Very closed, secretive
guarded and cautious

Open, sharing, valid
information shared

0 | 10
                                         5

No one listens, can't
hear anyone but self

Active listening and high
interest in what others
are saying

0 | 10
                                         5

---

[*]By Kenneth L. Murrell. Department of Management, University of West Florida, Pensacola,
FL. Used with permission.

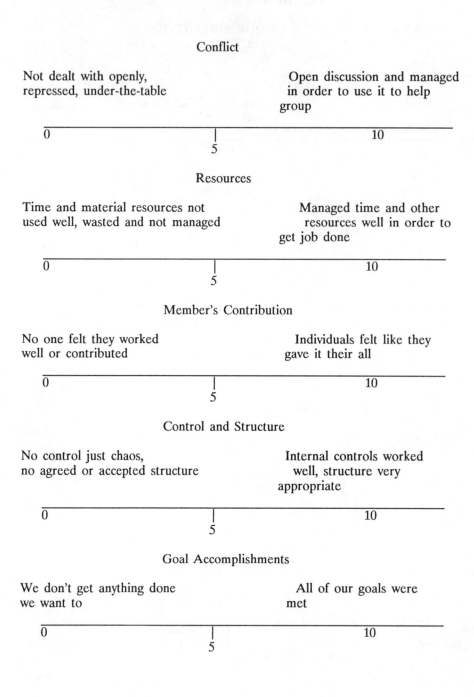

Conflict

Not dealt with openly,
repressed, under-the-table

Open discussion and managed
in order to use it to help
group

0   5   10

Resources

Time and material resources not
used well, wasted and not managed

Managed time and other
resources well in order to
get job done

0   5   10

Member's Contribution

No one felt they worked
well or contributed

Individuals felt like they
gave it their all

0   5   10

Control and Structure

No control just chaos,
no agreed or accepted structure

Internal controls worked
well, structure very
appropriate

0   5   10

Goal Accomplishments

We don't get anything done
we want to

All of our goals were
met

0   5   10

APPENDIX J

ROLE FOR FRED OR FRANCINE

Foremost, you are concerned about turning this place around. You were brought in to straighten up this unit. This Division is important to the Company that is why you have been given so much autonomy. Furthermore, you want to get this on track as soon as possible so that you can return to the Western operations.

To help you clean up this operation, you have brought in some top people of which this particular subordinate is one of the best. Even though you respect this person, there is one problem. He/she has been to too many of these 'human relations' courses and you feel tends to be a bit too 'soft' on subordinates. You think this is clearly demonstrated in not firing Rae.

So it is out of your desire to turn this organization around and because YOU BASICALLY WANT TO HELP this subordinate, that you are putting on all this pressure to fire Rae. You don't want to see your subordinate waste all this time and effort trying to prop up a poor performer when it would be possible to pull in a really top manager.

THIS IS IMPORTANT: Be as coercive and threatening as you can be. Yell, badger, interrupt and rant and rave. Warn him that he will be held accountable for Rae's performance, etc., etc. In other words, pull out all the stops in trying to get the subordinate to fire Rae.

There are only two limitations. First, you, personally, won't "order" the subordinate to fire Rae, you are only "telling him to do so" (so if the subordinate asks, "Is this an order?" change the subject). Second, if the subordinate says, "OK, you fire Rae," change the subject.

FINALLY: There is only one condition when you will back down and stop badgering Rae (which is the subordinate's objective). If the subordinate says: "Look, Rae is my subordinate, not yours. I will be responsible for her performance. If you, Fred, have any problems with Rae's performance, you see me about it but stop badgering her."

[This statement: a) recognizes the rules and structure of the organization and b) has the subordinate accept responsibility for his/her jurisdiction. Both are forms of legitimate power.]

If the subordinate tells you that, you may still grouse and grumble, but you will back down.

APPENDIX K

TOP SECRET
ARAK
Negotiation Information

Preface

This document contains the information that you as a negotiator will need for the conference. It describes the scoring system, security, and goals of Arak for each area.

Scoring

You are to represent Arak in the negotiations over the disputed zone. Naturally the government of Arak expects you to do the best you can for the citizens. To assist you in meeting the desires of the citizens the government has designed a point system that indicates the value of the issues as accurately as they can be estimated. Your goal is to maximize the total number of points for the whole negotiations.

Security

The disclosure of TOP SECRET information from the "Goal" sections that follow is left to your discretion during the negotiations. The following Area discussions are divided into three sections: Descriptions, Goals, and Intelligence.

Descriptions. All description are common knowledge.

Goals. All goal sections are TOP SECRET. These are the intentions and priorities of Arak. They also provide additional information which is not available or known to Barkan.

Intelligence. These sections are the result of espionage which has been conducted. Information about Barkan is presented that may be useful during negotiations.

Area I

Description. This is a choice food producing area, forest products resources area and a potential source of bauxite (aluminum ore). The area is 50 miles wide and approximately 90 miles long.

Goal. Ownership of this area can help overcome several major problems faced by Arak. They are: insufficient food for Arakians, a balance of payments deficit, and a diminishing supply of timber for the house building industry. In addition, it could provide a source of raw material for the country's developing industrial base.

There have been severe shortages in three of the last ten years resulting in malnutrition of approximately three million school-age children. Naturally the solution to this problem is a high priority for Arak. The second problem is the balance of payments deficit. Because of the recent food shortages Arak has run up a large deficit and its credit rating is quite poor in the worldwide monetary market. It is crucial that Arak overcome this deficit by developing an export business.

The townships in the central part of Area I are particularly well suited to potato production although potatoes can be grown successfully anywhere in the valley. Potatoes are central in the diet of Arakians. Other food crops can be grown at various places throughout the area. It is very important to obtain as much land as possible to alleviate the threat of malnutrition to Arakian school children.

Arak is well known for its pure grape juice which it exports when Area I is in its possession. Export of this juice brings in substantial revenue and adds immensely to the prestige of the country. Much of Area I is ideally suited for highly profitable production of both juice and table grapes.

Arak is attempting to provide housing for all of its population but it is facing a diminishing supply of timber within its present borders. If you can gain control of most of the forest land, you can assure adequate housing for Arakians. Without a sufficient supply of timber many Arakians will remain in substandard housing.

The Ministry of Agriculture and Natural Resources has assigned a point value to each of the townships to indicate the relative value of each in solving Arak's problems. These are indicated in the TOP SECRET map. The Ministry estimates that if you gain control of any combination of townships worth 140 to 160 of the 248 points, then Arak will be free of food shortages, will be able to export juice, and will be able to adequately house the population.

Based on these estimates the Prime Minister has instructed you to try to obtain the maximum number of points you can for your country.

Intelligence. Because of the highly productive and useful nature of this area you can expect Barkan to be very interested in this area, or at least very resistant to the idea of giving up all or part of this area.

Area II

Description. This is a very arid region which, until recently, was largely unknown. Because of the remoteness of this region little development has taken place. The area is 50 miles wide and 90 miles long. Ten years ago Cordan erected Steeltown about 25 miles outside this region. Cordan has never made any move to take over this region and remains friendly to both Arak and Barkan.

Goal. Arak has been put in a very difficult position in recent years. The need for steel has been acute in the past 10 years. Production of farm machinery, heavy equipment for construction, and defense weapons have all depended on a regular supply of quality steel into Trade City, 50 miles north of Area II.

Since the erection of Steeltown in Cordan, Arak has traded vigorously for the steel produced. This has been marginally satisfactory in the past but it presents Arak with two problems: unpredictable quality steel and a balance of payments deficit with Cordan.

Historically, 15% of the steel shipped from Steeltown has not passed the quality inspections. This occurs because Steeltown is operating over capacity and so cannot monitor adquately.

The trade has been secured primarily through the mining of a small iron ore deposit northeast of Trade City, about 75 miles from Steeltown. Ore is sold to Steeltown from this deposit at $5.00 per ton and steel is purchased for $25.00 per ton. This has caused a serious balance of payments problem and the rapid depletion of this small ore deposit. It is estimated by the Ministry of Agriculture and Natural Resources that at current rates of mining this deposit will be depleted at the end of two years. Consequently, an intensive search was made for a new ore deposit. An extremely large deposit was located. However, it is 100 miles south of Trade City, right on the border of Barkan. Knowledge of this deposit has been kept TOP SECRET and it is known that Barkan is not aware of this important resource. If this deposit could be obtained, trade with Cordan would continue and the balance of payments problem could be resolved.

Arak has long desired to produce its own steel, but it has not had all the necessary factors of production. It does have an ore deposit 900 miles north (not on map) but it can not exploit it because the iron ore and coal must be within 150 miles of each other to be economically useful. The

Ministry of Industry advises that due to slowdowns in other fields Arak has an abundance of skilled workers who could man a steel plant, but there is a serious question whether Arak has the technical skills to build a steel plant.

The Ministry of Industry found it impossible to anticipate all the solutions you, as a negotiator, might devise but to help you weight the issues in Area II the Ministry advises that:

1. A solution which almost certainly will provide for delivery of high quality steel for the long run (20 years) is worth 100 points.

2. A solution which probably will provide for delivery of high quality steel for the long run is worth 70 points.

3. A solution which reduces the deficit with Cordan is worth 40 points.

4. No solution is worth zero points.

Intelligence. The goals and priorities of Barkan are not known. However, it is known that Barkan receives at least some of its steel from Cordan. Also, it is estimated that steel is important to the welfare of Barkan, as it is with most developing countries.

Time for the Conference. The conference is scheduled to last thirty minutes. A treaty must be completed and signed by both negotiators by the end of the conference to prevent war between Arak and Barkan. Failure to prevent this war will result in no points for you as a negotiator.

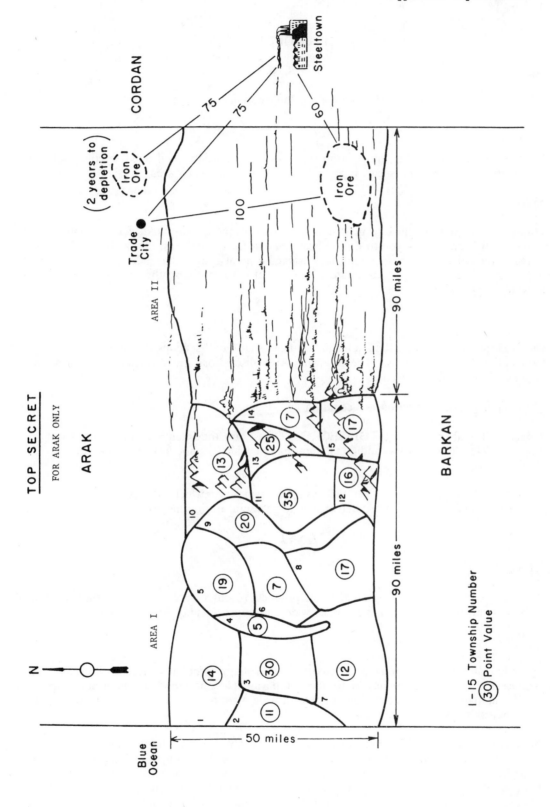

APPENDIX L

TOP SECRET
BARKAN
Negotiation Information

Preface

This document contains the information that you as a negotiator will need for the conference. It describes the scoring system, security, and goals of Barkan for each area.

Scoring

You are to represent Barkan in the negotiations over the disputed zone. Naturally the government of Barkan expects you to do the best you can for the citizens. To assist you in meeting the desires of the citizens the government has designed a point system that indicates the value of the issues as accurately as they can be estimated. Your goal is to maximize the total number of points for the whole negotiations.

Security

The disclosure of TOP SECRET information from the "Goal" sections that follow is left to your discretion during the negotiations. The following Area discussions are divided into three sections: Descriptions, Goals, and Intelligence.

Descriptions. All description are common knowledge.

Goals. All goal sections are TOP SECRET. These are the intentions and priorities of Barkan. They also provide additional information which is not available or known to Arak.

Intelligence. These sections are the result of espionage which has been conducted. Information about Arak is presented that may be useful during negotiations.

Area I

Description.

This is a choice food producing area, forest products resources area and a potential source of bauxite (aluminum ore). The area is 50 miles wide and approximately 90 miles long.

Goal.

Ownership of this area can help overcome several major problems faced by Barkan. They are: insufficient food for Barkanians, a balance of payments deficit, and a diminishing supply of pulpwood for its paper mills. In addition, it could provide a source of raw material for the country's developing industrial base.

There have been severe shortages in four of the last twelve years resulting in thousands of cases of rickets and anemia in preschool-age children. Naturally the solution to this problem is a high priority for Barkan. The second problem is the balance of payments deficit. Because of the recent food shortages Barkan has run up a large deficit and its credit rating is quite poor in the worldwide monetary market. It is crucial that Barkan overcome this deficit by developing an export business.

The townships in the central part of Area I are particularly well suited to wheat production although wheat can be grown successfully anywhere in the valley. Wheat is central in the diet of Barkanians. Other food crops can be grown at various places throughout the area. It is very important to obtain as much land as possible to alleviate the threat of disease to Barkanian children.

Barkan is well known for its quality fruit preserves which it exports when Area I is in its possession. Export of these preserves brings in substantial revenue and adds immensely to the prestige of the country. Much of Area I is ideally suited for highly profitable production of strawberries, peaches and various berries necessary for the production of preserves.

As a result of uncontrolled logging 50 years earlier, Barkan's own forests are presently being consumed faster than trees are being replaced. If you can gain control of most of the forest land in Area I, a steady supply of wood pulp can be obtained. This will keep the paper mills running while the traditional sources of pulpwood within the established border replenish themselves. Without a sufficient supply of pulpwood, the paper mills will close down and over 5000 employees will be laid off.

The Ministry of Agriculture and Natural Resources has assigned a point value to each of the townships to indicate the relative value of each in solving Barkans problems. These are indicated in the TOP SECRET map. The Ministry estimates that if you gain control of any combination of townships worth 140 to 160 of the 248 points, then Barkan will be free of food shortages, will be able to export preserves and will have sufficient pulpwood.

Based on these estimates the Prime Minister has instructed you to try to obtain the maximum number of points you can for your country.

Intelligence. Because of the highly productive and useful nature of this area you can expect Arak to be very interested in this area, or at least very resistant to the idea of giving up all or part of this area.

Area II

Description.

This is a very arid region which, until recently, was largely unknown. Because of the remoteness of this region little development has taken place. The area is 50 miles wide and 90 miles long. Ten years ago Cordan erected Steeltown about 25 miles outside this region. Cordan has never made any move to take over this region and remains friendly to both Arak and Barkan.
Goal.

Barkan has been put in a very difficult position in recent years. The need for steel has been acute in the past 10 years. Production of machine tools, trucks, heavy equipment for construction, and defense weapons have all depended on a steady supply of raw steel into Skill City, 50 miles south of Area II.

Since the erection of Steeltown in Cordan, Barkan has traded vigorously for the steel produced. This has been marginally satisfactory in the past but it presents Barkan with two problems: irregularity of delivery and a balance of payments deficit with Cordan.

Historically, approximately 10% of the orders of steel from Steeltown have arrived more than three months late. This occurs because Steeltown is operating over capacity and so incurs frequent breakdowns.

The trade has been secured primarily through the mining of a small coal deposit southeast of Skill City, about 75 miles from Steeltown. Coal is sold to Steeltown from this deposit at $5.00 per ton and steel is purchased for $25.00 per ton. This has caused a serious balance of payments problem and the rapid depletion of this small coal deposit. It is estimated by the Ministry of Agriculture and Natural Resources that at current rates of mining this deposit will be depleted at the end of two years. Consequently, an intensive search was made for a new coal deposit. An extremely large deposit was located. However, it is 100 miles north of Skill City, right on the border of Arak. Knowledge of this deposit has been kept TOP SECRET and it is known that Arak is not aware of this important resource. If this deposit could be obtained, trade with Cordan would continue and the balance of payments problem could be resolved.

Barkan has long desired to produce its own steel, but it has not had all the necessary factors of production. It does have an iron ore deposit 700 miles south (not on map) but it can not exploit it because the iron ore and coal must be within 150 miles of each other to be economically useful. The Ministry of Industry advises that Barkan has the technical skills to build a steel mill but that there are not enough skilled steel workers to fill all the positions in a steel mill.

The Ministry of Industry found it impossible to anticipate all the solutions you, the negotiator, might devise but to help you weight the issues in Area II the Ministry advises that:

1. A solution which almost certainly will provide for reliable delivery of steel for the long run (20 years) is worth 100 points.

2. A solution which probably will provide for reliable delivery of steel for the long run is worth 70 points.

3. A solution which reduces the deficit with Cordan is worth 40 points.

4. No solution is worth zero points.

Intelligence.

The goals and priorities of Arak are not known. However, it is known that Arak receives at least some of its steel from Cordan. Also, it is estimated that steel is important to the welfare of Arak, as it is with most developing countries.

Time for the Conference. The conference is scheduled to last thirty minutes. A treaty must be completed and signed by both negotiators by the end of the conference to prevent war between Arak and Barkan. Failure to prevent this war will result in no points for you as a negotiator.

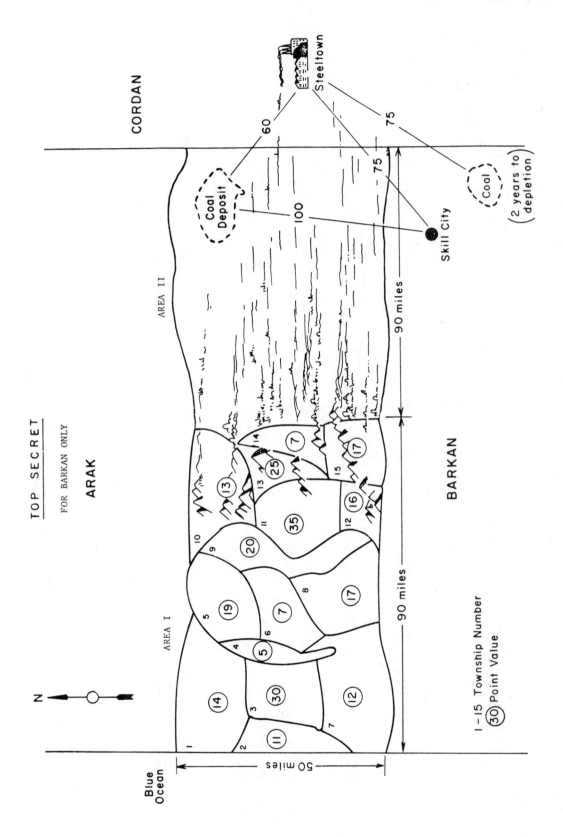

TOP SECRET

FOR BARKAN ONLY

ARAK

CORDAN

Steeltown

Coal Deposit

60

75

75

100

Coal

(2 years to depletion)

Skill City

AREA II

BARKAN

90 miles

AREA I

90 miles

50 miles

Blue Ocean

N

1–15 Township Number
30 Point Value

APPENDIX M

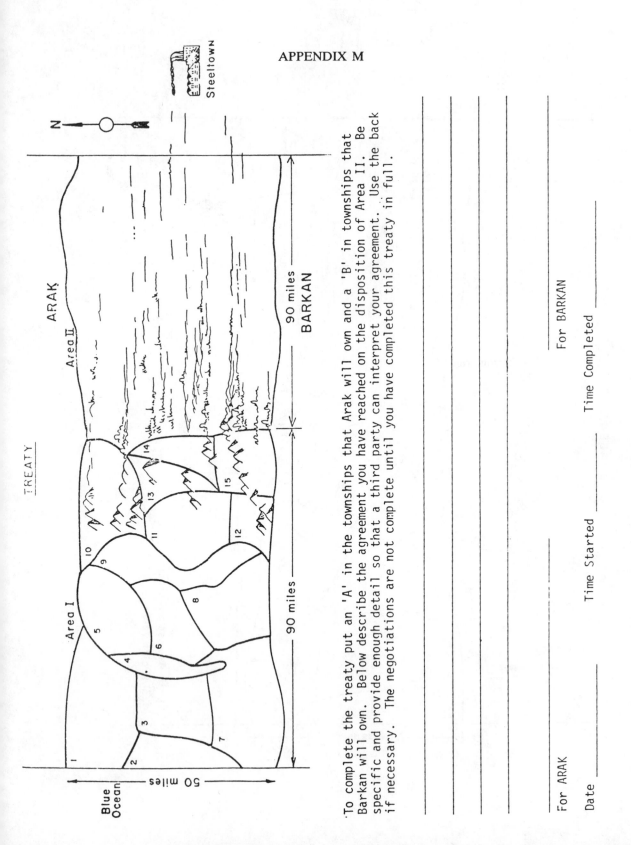

To complete the treaty put an 'A' in the townships that Arak will own and a 'B' in townships that Barkan will own. Below describe the agreement you have reached on the disposition of Area II. Be specific and provide enough detail so that a third party can interpret your agreement. Use the back if necessary. The negotiations are not complete until you have completed this treaty in full.

For ARAK _____   For BARKAN _____

Date _____   Time Started _____   Time Completed _____

APPENDIX N

SCORING PROTOCOL

Area I Scoring: Sum the points for each negotiator.

Area II Scoring:

100 pts.   A solution which <u>almost certainly</u> solves the steel problem will include access to both of the mineral resources (coal and iron) in Area II plus the use of Arak's technological skills for building a steel mill and Barkan's skilled workers to man the plant. (It is possible for one negotiator to gain all of the resources and the opponent to end up with none but the possibility is remote.)

70 pts.   A solution which probably solves the problem is one that falls short of the above but does better than simply gaining access to one resource (as below). This includes any solution which provides partial to full access to both mineral resources but does not include the indication of plans to share technology and skilled labor. Some examples are:

1. Full ownership of both iron and coal.
2. Full ownership of one resource and half of the other.
3. Partial ownership of both iron and coal.
4. Sharing "rights" to both or "joint exploration" of the area.

40 pts.   A solution which eliminates the balance of payments deficit is full or part ownership of one resource. There is no indication of any sharing of resources or sharing of technology and manpower. Some examples are lines drawn in Area II like this:

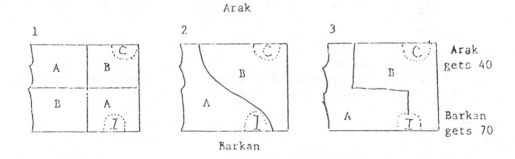

0 pts.   No solution.   The negotiators reach no agreement or one negotiator relinquishes all rights in Area II.

APPENDIX O

ROLE DESCRIPTION FOR "THE PRESIDENT'S DECISION"

ROLE SHEET: JOHN/JANE WARD, PRESIDENT

You are president of the ABCO Manufacturing Company and have held this position for the past two years. In your previous position as controller, you advised the president on fiscal and policy matters and gained a close knowledge of the inner workings of the company. As president your duties are much broader and more complex. You now have final responsibility for policy formulation and execution in such diverse fields as procurement, manufacturing, sales, finance, product development, personnel, public relations, and various other aspects of business operation. To a large extent, the progress of the company and your own success or failure as president depend on your making wise decisions. You get a certain amount of credit when things go well but you also take the blame when they go wrong.

One of the most difficult problems you have had to deal with since you became president is whether to expand operations. Within the company and among your close business associates, there are conflicting views on the matter. Those who are opposed to expansion contend that real estate and building values are seriously inflated and that the cost of new equipment is out of line. A further argument is that the television and other electronics sales are highly sensitive to economic conditions. Since company reserves are low, you would have to obtain the necessary funds through stock sales or mortgage loans, and the present financial condition of the company does not place it in an advantageous position for such financing. Furthermore, it would be some time before returns from expansion would begin to pay off to any great extent, and an early business slump could wreck the company.

While there are a number of people in the company who favor immediate expansion, all of them tend to see things in terms of their own particular area of the business and none are in a position to have a broad, overall perspective. Nevertheless, in casual discussion of the matter, they have come up with some impressive facts and arguments in favor of setting up a new plant. One contention, for example, is that the present four-story, thirty-year-old building is not adapted for modern straight-line production methods. Not only is it expensive to heat and light but it lacks the flexibility needed for efficient changeovers to meet production requirements. In addition, it has been necessary to turn down two or three large orders in the past because of insufficient capacity to meet production deadlines. Then there is the contention that a lack of growth is damaging to morale and that good people tend to become discouraged and leave to go with larger or faster growing companies where opportunities are greater.

During the past several months, you tried to keep an open mind to both points of view and, despite the risks, you were becoming convinced that on a long-term basis, expansion was the better course to follow. You have been making headway toward getting the company back on its feet, but, as things are, it is a slow, uphill struggle. Nevertheless, you think that given unfavorable circumstances, the progress you have made is as satisfactory as can be expected.

Despite your best efforts over the past two years, the board of directors informed you late yesterday that they had voted to give you one more year in which to show some results or else resign. You knew that certain members of the board were becoming impatient. However, this action was totally unexpected and came as a real shock. Obviously, expansion is out of the question if results have to be shown within a year. It would take longer than that to make the necessary financial and other arrangements to construct a new plant and get it into operation. The only possible course of action is to play it safe and hope for the best. With a few good breaks and strict belt tightening throughout the organization, it may be possible to demonstrate the desired results within the deadline set by the board. Certainly this is not the time to take chances. Your decision not to expand must be announced immediately. As a first step you have called a meeting of your three vice-presidents for 3 p.m. Your purpose is to check with them to see whether anything has been overlooked in arriving at your decision. It is now three o'clock and time to begin.

ROLE SHEET: WILLIAM CARSON, VICE-PRESIDENT, MANUFACTURING AND PRODUCT DEVELOPMENT

You are vice-president in charge of manufacturing and product development of the ABCO Company. When you moved into this job from that of plant superintendent two years ago, you had high hopes of streamlining operations and you have been able to accomplish a good deal. For years the previous management had refused to spend money on manufacturing facilities, following a penny-pinching practice of patching and fixing and making you do the best you could with inferior outmoded equipment and methods. Through your influence with Ward, you have been able to make a number of changes in layout and methods. By carefully shopping around, you have been able to get good buys on several pieces of secondhand but fairly modern equipment. In addition, you have set up a new product-development laboratory. This is a must if the company is to compete with the larger companies and their staff of research people, both in bringing out new products and in working out designs to simplify production. The company is slowly getting back on its feel and, in large part, this is due to the reduced unit costs you have been able to achieve in manufacturing.

However, you have gone just about as far as you can in this direction, and what is needed now is a new, modern plant. The present four-story building was satisfactory for its purpose thirty years ago, but with newer, integrated assembly-line procedures, all operations should be on one floor. The layout of the present building is awkward for moving things along form one process to the next and creates a lot of needless delay in changeovers when you have new orders to fill. It is also costly to light and to heat, and the construction on the upper floor is not strong enough to support some of the new heavy equipment where you could use it to the best advantage. You have urged Ward repeatedly to expand into a modern building and purchase new equipment; although Ward has always given you a fair hearing, you cannot get a commitment concerning your plan. Ward is a good accountant but doesn't know the manufacturing end of the business very well and seems to be a fence straddler. This may be because Ward was not experienced in administrative work before becoming president. As controlled, Ward learned company operations from a fiscal angle, but merely advised the former president and did not have to make the final decisions. Now that Ward is on the firing line and has to stand or fall on his/her own judgement, he/she seems to have difficulty in making up his/her mind about things. You have given Ward the best advice you can and you want to help move things along faster, but Ward has to make up his/her mind to expand or else the company will no longer be able to meet competition.

Ward has called a meeting with you and the other two vice-presidents in the office for three o'clock today. Ward has these meetings at fairly frequent intervals. You don't know what he/she has in mind but you hope he/she has finally agreed to go ahead with the new plant. Almost anything would be an improvement over the one the company is in now.

ROLE SHEET: JAMES/JANE JACKSON, VICE-PRESIDENT, SALES

You are vice-president in charge of sales and came to the ABCO Company five years ago. Before that, you were one of the assistant sales managers of a division of one of the large electrical manufacturing companies. Stepping into the vice-presidency of the ABCO Company meant quite an increase in salary and responsibility and it seemed that there was a real opportunity to do a good job and make a name for yourself. Five years ago, the company had no real sales organization and was losing ground rapidly. One of your first moves was to make an effort to recapture the market and to expand further. This took a lot of work and you had a struggle to win over the old management to your ideas. Now there are sales offices in most of the principal Eastern cities where ABCO products are in demand by manufacturers, and a fairly strong organization has been built up. The reorganization two years ago had its advantages in that Ward gave you more freedom to operate than you had enjoyed previously. Ward is doing a fair job as president in some ways but seems to be rather unimaginative. Ward always gives your ideas a fair hearing, but in the end he/she seems to shy away from new advertising campaigns. During the past two years, Ward has taken the steam out of some of your best promotional ideas simply by delaying action on them until too late. One of the things you have been pushing, for example, is an expansion of plant facilities. In the past year you have lost several big orders when Carson said he/she couldn't possibly meet the deadline set by the customers. There may have been something to what Carson calls "unreasonable deadlines" in one or two instances; however, it begins to look more and more as though Carson isn't fast enough on his/her feet to make the necessary changeovers in manufacturing and Ward refuses to push him/her. Carson seems to be Ward's fair-haired person. With a new modern plant, there could be no more excuses and you could take advantage of the breaks when big orders come in. It would help a lot too, if those in charge of product development would get to work. They have been set up for two years now and despite the ideas for new things that your salesmen have been funneling in to them, they haven't shown any progress. A small company like this must have new and better products to offer if it is to compete for new markets. That way the newspapers and trade journals give you a lot of free publicity, and the salesmen have a chance to get a foot in the door of potential customers. The main thing, however, is to get a new plant so that larger orders can be handled. Turning down the big ones -- as you had to do several times in the past -- is what hurts, and it demoralizes your sales force.

Ward has been receptive to your arguments for expansion, and there has been increasing evidence lately that he/she is ready to take action. Today at three o'clock there is to be a meeting in Ward's office with you and the other two vice-presidents. Apparently Ward is about to announce plans for the new plant, because his/her secretary told you over the phone that Ward wanted you to review in your mind, prior to the meeting, all the pros and cons on the matter of expansion. You are on your way to Ward's office now.

ROLE SHEET: RUSSEL/ROBERTA HANEY, VICE-PRESIDENT, PERSONNEL AND INDUSTRIAL RELATIONS

You are vice-president in charge of personnel and industrial relations, and have held this position since you moved up from the job of personnel director a year and a half ago. All the usual personnel services such as recruitment, hiring, promotions, training, and contract negotiations are handled through your office. On a policy basis, you have set up your office to serve three main functions. One is to prevent as many personnel problems as possible and assist the supervisors with those that arise. Second, you advise the president, Ward, on personnel matters. Third, you are responsible for maintaining a competent work force in which the employees get along well with each other and do a good job.

One of the things you were able to get underway as personnel director was an individualized program of training and work experience for promising young college recruits. Even though the conservatism of the previous management stymied their progress in many ways, you were able to obtain a few good people each year. Then when the reorganization took place two years ago, a considerable number of these graduates were able to move up a notch. This left a number of vacancies at the trainee level which you were able to fill by going out to the colleges. However you are now faced with the same problem you had previously. The company isn't growing and many of the people you brought in a few years ago who were not ready to move up during the reorganization are becoming impatient. You cannot hold out much promise to new college graduates because there just isn't any place for them to move up in the company, and there won't be any new opportunities unless the company expands its operations. Meanwhile, some companies are picking them off one by one. If this is allowed to continue, the management at the middle and lower levels will be second rate again in a few years. Unless the company can offer good people some inducements to stay, there will be crippling losses in many key positions -- the company simply cannot afford that and stay in competition. As far as you can see, expansion is absolutely essential if the company is to keep these employees.

Ward has sent word that there is to be a meeting at three o-clock in his/her office and that Carson and Jackson are also to be there. Since Carson is in charge of manufacturing and Jackson in charge of sales, it looks as though Ward may be ready to announce plans for the new plant.

APPENDIX P

ON USING THE CLASSROOM AS AN ORGANIZATION[*]

Advice to Students

The organizational simulation you will be taking part in reflects some of the issues which you will have to confront in any organization you work for. In order to help understand the purpose of this simulation and to prepare you for some of the experiences involved you should read the information below carefully.

Groups
Groups are a basic element of organizations. One of the most difficult things that students find on entering full-time work is developing the kinds of interaction that enable them to deal with this new environment. You should look out for how differences in background factors, personal interaction styles and motivation affect how your group works. Remember, how well you do in this simulation, as in the real world, depends on your group not just you. All groups experience problems during their development and while becoming cohesive. Try to understand what is going on both intuitively and by using formal models. Try out different strategies to deal with issues. Most of all consider what you are doing as a member of your group.

Performance
Your group performance will be assessed by other groups in the organization and they will be allocating resources to your group manager. Remember that your group is going to be viewed as a unit, so not only does your own performance count, but also other individuals in the group. You have a responsibility for the overall group performance. The manager will allocate rewards individually and part of the manager's responsibility will be to ensure that rewards are equitable. Often in this simulation, managers overallocate rewards and the manager's perceptions may be different to those of the groups that are evaluating you. You will need to deal with these conflicts in a constructive way.

Interactions
You will be dealing with what has been called "tacit knowledge" in this class. There appear to be three important elements that distinguish good performers from bad performers. These are:

1.   Managing Self - Knowledge about self motivation and self organizational
     aspect of performance - e.g., procrastination.

2.   Managing tasks - Knowledge about how to do work related tasks well.

3.   Managing others - Interaction with peers.

These are important management tasks and you will be faced with a number of situations where the development of these skills will be important.

Remember you are working in an organization so things may not be structured as you want them. You will be presented with problems so that you can develop strategies to deal with them. Your performance is going, in part, to be dependent on other people and there will be times when you will be frustrated and make mistakes. Learning to deal with these issues is an important part of this simulation and will be a large part of what you will be learning. Keeping a journal during this simulation will help you with this learning. Write down your experiences, how you dealt with issues, your reactions to events. By writing these down you will be making your thoughts concrete

---

[*]By John Betton. Used with permission.

and will also find, as you read back over your journal, that you will gain a perspective on yourself which will help you understand the kinds of interaction you will face in this class. What you learn and how well you do in this class is in part going to be a function of whether or not you are able to deal effectively with a changing environment and your ability to use your intellectual and emotional resources in this environment.